CHRISTIAN SATISFACTION IN AQUINAS

Towards a Personalist Understanding

Romanus Cessario, O.P.
Dominican House of Studies
Washington, D.C.

UNIVERSITY
PRESS OF
AMERICA

Copyright © 1982 by
University Press of America, Inc.
P.O. Box 19101, Washington, D.C. 20036

Printed in the United States of America

Library of Congress Cataloging in Publication Data

Cessario, Romanus.
    Christian satifaction in Aquinas.

    Bibliography: p.
    1. Satisfaction--Religious aspects--Christianity--
History of doctrines--Middle Ages, 600-1500. 2. Thomas,
Aquinas, Saint, 1225?-1274. I. Title.
BT263.C47 1982   232'.3   81-43836
ISBN 0-8191-2557-1
ISBN 0-8191-2558-X (pbk.)

FRATRIBUS

ORDINIS FRATRUM MINORUM CONVENTUALIUM

EX PROVINCIA SANCTI ANTONII

STUDIORUM CAUSA FRIBURGI HELVETIORUM DEMORANTIBUS

ANNIS 1976-1979

AMICUS AMICIS FRATERQUE FRATRIBUS SUIS

ACKNOWLEDGMENTS

I wish gratefully to acknowledge the help of the Reverend Colman E. O'Neill, O.P., in bringing this study to completion. Father O'Neill's own published works have already contributed to a better understanding of the personalist perspectives of Saint Thomas's sacramental theology, notably Meeting Christ in the Sacraments (1964) and New Approaches to the Eucharist (1967), as well as to a deeper appreciation of the profound theological implications of the Summa theologiae by his edition of the tertia pars, qq. 16-26, published under the title, The One Mediator (1965). The present volume owes its inspiration to Father O'Neill and may be viewed as an effort to apply his personalist hermeneutic to another area of Saint Thomas's teaching, that of satisfaction.

I wish also to express my gratitude to other fellow-Dominicans for their generous help: to Fr. Boniface Ramsey and Sr. Mary Schneiders, for their long hours of work in editing the text; to Sr. Francis Assisi Loughery for her careful proofreading of the final copy and to Fr. Larz Pearson who willingly shared with me his own extensive knowledge of the doctrine of Saint Thomas and offered many helpful suggestions, especially for the Introduction. Finally I acknowledge my debt to the Community of the Albertinum in Fribourg for the many kinds of assistance which they so graciously offered me during the course of my stay there.

Romanus Cessario, O.P.

Washington, D.C.
Easter Sunday, 1980

TABLE OF CONTENTS

INTRODUCTION

The theological act is an act of historical understanding in two respects. First of all, it bears upon a content that has been historically transmitted within the Christian tradition, beginning with the Scriptural witness and proceeding thence through its transmission in the intervening doctrinal and theological witnesses. Its objective, therefore, is a set of claims about history that have themselves been historically mediated. At the same time, theological exercise is historical in another sense. For it queries the testimonial materials received from the past tradition in light of its present historical situation. Its retrieval of the past is not an historically neutral one, consisting simply in an immediate attainment of past meanings and explanations. Rather, the encounter is within the perspective of concerns that are contemporary with the theological act itself. Such encounter is truly critical and measures up to the scientific charter of theological inquiry when the circuit is closed, as it were--i.e., when the perspective of the past and that of present theological inquiry are permitted to be mutually illumining.

The Christian claims about salvation and about the role of Jesus of Nazareth in God's final and definitive deed of saving humanity have been subject to a variety of understandings, explanations and analogies during the course of the Christian millenia. Those claims and their various renderings have a doctrinal and theological history, within which Saint Thomas Aquinas occupies a position that is scarcely negligible. If one may be permitted a generalization about that received tradition, its operative perspectives seem to have been objectivist in large measure, employing, for example, in the discussion of the Incarnation, the notion of "common nature assumed" as a central conceptuality.

Yet these are exactly the sort of perspectives that do not immediately fit in with the contemporary situation of the theological act in its attempt to penetrate and appropriate the received historical tradition. Whatever critical reservations might be levied, the simple fact is that the contemporary situation of the theological act is marked by different perspectives. The first of these perspectives, dominant since Descartes, is that of the dynamism of the subject as in some measure creative of the meaning and value of his interactions with the world. Closely allied to this subjectivist interest and the personalist concerns which it generates is the emergence of historical understanding: the recognition that human being is not simply historical being; that what is distinctively human is best recognized in those dimensions in which human being stands out from common nature and purely temporal succession.

This difference in perspectives is the starting-point of any theological exercise directed toward recovering the Christian soteriological tradition. The practitioner of theological inquiry will enter upon his enterprise shaped by his contemporary perspective to some extent. And, due to this initial difference in perspectives between the past tradition and present inquiry, the initial encounter will be marked by a certain experience of the "foreignness" of the received tradition. The genius of the theological exercise is, of course, to discover certain basic intelligibilities in the tradition without too facilely eliding the difference of perspectives.

Saint Thomas Aquinas's soteriological model of satisfaction is the case at hand in this dissertation. Its basic perspective appears alien at first and any number of authors have taken up the challenge to explain why.[1] It further suffers from the baggage of the native resonance of the satisfaction theory of Anselm's Cur Deus homo? and from its later conflation with substitutional theories of Christ's saving work.[2] As in all theological activity, the goal of this work will be to effect a merging of perspectives, such that the distinctive perspective of Saint Thomas's account of the satisfactory character of Christ's work be respected and yet that its latent resonances with the contemporary situation of theological activity might be illumined and recovered. For example, although the notion of "common nature assumed" with all of its connotations alien to contemporary thought-forms does function in Saint Thomas's account of Christ's satisfactory work, nevertheless this notion is in some respects only a preliminary element of explanation. The human nature assumed by the Word is that whereby he is "homoousios hēmin," in the phrase of Chalcedon; it is a factor explaining ontic accessibility and communion between Christ and other human beings insofar

xiv

as all agree in possession of this nature. More importantly, however, this ontic communication is only the arena for a mode of union that is based not simply upon the commensurability of natures, but rather a mode of union that is preeminently <u>personal</u>: fundamentally and hypostatically so in the case of the Word's union with his human nature and intentionally so, by way of the personal activities of supernatural knowing and loving, as the union in which both Head and members are conjoined. What is salvifically significant is what transpires between the persons who are the subjects of a common nature.

The professional theological career of Saint Thomas Aquinas spans some twenty years of preaching, teaching and writing. During this period of time Saint Thomas produced some one hundred works.[3] Since the appearance of the <u>Index Thomisticus</u> in 1973 the student of Saint Thomas has had at his disposal a research tool which allows him to study the texts of Saint Thomas in a more thorough-going manner than was possible for previous generations of scholars.[4] Although primarily a tool for linguistic research of the middle ages, the <u>Index Thomisticus</u> is an invaluable tool for research in theology as well--a fact noted by Walter Brugger among others.[5] The presently published sections of the <u>Index</u> provide the student of Saint Thomas immediate access to the some 1,200 places where throughout the course of his writings he uses some form of the Latin words "satisfactio" or "satisfacio."[6]

The initial step in researching this dissertation consisted in a careful examination of the references in the Thomistic corpus where some form of the word "satisfaction" appeared. Setting aside those places where the word was used to denote something other than the satisfactory character of Christ's work or the penitential satisfactions of the members of Christ (as when the verb "satisfacio" is used to mean to respond to a question),[7] two basic areas of theological discussion emerged as those in which Saint Thomas had frequent recourse to the notion of satisfaction. The first area is that of the salvific work of Christ in which Saint Thomas employs the model of satisfaction as a tool of theological explication for understanding the nature of God's saving deed in Christ. Closely allied to this first area of discussion is a second: the satisfaction accomplished by the members of Christ, that is, how the final and definitive salvation accomplished in Christ is mediated to those who by reason of their being a part of God's plan of salvation are incorporated in some way into the person of Jesus Christ. The biblical image of head and members has been adopted in this dissertation as a convenient conceptuality for organizing the materials in such wise as to reflect both the different contexts in which Saint Thomas discusses the notion of satisfaction and something of their intimate connection.

The second step followed in the preparation of this present work was to organize the materials in such a way as to acknowledge the chronology of Saint Thomas's works and to take into account the fact of development of thought in the author himself. Some accommodation to this basic principle of presenting the works of Saint Thomas in chronological order is required because of the nature of the works themselves, for example, the commentaries on Scripture, which seemed more appropriately treated in a single chapter at the beginning of the work, or because of the difficulty in determining the exact chronology of certain works which, in some cases at least, were composed simultaneously. In general, however, the major systematic treatises are examined chronologically to the extent that the consistent application of this principle aids a coherent presentation of Saint Thomas's doctrine.

The third step involved the retrieval of the several controlling perspectives which marked Saint Thomas's theology of satisfaction as a distinctive and original contribution to the development of Christian soteriology. The elements of this perspective emerge gradually and with various imports, determined largely by the nature of the work in which satisfaction is discussed and the given work's relation to his mature thought, which, it becomes increasingly apparent, is clearly contained in the Summa theologiae. The aim of this thesis is to show that Saint Thomas's contribution to the development of and adequate satisfaction-model for theological use in the discussion of the saving death of Jesus Christ is a distinctive one. It should not be assumed that it is a simple restatement of Anselm's satisfaction-theory, as Gustav Aulén, for one, does assume,[8] nor that it is easily drawn into service to support penal substitution theories.

Saint Thomas's theological clarification of the satisfaction-model is marked by the same emphases which are found in his mature works, foremost among which is a strong desire to accentuate the personal character of God-man relations as they are realized in the person of the incarnate Word. Drawing upon the richness of the various testimonial witnesses available to him, Saint Thomas fashioned a satisfaction-model which derives both its explanatory elements and deepest meaning and vitality from a vision of the saving work of Jesus Christ as actualized in the individual believer in order to move him forward on his journey to beatific fellowship. Central to this explanation is the notion of the reformation of the image of God in man which, with all of its dynamic resonances in Saint Thomas's account, is accomplished through the free exercise of satisfactory acts in the personal sin-marked histories of believers precisely as such acts are suffused with and undergirded by the eminent satisfaction of Christ. This scheme serves to highlight the unconditional priority of the divine action at the heart of the discussion, for it is God who is acting in Jesus to complete his plan for salvation.

It is extremely important to bear in mind in any discussion of a given part of Saint Thomas's theological synthesis how he understands the nature of the divine essence and how that shapes his conception of divine activity ad extra. God does not act in order to acquire some new perfection as an end or goal. Rather, as ipsum esse subsistens, his ontological transcendence is the root of the sheer liberality and graciousness of all his activities with respect to the non-divine. Thus the sole reason why God operates ad extra is to be sought in the divine reality itself, that is, the sheer communicative good that is his being. Such operation is above all ordered to the bestowal of triune communion in that good upon the rational creature, who bears the image of that communion in his constitution and as his destiny. The achievement of this personal communion as a surpassing gift and in the face of human historical sin is the core-reality that Saint Thomas develops his satisfaction-model to explain and the meaning he fathoms in the words of Saint Paul, "in Christ God was reconciling the world to himself."[9]

Satisfaction, therefore, is not something that God requires of man, or even of Jesus, as a condition for accomplishing his saving plan. Rather it is the means whereby God in very fact accomplishes his plan to bring all men into loving union with himself. It is man and not God who is changed by satisfaction. For, on the one hand, the increment and restoration of perfection designated by the term "satisfaction" pertains entirely to the human creature; by contrast, the communication of that increment pertains with absolute priority to the divine goodness and mercy penetrating the human creature with God's own love. It is, then, the individual, in the historical and social dimensions of his personhood, who in the progressive reformation of his God-like image (in the present order of things marred by the sin of Adam as well as by personal sin) is gradually changed into being what God intends his creature to be. [10]

In order to accomplish the purpose of this dissertation the results of the research have been divided into six chapters. The first chapter is introductory in scope; in it the professional career of Thomas Aquinas is reviewed and the works in which he speaks of satisfaction are discussed as to purpose and general theme. The recent study of James Weisheipl, _Friar Thomas D'Aquino_,[11] has been adopted as a standard for both the biographical details of Saint Thomas's life and for establishing the authenticity and dating of his works. It should be noted, however, that questions in either area which are a subject of debate among scholars do not substantially affect the conclusions of this dissertation.

The second chapter is devoted to Saint Thomas's commentaries and _reportationes_ on the scriptures. As already noted, these have been collected into a single chapter without regard for their position in the chronological list of his works and placed at the beginning of the dissertation. This was judged in the best interests of the work because the material concerning the satisfaction of Christ and of the members drawn from the scriptural commentaries could be better presented and more accurately analyzed in a global fashion, rather than introducing small snippets throughout the work. Such a manner of presentation also emphasizes the central role which commenting on the inspired texts played in the development of Saint Thomas as a theologian and, consequently, avoids the impression that the Bible was of peripheral or secondary importance to the theological task of systematization for a thirteenth-century _magister_ such as Saint Thomas. In addition, the fact that the scriptural commentaries are among the most difficult of Saint Thomas's works to assign a precise date of composition to argued for this manner of presentation.[12]

The third chapter concentrates exclusively upon the first theological synthesis of Saint Thomas, the _Scriptum super Sententias_. In this work Saint Thomas employs some form of the word "satisfaction" nearly 700 times in the course of commenting on the _Sentences_ of Peter Lombard; thus a considerable amount of material required consideration. Furthermore, the _Scriptum_ remains the only systematic work in which one finds a detailed discussion of satisfaction as one of the principal parts of the sacrament of penance. The corresponding section of the _Summa theologiae_ was not completed; in fact it was terminated at the brink of just such a discussion. For this reason, although the _Scriptum_ is an earlier rendition of satisfaction-themes in Saint Thomas's theological enterprise and will be subject to revision and to the introduction of new understandings as that enterprise advanced, the fact remains that the very wealth and variety of his treatment in the _Scriptum_ affords it an important place in ascertaining Saint Thomas's teachings. Hence the _Scriptum_ is an important text for beginning a study of satisfaction, especially as it is related to the virtue of justice.

The fourth chapter considers works which were composed between the two major theological syntheses, the _Scriptum_ and the _Summa theologiae_. In works such as the _De veritate_, the _Summa contra gentiles_ and the _De rationibus fidei_, one finds a consideration of the notion of satisfaction that is guided and amplified by the distinctive intention of these works (e.g., apologetic in the case of the latter two). In the _De veritate_, the notion is addressed more obliquely and by reference to certain closely allied notions such as the grace and merit of Christ as head. The works of this period exhibit some of the distinctive perspectives of Saint Thomas's theology that will shape the final contours of his satisfaction-model contained in the _Summa theologiae_. By way of preface to this exposition there is an examination of Saint Thomas's notion of sin viewed from the aspects of _poena_ and _culpa_ as he developed it in the _De malo_. The need for a more focused and extended treatment of the constituents of sin as Saint Thomas understands them was judged necessary because of its import for his satisfaction-model.

The final chapters, five and six, treat the _Summa theologiae_, the work of Saint Thomas's theological maturity. Within its restricted scope, the present study confirms the long-held belief that the most articulate expression of his thought is to be found within its pages. Concentration upon the _Summa_, however, has not always served the best interests of

Thomistic studies. The emergence of an historically-minded approach to Aquinas's thought since the end of the last century has underlined the importance of studying Saint Thomas within his historical situation and in the context of possible development within his own thought. Suffice it to observe the objectivist perspective for which Thomism is currently and frequently criticized--and which accounts for its initial appearance of "foreignness"--is oftentimes the result of having read Saint Thomas in an abstract and ahistorical way rather than having adverted to the full dimensions and texture of his thought as it develops throughout his writing career. Nevertheless, given the systematic integrity of the Summa theologiae as a whole, no attempt will be made to discriminate between the various chronological periods of the extended composition of its parts; rather, the treatment will proceed as an ensemble.

The formally christological questions of the tertia pars are the subject of chapter five. They are introduced by material from the prima secundae in which a more fully developed notion of punishment as restorative is found and in which a marked personalistic development of these themes seems to prepare for Saint Thomas's development of satisfaction in the tertia pars. It is in the course of treating questions forty-six through fifty-five of the tertia pars (devoted to the passion and death of Christ) that the argument that satisfaction is the guiding model or key-notion in Saint Thomas's theological explanation of the mystery of Christ's salvific death is advanced.

Chapter six is intended to be a summary chapter in which the perspectives of Saint Thomas's theology of image-restoration accomplished through satisfaction are put into sharp relief. This is done by setting this doctrine into the concrete, historical dispensation of salvation-history as a history of both sinful rejection and overriding divine grace, as a history ruled by a plan rendering satisfaction possible in a variety of historical modes, culminating in the Christian economy. As a last point of discussion, the sacraments of baptism and penance are examined as they are sign-actions mediating the satisfaction of Christ. However, at this point the primary focus is not analytical but synthetic, and so the final chapter should not be read as a minor treatise on Thomistic sacramental theology but, rather, as a summary of the entire dissertation, stating how the satisfaction of Christ is a fulfillment of God's saving plan in the believer: "For in him all the fulness of God was pleased to dwell, and through him to reconcile to himself all things, whether on earth or in heaven, making peace by the blood of his cross."[13]

CHAPTER I

THE ACADEMIC CAREER OF SAINT THOMAS
AQUINAS AND A BRIEF INTRODUCTION
TO THE WORKS IN WHICH HE
SPEAKS OF SATISFACTION

1252-1256: Sententiarius at Paris:
Scriptum Super Sententias

God graced his teaching so abundantly that it
began to make a wonderful impression on the
students. For it all seemed so novel--new
arrangements of subject matter, new methods
of proof, new arguments adduced for the
conclusions; in short, no one who heard him
could doubt that his mind was full of a new
light from God.

Thus one of the earliest biographers of Saint
Thomas, Bernard Gui,[1] described the success of Saint
Thomas's early teaching at the University of Paris.
The period 1252-1256 can best be described as a time
for graduate studies in the life of Saint Thomas.
During that time he carried out the duties of a bachelor, among the most formidable of which was the preparation of a scriptum based on the standard theological
textbook of the day, the Sentences of Peter the Lombard. Father Weisheipl has rightly compared the
production of such a scriptum to a modern Ph.D. thesis
in the United States; this was the way in which the
young scholastic theologian proved his skill and
secured his professional standing.[2]

A study of the role played by the Sentences
of Peter the Lombard in the development of western
theology belongs to the history of medieval theology
(although commentaries were being written well into the
17th century).[3] Suffice it to observe that this
popularity was due to the steady course which this
fundamentally conservative theologian tried to steer
between the extreme rationalism characteristic of the
school of Abelard and the extreme positivism found in
the theological approach used by the monastic schools.
The Lombard took the collected sayings (sententiae) of
the authorities and organized them. Taking his cue

1

from Saint Augustine, who wrote that all theological teaching is either of "things" or of "signs,"[4] he arranged his material around four cardinal points of the Creed, namely, the Trinity, the Incarnation, creation and sin, and finally, the sacraments and the Four Last Things. The first three belong to the category of "things" and the last one to that of "signs."

A good indication of the new approach about which Bernard Guy speaks is that Saint Thomas changed the principle of organization when he set about to compose his own work: he abandoned the Augustinian "things-signs" approach and, acting upon a suggestion made by the Franciscan theologian, Alexander of Hales,[5] divided the Lombard's book into two sections of two books each. The former he labeled the exitus (the coming forth of creatures from God) and the second, the reditus (the return of all things to God), a bold move on the part of a young bachelor. He departed from the traditional approach, one hallowed by no less an authority than Saint Augustine, and opted to follow the lead of thinkers, some of whom, like Plotinus, were outside of the Christian tradition.

Despite the freshness of outlook which characterized the teaching as well as the writing of the young sententiarius, the Scriptum super Sententias remains a first major work. It is evidently not a final statement of Saint Thomas's theological synthesis. In fact, shortly after his death concordances were prepared to mark the difference between what Saint Thomas said in the Scriptum super Sententias and how he speaks in the Summa theologiae. However, it should be noted here that not every subject Saint Thomas treats in the Scriptum super Sententias is treated in the Summa becaue of the unfinished character of the latter work. Hence, certain subjects find their only comprehensive systematic treatment in the Scriptum super Sententias. This is important for the present study, since one such subject is the treatment of penitential satisfaction.

The work as we have it was completed around 1256.[6] It is a polished piece of writing and not merely an edited set of notes used for classroom lecturing. Its four boooks are subdivided into distinctions, questions, articles and sometimes even "quaestiuncula," or sub-questions. The issues which are discussed in these units bear some relation to the corresponding text of the Lombard, but fundamentally

2

they are independent discussions in themselves, intelligible apart from the text of the original author. Rightly, then, is the work referred to as a <u>scriptum</u> or a "writing" on the <u>Sentences</u>, rather than a commentary on them.

Perhaps the most important thing to understand about a work like the <u>Sentences</u> of Peter Lombard is the attitude of the Middle Ages toward authority, that is, "approved sources." There is no brief way to summarize the attitude of theological writers toward those eminent men of the Christian tradition (and even outside of the Christian tradition) who had preceded them. One need only observe that what had gone on before was important, whether it was the theological tracts of Saint Augustine or the biblical commentaries of Saint Jerome or even the more recent discussions by such men as Ivo of Chartres or Saint Anselm of Canterbury. This consciousness of the past could have been restrictive and have limited the development of theology by fostering a servile spirit toward its authorities. Nor would one be hard put to cite examples where this in fact happened. It is, then, a sign of Saint Thomas's genius that even from the start of his theological career, he was able to deal respectfully with the authorities and at the same time still find freedom to develop his personal thinking.

Since it is a systematic work, considerable attention will be given to the <u>Scriptum super Sententias</u> in the course of this study. A sustained look at Saint Thomas's teaching here will also allow a comparison between his initial doctrine on satisfaction and whatever development might have taken place between this early work and the completion of the <u>Summa theologiae</u>.

<u>1256-1259 Regent Master in Theology at
Paris: De veritate; Quaestiones de
quodlibet; Super Matthaeum;
Super Isaiam; Contra
impugnantes</u>

During the spring of 1256 Saint Thomas left the ranks of the bachelors of theology at the University of Paris and was granted the title of master in theology. This was an exciting moment at the University of Paris. The antimendicant controversy was at its height. Shortly after his inception as a master, Saint Thomas was obliged to take time away from his formal classroom preparation in order to formulate a rebuttal to those forces at the University that wished to restrict the presence of religious clergy among the teaching body. The result of that effort is his work, Contra impugnantes Dei cultum et religionem, a rather long polemic directed against the quite vitriolic remarks contained in the De periculis novissimorum temporum of William of Saint-Armour, leader of the antimendicant forces. Save for a passing reference, this work will not figure in this study, dealing as it does with questions related to the apostolic activity of religious orders and their right to exercise certain apostolic functions within the Church.

Once Saint Thomas assumed the role of a master at the University of Paris he was obliged to perform the two basic duties of that office, namely, to lecture on the Bible and to determine, that is to say, resolve in a scientific way, theological questions of his day. A third duty was the preaching of sermons at the University.[7] This present study does not allow a digression on the methodology of medieval teaching; for this specialized area several excellent studies are available.[8] This study will, however, have occasion to examine writings dating from Saint Thomas's first Paris regency which are representative of both of the academic functions of the master in theology.

In pursuing our examination of those texts that treat of christological satisfaction, the central work dating from this period will be the disputed question, De veritate. In particular our focus will be upon those sections of the work which belong to Saint Thomas's third year of teaching (1258-59) and which deal with the subject of the human will and the effect of the grace of Christ upon it (Qq. 21-29). Besides the regularly scheduled academic disputations (of which the De veritate is an example) there was another kind of disputation to which the master was obliged. This was the so-called quodlibetal disputation held twice yearly, during Advent and Lent, at which students and other members of the faculty of theology could raise questions of personal interest. Saint Thomas's Quaestiones de quodlibet cover a broad range of subjects; of those questions belonging to his first Paris regency only some incidental remarks touch upon the notion of satisfaction.

The obligation to read (legere) and to comment upon the sacred Scriptures was the backbone of magisterial teaching at the University of Paris during the

13th century. The title <u>magister in sacra pagina</u>, as Father Weisheipl observes, was the most ancient designation of a medieval theologian.[9] The scriptural commentaries of Saint Thomas are among the most eloquent testimony to his spirituality as well as his theological competence. The dating of these commentaries is a subject of dispute among scholars, though it seems reasonably sure that <u>Lectura super Matthaeum: Reportatio</u> belongs to the period presently under discussion. The details of this particular work's publication are complex; however, those sections of the <u>Lectura</u> pertinent to our study do not seem to be part of the passages of questionable authenticity.[10]

A second biblical commentary to be examined is the <u>Postilla super Isaiam</u>. The dating of this work is especially difficult. The Leonine editors claim that it is the first theological work of Saint Thomas.[11] Father Weisheipl, however, rejects their line of argumentation, founded on the existence of a small autograph section, and assigns this work to the second period of Saint Thomas's academic career instead of the first. The question, however, is not of great moment for this study since the sole reference to christological satisfaction does not contribute to its doctrinal development. This passage is, however, a beautiful one from the pen of a young theologian and for this reason it will be presented in full. Reference to the scriptural commentaries also serves to remind us of the solid biblical foundation, the "underpinning of the rest," as the medieval author put it,[12] which is to be found underlying the elaborate superstructure of medieval theology. Citations from the scriptural commentaries, then, should give pause to those who would rashly characterize the theology of Saint Thomas as too rational, or speculatively divorced from the revealed sources of the Christian faith.

1259-1268: In Service to the Church in Italy: Summa contra gentiles; De rationibus fidei; in Job; De malo; Summa theologiae, Prima pars

Having completed his three-year term as master of theology, Saint Thomas Aquinas left Paris and, as the custom of his Order dictated, returned to Italy where he had first entered the Friars Preachers. An exact chronology of the next ten years of his life is difficult to establish, due, in part, to scanty documentation. We do know, however, that Saint Thomas did spend all of the time in Italy either in service to the Dominican Order or to the papal curia. The following chronology will help locate Saint Thomas during the period presently under consideration:

Fall 1259	at Paris
1260 to fall 1261	at Naples
1261 to fall 1265	at Orvieto (papal curia)
1265 to summer 1267	at Rome
1267 to fall 1268	at Viterbo (papal curia)

Prior to having completed his term at Paris, Saint Thomas was asked to begin a new kind of apostolate of the pen which he would continue once he left the classroom. Dominican missionaries were working in Spain and North Africa with Moslems and Jews, many of whom had assimilated a great deal of the new Aristotelian learning. These missionaries had need of help in responding to the objections posed by such men in the course of evangelization. Tradition has it that the saintly Dominican, Raymond of Peñafort, asked his brother, Thomas Aquinas, to compose a work that would be serviceable to the missionaries who had to face the many difficulties which the Moslem and Jewish believers posed with respect to the truths of the Christian religion.[13] The Summa contra gentiles is the fruit of this request. While primarily apologetic in purpose, the Summa is more than just a missionary manual. Father Chenu has written that this work "offers itself as a defense of the entire body of Christian thought, confronted with the scientific Greco-Arabic conception of the universe."[14] It is an apologetic theology. Although scholars agree that Saint Thomas began this work in Paris, exactly how much of the manuscript was completed when he arrived in Italy is a subject of debate.[15] We do know that he completed the text while at Orvieto sometime during 1264.

About the works written by Saint Thomas during this Italian sojourn Father Weisheipl has this to say: "All of his writings should probably be seen as an act of apostolic service to the intellectual needs of the Church and the needs of men seeking the truth."[16] In this he echoes the words of the medieval chronicler, Tolomeo of Lucca, who remarked that after Saint Thomas had left Paris he came to Italy where he wrote "many useful works."[17] Certainly among the most useful is the Summa contra gentiles.

The work is divided into two unequal parts, the first of which (Books I-III) deals with truths about God that can be known by human reason alone, and the second (Book IV) with truths that are known only by revelation. The present study will have occasion to look at both parts. The lengthier discussion, as might be expected, will be found in Book IV, where the Incarnation is treated. However, in Book III some remarks about satisfaction are also to be found. The larger context for these latter remarks is the question of the need mankind has for divine help in reaching beatitude. Turning to Book IV, as has been noted, we come to the questions which deal with the Incarnation and related truths of faith. Refusing to make a philosophical summa out of Books I-III, Father Chenu insists on a theological order for the entire Summa, and he cites Saint Thomas in support of his contention. Towards the beginning of Book II, Saint Thomas writes that ". . . . after what has been said in Book I about God in Himself, there remains to continue with the things that come from Him."[18] Among those things which come from God is the God-man, and with Christ we arrive at those truths which are the most hidden of the Christian faith and which are not accessible to reason alone.

A short time after Saint Thomas had finished the Summa contra gentiles, another opportunity to render service to the intellectual needs of the Church presented itself. A Christian missionary in Antioch requested help in responding to some objections to certain truths of the Faith that he had encountered while working with Saracens, Greeks and Armenians. Although he had recently finished a full treatment of such questions in the Summa contra gentiles, Saint Thomas wrote a long reply to the unidentified Cantor of Antioch. The work has come down to us as the De rationibus fidei contra Saracenos, Graecos et Armenos ad Cantorem Antiochiae. Only one of the five questions posed by the Cantor deals directly with the question of satisfaction.

Saint Thomas prefaces this work with a caution about not trying to prove truths of the Faith that are beyond reason's ability to comprehend; such an effort is destined only to bring ridicule to the Faith. The missionary can, however, show that nothing which Christians hold by faith contradicts human reason.[19] The problem posed by the Cantor, which is relevant for us, is as follows: The Saracens say that Christ could

7

not have died for the salvation of the world, for if he were divinely omnipotent he could have saved the human race by other ways and have prevented man from sinning.

In responding, Saint Thomas will observe that when speaking about what God has done one can only seek to establish the suitability for what we know to be the case. One cannot begin to consider all the other ways that might have been possible, or that God could have chosen; to do so would be to ignore the fundamental truth that, in fact, God did choose a particular way of doing something, whether it be how he chose to save the world or how many stars he chose to put into the heavens. Since all who worship God, including the Saracens, revere him as supremely good and providential, men of faith will seek to find out why the way God chose to do something is the best way and not seek to discover why some other way would have been better.

Another observation which Saint Thomas makes in the course of this response is of equal interest to this study, especially in light of what has been said above about the role that prayerful reflection plays in discerning the wisdom of God's actions. In the seventh chapter of the De rationibus Saint Thomas writes:

> If a man will devoutly consider the suitabil-
> ity of the Passion and Death of Christ, he
> will find there such an abyss of wisdom that
> more and greater things will continually
> reveal themselves to him. To such a man the
> truth of Saint Paul's words will be manifest
> --". . . but we preach Christ crucified,
> a stumbling block to Jews and folly to
> Gentiles, but to those who are called,
> both Jews and Greeks, Christ the power
> of God and the wisdom of God." And again
> --"For the foolishness of God is wiser than
> men . . . ." (I Corinthians 1:23-25).[20]

This, I believe, is an important point to underscore in any discussion of scholastic theology--be it that of Saint Anselm of that of Saint Thomas. It reminds the student or Saint Thomas's theological writings that the reasons which he gives for those truths of the Faith (which themselves are accessible only in the light of the Faith) are the fruit of prayerful meditation and reflection on the mysteries of the Faith. They do not represent an attempt to dissolve those mysteries with arguments or subtleties that might appear facile or even glib to those who do not understand this method.

During part of the time that Saint Thomas was writing the Summa contra gentiles, he lived at the Dominican priory at Orvieto. At that time the curia of Pope Urban IV was also located there. It has already been noted that Saint Thomas aided this Pope, especially during his attempt to heal the division between eastern and western Christianity.[21] While Saint Thomas was in service to the Pope he also served the intellectual needs of his Dominican brothers in Orvieto. The commentary Expositio in Job ad litteram is the fruit of that service.

The Constitutions of the Dominican Order indicated that the "lector" of the convent, the post held by Saint Thomas at the time, was regularly to expose and comment upon the books of the Old and New Testaments. The text that is extant of the Expositio in Job is a well-documented one and therefore scholars assume that it is not simply a copy of Saint Thomas's personal notes but rather a polished and reworked text.[22] In the prologue to the Expositio, Saint Thomas explains that his intention is to comment on the Book of Job "secundum litteralem sensum"; that is, he will not attempt to develop a spiritual exegesis. In his opinion such a work had already been adequately accomplished by Saint Gregory the Great in his Moralia, which was well-known to medieval theologians.

After a provincial chapter of the Roman Province held in 1265, Saint Thomas was asked to establish a school for young Dominicans in need of special training for their work in the Order. Accordingly he opened a small-scale provincial studium at the Convent of Santa Sabina, the Dominican headquarters in Rome. Father Weisheipl, aware of the disputes among scholars on this point, makes the De malo the fruit of disputations held during the academic year 1266-1267, when Saint Thomas was at Rome. One does not find a discussion of satisfaction as such among the articles of the Disputed Questions, De malo. Our interest in it derives from the discussion of the results of evil, namely, culpa and poena, which are subjects directly related to that of satisfaction.

It was also at this time that Saint Thomas conceived the idea of his major theological work, the Summa theologiae. Apparently, in the course of teaching theology to the young students at Rome, Saint Thomas came to realize the shortcomings of the Sentences of Peter Lombard as a standard textbook for beginners in the theological science.

9

We have considered how newcomers to this teaching are greatly hindered by various writings on the subject, partly because of the swarm of pointless questions, articles, and arguments, partly because essential information is given according to the requirements of textual commentary or the occasions of academic debate, not to a sound educational method, partly because repetitiousness has bred boredom and muddle in their thinking.[23]

He may have even thought of revising the Scriptum super Sententias in an effort to make the subject matter easier for his young charges to comprehend. In fact, however, he conceived the idea of an entirely new textbook for beginners and sometime during the year 1266 he began work on the Summa theologiae.

The question of the structure of the Summa is one that is a matter of discussion to this day.[24] A complete exposé of the central conception behind Saint Thomas's chef d'oeuvre is beyond the scope of this present work. One point, however, is worth underscoring. There is to the Summa theologiae of Saint Thomas Aquinas a kind of organic unity--what Father Gilby refers to as its "biological temper"[25]-- that will not permit any single part of the whole to be correctly understood in isolation. The author himself has provided his reader, in the form of prologues attached to the beginning of each major part of his work, with aids to grasping the scope of a particular section. An examination of these prologues provides an idea of the general thrust to a given section of the Summa and establishes the broader theological context within which Saint Thomas speaks about satisfaction.

"The fundamental aim of holy teaching," writes Saint Thomas, "is to make God known, not only as He is in Himself, but as the beginning and end of all things and of reasoning creatures especially." Accordingly he announces his intention to treat of three main topics which correspond to the three major divisions of the Summa:

First, of God;
secondly, of the journey to God of reasoning creatures;
thirdly, of Christ, who, as man, is our way to God.[26]

10

Father Chenu states his conviction that Saint Thomas's appeal to the Platonic scheme of emanation and return is crucial to understanding what he is about in the Summa theologiae. "Since theology is the science of God," Chenu writes, "all things will be studied in their relation to God whether in their production or in their final end, in their exitus et reditus."[27] Recall that this theme had already been used by Saint Thomas in his restructuring of the Sentences of Peter Lombard.

The entire prima pars was written during Saint Thomas's stay in Italy. Although the idea for writing the Summa was conceived in Rome, a good deal of the prima pars, at least the treatise on man, was written at Viterbo.[28] At the request of a provincial chapter Saint Thomas moved to this city during the summer of 1267. During his stay there Saint Thomas would profit from the company of a fellow Dominican, William of Moerbeke, who was also in the service of Clement IV's curia at Viterbo, and who was in the process of translating Greek theological and philosophical texts into Latin.

When the principal topics of the prima pars are identified it is possible to recognize certain elements which support Father Chenu's conviction that it is here that Saint Thomas develops the exitus theme.

> The treatment of God will fall into three
>   parts:
> first, his nature;
> secondly, the distinction of persons in God;
> thirdly, the coming forth from him of crea-
>   tures.[29]

However it is possible to cite other elements in the prima pars, e.g., the discussion of the beatific vision (Q. 12) or on goodness (Q. 5), which call for caution in applying Father Chenu's schema too rigidly and which might suggest that it is an over-simplified explanation of Saint Thomas's masterplan for the Summa.[30]

Nonetheless, the main tracts of the prima pars, namely, the one God, the Trinity, and creation are clearly evident in this breakdown. Apart from the noteworthy exception of the block of questions in which Saint Thomas comments upon what the Scriptures say about the six days of creation (Qq. 67-74), the development of these tracts does not follow the method of a scriptural commentary. Direct references to the biblical text, however, appear constantly. There is a dynamic at work in the structure of the _Summa theologiae_ which explains this procedure and which is a crucial one for this present study.

Saint Thomas, along with the tradition of the Church, was convinced that Christian revelation furnishes grounds for speculation on God and possesses a sacred scripture which is the written record of revelation. His aim was to combine into a single _sacra doctrina_ both a study of salvation history and a speculative investigation of what that sacred history teaches. The Incarnation is an event of salvation history and, as such, a contingent happening.[31] It enters into the pattern of the _exitus-reditus_ as a free act of God. Saint Thomas envisioned nothing untoward in describing the ontological relations which exist between the created universe (and primarily man) and God without first making reference to the actual way in which God chose to unfold the plan of salvation in human history. On the contrary, he judged it "a sound educational method" and therefore an aid to teaching and understanding the biblical revelation.

In light of this mentality, Saint Thomas will not be embarrassed, for example, to talk about the life of man uplifted in grace (_secunda pars_) before he talks about the One Mediator of that grace (_tertia pars_). He will have already announced that man's destiny is indefinitely above what his natural powers can achieve, that it is nothing less than union with the Triune God and, as such, demands that man be elevated above the level his natural capacities make it possible for him to reach. However, he will not be able to talk significantly about satisfaction before his treatment of Christ (_tertia pars_) because satisfaction is linked to the contingent, historical fact of Christ's passion and death on the Cross. "The Incarnation was not absolutely necessary for the restoration of human nature, since by his infinite power God had many other ways to accomplish this end," writes Saint Thomas in the _tertia pars_.[32]

1269-1272:   Second Parisian Regency:
Compendium theologiae; Pauline
Commentaries; Super Johannem;
De virtutibus; Quaestiones de
quodlibet; De perfectione
spiritualis vitae; Summa
theologiae, Secunda
pars

In November of 1268 the Master General of the Dominican Order, John of Vercelli, informed Saint Thomas that he would have to return to Paris in order once again to occupy the second Dominican chair at the University. Foremost among the reasons for this extraordinary request (as a matter of principle, reappointments were not the usual procedure) was the renewed offensive of the antimendicant forces at Paris, this time led by the archdeacon of Tournai, Gérard d'Abbeville. The Dominican Order felt it necessary to have a competent friar in Paris in order to refute the charges and accusations leveled against the mendicant orders by their opponents and to defend the rights and privileges of these orders threatened by such attacks. Thomas Aquinas left Italy with some companions and arrived in Paris shortly after the beginning of the new year, 1269.

The fact that Thomas reached Paris only after the academic year was well under way confirms, in Father Weisheipl's view, the fact that there was something urgent about his reappointment. Once having arrived at Paris he assumed the professional duties of a regent master in theology. The three and one-half years that followed are judged by many to be the most productive years in Saint Thomas's life.[33] Many who have studied Saint Thomas's works closely are convinced that a significant development takes place in his thought during this period. While the development is easy to remark it is less easy to explain. One scholar's description of the change is worthy of note for this study: Father Gauthier has written that during this period Saint Thomas was induced to mitigate the stress on intellectualism that he had earlier displayed.[34] Father Weisheipl is in agreement and further suggests that Thomas's return to the classroom and contact with young students and their needs was a factor in this development.[35]

As a regent master in theology Saint Thomas was once again required to perform the threefold duties of a master, namely, to lecture on the Bible, to preside

13

over public disputations of the ordinary as well as of the quodlibetal kind, and to preach sermons at the university.

"He wrote on all the Epistles of Paul, which he valued above all writings, the Gospels alone excepted; and while engaged on this work at Paris, he is said to have had a vision of the Apostle," wrote the chronicler of Saint Thomas, William of Tocco, in his Hystoria beati Thomae.[36] The Expositio et lectura super Epistolas Pauli Apostoli is one of Saint Thomas's works whose provenance, date and manner of composition are especially difficult to determine. Noting the agreement of some contemporary witnesses on this point, Father Weisheipl argues that Saint Thomas lectured on these epistles at Paris.[37] One can only say with certitude, however, that the Commentary on the Letter to the Romans and part of the Commentary on the First Letter to the Corinthians were completed during the second Paris regency. This part of the expositio was corrected and edited by Saint Thomas himself and, at least as far as Romans is concerned, manifests a polish and completeness lacking in those sections of the work which are simply a reportatio.[38] From I Corinthians 7:10 until the end of the Epistles of Saint Paul (including the Letter to the Hebrews) the published text is the work of Reginald of Piperno as he recorded the lectures of Saint Thomas that were given at some moment of the latter's career. Among all of Saint Thomas's commentaries on Scripture, those on the Pauline corpus, especially, as could be expected, on Romans, provide the richest source for his teaching on the theology of satisfaction.

The second biblical commentary dating from this period that makes reference to satisfaction is the Lectura super Johannem: Reportatio. As with the commentary on Romans and the first seven chapters of I Corinthians, Saint Thomas corrected the reportatio of his classroom lectures.[39] Because of the interest and financial support of a student and admirer of Saint Thomas, Adenulf of Anagni, the text seems to have received special attention and thus, in the opinion of some scholars, holds a special place among Saint Thomas's scriptural commentaries. Like the Lectura super Matthaeum: Reportatio of the first Parisian regency, this theological commentary on John does not contribute a great deal to the development of our subject. It does, however, advert to both penitential and christological satisfaction in commenting upon some similar passages in the Vulgate text of both Gospels.

14

The results of Saint Thomas's academic disputations held during his second regency are somewhat easier to pinpoint as to date of composition. The ordinary academic disputation is represented by the De anima, which does not figure in our present investigation, as well as by the short disputations collected under the title De virtutibus (In communi, De caritate, De correctione fraterna, De spe, De virtutibus cardinalibus). These latter parallel the discussions of the same subjects in the secunda pars of the Summa theologiae, which was also among Saint Thomas's occupations at this time. The second and third of these disputations (De virtutibus) offer some remarks on satisfaction that will be of interest to our study.

The Quaestiones de quodlibet of this period are still subjects for further research. Questions 1 to 6, as well as number 12, are commonly assigned to this period of Saint Thomas's life.[40] Of special interest to this study will be Quaestio 2 which, according to Father Weisheipl, was held at Christmas 1269, and Quaestio 3, held at Easter of the following year. Quaestio 12 is a reportatio found after Saint Thomas's death and later added to the collection; the sole reference to satisfaction is of passing interest.

Among the first works completed by Saint Thomas upon his return to Paris and one whose date is well-established is a polemical work, De perfectione spiritualis vitae, published in the summer of 1269. It was a response to Gérard d'Abbeville's Contra adversarium perfectionis christianae. We have already seen passing reference to satisfaction in the Contra impugnantes, Saint Thomas's response to Gérard's mentor, William of Saint-Amour. Now a somewhat more developed doctrine is presented concerning not just the role that satisfaction plays in the life of a religious, but how the religious life can be understood as a supremely satisfactory work. This theme will be found reflected elsewhere in the writings of this period. It certainly is a clear example of development in the thought of Saint Thomas as regards the penitential character of satisfaction.

By way of contrast to the aforementioned work, the Compendium theologiae ad fratrem Reginaldum socium suum is perhaps impossible to date exactly. It was written for the faithful friend and assistant of Saint Thomas, Reginald of Piperno, who was responsible for so much of the transcription of Saint Thomas's notes and lectures. It was Saint Thomas's wish that Reginald have a summary of the principal teachings of the Faith at his disposal. This "doctrina compendiosa" was to have been organized around the three theological virtues in which, as Saint Paul teaches, consists the whole perfection of the Christian life.[41] The work, however, was never finished due (as an editor's note makes clear) to Saint Thomas's death. Modern scholarship tends to assign an early date for the beginning of this work. The style of the Compendium, as well as the purpose for which it was written, does not make it a work which contributes significantly to the development of Saint Thomas's theological teaching; one does find, however, succinct recapitulations of his thought that serve as useful summaries.

Although it is clear that Saint Thomas began the secunda pars of his Summa theologiae at Viterbo prior to his return to Paris, the major part of the work on this section was accomplished during the second Parisian regency. A great deal of study has been given to determine the exact dates of composition; the results of this work are available elsewhere, but not pertinent to our present purpose.[42] It has been said that the secunda pars is Saint Thomas's most original contribution to theological literature.[43] As with the prima pars, we will study the prologue to the secunda pars in order to gain some idea of the scope of the discussion which Saint Thomas undertakes in this, the longest section of his Summa theologiae.

In the prologue to the secunda pars Saint Thomas writes:

> Man is made to God's image, and since this implies, as Damascene tells us, that he is intelligent and free to judge and master of himself, so then, now that we have agreed that God is the exemplar cause of things and that they issue from His power through His will, we go on to look at this image, that is to say, at man, as the source of actions which are his own and fall under his responsibility and control.[44]

Father Gilby has paraphrased the idea behind the secunda pars as follows: It "considers the returning home of human creatures to God by their own proper activities in the life of their grace-uplifted nature."[45]

The following is a breakdown of the four topics which make up the subject matter of the first part of the secunda pars.

The first topic is that of the destiny of human life, or the "returning home . . . to God," (Qq. 1-5) in which Saint Thomas clearly identifies man's destiny and his ultimate happiness with his possession of the beatific vision. "There can be no complete and final happiness for us save in the vision of God," he writes in one of the opening questions of the secunda pars.[46] This unequivocal assertion at the head of the discussion that follows gives to that discussion its fundamentally theological character. The secunda pars can be considered an essay in part of Christian anthropology. Nevertheless, "sacra doctrina is centered on God," as Gilby writes, "and loses nothing of its singlemindedness when it also extends to his friends and creatures."[47] Recall, too, that it is the Triune God, already spoken about in the prima pars, with whom man's complete happiness demands that he seek union.

A second topic of the secunda pars is the image of God in man. This subject had already been introduced in the prima pars (Q. 93) where man's being created "ad imaginem et similitudinem Dei" received a thorough theological analysis. In the present section man's activity will be discussed by examining the nature of human acts (Qq. 6-21) and the emotional life of man (Qq. 22-48). The theological axiom, "man is made to God's image," is one which enjoys a solid foundation in the New Testament as well as considerable elaboration in the patristic tradition.[48] The restoration of the image of God, marred by sin in fallen man, is a way of describing salvation and the work of Christ. Saint Thomas will make rich use of this analogy to explain the results of satisfaction. His reference to man as God's image at the very beginning (prologue) of the secunda pars is an indication that, even as Saint Thomas developed his analysis of the structure of Christian life, the economy of salvation was a guiding principle of his reflection.

The third topic is comprised of a discussion of the virtues and vices in general (Qq. 49-70) and sin (Qq. 71-89). Man is the "source of actions which are his own and fall under his responsibility"; this is to say, he is free and (though this is not the same thing for Saint Thomas) able to choose between the good and evil. His ultimate happiness is not forced upon him; rather he chooses it freely "by his own proper activity."

The fourth topic found in the first half of the secunda pars is that of grace. The closing questions treat the Law of the Old and of the New Dispensation (Qq. 90-108) as well as the life of "grace-uplifted nature" (Qq. 109-114). We have already had occasion to comment upon Saint Thomas's purpose in placing this discussion of grace at this particular turn of the Summa's development. It is interesting, however, to contrast the mode of presentation used by Saint Thomas and that which is found in the Scriptures. Both the Summa and the New Testament speak about man's happiness or salvation. The Summa speaks first about the work of grace which conforms man to the trinitarian life of the Godhead. This conformity, begun here on earth, reaches its perfection in the union which is designated as the beatific vision. Subsequently, the Summa presents the person of Jesus Christ, the mediator of the saving grace, through whose causality man receives the grace which remains a gratuitous gift from God.

The second part of the secunda pars continues a more specific discussion of the virtues and vices. "Having set out the general theory on vices, virtues and other topics related to morals, we must turn to specific details about each."[49] Thus Saint Thomas introduces this section of his Summa. It is significant to note that at the same time that Saint Thomas was working on the secunda pars he was also reading the Nicomachean Ethics of Aristotle and commenting upon that.[50] Taking his cue, then, from Aristotle, he chose to organize this section of his work around the virtues. Another reason, as he explains in the prologue, was to be concise and to avoid repetition. Above all Saint Thomas's concept of Christian life as a growth from grace to glory, of beatitudes and not simply as obeying commandments, accounts for his decision to describe the moral life in terms of the virtues.

The largest number of questions is devoted to the virtues which touch upon the lives of all men (Qq. 1-179); a shorter number treats of the virtues which pertain to men and women in various callings, or states of perfection (Qq. 180-189). Along with the virtues, the corresponding Gift, the opposite vices, and the applicable precepts, affirmative or negative"[51] are also discussed. It is said today that the secunda pars constitutes the moral theology of Saint Thomas. Such a concept is foreign to the thought of the author for whom the entire Summa theologiae was an integrated whole, a single essay on the sacra doctria. To read the secunda pars in this way would also tend to isolate its contents from the christological context in the Summa. Such a misreading would be especially harmful for our study since the discussion of sin and its consequences is found in the secunda pars. Satisfaction is required because of the reality of sin, caused by man, and its effects. In addition, several references to penitential satisfaction are found in the secunda pars in connection with the acts of virtue that are the traditional forms of external satisfaction, e.g., prayer, fasting and almsgiving, as well as in connection with the religious state of life.

1272-1273: Regent at Naples: Summa theologiae, Tertia pars; Super Psalmos; Sermons

Sometime after Easter of 1272 Saint Thomas left Paris with his companion, Reginald of Piperno. He assisted at the installation of his successor as master, Romanus of Rome, and left for his native Dominican province of Naples with some questions of the tertia pars of his Summa among his belongings. Once at Naples he took up residence at the Convent of San Domenico where, for the next year and a half, he would continue his university duties on a smaller scale. He did not, however, diminish his efforts, as testimony from his canonization process indicates: he was "always studying, lecturing or writing for the good of his fellow Christians."[52]

The central occupation of Saint Thomas's writing during this period was the tertia pars of the Summa theologiae. However, some other writings date from this period which make incidental reference to satisfaction and thus are of interest to this study. Foremosts among them is the commentary which Saint Thomas began on the Psalter. The work is a reportatio made by Reginald. Prior to 1880 the series consisted of the commentaries on Psalms 1 to 51; in that year a researcher discovered the commentaries for Psalms 52-54.[53] It is believed, on the basis of a copyist's note, that Saint Thomas abruptly terminated this work along with the Summa theologiae.

À second group of writings which are of minor interest to this study are frequently cited as opuscula; in fact, they are reportationes of sermons that Saint Thomas delivered in the Church of San Domenico during the Lent of 1273. The present scholastic form of these sermons betrays somewhat their original style. They were preached in the vernacular and recorded in Latin notes from which the current text was composed. Those of interest to this study are the Collationes super Credo in Deum, the Collationes super Pater Noster and the Collationes de decem praeceptis.

By far, however, the most outstanding accomplishment of this final period of Saint Thomas's academic career is the work that he was able to complete on the tertia pars of the Summa theologiae. The story of his experience before the crucifix in Saint Nicholas's Chapel of San Domenico is well-known. Father Weisheipl's account, based on the documentary evidence, is well worth reading, though his interpretation of Thomas's experience as a nervous breakdown might not be shared by all. Whatever the cause, the effect is well-known: "Reginald," said Saint Thomas, "I cannot, because all that I have written seems like straw to me."[54] The Summa theologiae breaks off with question 90, article 4 in the course of the discussion of Penance, which is unfortunately prior to the projected, detailed discussion of penitential satisfaction. Saint Thomas did, however, complete the formally christological questions (Qq. 1-59).

The prologue to the tertia pars clearly outlines both Saint Thomas's vision for the entire section as well as what he intended to be the theme of his discussion of the person and mysteries of Christ:

> Our Savior, the Lord Jesus Christ, as he was according to the angel's witness, saving his people from their sins, showed in his own Person that way of truth which, in rising again, we can follow to the blessedness of eternal life. This means that after our study of the final goal of human life and of the virtues and vices, we must bring the entire theological discourse to completion by considering the Saviour himself and his benefits to the human race.[55]

We have already remarked how Saint Thomas's desire to introduce an ordo disciplinae into sacred history moved him to structure his Summa around the Platonic

20

exitus-reditus theme. The tertia pars does not abandon that design but, on the contrary, complements it with a discussion of the actual way in which God chose to carry out the return of the human creature, indeed of all creation, to himself. The ordo disciplinae will now seek to find suitable reasons for the "facts" or the data of the revelation accomplished in Jesus Christ. This is what G. Lafont refers to as "the economic necessity of the Incarnation."[56]

The mystery of the Incarnation, however, encompasses more than the mystery of the person of Jesus Christ in itself. The benefits which he brought to the human race must also be discussed. In the prologue Saint Thomas also suggests that a complete consideration of the economy of salvation requires three main headings, which would have corresponded to the three principal parts of the tertia pars:

> First, the Saviour himself;
> secondly, his sacraments, through which we attain salvation;
> thirdly, the goal of life without end that we attain through Christ by our resurrection.[57]

The first division is subsequently divided into two main parts: on the mystery of the Incarnation, in which God became a man for our salvation (Qq. 1-26), and on what was done and suffered by our Saviour, that is, by God Incarnate (Qq. 27-59). It is because Christ is both the Divine Word and man that what he accomplishes has significance. No mere study of "functional" christology is adequate to penetrate into the mysteries of Christ's life. One must, as far as human reason is able, seek to understand something of who Christ is and how the perfect nature of God and human nature are united in the person of the Word.

Question 26, which is devoted to the office of Christ as Mediator, is a pivotal one. The fact that it is among the briefest in the Summa, Father O'Neill explains, "would appear absurdly out of proportion if it were not understood that the whole remaining part of the work, dealing with Christ's mysteries and the Church of faith and of the sacraments, is an examination of Christ's actual mediation."[58]

In the prologue to the tertia pars Saint Thomas introduces the Savior, Jesus Christ, as one who showed to man "a way of truth" which he "can follow to the

21

blessedness of eternal life." This way of truth which Christ shows to us is in fact the way of the reditus; it is the route that leads the creature back to God from whom he has come. The metaphor of "way" is a dynamic one; it emphasizes growth in Christ, positive advance towards the promised goal of perfect union with God.

It is to the blessedness of eternal life, that is, the vision of the Blessed Trinity (already treated at the beginning of the Summa and at the beginning of the secunda pars), that Christ summons a fallen humanity, itself unable to attain such an elevated goal because of its sin. Significantly, then, does Saint Thomas choose his introductory words from the 14th chapter of John's Gospel where Christ speaks about himself as "the way, and the truth, and the life." He is the Way along which man is led to his final goal of eternal life; Christ is the Way in which the image of God in man, marred but not effaced by Adam's sin, is restored to its original condition.

The present order of salvation, however, is one in which man is redeemed from sin in order to be able to have access to beatitude. Saint Thomas's employment of the Gospel of Saint Matthew in the prologue to the tertia pars is significant for this important, if subsidiary, theme of his christology.

> Joseph, son of David, do not fear to take Mary your wife, for that which is conceived in her is of the Holy Spirit; she will bear a Son, and you shall call his name Jesus, for he will save his people from their sins.[59]

This aspect of the tertia pars will be an important focus of our study. The way by which man returns to God is a way of satisfaction for sin; of satisfaction accomplished by Christ the Head and of satisfaction applied to his members.

CHAPTER II

THE BIBLICAL COMMENTARIES: THEOLOGIZING
OUT OF THE REVEALED WORD

Principles of Saint Thomas's Biblical
Interpretation

The success of the Summa theologiae and, in
general, of the other systematic compilations of Saint
Thomas has for a long time turned attention away
from the contents of his scriptual commentaries.
Nonetheless it remains an historical fact that, as a
13th century master of theology, Saint Thomas's principal professional responsibility was the teaching of
the Bible.[1] An examination of the fruits of his
lectures on the Old and the New Testaments serves as a
suitable and perhaps indispensable introduction to a
study of his systematic works. Such a procedure also
reminds the reader of Saint Thomas that his theology
is not divorced from the revealed Word of God, nor is
it one in which the Scriptures are accorded only
ornamental status, while the true inspiration derives
from non-Christian philosophy.

Regarding Saint Thomas's exegesis there is a
difficulty that has to be dealt with squarely from
the beginning: it is, in a word, obsolete by modern
standards. Does such an obsolete interpretation of
the Bible invalidate Saint Thomas's whole theology,
especially when it is presented as a systematic reflection on the revealed data of Scriptures? A lengthy
discussion of these issues is outside the scope of this
present work; however, a concise paragraph from an
essay by Father Edmund Hill offers a distinction which
I think is correct and which allows a student of Saint
Thomas to read and to use his scriptural commentaries
without too much apology for the kind of interpretation
contained therein. Speaking about the doubt as to the
value of Saint Thomas's theology that might occur to a
modern reader who was aware of the developments in
scientific exegesis when he encountered Question 102 of
the prima pars (which treats of the Garden of Eden),
Father Hill writes:

I would save the validity of St. Thomas's theology against this sort of doubt by saying that his interpretation of Scripture uses techniques that are indeed obsolete, and therefore produce many results that are obsolete, but is controlled by principles that are of the essence of the Catholic tradition of reflection on Scripture, and therefore produces a work that is essentially valid.[2]

Father Hill goes on to say that, despite H. de Lubac's assertion to the contrary, he would personally cite Origen as an example of a theologian of genius and admirable Christian devotion, whose work was essentially invalidated by wrong principles of interpretation introduced from outside into the Catholic possession of Scripture.

Father Hill's distinction between Saint Thomas's "principles" and his "techniques" requires further clarification. There is no need to belabor the point that the techniques of a 13th century exegete are largely obsolete after several centuries of progress in the development of textual and historical research. Nor did such a judgment of obsolescence await the significant advances made in higher criticism of the Scriptures in this century. Erasmus depreciated the value of Saint Thomas's theology on the grounds that he was ignorant of the biblical languages.[3] One need but recall the tools that were wanting to Saint Thomas and his contemporaries--critical editions of the biblical texts, personal acquaintances (in Saint Thomas's case, at least) with the biblical languages, handbooks and dictionaries on ancient civilizations and culture, etc.--to realize that the exegetical techniques which he employs in the study of the Scriptures are different from those used by modern theologians.

His principles for reading the Scriptures, however, are quite another matter; they retain their validity to this day. In one of his quodlibetal questions, Saint Thomas clearly describes a fundamental principle which underlies his understanding of what the Scriptures are:

The Scriptures are meant especially to show us the truths which are necessary for salvation. The manifestation or the expression of these truths is able to be

24

accomplished either by means of words or by means of things; the words, in effect, designate the things, and these things themselves are able to be figures of other realities. The Author of all things has the power not only to use words to designate things, but also to use things in a way that they signify other things. It follows that in the Scriptures, the truth manifests itself in a double fashion: first, the words yield certain realities--that is the literal sense; and second, these realities become figures of other realities--that is the spiritual sense.[4]

The same principle is more succinctly put in the De potentia, where Saint Thomas says that if there is a truth which seems suitably expressed by a passage of Scripture which the author of the text did not understand, one should not doubt that it was understood by the Holy Spirit, who is the principal Author of the Bible.[5]

It is Saint Thomas's conviction of the revelational intention of the divine Author, in the manifestation of which both the literal sense[6] and the spiritual senses are intrinsically bound together, that guides his approach to the reading of the Bible. It is commonly held by historians of medieval exegesis that Saint Thomas's use of the Bible is notable for its sobriety regarding the use of the spiritual sense. In this regard C. Spicq does not hesitate to call Saint Thomas a "revolutionary figure." In his Esquisse d'une Histoire de l'Exégèse Latine au Moyen Age Father Spicq writes:

Saint Thomas insisted less than the better part of his predecessors on the spiritual senses. . . . Thanks to his analysis of the modes of signification of the signifying words, and of the things signifying and signified, he gave to literal exegesis its full value, and reduced considerably the interest in mystical interpretations during the High Middle Ages.[7]

This attitude of respect for the literal sense of the Scriptures is a basic principle, although applications of a spiritual sense to various texts of Scripture need not be a cause for disquiet on the part of a contemporary reader of Saint Thomas's theology.

There is nothing hidden in any text of the sacred scriptures that is not manifestly expounded elsewhere in them; whence expositions of the spiritual sense ought always to have a foundation in some other literal exposition of the scriptures, and thus one guards against error.[8]

The texts to be examined in this section will offer a sampling of the various kinds of scriptural senses employed by Saint Thomas. Certain of these could give rise to the kind of doubt which Father Hill addresses in his essay. Unquestionably the contemporary student of the Bible enjoys countless advantages which aid his work that the medieval magister in sacra pagina did not enjoy. Seen, however, against the background of the medieval theologians' devotion to the Word of God (for the understanding of which Beryl Smalley's book, The Study of the Bible in the Middle Ages, is an invaluable tool),[9] there seems little reason to doubt the doctrinal solidity of the teaching which emerges from their scriptural commentaries. It would be absurd for a Christian believer who understood the opening lines of Hebrews 1:2--"but in these last days He has spoken to us by a Son,"--to think that the key for unlocking the true meaning of the Word of God could have been hidden for nineteen centuries.

The Satisfaction of Christ the Head

Postilla super Isaiam: A Biblical Christology

Another characteristic of scholastic exegesis, which contemporary theologians could regard as unusual, is the custom of slipping, almost imperceptibly, from exegesis to systematic theology. Thus, while the bulk of the Postilla super Isaiam is devoted to the division and explanation of the text "ad litteram"--for such was the basic scholastic method of reading (lectio) the Scriptures to the students, each of whom did not possess a personal copy of the Bible--there are theological digressions periodically written into the text. A good example of this is found in the ninth chapter of the commentary where Saint Thomas discusses Isaiah 9:6: "For to us a Child is born, to us a Son is given; and the government will be upon his shoulder." Three theological notes are given to explain the phrases "a Child is born" ("Parvulus natus est"); "to us . . . is given" ("datus est nobis"); and "upon his shoulder" ("super humerum eius"). Each of the notes is, in fact, a brief excursus on biblical christology.

The first note describes the abasement of Christ involved in the Incarnation (<u>kenosis</u>). While he does not refer to the great christological text in <u>Philippians</u> 2:5-11, one has the feeling that Saint Thomas has grasped the flow of Saint Paul's thought: the Incarnation signifies a voluntary humiliation on the part of the Son who did not carry his divine prerogatives into his human existence. Significantly absent from Saint Thomas's remarks is any reference to the metaphysics of the Incarnation.

> With respect to the words "Parvulus natus est," it should be noted that Christ is called a little one first as regards his birth because of his age: "And going into the house they saw the Child with Mary his Mother" (Matthew 2:11); second, as regards his possessions, since he was poor: "For you know the grace of Our Lord Jesus Christ, that though he was rich, yet for your sake he became poor" (II Corinthians 8:9); third, as regards his heart, since he was humble: "Learn from Me; for I am gentle and lowly in heart" (Matthew 11:29); fourth, as regards his vile death: "Let us condemn him to a shameful death" (Wisdom 2:20).[10]

The second note suggests nine ways in which Christ can be thought of as "for us;" one might consider this Saint Thomas's way of sketching a functional christology.

> Noting the phrase "datus est nobis," it can be said that Christ is given to us first as a brother: "O that you were like a brother to me, that nursed at my mother's breast!" (Song of Solomon 8:1); second, as a doctor: "Be glad, O sons of Zion, and rejoice in the Lord, your God; for he has given you a doctor of justice" (Joel 2:23); third, as a watchman: "Son of man, I have made you a watchman for the house of Israel" (Ezekiel 3); fourth, as a defender: "He will send them a saviour and will defend and deliver them" (Isaiah 19:20); fifth, as a shepherd: "And I will set up over them one shepherd. . . . and he shall feed them" (Ezekiel

27

34:23); sixth, as an example for our activities: "For I have given you an example, that you also should do as I have done to you" (John 13:15); seventh, as food for wayfarers: "The bread which I shall give for the life of the world is my flesh" (John 6:52); eighth, as a price of redemption: "The Son of man came not to be served but to serve, and to give his life as a ransom for many" (Matthew 20:28); ninth, as a price of remuneration: "To him who conquers I will give some of the hidden manna" (Revelation 2:17).[11]

Having first described the ways in which Christ "emptied himself" (Philippians 2:7) and, secondly, listed several ways in which the mission of Christ is directed toward mankind, Saint Thomas turns his attention to the final phrase--"super humerum eius." This provides him with the occasion to speak about the roles that are given to Christ in salvation history: he is a priest who satisfies and a victor who is glorified. One recognizes here a reflection of another Pauline antithesis, in addition to that of the kenosis found in Philippians 2:5-11; to the abasement of Christ there corresponds his exaltation.

> Similarly it should be observed concerning the words "super humerum eius" that God placed upon the shoulders of Christ first sins, as upon one who satisfies, as Isaiah says: "And the Lord has laid on him the iniquity of us all" (Isaiah 53:6); second, a key, as upon a priest: "And I will place on his shoulder the key of the house of David; he shall open, and none shall shut" (Isaiah 22:2); third, principality, as upon a conqueror: "And the government will be upon his shoulder" (Isaiah 9:6); fourth, glory, as upon one who triumphs: "And they will hang upon him the whole weight of his Father's house" (Isaiah 22:24).[12]

Although this long selection from the commentary on Isaiah contains but a single direct reference to satisfaction, it is worth a sustained look in order to emphasize the scriptural foundation to Saint Thomas's theological reflection and synthesis. The validity of his work, especially his future christology, is better appreciated when one is aware of his acquaintance with and rich use of the biblical material. Of course it is the text of the Latin Vulgate that offers him the opportunity to develop this synthesis. Certain terms found in the Vulgate text will disappear in later translations of the Scriptures--for example, the term "doctor" in the verse from Joel.[13] A newer translation often does not surrender itself to the same kind of appropriation as the text used by Saint Thomas. Our concern here is not, however, to raise further questions concerning Saint Thomas's biblical scholarship--still less his knowledge of the biblical languages. It is, however, to point out his familiarity with the standard Bible of his day. Granted the limitations placed on him by reason of the available text and the state of 13th century biblical scholarship, what emerges from this small excerpt of an Old Testament commentary is the picture of a teacher of sacred doctrine thoroughly aware of the inspired source of his science and fully at ease in using it. If we take into consideration for a moment the opinion of the Leonine authorities that this work could be the very first of Saint Thomas's theological endeavors, one cannot but be struck by the appreciation for the Sacred Scriptures which it shows.

The Commentaries on the Gospels of
Matthew and John: The Allegorical
Sense of the Scripture -
Christ and the
New Adam

There are several texts from the commentaries on the Gospels which deal with the satisfaction of Christ; they also serve as quite clear examples of what Saint Thomas calls the spiritual sense of Scripture. In the first question of the <u>Summa theologiae</u> he writes that in addition to the literal sense of the Scriptures there exists a spiritual sense which is sometimes called the mystical sense.[14] This spiritual sense lies not directly in the significance of the words as does the literal sense, but in the symbolism of the things they deal with. When the things under consideration are those of the Old Law which signify things of the New Law, that particular kind of spiritual sense is referred to, according to medieval usage, as allegorical sense.[15] The three texts which follow all touch upon some circumstance of Christ's passion, whether the instrument of his death, the time of his suffering or the place where he suffered. Each, in turn, suggests an allegorical interpretation of some Old Testament passage.

In the commentary _Super Matthaeum_, for example, Saint Thomas comments on Matthew 27:35: "And when they had crucified him." He observes that death by crucifixion was a fitting way for Christ to have satisfied for the sin of Adam, who had sinned "in ligno," that is to say, by eating of the fruit of the tree ("de ligno") of the knowledge of good and evil.[16] As is often the case in spiritual exegesis, a third citation is employed to help establish the significance of the Old Testament text for the New Testament. In this instance Saint Thomas quotes Wisdom 14:7: "For blessed is the wood by which righteousness comes." Thus, in accord with a tradition in Christian piety, Saint Thomas affirms that Christ's desire to suffer "in ligno," and thereby to satisfy for the sin of Adam, is symbolized by an element of the biblical narrative of original sin.

Another detail of the original sin story that surrenders itself to spiritual interpretation is the time of Adam's sin. Saint Thomas asserts that the sin of Adam must have taken place in the afternoon since it is written in Genesis 3:8 that, having sinned, Adam and Eve "heard the sound of the Lord God. . . in the cool of the day." The time of Christ's passion and death was clearly the afternoon as well, as the words of Matthew 27:45 indicate: "Now from the sixth hour there was darkness over all the land until the ninth hour."[17]

A third detail of the passion that is understood by Saint Thomas as signified in the Genesis narrative is the circumstance of place. In the _Lectura super Johannem_ he recalls that the sin of the first man was committed in a garden--"paradise" being interpreted as a "garden of delights" ("in paradiso voluptatis"). It is significant that in satisfying for such a sin "Christ was captured in a garden, suffered in a garden and was buried in a garden."[18]

Another variety of the spiritual sense of scripture, the analogical, "when the things that lie ahead in eternal glory are signified,"[19] is employed to derive further meaning from the garden theme. Since the Church is sometimes referred to as an enclosed garden, Saint Thomas sees the Church as spiritually signified by the garden of Christ's passion.[20] In another example of the same kind of spiritual interpretation, heaven itself is signified by the garden image, since by his passion Christ leads mankind to its final destiny, which is another kind of garden of delights, or paradise, as Luke 23:43 says: "Today you will be with me in Paradise."[21]

These three examples of Saint Thomas's spiritual exegesis, apart from illustrating the kind of biblical interpretation fruitfully employed by the medieval theologians, serves to adumbrate the theological development of satisfaction found in his other biblical commentaries, especially on the Pauline corpus, as well as in his systematic works. Well has Father Chenu written: "The magister in sacra pagina begets the magister in theologia; exegesis begets scholasticism."[22]

The brief excerpts already examined suggest two points fundamental to Saint Thomas's theologizing on Christ. The first point is that the satisfaction made by Christ on the cross is necessary by reason of the sin of Adam and all the sins subsequent to that original sin. In Super Matthaeum Saint Thomas comments on Matthew 26:38--"Then he said to them, 'My soul is very sorrowful, even to death'"--and says that Christ added "even to death" to indicate that by his death he would satisfy for the present crime of his betrayal as well as for all other sins.[23] The second point is that the satisfaction accomplished by Christ makes it possible for man to reach his supernatural end, whether that be presented as the establishment of a community of salvation, the Church, or as the opening of the gates of heaven, as in the promise to the Good Thief. When Saint Thomas speaks about the Church as a community "consecrated" by the blood of Christ, as the community of the Elect, his meaning is eschatological. For this reason I suggest that the spiritual interpretation of the Church as an "enclosed garden" is an employment of the anagogical variety of spiritual interpretation.

The Commentaries on the Letters of
Saint Paul and on Hebrews

Christ as "Propitiatio" for our sins

To say that Saint Thomas repeatedly refers to the satisfaction of Christ as something necessary because of the sins of mankind is to say that he focuses attention onto one of the principal elements of the primitive gospel preaching. C. H. Dodd points out that when Saint Paul wished to give authenticity to his teaching he simply reminded his audience of the gospel which underlay it all.[24] In I Corinthians 15:1-3 he writes: "Now I would remind you, brethren, in what terms I preached to you the gospel, which you received. . . . For I delivered to you as of first importance what I also received, that Christ died for our sins in accordance with the scriptures." The following texts from Saint Thomas's biblical commentaries discuss Christ's expiation for our sins.

Saint Thomas's commentary on Romans 3:23-26 offers him the occasion to treat on the expiatory character of Christ's satisfaction. Saint Paul writes: "They are justified by his grace as a gift, through the redemption which is in Christ Jesus, whom God put forward as an expiation." (Romans 3:24) In his commentary, Saint Thomas states his teaching on the need for the satisfaction made by Christ. Commenting on the phrase, "through the redemption which is in Christ Jesus" Saint Thomas writes:

> It is as if someone, having committed some fault, became indebted to the king and was obliged to pay a fine. One who paid the fine for him would be said to have redeemed him. Such a debt was owed by the whole human race because of the sin of the first parents. So it was that no other one apart from Christ was able to satisfy for the sin of the whole human race, since he alone was free of every sin.[25]

Such theological glosses on the text, inserted into the _lectura_, are characteristic of a well-developed commentary such as that on Romans; they afford an opportunity for the student of Saint Thomas to see what particular texts of the New Testament moved him to theologize on a given topic such as satisfaction. Noteworthy in this particular excerpt is the fact that Saint Thomas cites the sinlessness of Christ as the reason why the satisfaction which he accomplished was an efficacious one for the human race.

Saint Thomas continues his commentary, noting that there is no other source of redemption possible for us, indeed "not with perishable things such as silver and gold" (I Peter 1:18). Christ alone is our redemption since it is he "whom God put forward as an expiation (propitiationem)." It is this designation of the sinless Christ by God to which Saint Thomas attributes the efficacy of Christ's satisfaction as our

justification and as our redemption.[26]   "Because
God had ordained him for this according to his own
counsel," continues Saint Thomas, "who accomplishes all
things according to the counsel of his will."[27]   This
reference to Ephesians 1:9-11 recalls the mystery of
God's purpose in the world, his age-long purpose
to call all men to share in the fruits of Christ's
redemptive work.

It is the term "propitiatio" of Saint Thomas's
Latin Vulgate Bible that spurs him to interpret this
and other texts in tems of satisfaction: to say
that Christ satisfies for us is to say that he expiates
for our sins.   For example, when the Psalmist cries,
"Propitius esto peccatis nostris,"   "Forgive our
sins!," he is crying out for the satisfaction accomplished by Christ.[28]   When the First Letter of John
2:2 refers to Christ as "the expiation (propitiatio)
for our sins," it is because he has satisfied for
us.[29]   Or when Saint Thomas, according to the principles of spiritual exegesis, recalls the instruction
contained in Exodus 25:17 to put the mercy seat (propitiatorium) over the ark, it is Christ our expiation who
is being put over the ark of the Church.[30]

The expiatory value of Christ's death in Saint
Paul's writings is closely associated with the liturgy
of sacrifice.   L. Cerfaux refers to Romans 3:23-26 as a
particularly important passage where this connection is
made.   Speaking of Christ, Saint Paul says that it is
he "whom God put forward as an expiation by his blood."
Saint Thomas adds, "It is only through the Blood of
Christ that both the sins of the present as well as
those of the past are able to be forgiven."[31]   The
efficacy of Christ's blood to wipe away man's sins is
realized only when man has faith in the power (virtus)
of the Blood of Christ.

A fuller explanation of what it means to have
faith in the power of Christ's Blood is found when
Saint Thomas comments on the next phrase of Romans
3:25--". . . to be received by faith."   Apropos of this
line he writes:

> This death of Christ is applied to us by
> faith, by which we believe that the world has
> been redeemed by his death--Galatians 2:20:
> "I live by faith in the Son of God, who loved
> me."   For even among men, satisfaction by one
> for another is without worth, unless such
> confidence is present.[32]

It is in his commentary on the Letter to the Hebrews, however, that Saint Thomas is able to develop the implications of the sacrificial character of Christ's satisfaction. At the very beginning of Hebrews 1:1-4 Christ is referred to as making "purification for sins." Saint Thomas comments that among the ways this can be understood is that on the altar of the cross he satisfied for the punishment (reatus poenae) encumbent upon man because of sin.[33] On the fifth chapter of Hebrews, which resumes the theme of Jesus the high priest, Saint Thomas comments that it is Christ himself who is the priest and who, according to the command of Leviticus 4:26, sees to the carrying out of sin offerings.[34]

The commentary on Hebrews continues by remarking that "every high priest is appointed to offer gifts and sacrifices. . . . Hence it is necessary for this priest to have something to offer."[35] It is Christ himself who is the offering, writes Saint Thomas, and because he was without sin he fulfilled the Old Testament exigency that the offering be without spot or blemish. There is a further congruence in the role of Christ as hight priest, namely, that a man is able to satisfy for mankind's sins. By the sacrifice of the cross Christ offers himself in satisfaction for the sins of his brothers and sisters. Such an efficacious sacrifice having been absent prior to the time of Christ's death is the reason, according to Saint Thomas, why the sacrifices of the Old Law, offered by those who were sinners, did not "perfect the conscience of the worshipper" and were not truly satisfactory. By contrast, the sacrifice offered by Christ, who alone was sinless, was acceptable and accomplished true satisfaction.

Just as it is a commonplace to say that Christ died for our sins, so an equally familiar element of the New Testament teaching is that Christ's death destroyed death.[36] In his commentary on II Timothy 1:10 Saint Thomas explicitly equates Christ's having destroyed death with his having satisfied for our sins.[37] This theme is continued and elaborated in the commentary on Hebrews 2:14-16, where the inspired author discusses another consequence of Christ's having assumed a human nature: "Since therefore the children share in flesh and blood, he himself likewise partook of the same nature, that through death he might destroy him who has the power of death, that is, the devil, and deliver all those who through fear of death were subject to lifelong bondage."

Careful to dissociate himself from early medieval "rights of the devil" theories and with an eye to refuting them, Saint Thomas distinguishes the ways in which the devil might be said to have some power concerning death. A judge can be said to have dominion over death when, as in inflicting death, he commands a capital punishment. A thief, too, can be said to have a certain dominion over death but only in the sense that he has merited it by his crimes; he has a "right" to death. It is in this second (perhaps somewhat forced) sense that the devil led man to death.[38] Christ's redemptive death destroys the devil's ill-gotten right concerning death. Indeed the devil would have presumed to extend this effect of sin even to Christ himself, but the power of the sinless Christ's own death justly conquers the power of the devil. As a result of this victory man is freed from the devil's bondage, that is, from the servitude of sin.

In his commentary on the kenosis hymn of Philippians Saint Thomas makes another comparison between the roles played by the devil in seducing man away from God and the role played by Christ in leading man back to God. Commenting upon Philippians 2:6--"though he was in the form of God, Christ did not count equality with God a thing to be grasped" (rapinam)--Saint Thomas remarks that one can contrast the humility of Christ, who, though he was God, sought to lower himself, with the audacity of the devil and man, who, filled with pride, sought to grasp (rapina) at divinity. Christ, indeed, was entitled to such a holding on to divinity since he knew well who he was; neither the devil nor man, on the contrary, was entitled to such a rapine. It was for the sin of pride that Christ satisfied, concludes Saint Thomas, appropriating to Christ the words of the psalmist--"What I did not steal (non rapui), must I now restore?".[39]

A commentary on Ephesians 1:7-8 enlarges on the meaning of expiation or removal of sins (remotio peccati) as equivalent to the satisfaction of Christ: "In him we have redemption through his blood, the forgiveness of our trespasses, according to the riches of his grace which he lavished upon us." Saint Thomas notes, having recourse to technical theological terms, that there are two things which separate fallen man from God: the one is sin itself (macula peccati) and the other is a debt of punishment (noxa poenae). Christ's satisfaction is sufficient to remove both obstacles to man's union with God. "In him we have our redemption," writes Saint Paul, and that redemption, according to Saint Thomas's interpretation, means liberation from the stain of sin. Christ also satisfied to the Father and, because of his death, the debt to punishment encumbent upon us as sinners is abolished.[40]

This salvation which Christ procures for mankind is "according to the riches of his God's grace," which means that God bestows gratuitously on an unworthy people the redemption and sanctification which is accomplished by the satisfaction of his Son.[41] Indeed Saint Thomas does not hesitate to call this grace a superabundant one (ex superabundanti gratia) because God was willing to safeguard the honor of the human race at the price of his Son, whose death, after the fashion of justice (quasi per justitiam), liberated man from the servitude of sin.[42] The implications of this being bought back, that is redeemed instead of simply liberated, will be discussed in the systematic works.

Liberation from sin, however, is only one side of the effect of Christ's redemptive work. Man is also turned toward God and, in effect, reunited with him. It is this aspect of satisfaction that Saint Thomas speaks about in commenting on Ephesians 2:16 where Saint Paul talks about redemption as "bringing the hostility to an end." Saint Thomas's observation is a simple one: "Christ sufficiently satisfied for our sins; the price being paid, it follows that reconciliation should occur."[43] It is to this aspect of Christ's satisfaction to which we now turn.

Christ is our "Reconciliatio"

In the previous section we have seen that Saint Thomas emphasized the subjective state of Christ, his sinlessness, as a reason for the efficacy of the satisfaction which he accomplished. In commenting on the words of Saint Paul in Romans 5:8ff, "But God shows his love for us in that while we were yet sinners Christ died for us," he offers another reason for this efficacy. The satisfaction of Christ finds its value not only in the shedding of his sinless blood but also in the love with which these sufferings were borne. This shift to the love of Christ is not an abrupt one, however. For whereas in the previous section Saint Thomas spoke of the sinlessness of Christ (and not simply blood-shedding), he now turns to a deeper aspect of that sinless state, his love. One sign of the love with which Christ bore his sufferings is that he died

36

for us while we were still at odds (inimici) with God. "The very death of Christ itself shows God's love for us, because he gave his Son that he might die in order to satisfy for us."[44] God's love, then, is revealed in Christ's saving action.

Were it not for Christ's love, asserts Saint Thomas, Christ's death would not have had the salvific value that it did. If one were to consider the death of Christ as a mere natural phenomenon there would be nothing acceptable about it to a God who "does not delight in the death of the living."[45] It would be even less acceptable if one were to consider the death of Christ as the result of murder; that would be in fact displeasing to God. However, if one considers Christ's loving and obedient acceptance of death then it takes on positive meaning.

> From this was the death of Christ meritorious and satisfactory for our sins, and as such acceptable to God, adequate for the reconciliation of all men, even of those killing Christ, some of whom were saved by his very prayer, when he said: "Forgive them, for they know not what they do."[46]

Here is the heart of the matter: it is the will of Christ formed by love and by obedience which gives his death saving significance.

"For if while we were enemies we were reconciled to God by the death of his Son, much more, now that we are reconciled, shall we be saved by his life" (Romans 5:10). The fruit of the satisfaction accomplished by love is the reconciliation of God and man, a reconciliation made possible by the removal of the offense that heretofore separated them. Saint Thomas has recourse to an argument from human experience to support his conclusion. The unique character of Christ's love is shown when one considers that in human affairs one is certainly less disposed to do good to an enemy unless some form of reconciliation has already taken place. Christ, however, died for sinful mankind. The full impact of the reconciliation which the death of the sinless Christ accomplished is suggested when Saint Thomas writes that "even now we are joined to God through faith and charity."[47] Reconciliation, then, should not be considered merely as the removal of some obstacle which previously separated two parties, but as something positive because the satisfaction made by Christ results in man being given a positive share in his (risen) life.

Saint Thomas's teaching on the ability of one person to make satisfaction for another is an integral element of his doctrine on satisfaction. Fuller discussion of this issue awaits the systematic works. However, the standard biblical text to which Saint Thomas refers many times as grounds for the validity of such vicarious satisfaction is Galatians 6:2, "Bear one another's burdens, and so fulfill the law of Christ." In his commentary on this adage of Saint Paul, Saint Thomas spells out three ways in which such an injunction might be carried out. The third of these ways is of concern to this study, namely, "by satisfying for the punishment owed another, by prayers and good deeds.[48] In support of this interpretation he cites Proverbs 18:19: "A brother helped is like a strong city."

The satisfaction, accomplished by Christ's passion, borne in love, results in our being reconciled to God, in our being in harmony with him. Though sin established man in a state of estrangement from God, blocked from attaining the destiny which God intended for his creature, the redemptive work of Christ results in man's now being able confidently to hope for that destiny which is union with God. In the commentary on Romans Saint Thomas speaks about such reconciliation in connection with verse 5:11, "we also rejoice in God through whom we have now received our reconciliation." Significantly for our discussion of Saint Thomas's biblical commentaries, this section of the fifth chapter of Romans comes just before Saint Paul's development of the Adam-Christ analogy. It should be noted, however, that Saint Thomas does not lose sight of the final goal of reconciliation in Christ which is union of man with God.

The commentary on II Corinthians 5:18 provides another occasion for Saint Thomas to elaborate on reconciliation, "All this is from God, who through Christ reconciled us to himself and gave us the ministry of reconciliation." Here Saint Thomas outlines two benefits which result from the work of Christ, the one a general benefit for all men and the other a special benefit given only to the Apostles. The general benefit is none other than the reconciliation itself: "For men were enemies of God because of sin; Christ, however, took away this enmity from their midst by satisfying for sin."[49] To use another term for this reconciliation, Saint Thomas suggests that Christ establishes concord between God and man.[50] In the commentary on Hebrews 8:2-6 Saint Thomas describes the reconciliation as a union when he writes that all those for whom Christ's expiatory sacrifice was offered are united to God.[51] A special benefit, also the result of reconciliation, is given to the Apostles. It is the ministry of reconciliation for others: the Apostles are to be the channels through which the effects of Christ's satisfaction are given to the world. The Apostles are the conduits of this union, this concord between God and man.[52]

This mention of a ministry of reconciliation given to the Apostles brings the discussion of Saint Thomas's biblical commentaries to the next topic, namely, the satisfaction of the members. Before that, however, a brief recapitulation of the teachings of Saint Thomas that emerges from the places in his commentaries on the gospels, the Pauline corpus and the Epistle to the Hebrews is in order. Perhaps no better recapitulation is possible than to say that the Adam-Christ typology is the inspiration behind Saint Thomas's talk about satisfaction. Sin and death for all men followed upon Adam's pride and disobedience; satisfaction and reconciliation for all men is the result of Christ's love and suffering in obedience to his Father's will. Because of the satisfaction accomplished on the cross all men can reach the beatific destiny intended for them by God. It is this fundamental picture of Christian salvation as it is found in the New Testament which guides Saint Thomas's systematic treatment of Christ's satisfaction.

The Satisfaction of the Members

Expositio in Job "ad litteram":
Penitential Satisfaction and
the Moral Sense of
Scripture

In the prologue to his commentary on Job Saint Thomas explains that his intention is to comment on Job "secundum litteralem sensum." We have already remarked that he decided against developing the spiritual sense because that had been done adequately by Gregory the Great more than six centuries previously in his Moralia.[53] Besides respectfully declining to repeat

the work already accomplished by Gregory, Saint Thomas,
by declaring his intention to follow the literal sense
of Job, also separates himself from the mentality of
others whose commentaries on Job preceded his. For
example, the writer of the anonymous Victorine letter
(an instruction to a young monk about to begin his
theological education in the monastic tradition)
roundly denied that the book of Job had any useful
literal significance and counseled that it be read only
with reference to Christ and his Church.[54]

In a clear break with this tradition of interpreting Job, Saint Thomas immediately identifies the
literal theme or purpose of the book: it is "to
demonstrate through probable reasons that human affairs
are subject to divine providence."[55] As B. Smalley
observes, "Thank to his 'compendious' treatment, the
'purpose' never disappears behind the exposition of
isolated texts."[56] While Saint Thomas acknowledges
that one who undertakes a commentary on Job will
be bound to try to explain how the sufferings and
afflictions of the just man can be reconciled with an
all-good Providence, the traditional theme of patience
does not figure in his commentary.

Saint Thomas's intention to be guided by the
literal meaning of the text of Job does not imply that
he will avoid all spiritual interpretation in his
commentary. Rather, he will refrain from offering the
kinds of accommodated interpretation, indeed, the
sometimes forced explanations of the texts, already
amply provided by his predecessors.[57] On this point
Father Chenu has written:

> His reaction was a significant one, for it
> brought out the fact that theology was
> putting up a safety-catch against the multi-
> plying of figures and allegories without
> criterion or limits. It remains that, _de
> facto_, Saint Thomas did practice on his own,
> in his running interpretation of the texts,
> that classical type of interpretation wherein
> utilization of the Bible for spiritual
> purposes oversteps the explanation of the
> word of God.[58]

It should come as no surprise, however, that the
isolated references to satisfaction contained in the
Expositio in Job do not refer to the satisfaction of
Christ. It is the relationship of divine providence to
human affairs that is the subject of Job; when the

40

occasion to speak about satisfaction occurs, Saint Thomas does not employ the allegorical (messianic) spiritual sense, nor the anagogical (eschatological), but a third variety, the moral sense. Elsewhere Saint Thomas writes of the moral sense: it is brought into play "when the things done in Christ and in those who prefigure him are signs of what we should carry out."[59] It is the penitential satisfaction which "we should carry out" that is the subject of Saint Thomas's isolated remarks on our theme in his commentary on Job.

The first mention of satisfaction comes in the very first chapter of the commentary. In the biblical narrative, Job is said to offer sacrifices for his sons, after they had completed their cycle of feasting. Commenting on the line, "burnt offerings according to the number of them all (i.e., his sons)" (1:5), Saint Thomas notes the correspondence between the number of the sacrifices and the number of Job's sons. "Each sin," he writes, "should be expiated by a corresponding satisfaction."[60]

A second reference to satisfaction is found in the commentary on the seventh chapter, where Job is lamenting his state--"If I sin, what do I do to thee, thou watcher of men?" (7:20). This cry of human infirmity moves Saint Thomas to offer one of three reasons why it is proper, given man's weakness, that God should forgive our sins. "Man is unable to do anything condign by way of recompense for the offense which he has committed against God."[61] The underlying reasoning is that if God keeps so close a watch over man's actions he must realize that by human effort alone man, precisely because he is in a sinful condition, is unable to win forgiveness for his sins. Such, then, should not be a precondition for God's forgiveness.

Commenting on the eighth chapter, Saint Thomas has a third opportunity to speak about satisfaction, emphasizing the role of prayer as a satisfaction for sin. It is Job's friend, Bildad, who addresses him in the biblical text: "If you will seek God and make supplication to the Almighty." (8:5) This moves Saint Thomas to comment that "among the works of satisfaction prayer seems to be foremost."[62] It is the Latin word for supplication, deprecatus, in the Vulgate text which suggests to Saint Thomas the satisfactory work of prayer. Actually, this forms the second stage of a three-step plan (in Saint Thomas's view) offered by

41

Bildad whereby Job might win pardon and relief from his sufferings. Briefly put, the plan is to rise quickly from sin, make satisfaction for sin and be careful not to fall back into sin.

The last two passages which speak of satisfaction are found in the final chapter of the commentary. Saint Thomas reflects on Job's admission that he now understands the purposefulness of God's actions; he views Job as moved to a deeper awareness of his sinfulness. Saint Thomas comments: "The more a man considers the justice of God, the more he will be aware of his own faults."[63] Simply to be aware of one's sinfulness is not enough, however; satisfaction must be done. Job, moved by the fragility of human nature, acknowledges this when he says "Therefore I despise myself and repent in dust and ashes" (42:6). Saint Thomas comments on the fittingness of this conclusion by remarking that "a humble satisfaction is appropriate to expiate for the pride of man's thoughts."[64] This relationship between a humble spirit and the desire to make satisfaction is an important theological point; perhaps the most thought-provoking reflection on satisfaction to come out of this commentary.

Significantly, a similar observation is found in the single reference to satisfaction contained in a minor work of Saint Thomas, De regno. We know that it was written for a King of Cyprus, who apparently died before he had a chance to receive Saint Thomas's thoughts on governance.[65] In it Saint Thomas explains why a bad king, that is, a tyrant, is unable to make satisfaction. He writes:

> Such tyrants, bloated as they are with pride, are rarely sorry for their sins and rightly deserted by God; steeped in a desire for human adulation, they even more rarely are able to make suitable satisfaction.[66]

These remarks, both those in the commentary on Job and in the De regno, on the relationship between a humble spirit and the ability to perform penitential satisfaction are noteworthy. They indicate Saint Thomas's insight into the psychology that lies behind the practice of the faith; in this case, the fact that there is something required in man's spirit, namely humility, in order that he be disposed to acknowledge his need for satisfaction and subsequently seek to perform it. In the systematic works, such as the Scriptum super Sententias, this relationship between satisfaction and humility will be looked at from another perspective. The moral effects of satisfactory deeds on man's dispositions will be stressed; it is the performance of satisfaction (for example, that enjoined in the sacrament of Penance) that develops in man a humble and contrite spirit.

The last passage in Job which deals with satisfaction approaches the subject of christological satisfaction, dealing as it does with the intercession of a holy man for others. The remark comes as part of the commentary on what contemporary editors of the Bible call the epilogue, in which the ancient folktale, which has served as a setting for the biblical account,[67] reappears abruptly. The friends of Job have not spoken rightly of God and, in Saint Thomas's view, they have sinned greatly because theirs is a dogmatic error. Accordingly, in the biblical account they are asked to offer up a sacrifice of seven bulls and seven rams. Then the Lord instructs them to "go to my servant Job and offer up for yourself a burnt offering; and my servant Job shall pray for you, and I will accept his prayer not to deal with you according to your folly" (42:8).

Saint Thomas sees in this command a two-fold significance bearing upon satisfaction. First, God is affirming the principle that the one who sins must be the one who performs the satisfaction. Thus the three friends of Job are ordered to "offer up for yourselves" the required sacrifice. The second significance which Saint Thomas sees in the passage is perhaps of greater interest. The friends are asked to go to Job for his intercession. In Saint Thomas's mind this indicates that the sacrifice of sinners, or the satisfaction performed by them, can need the help of a holy man --"but your satisfaction needs the intercession of a faithful man."[68] Because Job's prayers are added to the satisfaction undertaken by the guilty friends, they will escape their due punishment. This teaching that the satisfaction performed by a guilty party can be validated, as it were, by the intercession of an innocent friend adumbrates the relationship which Saint Thomas describes between the perfect satisfaction of Christ and the various penitential satisfactions undertaken by his members.

Commentaries on the New Testament: Satisfaction in the Context of the Sacraments of Baptism and Penance

The relationship between the satisfaction of Christ the Head and the satisfaction of the members, especially as the latter is carried out within the context of the Church's sacramental system, is a subject that will be clarified in the systematic works of Saint Thomas, especially the _Summa theologiae_. For the moment there are a group of New Testament texts that offer Saint Thomas the occasion to speak, according to the principles of one kind of spiritual interpretation or another, about penitential satisfaction in connection with the sacraments of Baptism and Penance.

In the first of these texts, a commentary on Romans 11:29, "The gifts and call of God are irrevocable," Saint Thomas finds the occasion to distinguish between the need for external works of satisfaction in the sacrament of Penance and the fact that in Baptism such satisfaction is superfluous. He writes that although contrition of the heart, or interior penance, is required of an adult who seeks to be baptized, an external penance is not demanded of such a one.[69] Baptism, drawing on the regenerative power of Christ's passion, works _per modum cuiusdam generationis_--it is birth in Christ--and for this reason it removes whatever there is of the _poena_ which is the result of sin. The sacrament of Penance, by way of contrast, works _per modum sanationis_. The healing process involved in this sacrament does not require that all of the effects of sin be removed immediately and, therefore, external works of penance, or satisfaction, are enjoined by the priest so that the penitent himself might cooperate in the process of his own integral healing.

In commenting upon II Corinthians 7:10, "For godly grief produces a repentance that leads to salvation and brings no regret, but worldly grief produces death," Saint Thomas has occasion to speak about the traditional threefold division of the sacrament of Penance, "contritio cordis, confessio oris, satisfactio operis."[70] Godly grief, writes Saint Thomas, brings no regret or, according to the Vulgate text, leads to lasting salvation (_in salutem stabilem_) because it moves man to undertake the other two parts of the sacrament of Penance.

44

A different light is thrown onto the relationship between the three parts of the sacrament of Penance in a discussion of I Corinthians 11:27--"Whoever, therefore, eats the bread or drinks the cup of the Lord in an unworthy manner will be guilty of profaning the Body and Blood of the Lord." Saint Thomas lists three ways in which a person might approach the Eucharist in an unworthy manner. Only the third way is of interest for this present study, since it deals with the case where sacramental confession and satisfaction is not possible before receiving the Eucharist. Should one who has committed a mortal sin approach the Eucharist, he would be guilty of profaning the Body and Blood of the Lord. However, it might happen that under certain circumstances such an individual could not confess his sins and perform a satisfaction for them. A simple act of contrition would suffice in this case, since by such an expression of sorrow the will to sin is taken away.[71] While Saint Thomas acknowledges that such a preparation should not be the regular (<u>regulariter</u>) one for receiving the Eucharist, it is nonetheless an adequate one.

Apart from the welcome flexibility that such an opinion exhibits, there is a more profound theological meaning underlying this resolution of a practical, moral dilemma. There are two effects consequent upon a morally bad act: the first is the stain of sin (<u>macula peccati</u>) and the second is the punishment due to sin (<u>reatus poenae</u>). In his commentary on Psalm 50, Saint Thomas explicitly says that when David asked to regain the innocence he had lost by turning away from God, he sought "first that the evil or sin be removed and second that the effect of sin be removed."[72] The essential act of conversion is an act of charity precisely because the sinner turns toward God from whom he had been estranged and this removes the <u>macula peccati</u>. Penance, on the other hand, as it regards past sins and their <u>reatus poenae</u> is an act of the virtue of justice. Saint Thomas has no hesitation in allowing someone who has turned to God in charity to receive the Eucharist, even though such an individual (due to external circumstances) has not had the occasion to express sorrow for his sins by sacramental confession and subsequent satisfaction.

Some indication of the role that satisfaction plays in the healing of the effects of sin can be seen in the commentaries on the Gospel of Matthew and John. Commenting on the cure of the paralytic in Matthew 9:1-8, Saint Thomas writes:

There were three things about the sick man:
he was lying on his bed, he was carried by
others, he was unable to walk. Because he
was lying down Christ said "Rise"; because he
was carried in, Christ commanded that he take
something up--"Take up your bed"; because
he was unable to walk, Christ said "Rise and
walk."[73]

Then Saint Thomas offers a spiritual interpretation,
according to the moral sense, of what this episode
means for the Christian who has sinned:

Likewise to the sinner lying in sin it is
said "Rise" from your sin by contrition;
"Take up your bed" by satisfaction; "And go
home" into the house of eternity, or a clean
conscience.[74]

A commentary on a similar healing miracle of
Christ, the cure of the man at the pool of Bethzatha in
John 5:1-9, offers another occasion to examine the role
of satisfaction in the healing of the effects of sin.
The verse in question is similar to that commented on
in the above text from Super Matthaeum; John 5:8 reads:
"Jesus said to him, 'Rise, take up your pallet and
walk.'" The spiritual interpretation of the first two
elements of the command is identical to that found
in the commentary on Matthew. First the Lord commands
the sick man to rise, and this is interpreted as an
injunction to rise from sin (recedendo a peccato).
Second, he is told to take up his pallet as a means of
satisfying for his sins. "For by the pallet, on which
a man lies, is signified sin. When a man picks up his
pallet he is carrying the burden of penance imposed on
him for his sins."[75] As usual a third text is employed
to establish the link between the figure and the
spiritual interpretation; here it is Micah 7:9: "I
will bear (portabo) the indignation of the Lord because
I have sinned against Him."

The third injunction given to the paralytic is
that he walk. Saint Thomas interprets this detail as
meaning that the man who has confessed his sins and
performed his satisfaction must now continue to advance
in goodness (proficiendo in bono). In the following
paragraphs of his commentary, Saint Thomas gives a
résumé of Saint Augustine's interpretation of this same
gospel incident. The details of their allegorizations
differ, but the two authors are in agreement on the
final point, namely, that the command of Christ to the

paralytic--"Walk"--indicates that the reason man is freed from sin is so that he will be able to move once again toward his final and proper destiny, which is union with God.

This detail is noteworthy since its suggests the larger theological framework into which Saint Thomas will place his theology of satisfaction. The part of that framework pertinent to the present discussion is man's desire to reach his supernatural goal of union with God. The forgiveness of sins and the satisfaction for them are not ends in themselves; they are steps in the process of fallen man's return to God. The healing that is accomplished by satisfaction rectifies the disorders in man caused by sin and remaining even after conversion, and it redirects his efforts toward realizing his final goal of beatitude. In light of the anagogical interpretation given to Christ's command to the paralytic, "Walk," one better understands the reason for Saint Thomas's flexibility with regard to the reception of the Eucharist (the pledge of man's future glory) by one who has turned back to God in sorrow but has not had the opportunity to confess and satisfy for his sins.

Postilla super Psalmos: Satisfaction Produces a Joyful Spirit

The full effect of the sinner's turning toward God and its ratification in the sacrament of Penance is clearly described by Saint Thomas in his commentary on the psalms, especially on Psalm 50, the Miserere. This psalm, which was frequently employed in the liturgical and para-liturgical prayer of the medieval Dominican priory, is the eloquent testimony of David's remorse for his sin. The title, found in Saint Thomas's Vulgate text, indicates the occasion for its composition: "A psalm of David, when Nathan the prophet came to him, after he had gone in to Bathsheba."[76] Saint Thomas notes that the very number of the psalm, 50 in the Vulgate enumeration, corresponds to that of the jubilee year, when, according to the precepts of Leviticus, all debts were forgiven. This is highly appropriate, says Saint Thomas, since this psalm treats of the "full remission of sin."[77]

The Miserere, then, is a psalm which will offer Saint Thomas the occasion to speak about the full cycle of Christian sorrow and reconciliation. One should not be surprised that the commentary on the psalms provides the occasion for such a complete discussion of theological matters. In the prologue to his commentary, Saint Thomas writes that in Psalm 50, in addition to the traditional threefold division of the sacrament of Penance, a fourth part is mentioned:

> This fourth element is the effect of penance, in which it is shown how penitence restores man to a perfect state. Therefore among all the other psalms this one is most frequently used by the Church.[78]

The phrase "restores man to a perfect state" ("restaurat hominem ad perfectum") expresses what is the ultimate goal of reconciliation. The importance of this teaching is better realized in light of the biblical and patristic doctrine of man as God's image, to which Saint Thomas has frequent recourse in his systematic works; indeed it forms a _leitmotiv_ of his anthropology and christology. The restoration of man to the perfect image of God in which he was created is a theological idiom for the fullness of salvation made possible by the salvific work of Christ.

Nor is there reason for surprise that Saint Thomas understands the psalms as clearly referring to the person and the work of Christ. In the prologue he lays down the principles of interpretation that he will follow throughout his commentary, namely to follow a principle of Saint Jerome,

> who in his commentary on Ezechiel gave us a rule which we will follow in our exposition on the psalms, namely, that the happenings recounted in the psalms should be interpreted as saying something either of Christ or of the Church.[79]

Nonetheless Saint Thomas is flexible enough to draw lessons directly from the experiences of David, whose conversion and repentence is the setting for the psalm. For example, Saint Thomas uses David as a warning for us. If David, he writes, who was blessed with such a special relationship with God, could turn and sin against him, then we have every reason to be on our guard against falling into sin. In another section of the commentary he makes a similar remark. Writing on Psalm 37:5, "My wounds grow foul and fester," Saint Thomas warns that the danger of recidivism is a real one, just as scar tissue is prone to infection.

Satisfaction, he notes, is a means of healing the wounds of sin; it strengthens man against future temptation.[80]

The _Miserere_ is David's prayer for mercy. The mercy for which he asks is identified with the divine goodness, as it regards the miserable state of the sinner. In effect, then, it is God himself whom the sinner seeks by his cry for mercy. The twofold effect of sin must be removed, however, if the sinner would approach God. When David prays to be washed thoroughly from his iniquity, Saint Thomas understands that he asks to be cleansed from both the stain of sin (_macula peccati_) and its punishment (_reatus poenae_). In effect David says, "I ask that you grant me a reprieve from punishment, but also that you cleanse me of the stain of sin."[81]

Punishment being a consequence of sin, satisfaction is required. Since all men find themselves born into a sinful condition, no one is able to receive full remission of his sins apart from making satisfaction. In a comment on the verse of the psalm, "Behold, thou desirest truth in the inward being," Saint Thomas writes with perception about the relationship between the willingness of a sinner to make satisfaction and his willingness to accept the truth of his sinful condition. He writes:

> _Ecce enim veritatem dilexisti._ The one who wants to satisfy must love that which God loves. God however loves the truth of the faith: John 18:37, "Everyone who is of the truth hears My voice." Likewise God loves justice: Psalm 88:15, "Steadfast love and faithfulness (_veritas_) go before thee." Such love of truth and justice is required in a penitent in order that one might be punished in those very things in which one has failed."[82]

Even the hyssop, with which the Psalmist asks to be purged of his sins, is a symbol for Saint Thomas of the humility which is required for an authentic act of repentance. He notes that the hyssop plant grows close to the ground and thus fittingly symbolizes the faith which is accompanied by humility and which is such an essential predisposition for performing satisfaction. The actual sprinkling, or symbolic cleansing, with the hyssop branch is interpreted as a reference to the sprinkling of the blood of Christ of which I Peter

1:2 speaks: ". . . sanctified by the Spirit for obedience to Jesus Christ and for sprinkling with his Blood. . . ."

Such an effective cleansing gives the Psalmist hope for a full restoration. In the present case, David awaits the return of his prophetic gifts as well as the joy that comes from a clear conscience. The theme of joy being given back to the repentant sinner is an important one in the interpretation of the Miserere as it is in the theology of Christian reconciliation. In his commentary on the Beatitudes in Matthew 5:4, Saint Thomas interpreted "Blessed are those who mourn, for they shall be comforted" as an indication of the comfort, indeed, the consolation of joy, that comes to one who mourns for his sins.[83] Commenting on the verse of Psalm 50, "let the bones which Thou has broken rejoice," he writes:

> Through the sadness of repentance the heart of man is broken: and therefore when men are happy it means that the bones that were broken themselves share in the joy.[84]

It was this joy, which comes from a clear conscience, which the Psalmist had lost by his sin. The false delight that accompanied David's sin with Bathsheba was not the joy which the Gospel promises, as Saint Paul was obliged to remind the Romans in a similar context "for the kingdom of God is not food and drink but . . . joy in the Holy Spirit" (Romans 14:17). Saint Thomas continues:

> This kind of joy the Psalmist had lost and therefore he asks that it be restored to him, when he says, "Redde mihi laetitiam"--not carnal joy, but the joy "Salutaris tui," that is, of your salvation. Another text has "laetitiam Jesu," namely the joy of the Savior, through whom the remission of sins is accomplished.[85]

It is the redemption, accomplished in Christ, that is the source for the Psalmist's hope for true joy. In the prologue Saint Thomas has written that the subject matter for the psalms is "all the works of the Lord."[86] The "right sacrifices" of the Miserere are understood as referring to the sacrifices of Christ on the cross. It is Christ's satisfaction that gives joy to the repentant sinner. These texts from the Postilla super Psalmos conclude our examination of

Saint Thomas's biblical commentaries. It is significant that in a final text from the commentary on Psalm 50 the joy of salvation which is given to the penitent David is understood as a teaching on the beatific vision. David has learned the lesson of God's plan to bring all men to himself, the truth of man's call to the beatific contemplation of the Godhead (speculatio veritatis ad beatam contemplationem). Indeed this brief discussion in the prologue when he writes that "everything which pertains to the purpose (ad finem) of the Incarnation is so clearly treated in this work that it might almost be looked upon as a gospel rather than as a prophecy."[87]

Conclusion

The method that has been employed to examine Saint Thomas's scriptural commentaries, namely to look at those texts in which he speaks of satisfaction, does not result in a systematic presentation of his theology of satisfaction. However the major themes which are included in this systematic treatment do emerge and it will be beneficial to list these by way of conclusion.

Attention is first drawn to the explicit references to the satisfaction of Christ which appear throughout the commentaries on the biblical texts. The long text from the Postilla super Isaiam is a good example. It places the satisfaction of Christ into the broader framework of a biblical christology in which the various aspects of the person and work of the Savior are described by continuous reference to other biblical texts. Such a descriptive presentation takes into account the titles of Christ, his manner of life, his relationship to God and the effects of his saving activity. This is a significant text because it disputes in part a criticism that is frequently made (by Aulen, for example, in his Christus Victor)[88] that the scholastic tradition, including Saint Thomas, over-emphasized the expiatory explanation of Christian redemption and paid little attention to its other dimensions, notably exaltation christology which enjoys such a prominent place in the earlier tradition, especially in the East.

Other references, especially in the commentaries on the New Testament, point out Christ's subjective state and describe the dispositions in him which made his work efficacious. His love, obedience and humility are what account for the value of his blood-shedding and other physical sufferings. It is the death of the sinless Christ that breaks the cycle of sin (caused by Adam) and makes it possible for those who are united to him to themselves perform satisfactory works. The same internal dispositions in the Christian believer move him to actively engage in works of satisfaction and even to undertake such works for others who presumably do not possess the same dispositions in an adequate degree, as Job's prayers made those of his friends efficacious.

There is, too, a positive value to satisfaction in addition to its reparatory value (propitiation). The satisfaction of Christ makes it possible for man to reach his final goal of beatitude by a participation in the (risen) life of Christ himself. The individual satisfactions which are performed by the members of Christ, within the framework of the ministry of the Church, contribute to the gradual reformation of the image of God in the believer. In this regard there is a reciprocal relationship between the internal, subjective dispositions of the believer and his external works of satisfaction. Humility, obedience (to a confessor, for example) and love move one to recognize his need for satisfactory acts; the performance of satisfaction increases the individual's awareness of his sinfulness and his need to continue in the path of satisfaction.

A member of Christ, incorporated into him by Baptism, enters more deeply into the mystery of Christ's satisfaction and thereby into the very life of God. The ultimate goal of eternal union with God is already begun in the pilgrim believer as he moves from grace to glory.

CHAPTER 3

INITIAL ORGANIZATION OF MATERIALS IN THE SCRIPTUM SUPER SENTENTIAS: A GROUNDWORK FOR FURTHER DEVELOPMENT

Scriptum super Sententias, Book Four: A Dialectic Between Two Classical Definitions of Satisfaction

Although Saint Thomas chose the exitus-reditus theme as the basic plan for both the Summa theologiae and his commentary on the Sentences of Peter Lombard, the fact remains (and Father Chenu insists that the fact should be appreciated) that there are crucial differences between the detailed structure of Saint Thomas's first effort at systematic theology and the final work of his academic career.[1] The intellectual and spiritual development that went on in Saint Thomas's during the more than ten years that separate the completion of the Scriptum super Sententias and the beginning of the Summa theologiae account for the commonly held opinion that the latter work represents Saint Thomas's definitive theological opinion on a given subject. While there is undoubtedly a great deal of truth in such an opinion, it is an historical fact that for the first two centuries of Thomism the Scriptum super Sententias was the book to which Thomists spontaneously referred, as the work of Capreolus bears witness.[2] Apart from the intrinsic value of Saint Thomas's early thoughts on theology, the Scriptum super Sententias (because of the unforeseen interruption of the Summa theologiae) possesses another advantage, namely, the systematic discussion of subjects not treated in the unfinished Summa.

One such subject is a complete treatment of the sacrament of penance.[3] Significantly the treatment of the sacrament of penance in the Scriptum is also one of those places where a different ordering of questions indicates a different theological perspective from that in the Summa. Taking his lead from the Lombard, Saint Thomas places his discussion of the justification of the sinner within the context of the sacrament of penance; that is to say, in the context of the role played by the sacraments in such a conversion. The theological stress, then, is on the concrete, historical economy of salvation in the Church.[4] In the Summa theologiae, however, the question of the justification of the sinner is separated from the christological-sacramental discussion of the tertia pars. In keeping with the more closely worked-out plan of the later work, Saint Thomas discusses justification as part of the treatise on man's rebirth in grace in the first part of the secunda pars. This transfer of the treatise on justification is a good sign of Saint Thomas's preference for the ordo disciplinae in the Summa theologiae (where the discussion of grace and justification is placed next to that of original sin) over the order of sacred history, still operative in his commentary on the Sentences (where the discussion of justification is separate from that of the sin which makes it necessary).

It is within, then, the context of the sacrament of penance, which is "ordained to the removal of evil, which comes about as a result of the things we do in this life,"[5] that an excursus on the notion of satisfaction is found. According to the custom of the day the choice of questions to be discussed in connection with the reading of the Lombard's text was directed not only by scientific necessity but also by current interest among theologians. It is supposed that the young bachelors were directed in their choice of questions by the masters at the university. Thus it is not methodologically unsound to lift the discussion of satisfaction out of the 15th distinction of Book Four in order to get an overall grasp of Saint Thomas's first synthesis of thought. He himself writes in the introduction to this distinction: "Here one should inquire about satisfaction and its parts; whence there are four things that are discussed, the first of which is satisfaction itself."[6]

The Definitions of the Liber
ecclesiasticorum dogmatum
and of Cur Deus homo?

Given the fact that the Sentences of Peter Lombard are basically a compilation of important theological texts, one is not surprised by the fact that Saint Thomas develops his notion of satisfaction by commenting upon two definitions that had become commonplace in the theological tradition of his time. The first definition comes from the Liber ecclesiasticorum

54

dogmatum. Regarding the question whether Saint Thomas knew who the author of this book was, the research of Father Weisheipl is comprehensive. This work was generally attributed to Augustine by all of Saint Thomas's contemporaries, but it was actually written by Gennadius of Marseille (c. 470). It seems that Saint Thomas always referred to this work without author and the few exceptions to this practice are probably the result of interpolations. The reference in Quodlibet 12,10, "Sed ille liber non est Augustini, sed Gennadii" is obviously a marginal gloss.[7] As a result of its supposed Augustinian authorship, the definition was held in high regard in the Middle Ages: "Satisfactio est peccatorum causas excidere, et eorum suggestionibus aditum non indulgere."[8] Satisfaction aims at cutting out the root causes of sin and strengthening one against its enticements in the future.

The second definition is that of Anselm in the Cur Deus homo?: "Satisfactio est honorem Deo impendere."[9] Satisfaction gives to God an honor that is due him. The dialectic that Saint Thomas develops between these two definitions makes it possible to get an overall grasp of his notion of satisfaction as it is developed in the Scriptum. As noted, the context for the development is a discussion of penitential satisfaction and its three traditional expressions --almsgiving, fasting and prayer. Three questions are discussed in XV.1.1.a.b.c.: (1) whether satisfaction is a virtue or an act of virtue; (2) whether satisfaction is related to the virtue of justice; and (3) whether the pseudo-Augustine's definition of satisfaction, cited above, is a fitting one.

The response to the first question clearly establishes that satisfaction is an act of virtue. The reason for this is that satisfaction fulfills the essential requirement of an act of virtue or at least of a moral virtue, namely, that it has to do with establishing a mean between two extremes. "And because equality is a mean," says Saint Thomas, "which is implied in the very term 'satisfaction' (for one does not speak of something as satisfactory except insofar as it has some proportioned equality to something else), it is obvious that satisfaction, formally speaking, is an act of virtue."[10] None of the objections overrides this fundamental reason for making satisfaction an act of virtue. Neither the fact that satisfaction is not always something about which one has a choice[11] nor the fact that at times it can be enjoined on one quite ill-disposed to make it destroys its virtuous character since one is free to consent to obligation (and thereby make it a free act). In the case of a satisfaction being imposed by a third party, it is only necessary that the one ordering be free.[12]

If, then, satisfaction is an act of virtue, what is the virtue? It would seem that it is an act of charity since the reconciliation which it produces is related to love.[13] Or perhaps it is an act of prudence since the one who makes satisfaction for some past offense will be suitably reminded about similar failure in the future--which is a function of prudence.[14] Neither of these connections is as fundamental to satisfaction as the fact that it is linked to something that is due another. Here Saint Thomas quotes Anselm's "Satisfactio honorem debitum Deo impendit." Thus satisfaction gives to God an honor that is due him, and justice is the moral virtue which governs things that are due another.

The response to the XV.1.1.b explains why satisfaction belongs to justice. Referring to Aristotle's discussion of rectificatory justice in book five of the Nicomachean Ethics, Saint Thomas notes that the adverb satis, meaning "enough" (from which, of course, the term "satisfaction" is derived), actually refers to the kind of proportioned equality which is the mean of justice. "This, then, is what the just is," writes Aristotle, ". . . . the proportional; the unjust is what violates the proportion."[15] When speaking of satisfaction, this proportioned equality--we may simply call it an equilibrium--is established in the one actually performing the satisfactory deed. Thus Saint Thomas ranks satisfaction as part of that justice which is found between one individual and another, or what the scholastic tradition has called commutative or rectificatory justice. Properly speaking, however, satisfaction reestablishes an equilibrium that was not lost so much by the taking away of another's goods as by a hurtful action which has upset the right relation which should exist between one person and another. Hence satisfaction presupposes that something has gone wrong in the past--that some offense has upset the equilibrium. This reference to the past leads Saint Thomas to observe that the particular part of justice that is involved here is vindictive justice, to which the virtue of penitence is in some way allied. The conclusion of this discussion is that satisfaction, since it implies the restoration of a due equilibrium, unbalanced because of some past offense in the one satisfying, can rightly be said to be an act of the virtue of justice and, more particularly, that part of justice which is called penitence.

Having completed this prefatory discussion, Saint Thomas is ready to expose a fuller and more complete description of what satisfaction is by referring to the two traditional definitions mentioned above. The question is posed: In light of what we have already seen about satisfaction, is the definition given by the Liber ecclesiasticorum dogmatum a fitting one? The second definition, that of Anselm's Cur Deus homo? is given a less prominent place in the discussion. In the fifth objection of XV.1.1.c. Saint Thomas notes that the Anselmian definition, i.e., satisfaction gives to God an honor that is due him, does not seem to correspond at all to that of the Liber, i.e., satisfaction aims at cutting out the root causes of sin and strengthening one against its enticements in the future. Despite the fact that the context of the discussion might lead Saint Thomas to favor the "moral" definition of the Liber, an historical reason explains why he preferred what he considered to be the opinion of Augustine to that of Anselm. In the hierarchy of authorities current at Saint Thomas's time Augustine was numbered among the "ancient, saintly Fathers," while Anselm was young enough to be still counted among the "modern masters"--a group who from the beginning of the 12th century came to be regarded as having some limited authority in determining theological discussions.[16]

Saint Thomas takes the occasion of this discussion to underline the twofold end accomplished by satisfaction which will become a standard part of his future discussions on the subject. The fundamental discrepancy between the Liber's definition and that of Anselm is that the former speaks of satisfaction in relation to the causes and effects of sin, whereas the latter speaks about it as redressing an injury. The Liber defines satisfaction as aiming to cut out the root causes of sin and to strengthen one against enticements to similar sin in the future, while Anselm speaks of it as restoring to God some honor to which he has a claim.

As an aid to resolving the supposed discrepancy Saint Thomas turns to Aristotle, who writes in the Nicomachean Ethics:

. . . if the virtues are concerned with actions and passions, and every passion and every action is accompanied by pleasure and pain, for this reason also virtue will be concerned with pleasures and pains. This is indicated also by the fact that punishment is inflicted by these means; for it is a kind of cure, and it is the nature of cures to be effected by contraries.[17]

This insight provides Saint Thomas with a cue for advancing his dialectic and for developing his discussion of satisfaction. There is in fact a twofold purpose in making satisfaction. Not only is satisfaction aimed at reestablishing an equilibrium upset by some prior offense but it is also concerned with guarding against repeating the same offense in the future. "Satisfaction," writes Saint Thomas, "which is an act of the virtue of justice, carrying a penalty, is a medicine: it cures past sins and guards against future ones."[18] The curative and the preventative aspects of satisfaction will remain important parts of further discussion on the subject.

In light of the text from Aristotle, Saint Thomas can provide an explanation that will reconcile the two traditional definitions. Observe how the metaphor of the medicine with its curative and preventative properties serves as a key image in the dialectic. Saint Thomas writes:

Satisfaction can be defined in two ways. One way is with respect to past faults, which it heals (curat) by recompense; thus it is said that satisfaction is a recompense for injury according to justice's measure. This is also expressed in Anselm's definition that satisfaction gives to God an honor due him, due because of a fault committed. Satisfaction can also be defined with regard to future faults, from which one is preserved (praeservat) by satisfaction.[19]

The metaphor of the medicine, like all analogies, limps. A qualification is needed to avoid misunderstanding the differences between healing the body and healing the whole human person. While it is true that one can cure physical disease by eliminating the causes of the disease, spiritual "disease" or sin is concerned with deeper roots of the personality. Our free will cannot be forced. Thus pseudo-Augustine's "peccatorum causas excidere" should be understood as eliminating or shunning the cause of previous sins, while the "eorum suggestionibus aditum non indulgere" is understood as the tempering of free will with respect to future temptations.

In the responses to the objections of XV.1.1.c. Thomas clarifies some issues that demand further precision. For example, one should not be led to believe that satisfaction eliminates the remote causes of sin, the so-called fomes peccati. Rather it directs its healing character to the more proximate concupiscences that have been aroused by past actual sins as well as to the external occasions of sins which are regulated by satisfactory penances. In another response Saint Thomas throws some further light onto the reciprocal relationship between redressing a previous injury and preventing a repetition of the same. He says:

> Being careful about the future is a kind of recompense for the past since one is dealing with the same thing [sin], only in different ways. In being mindful of our past we detest the causes of sin because of the sins we have committed; our aversion is motivated by sin itself. Whereas in being careful about the future our aversion is directed to the causes of sin, so that when they have been removed we might more easily avoid the sin itself.[20]

The text just analyzed, XV.1.1., is a fundamental article for Saint Thomas's understanding of satisfaction at the time of the Scriptum super Sententias. He has located satisfaction as a good act, an act of virtue. It is an act of that part of the virtue of justice which is called penitence, since it deals with redressing past faults. He has examined the two traditional definitions and developed a dialectical understanding of satisfaction by reconciling them around the metaphor of medicine. Prior to investigating his discussion of the possibility of a creature making satisfaction to God it would be helpful to examine a question allied to the present one, namely, whether there is a difference between satisfaction and restitution, which, like satisfaction, is also an act related to the virtue of justice. The reason for this is that the notion of satisfaction is more clearly defined in this way.

Satisfaction: More than Restitution

Saint Thomas begins XV.1.5a by citing some reasons why one might be led to think that restitution is indeed a part of satisfaction. For example, since satisfaction reconciles a person to both God and one's neighbor and since restitution reconciles one person with another, then there must be some connection. Or, satisfaction is accomplished by doing something contrary to the sin committed (e.g., one satisfies for gluttony by fasting), but restitution as well is a kind of contrary since it is opposed to taking something which does not belong to one. Furthermore, Saint Ambrose is credited with saying that true penance is to stop sinning, but restitution is a kind of cessation of sin since one stops holding onto that to which another has the right. Accordingly, restitution--and, for that matter, satisfaction too--are parts of the virtue of penitence.

It is the argument to the contrary which is the most interesting: Saint Thomas simply says, quoting Saint Anselm, that satisfaction is made to God; restitution, on the other hand, is made to one's neighbor; therefore, restitution is not a part of satisfaction. Further explanation is found in the solution. The principle of division is quite clearly put: restitution deals with restoring some external goods that have been taken; it deals with restoring the equilibrium disrupted by some thing, e.g., theft of property. Satisfaction deals not with external goods but with actions and attitudes wherewith one perpetrates an injustice. Thus Saint Thomas envisions the possibility of the one being made without the other, as when someone, unable to make restitution, humbles himself before his neighbor because of some contumacious word or deed. The opposite could also be the case when, for example, someone who had robbed his neighbor made restitution by restoring the ill-gotten goods but refused to satisfy for the sorrow caused by the violent act of robbing.

The conclusion to this discussion is that, simply speaking, restitution is not a part of satisfaction but a preliminary step. Saint Thomas further observes that the one who restores what is owed to another (given that he has unjustly taken it) is not reconciled by that simple act to his neighbor; he is obliged to do something further than merely restoring the goods. For example, he must humble himself in some way. Nor is restitution exactly the contrary to stealing as fasting is to gluttony; rather it is merely restoring the right order of things, as eating moderately would be related to gluttony. The remaining quaestiunculae of XV.1.5 deal with the questions of to whom, by whom and how restitution should be made; they are not of interest to this study. What is important is that, by clearly distinguishing between restitution and satisfaction, Saint Thomas has shown that the latter involves more than simply reestablishing the balance of justice or regaining a status quo. Satisfaction is a question of redressing an offense.

Satisfaction Made to God: A Qualified Satisfaction

When, however, the offense that is committed is one against God, how can man hope to make satisfaction for the hurt caused by such an offense? This is the question treated in XV.1.2; it is obviously an important one for this study. In the single solution of the article Saint Thomas provides the needed clarification which explains how a creature can be said to make satisfaction to his Creator. Initial considerations would suggest that such a satisfaction would not be possible. Since, for example, the magnitude of an offense is judged according to the dignity of the one offended, sin has a kind of infinite character to it. Man, however, is unable to do anything infinite. Furthermore, being God's servants, we already owe him everything. With what could we make satisfaction to him? Even our time is committed to God's service, which means we would have no opportunity to satisfy. Finally, when one considers that a God-man was necessary to satisfy for original sin, how could a mere man hope to satisfy for grave, actual sins which are more malicious than original sin?

Yet there must be some way in which one can be said to satisfy God since God asks this kind of satisfaction (as in Luke 3:8, "Bear fruits that befit penance") and he would not ask us to do something that was impossible. Indeed, man is obliged to pay a twofold kind of debt: for the good things which he has received from God he owes thanksgiving and worship, and for the sins which he has committed he owes satisfaction. Yet, Saint Thomas observes, even the pagans were aware that when it came to thanking either one's parents or the gods no strict equivalence could be imagined; one could only do what one was able to do. The reason he offers for this is important:

"Friendship does not demand equivalency except as it is possible."[21] Thus when speaking about making satisfaction to God one must understand that the satis, the "enough," is not reckoned according to a strict quantitative measure but according to a certain proportion. This understanding covers both the definition of the virtues of justice as well as that of satisfaction.

The responses to the arguments outlined above complete the discussion. Three of them treat of the ways in which man, who already owes everything to God anyway, could even think of offering something extra in order to satisfy for an offense. Saint Thomas's approach is evenhanded: although one may have wasted time in the past for sinning, there is free time--time not owed to God by precept--for satisfying in the future. While it is true that man owes everything that he is capable of to God, this does not mean that he is obliged to do everything that he is capable of; in fact, in this life, since one is bound by so many different obligations, one would be concerned to fulfill those things that are commanded, while the things not commanded would be supererogatory and potentially satisfactory as well. Lastly, although it is true that man is God's servant, he is nonetheless a servant endowed with liberty, and so he can use his liberty to satisfy.

The response to the first objection, XV.1.2 ra/1, warrants emphasis. Saint Thomas explains how man can hope to compensate for an offense which does have a kind of infinity to it. He writes:

> Just as an offense has a certain infinity because of the infinite character of the divine majesty, so also the satisfaction takes on a certain infinity because of the infinite character of the divine mercy.[22]

This kind of satisfaction, however, is a work of grace. Man could not hope to satisfy to God apart from some manifestation of his mercy; that is, man's satisfaction being informed by grace (gratia informata).[23] This is a topic to which we will return when we discuss the question of how original sin differs in gravity from actual sin, which is the subject of the fifth objection in XV.1.2.

The conclusion of this discussion concerning whether man can adequately satisfy God pushes the development of the treatise on satisfaction to the limits of its larger theological context, namely, the relationship between man's satisfying God and the mediation of Christ. God is willing to accept a modified kind of equality, an equality proportioned to what man is able to do, in place of what strict justice would demand. This tempering of justice's demands for satisfaction made to God is an act of the divine mercy. Saint Thomas flatly rejects the opinion that man could satisfy God without the aid of grace. On the contrary, he acknowledges an opinion held by some that man's satisfaction for his sins only has value because of the value of the merit of Christ, and he appears to endorse it, although he maintains that, if grace were bestowed in some other way than through Christ, that would be equally effective for giving to a sinner's satisfaction the required infinite dimension.[24] We will have occasion to discuss this aspect of Saint Thomas's thought in the following section which treats of the satisfaction of Christ. There remain several other aspects of satisfaction in itself to be considered.

Satisfaction and Friendship

The first three quaestiunculae of XV.1.3 all deal with the same question, namely, in what way charity, the love of friendship, is related to satisfaction. The approach is somewhat indirect. The first question is whether a man can satisfy for one sin but not for another. The second is whether one who has confessed certain sins but then fallen into new ones can still continue to satisfy for the sins he has confessed. The third is whether one can reactivate the satisfaction made outside of charity once one has returned to the state of charity. Our concern here will not be so much with the particulars of the discussions, which have a practical importance all their own, but with seeing how Saint Thomas at each turn underlines the importance of friendship in making satisfaction.

The response to the first question is an unqualified "no," despite the objection that of those things which have no connection with one another one can be taken away independently of the others. For example, in the case of sin, one can commit one specific sin without committing all of them. The answer is negative because the making of satisfaction is not a mechanical act but the restoration of a relationship that has been broken by offense. "The removal of something offensive," says Saint Thomas in XV.1.3,a, "is a restitution of friendship; therefore if there is something which impedes friendship, even among men, satisfaction is not possible."[25]   Sin, however, breaks that love of friendship which should exist between God and man and thus it is impossible for man to satisfy for one sin and not for another.

The response to the second question is equally straightforward and negative despite the fact that some held the opinion that one could satisfy for forgiven sins even after one had sinned anew.   There is a slight change of nuance: When a person sins the equality of justice, which is a ground for friendship, is broken. In light of what was said above, namely, that the equality of justice with regard to God is less one of equivalency and more one of his accepting whatever proportional equality we can restore, it is absurd to think that God would go on accepting an inadequate redress once that bond of friendship has been broken by a subsequent sin.   The conclusion is simply that without love there can be no satisfaction.

The response to the third question is founded upon the same reasoning.   Satisfaction is based upon the supposition that one is pleasing to God and thus that deeds done outside the bond of friendship with him cannot qualify as satisfactory since they can in no way be said to proceed from love.   The same argument is used to show why good deeds done outside of charity merit nothing worthwhile of either temporal or eternal value, although Saint Thomas does allow them to play a role in leading man to seek the state of friendship with God.[26]   The point is clear enough.   The acts of satisfaction which a man makes to God are not isolated, mercantile exchanges that have an intrinsic value all their own.   These acts of satisfaction find their worth within a broader context; they are part of the relationship that exists between God and man which is the love of friendship or charity.   If an individual's satisfaction is to have any value or meaning, then the broader relationship must be a living one and not one that has been fractured or destroyed by some separate offense that would result in a man's being at enmity with God.

While, then, it is true that satisfaction can only be of value when it is achieved within this broader, permanent relationship of love, it is not true that one must unceasingly make satisfaction.   In this respect satisfaction differs from contrition, or sorrow, for sin.   In the context of the discussion of the justification of the unrighteous, Saint Thomas asks whether the whole of this life ought to be a time for contrition. One of the points of XVII.2.4. that seems to go against such a proposition is that contrition, like satisfaction, is a part of penance. However, one is not always obliged to make satisfaction; neither, then should one be obliged to be perpetually contrite for past sins. In the response to the fifth objection (after having shown why a man should maintain a contrite spirit throughout his lifetime) Saint Thomas replies that, although it is true that one is obliged only to accomplish the satisfaction that is given for a particular sin, nonetheless one is obliged to be consistently contrite for this same sin. Contrition, then, unlike satisfaction, has a permanent obligation attached to it.

There is a final reference which underscores somewhat dramatically the need for the bond of friendship, or charity, between God and man in order that satisfaction might be made. It is the discussion which Saint Thomas undertakes concerning the sacraments of the Old Law and their efficacy.[27] The argument of I.1.5 runs something like this: If it is impossible to satisfy without grace (that is to say, without this bond of friendship being present), how did the sacraments of the Old Law, which seem to have been satisfactory since they were prescribed for various sins (as is clear from the Book of Leviticus), gain their value? The only explanation is that these sacraments of the Old Law must have conferred grace. Having already explained[28] why these sacraments did not, in fact, confer grace, Saint Thomas explains how one might regard the sacrifices of the Old Law as satisfactory. Fundamentally the sacraments/sacrifices of the Old Law did nothing to take away the stain of sin (culpa) because at the time that they were offered there existed no bond of friendship between God and man that would have made them acceptable. Nonetheless, since they were burdensome in many instances, he does allow them some value, namely, that they were able to satisfy in part for the punishment (reatus) of sin.

This mention of the burdensome character of satisfactory actions brings us to a discussion of another characteristic of satisfaction. In addition to being performed within the broader context of the love of friendship, Saint Thomas also requires that the actions with which an individual accomplishes satisfaction cause him pain or be burdensome to him.

Satisfaction: Burdensome Task

Saint Thomas begins this discussion in XV.1.4.a.b by referring to the familiar definition of Anself's Cur Deus homo?, which states that "satisfaction gives to God an honor that is due him." He writes that if this is the case it does not seem likely that satisfaction would require painful or burdensome activity, since to give honor to someone does not demand that kind of behavior. In addition, it is said that God does not delight in our sufferings; thus one would not expect that he would be honored by painful or burdensome deeds.

The response to this question is worth a detailed look since it explains how it is that man can return or offer to God something owed him when, in truth, nothing can be taken from or lacking to God, in the first place. Recalling the image of the medicine, Saint Thomas writes that satisfaction looks backward to healing a past sin and forward to preserving one from a similar fall. He continues to show how both of these medicinal functions of satisfaction demand painful or burdensome acts. Redress or recompense, as we have seen, involves the restoration of a certain balance or equilibrium, and it is the burden of the one who has offended to make this restoration. In human affairs this restoration is brought about simply by taking from him who has more than is just and giving to him from whom something has been unjustly taken.

Since it is impossible for any creature to take something away from God, the restoration which satisfaction makes must be of a different kind. However, Saint Thomas cites the authority of Saint Anselm when he recalls that one does speak about sin as taking something away from God, namely, his honor. It is an axiom of the Cur Deus homo? that the sinner takes away from God the honor that is due him. That is what sin is--to take away from God what is his, to dishonor him.[29] The sinner, by his bad action, has robbed God of honor that would have been his due. Such would not have been the case had the sinner followed the way of justice and rectitude.[30] For this reason a sinner is bound to satisfy. The recompense can only be made by taking something away from the sinner and, at the same time, offering honor to God.

A good act of itself would offer honor to God but not take anything away from the sinner; indeed, it would perfect him, that is, it would add something to him. A painful act of itself would subtract something from the sinner but not offer honor to God. Hence in order for a true satisfaction to be made to God the act must be both good and painful. It must be good so that God will be honored and painful so that something will be taken away from the sinner. The conclusion to the solution simply recalls that, as far as satisfaction which looks to the future is concerned, painful actions have a preventative character (poenae medicinae sunt).

The responses to the objections are brief but important. Saint Thomas simply says that while it is true that punishment as such does not please God, punishment which is just does please him--not because it is painful but because it is just. It is precisely this kind of justice that Anselm is talking about. In fact there is no extended reference to the work of Saint Anselm in the XV.1.4a. However, in the response to the objection that Anselm's definition of satisfaction seems to allow merely good works to be satisfactory Saint Thomas clarifies the point. He writes: "What is owed (debitum) for sin is a redress of an offense which cannot be accomplished without punishment; and it is of such a debt (debito) that Anselm was speaking."[31]

The two remaining quaestiunculae are of interest for the issue at hand. The first, XV.1.4.b, deals with the question of "flagella," that is, the punishments which God allows to befall us but which are not of our own choosing. Can these acts of God be means of satisfaction? Saint Thomas's response is a simple one, inspired by a saying of Saint Augustine in the De Civitate Dei, which says that in the same affliction bad folk blaspheme God whereas the just praise and beseech him.[32] In his comment Saint Thomas explains that if we accept these punishments which are outside of our control, in a spirit of patience and penance, then they can be means of satisfaction for our sins. On the other hand, if one does not accept them in such a spirit, then they serve simply as instruments of vindication, as when one is forced to make recompense either by the judgment of someone else or by force.

The second quaestiuncula, XV.1.4.c, treats of the satisfactory value of prayer, addressing the objection that it seems to lack the characteristic of painfulness necessary for authentic satisfaction. Yet prayer, along with almsgiving and fasting, are the three traditional means of penance which the Church enjoins on sinners in order that they might make satisfaction.[33] We will simply record in the first place the way that Saint Thomas explains this threefold division of satisfaction, since it serves as a good summary of the principal elements of his definition (elements that he received from the Liber and Anselm) and is also a masterly example of how, without forcing his material, he weaves a single piece of cloth out of the various threads of theological traditions.

First, he cites the Anselmian element: Satisfaction should be such that it subtracts something from us for the honor of God. We have three kinds of possessions, or better, three kinds of well-being, namely, that of the soul--spiritual well-being; that of the body--corporal well-being; and our wealth--material well-being. Almsgiving aims at taking something away from our fortunes. Fasting affects our bodily well-being. Finally, prayer, while it cannot subtract or take away any of the good things of our soul which, in truth, makes us acceptable to God, does help us to surrender ourselves entirely to him and in that way takes us away from ourselves.

Then Saint Thomas invokes the two-part definition of the Liber, the first part of which says that satisfaction aims at cutting out the root causes of sin. According to I John, these root causes of sin are threefold--concupiscence of the flesh, concupiscence of the eyes and the pride of life. Against the lust of flesh Saint Thomas poses fasting; against the lust of the eyes, almsgiving; and, as a remedy to the pride of life, the humbling of man before God which is prayer. Satisfaction, according to this definition, aims at bolstering one's strength against sinning in the future. Every sin is committed either against God, and prayer warns against that; or against our neighbor, and almsgiving strengthens us against that; or against ourselves, in which case fasting serves as a preventative. This is a good example of the kind of synthesis which Saint Thomas develops in the Scriptum super Sententias. He takes two traditional definitions of satisfaction as well as three traditional penitential practices of the Church and integrates them to form a single theological teaching on satisfaction.

Still to be answered, however, is the related question of how prayer can be satisfactory since it does not seem to be painful. The response to the first objection of XV.1.4.c offers two ways of explaining the difficulty. First, one might consider that there are

68

two kinds of prayer--contemplative prayer which is altogether delightful, a kind of heavenly conversation that has nothing painful and therefore nothing satisfactory about it, and the prayer which is the cry of the sinner, a painful prayer which is satisfactory. Or another explanation might be that all prayer has a satisfactory value because, although it has a certain sweetness to it, it also afflicts the body. Here Saint Thomas quotes the authority of Gregory the Great, in observing that as the power of intimate love takes hold of us the power of the flesh is proportionately weakened. That is why when Jacob wrestled with the angel his thigh was put out of joint; he had seen God but went away limping. Saint Thomas gives preference to the latter explanation.[34]

The remaining three questions of distinction XV in the fourth book of the Scriptum treat in detail the principal ways of making satisfaction. Almsgiving, fasting and prayer enjoy a long-standing tradition in the history of the Church's spirituality and liturgy.[35] Saint Thomas appears to feel that this traditional threefold enumeration is adequate despite the fact that one is able to think of other works of satisfaction or penance that do not appear to be included in this listing, for example, pilgrimages and the discipline. In response to this objection Saint Thomas writes:

> Whatever is part of bodily affliction belongs to fasting; whatever is spent on the well-being of one's neighbor belongs to almsgiving; and whatever is offered to God in praise belongs to prayer.[36]

He devotes a separate question to each of these practices of the Church's penitential discipline, taking the occasion, as the methodology of the Scriptum super Sententias allows, to discuss matters of related interest. There we find such questions as "Can a wife give away her husband's goods as alms?" or "Can one eat twice on a fast day?" or "Is it right to pray to the souls in purgatory?"[37] When it comes to discussing the satisfactory character of these practices the explanation is somewhat standard. The response will show how the particular practice in question fulfills the twofold aim of satisfaction, namely, redress for a past offense and support against committing a similar fault in the future. Saint Thomas explains how each of the traditional practices in fact does take away something from the penitent and thus can be said to be a kind of recompense, and he likewise shows how each weakens the

69

power of concupiscence and thus can be said to be a kind of bolstering against a similar fall in the future. The details of these explanations are not pertinent to the present discussion.

A brief summation, however, of Saint Thomas's teaching on satisfaction in itself is possible. Satisfaction is an act of the virtue of justice, more particularly of penitence, which is that part of justice which deals with redressing past offense. It restores to God an honor lost by sin, even when the offense has been directed toward one's neighbor, since an offense against one's neighbor is also an offense against God. It also aims at weakening the dispositions to sin within us, and thus serves to strengthen us against a repetition of the same sin in the future. Since the satisfaction goes beyond mere restitution it can only be accomplished within the broader context of friendship. It is more than the restoration of something or the cessation from some hurtful activity; it is rather the rehabilitation of a relationship brought about by the redress of an offense. Thus there is no question of performing a bona fide satisfaction apart from God's help since "without charity there is no satisfaction."[38] The presence of charity, however, does not rule out the possibility of suffering. Satisfaction demands that he who performs it be separated from something that he cherishes in order that the equilibrium of justice be restored. But satisfaction is a Christian act and thus the very charity which prompts it can ease the penal character of the satisfaction, for the man who loves more suffers less. Far from decreasing the value of satisfaction, this increases it.

Satisfaction for Another

There is a final question contained within this section of the Scriptum super Sententias which is of interest for this present discussion on Saint Thomas's notion of satisfaction. In the many questions which treat of the effects of penance and of the temporal punishment due to sin Saint Thomas has the occasion to ask if one man is able to satisfy for another. While the working definition of satisfaction, developed from the two definitions, does not immediately suggest that one could satisfy for another, Saint Thomas is aware of Galatians 6:2, "Bear one another's burdens, and so fulfill the law of Christ," and he feels that somehow it should be possible.

70

He begins his explanation of this question by recalling the familiar twofold aim of satisfactory punishment, namely, to restore an equilibrium and to cure. With regard to the latter, which is satisfaction's preventative purpose, it is clear that one cannot satisfy for another since, as Saint Thomas succinctly puts it, "by the fast of one man, another's flesh is not controlled."[39] However, with regard to the former, namely the restoration of an equilibrium, one man can satisfy for another provided that he be in the state of charity so that his works can have such a satisfactory character. Interestingly enough, in response to a claim that when this is the case the punishment suffered by the surrogate should be greater than would have been the case had the guilty party performed his own satisfaction, he adds that, on the contrary, less punishment is required of a man who satisfies for another since there is greater love present in such an act. Furthermore, it is not necessary that one be incapable of making the satisfaction oneself.[40] A similar teaching is found when Saint Thomas discusses the suffrages that are offered for the dead. Just as one is able to satisfy for another living person, so also can one satisfy for the souls in purgatory.[41]

This discussion of the possibility of one man's satisfying for another completes the picture of satisfaction as presented in the fourth book of the Scriptum super Sententias. The methodology of this work has allowed us, with due respect for the plan underlying its organization, to extract a description of satisfaction from its pages. We are in a better position to understand the employment made of this notion in Saint Thomas's soteriology now that we have examined what must be the prime analogate for all satisfaction, namely, that which occurs among men.

This discussion of the possibility of one man's satisfying for another can serve as a transitional discussion as well, since it immediately raises the question of how Christ was able to satisfy for sinners. The christological questions are treated ex professo in the third book of the Scriptum super Sententias; in addition there are some texts pertaining to the satisfaction of the members which are yet to be examined in the fourth book where, because of the plan of the Scriptum, we were obliged to begin our investigation.

Scriptum super Sententias, Book Three:
New Perspectives on Traditional
Materials Concerning the
Satisfaction of Christ

The text which Saint Thomas chose as the theme for
the prologue to the third book of his Scriptum super
Sententias is taken from Ecclesiastes 1:7--"To the
place where the streams flow, there they flow again."
The Latin of the Vulgate, however, is necessary to
appreciate the use which Saint Thomas makes of this
verse in announcing the theme of his christological
discussions: "Ad locum unde exeunt, flumina revertun-
tur ut iterum fluant." This introductory essay is
built around the imagery of waters flowing from the
mountains. Saint Thomas writes that "high mountains
are among the noblest of creatures."[42] (Possibly he
had been especially struck by the alpine scenery which
he was able to view when travelling from Italy to
Paris.) The streams represent the inexhaustible
goodness of God, which is the ultimate source of the
being and existence of all things. The Incarnation is
a point of juncture at which human nature, having come
forth from God, is able to return to him, as the waters
return whence they came. It is Christ, the God-man,
who makes it possible for man, in whom the corporeal
and spiritual orders of reality unite, to return to his
Source. The waters that flow again, now from Christ,
in whom the divine and human natures are united,
represent the gifts and virtues which God bestows
on man. This image of coming forth and returning
(exitus-reditus) and the organization of materials
which it suggests, as has already been mentioned, is
unique to Saint Thomas: it is not part of the original
conception of the Lombard.[43] The third book, then,
of the Scriptum treats of the Incarnation as well
as the virtues and gifts which man receives because
of it.

The Necessity of the Incarnation: Cur
Deus homo? as Starting Point

I.1.2: The arguments

The first distinction of this book deals with
certain preliminary questions customarily discussed in
relation to the Incarnation; for example, whether it
was even possible, whether it occurred at the right
time and whether God would have become incarnate had
man not sinned. Our interest lies, however, in I.1.2:

"Was it fitting that God became man?" In this long article Saint Thomas is able to cite at least nine arguments that point to the conclusion that it was not fitting for God to become man. Since many of these arguments will reoccur throughout the systematic discussion of the satisfaction of Christ, the text of Saint Thomas is given in its entirety.

1. Just as goodness and evil are opposed, so are majesty and lowliness. It would have been unwise of God to associate with lowliness since his wisdom would have dictated that he avoid whatever is opposed to his majesty.

2. Furthermore, the sin of Adam and the sin of the angels were both sins of pride, yet God did not assume an angelic nature. Why, then, should he have assumed a human one?

3. There is a relation between creation and restoration, but God assumed no human nature to create. Why, then, did he assume a human nature to restore?

4. It would have been more fitting for God to show the greatness of his mercy than the severity of his justice. Mercy dictates forgiveness of sins without satisfaction. Thus God could have saved man without assuming a human nature and even have wrought greater praise from mankind since he manifested greater mercy.

5. A merciful God does not ask more than man can give. Yet man is able to satisfy in part for himself, and thus there was no reason for God to become man.

6. Furthermore, in this regard, man is able to make satisfaction for mortal sin. Thus he should be able to make satisfaction for original sin, since the latter is less malicious--as it is less voluntary--than the former.

7. Likewise, the First Parents satisfied for the original sin insofar as it was an actual sin on their part. Why could not man, then, have satisfied for original sin?

8. Furthermore, according to the Dionysian view of the world the angelic nature is placed between human nature and divinity. If man could not have satisfied sufficiently, then surely the angels would have been able to accomplish this.

9. Lastly, since the good of the entire human race is still a created good, it would not have been impossible for God to have created a creature whose goodness exceeded the good of the entire human race and who could have made up for the corruption of the human race. Thus it would not have been necessary or fitting that God became man.[44]

The presentation of the alternate position is contained in the sed contras. Although they do not necessarily represent the exact line of argumentation that Saint Thomas will develop in his solution in I.1.2, they do sketch in broad strokes the direction that argumentation will take. Since the very sed contra, which is particularly significant, paraphrases the argument of Cur Deus homo? we shall save it for last and examine the sed contra in reverse order. The fourth sed contra deals with the question of the devil's role in the Fall. Given the medieval tradition of ransom to Satan, the nuance here is important. Saint Thomas quotes James 4:6, "God opposes the proud. . . ." It was precisely this pride on the part of the devil which led him to envy man and to seek to enthrall him. This was unjust since man was created to be God's servant and not the devil's. "Thus it was entirely fitting," writes Saint Thomas, "that the all-powerful God oppose the devil's wickedness so that man might not only be snatched from his power but indeed be made his master."[45] Since there is no nature above the angelic except the divine it was entirely right for God to do this and to become man. Saint Thomas does not speak at all about any kind of "rights of the devil" but, on the contrary, about the injustice of the devil's enslavement of mankind.

The third sed contra simply quotes the Wisdom of Solomon 8:30--"But against wisdom evil does not prevail"--and shows how it was right for God to do all that he could to conquer the wickedness of the devil who had thrown mankind into such an unhappy state of sin and misery. The second sed contra is even simpler: The good of no single creature exceeds the good of human nature considered as a whole, and hence it would have been impossible for any creature to have made recompense for the whole human race.

The first sed contra is of special interest since it outlines the reasoning which guides Saint Thomas's discussion of satisfaction. The first half of the argument runs as follows: (1) It was not fitting that human nature, which is among the noblest of God's creatures, be frustrated in reaching its goal. (2) Such was the result of the original sin since by it man was deprived of beatitude. (3) To restore human nature required that the sin be dismissed--"but it is not just that a sin be dismissed without satisfaction."[46] The conclusion to this first half of the argument is simply that it was fitting that satisfaction be made for the sin which touched the whole human race.

The second half of the first sed contra continues: (1) Satisfaction cannot be fittingly accomplished except by him who ought to satisfy and who is able to satisfy ("nisi ab eo qui debet satisfacere et potest"). (2) He, however, who ought to satisfy is man, since it is man who sinned, and he who alone can satisfy is God.[47] The reason given here is that of Anselm, although Saint Thomas does not refer to him by name: Since every creature already owes his whole being to God, a mere creature could not satisfy; nor could man himself, since sin has left him unworthy. The conclusion is that in order that satisfaction be made for the sin of human nature (original sin) it is fitting that God become incarnate. Although Saint Thomas will offer his own nuances to the Anselmian doctrine of satisfaction, the principle enunciated in this sed contra, "qui debet et potest," remains a fundamental one for his systematic discussion of the satisfaction of Christ.

The solution: God's mercy, justice and wisdom

In the actual solution to I.1.2, Saint Thomas develops his response around the divine attributes of mercy, justice and wisdom. The response that he gives to the question posed by Saint Anselm is one marked by freshness and originality. Saint Anselm's argument stressed why man needed a God-man in order to be saved; Saint Thomas's emphasis is on the fittingness of the divine initiative to undertake man's salvation. It is not unusual that the arguments presented in the sed contras are not taken up in their original form in the responses. This shift of emphasis is not the only way, however, in which Saint Thomas modifies the argument of _Cur Deus homo?_ He begins his solution by explaining that in matters of faith demonstrative proof is impossible since faith, as Hebrews 11:1 says, is "of things not seen." Especially is this true of realities like the Incarnation which depend sheerly on the will of God. When treating of such things the student of theology may only show that something is not impossible or that it is appropriate. The warning is perhaps directed against the somewhat overly optimistic appearance of Saint Anselm's _necessariae rationes_. Father Chenu writes that "the School was always haunted by Anselm's _necessariae rationes_, but the masters, like Anselm, upheld these bold conceptions and necessary relationships only within the realm of mystery wherein faith had led them."[48] The arguments of convenience which Saint Thomas outlines for the appropriateness of the Incarnation are an example of another way in which he modified the theological approach of _Cur Deus homo?_

The three arguments all have a common supposition, stated by Saint Thomas as follows: "Since human nature has fallen, but was nonetheless reparable, it was fitting (_decuit_) that God repair (_repararet_) it."[49] This is true for three reasons: (1) The fullness of the divine mercy demanded the Incarnation since God's goodness obliged him to do what he could to restore fallen human nature, which, it must be added, remained reparable even after the Fall. (2) The immutability of God's justice, against which no one may sin without making satisfaction, demanded the Incarnation since only in that way could there be found among mankind someone who was able to make the required satisfaction. (3) Divine wisdom demanded that the way in which this reparation be accomplished be the most fitting. The most fitting way to bring about satisfaction was fully to restore human nature so that one who possessed that nature might the more easily find what he had lost. (If an angel had been chosen to save man, such would not have been the case, since man's beatitude would have been inferior to that of the angels.) Not only did the divine wisdom ordain that the restoration be complete or integral but that man's task of reaching God be made easy. Hence God chose to save man in a visible way since in this life man is drawn to things which he can sense externally. Thus, as the preface for the Christmas Mass reminds us, "through him whom we can see we are drawn to the love of the God whom we cannot."[50]

The responses: qualification of Cur Deus homo?

The responses to the objection of I.1.2 provide Saint Thomas with the occasion to complete the development of his treatment on the motive of the Incarnation. The notion of satisfaction and the doctrinal points which touch upon the necessity of a God-man to accomplish it adequately are treated in the responses to objections 3,4,5,6,7, and 9. The responses offer the opportunity to contrast Saint Thomas's teaching with that of Anselm, who used many of the same arguments in the course of his Cur Deus homo?

The response to the third objection is a good example. The fundamental Anselmian teaching that a God-man was required for satisfaction because only man owed (debet) satisfaction is behind Saint Thomas's explanation that the work of creation required no created instrument because it did not involve the making of satisfaction. The work of re-creation, however, did require such an instrument since without man the proper kind of satisfaction could not have been accomplished.

The fourth response replies to the objection that the demand for satisfaction appears to be contrary to the mercy of God. Saint Thomas involves a fundamental principle of this theology, namely, that there is no contradiction in God. Thus there is no contradiction between the mercy of God and his justice. In fact, Saint Thomas observes, a mercy which would eliminate justice would be a kind of foolishness rather than a virtue. The Incarnation manifests both the mercy and the justice of God. It manifests his mercy because the Incarnation is a greater demonstration of mercy, given all that it entails concerning the kenosis of the Word, than would have been the case had God chosen to absolve man without the satisfaction of the God-man. Likewise it manifests his justice since Christ does in fact satisfy justice's demands by his expiatory death. Saint Thomas appends two observations that are important. First, God, being the judge of all, had no choice but to fulfill the demands of justice and preserve its order. If he had done otherwise it would have given the impression that judges of a lesser order could follow his example and do likewise. Second, since God is goodness itself he alone has the right to vindicate, according to Deuteronomy 32:35, "Vengeance is mine, and recompense. . . ." All the more ought he to take vengeance on a sin committed against himself.

The three points given in this response to the question as to why God's mercy would not have been more manifest by a simple deliverance from sin rather than by satisfaction for it are drawn from I,12 of Cur Deus homo?, where Anselm answers the same question. There one finds that the Doctor of Canterbury appeals to the disorder inherent in forgiving a sin without punishment, to the incongruity of God's acting differently from that which is the rule of justice among men, to God's sole right to take vengeance and, finally, to the harmony of the divine attributes.

The response to the following objection is an example of a place where, rather than following Saint Anselm, Saint Thomas clarifies a detail of the former's theology that remains ambiguous in Cur Deus homo?. The fifth objection deals with the relationship between the gravity of the offense and the quality of the satisfaction for it. The teaching of the response is substantially that of the fourth book, where Saint Thomas describes how man can be said to make satisfaction to God. Saint Thomas distinguishes two ways in which the gravity of an offense might be considered. An offense can be looked at either in the perspective of an insult to the divine majesty or in the perspective of the harm that it causes man who sins. Considered from the first point of view, sin causes an effect of relatively infinite (infinitatem quamdam) magnitude precisely because of the infinite majesty that is offended. From the second perspective, however, sin's effect is decidedly finite, even in the case of the original sin, whose effects touch upon all mankind. This clarification is clearly an example of Saint Thomas's careful theological analysis of the reality of sin and of his willingness to correct what, at best, remains ambiguous in Anselm. In several chapters of Cur Deus homo? Anselm suggests that the salvific death of a God-man is required precisely because the sins of mankind are of infinite magnitude.[51] Saint Thomas's qualification, "a relatively infinite character," is an important refinement of Anselm's argument.

Saint Thomas continues his response by outlining the kind of satisfaction that must be made so that both of the effects of sin, the finite one and the relatively infinite one, can be accounted for. Satisfaction must first restore to man whatever finite good he has lost by sin and in the second place it must redress the sin because it is an offense against God. Grace is required to make adequate satisfaction because only grace, since it merits an infinite reward, can be said to give satisfaction the somewhat infinite value required to compensate for a somewhat infinite offense. Man alone is unable to satisfy for his sins because he has no claim to grace. God alone can give man what he needs to satisfy for his sins and his willingness to do so means that the demand for such grace-filled satisfaction is not an unjust one on God's part.

The sixth response deals with the difference between the satisfaction required for original sin and that for actual sin. Saint Thomas's purpose here is to explain why a God-man is required to satisfy for original sin. In responding to this question, however, he is led to confront a related question, namely, whether a man is able to satisfy for any sin apart from some relationship to Christ. The text of I.1.2 ra/6 suggests that he is hesitant to respond to the second question in the affirmative without qualification.

In the first place he describes two differences between original sin and actual sin, one regarding the origin of the sin and the other regarding its effects, or the kind of goods which the respective sins corrupt. With respect to the origin of sin, any actual sin possesses a far greater voluntariness to it and therefore is of greater vituperation than the original sin. The latter, says Saint Thomas, has a less well-defined beginning (one can even speak, in the individual, of a certain necessary character with respect to original sin)[52] and subsequently is less of a willed offense against God. With respect to the effects of the two kinds of sins, however, the contrary is the case. Original sin affects the entire human race while actual sin affects the good only of the one who commits it. According to Saint Thomas's terminology, actual sin is a greater fault (culpa), but original sin a greater evil (malum).

Accordingly, in line with Saint Anselm's principle that no individual creature could offer to God a good equal to or exceeding the good of the whole human race, no individual creature would be able to satisfy for the original sin which corrupted that goodness. Only one whose worth was more than that of the whole of human nature could restore the good lost by original sin. In the context of this discussion it would follow, as the following response makes clear, that Adam would have been able to satisfy for whatever there was of personal sin for him in the original sin, but not for the effect that his personal sin had on the human race.

As if to forestall misinterpretation, Saint Thomas qualifies his remarks in two ways. First he explains that even for the satisfaction of actual sin the aid of grace is required. This is in keeping with what was said above in the response to I.1.2 ra/5 concerning the need for God's grace to render man's satisfaction relatively infinite so that it would correspond to the relatively infinite offense against God that sin is. The second qualification deals with Christ's role as the mediator of such grace. Here Saint Thomas is somewhat hesitant. He simply acknowledges that certain theologians (among whom is Alexander of Hales)[53] are of the opinion that even the satisfaction made for personal sins is without value apart from the satisfaction made by Christ. The reason for Saint Thomas's hesitation on this point seems to be less on account of the issue of the mediation of Christ than on account of the issue of the satisfaction of the holy men who lived before Christ. The theologians to whom Saint Thomas refers appear to have taught that the satisfactions accomplished by the holy men of the Old Testament were efficacious because of their belief in the redemption that would be accomplished by Christ. Saint Thomas will clarify his position on the satisfaction of the Old Testament saints elsewhere in the discussion.

The response to the ninth objection treats of the question as to whether God could have created a hypothetical creature who would have been able to make the kind of satisfaction required. Such a creature's goodness would have to be of such magnitude that he would be able to return to God a good at least equal to that corrupted by the original sin. Saint Thomas offers three reasons why such an hypothesis is an unworkable one. The first two are of interest. The first is borrowed directly from Saint Anselm, namely, that every creature owes whatever good it possesses to God since he is the creator. Therefore there could be nothing supplementary wherewith any created being might make satisfaction. The second reason, as has already been defined by Anselm, is that satisfaction demands that at least an equal good--if not a greater good--be restored in place of what sin has destroyed. No creature could be created whose worth would exceed the good of human nature taken in its global sense.

In Saint Anselm the reason underlying his refusal to consider any creature capable of making the required satisfaction for original sin was his conception of the relationship between God and man, which was modeled upon that of a master and a slave. This relationship is not justified or explained but is presupposed as a given in the Cur Deus homo?. The master's right of possession and of free disposition of the servant, as well as the obligation of the slave to belong entirely to his master and to follow his will perfectly, are principles taken for granted by Saint Anselm; so he would reject satisfaction made by anyone whom God has created, no matter what his created goodness, since that goodness would derive entirely from God.

A final reason that Saint Thomas gives for not envisioning the work of our redemption as accomplished by a hypothetical creature of whatever amount of goodness, is the effect of the satisfaction accomplished by Christ. Man is elevated to an order that is above his natural order (ad gradum superiorem). If man is raised above the created order of things it is impossible to think that any created instrument would alone suffice to accomplish such a work. God alone could restore human nature. This final, brief reference to the beatific life to which man is called in Christ recalls the emphasis that Saint Thomas chose to develop in the solution to I.1.2., namely, the goodness of God in bringing about the Incarnation in order that man might reach his goal. Here too a significant contrast can be seen in the theological perspectives of Saint Thomas and Saint Anselm. The former is--and will continue to be--concerned to understand the satisfaction of Christ primarily as a manifestation of the divine goodness; the latter, to interpret it as a rectification of a divine order upset by sin.

This concludes the first introductory question on christological satisfaction. Almost the entire weight of the response to the question as to why it was fitting that the Son of God become incarnate is laid on the notion of satisfaction. This question has been treated in such detail because Saint Thomas will refer to the principles established here throughout his discussion of Christ's satisfaction in the third book. A brief résumé of the central points of the article will be useful.

The starting point of the discussion is original sin. The sin of the First Parents finds its malice in the fact that it, unlike the personal sins of others, affects the entire progeny of Adam, the entire human race. It is the sin of nature, which by reason of its communicability has a relatively infinite character to it. The result of this sin, like the personal sins of any man, is that one is unable to find one's completion

in God. Man is thwarted in reaching his ultimate goal.
The sin, however, not only affects man but is also an
offense against the infinite majesty of God. As such,
sin takes on a kind of infinite magnitude. In all of
this the devil has a hand since, moved by envy, he
enticed the First Parents to sin and ultimately to
enslavement.

The malice of the devil, however, is no match for
the wisdom of God. Moved by the incongruity of seeing
the noblest of his creatures blocked from reaching the
destiny for which he was made, God chooses a way that
will restore man to his lost dignity and make it
possible for him to reach the goal of beatitude. The
way that he chooses at once manifests his mercy and
preserves his justice. Since it is man alone who
should (debet) redress the original sin, since it is he
who committed it, but God alone who can (potest)
redress it, because of the kind of infinite character
inherent in this evil, it follows that one who is both
God and man is alone able to make the required kind of
satisfaction. In the Incarnation God's mercy is
manifest in Christ's taking on our human nature and
God's justice is safeguarded in Christ's suffering for
our sins. Because of the satisfactory act of Christ,
man is restored to union with God and is also able
effectively to satisfy for his own sins, since grace
suffuses these actions with the infinite character they
would lack of themselves.

The Satisfaction Accomplished by the Passion: Redemption not Liberation

The twentieth distinction of the Scriptum super
Sententias is the occasion for Saint Thomas to discuss
the relationship between the passion of Christ and the
satisfaction whereby man is liberated from sin. A
single question composed of five articles treats of
four subjects that are pertinent to the development of
this study: XX.1.1 treats the reparability of human
nature; XX.1.2 deals with whether another besides
Christ could have satisfied for human nature; XX.1.3.
considers whether satisfaction was appropriately
accomplished by the passion of Christ and XX.1.4
whether the human race could have been liberated in any
other way. An examination of these texts will afford
the opportunity to see how Saint Thomas, drawing on the
principles already established in I.1.2, talks about
the satisfaction that is brought about by the expiatory
death of Christ.

The entire christological discussion that lies in-between the first and twentieth distinctions makes frequent reference to the principles established in I.1.2. For example, the suitability of Christ's having assumed human flesh is frequently explained in terms of the need for someone of Adam's race to make satisfaction.[54] The unity of the person of Christ is sometimes shown to be necessary because there would otherwise be no single person who was both able (potest) and who ought (debet) to make satisfaction.[55] The passion of Christ is the moment par excellence of satisfaction (as will be seen in XX.1.3 as well), during which he showed his willingness to suffer by bearing the greatest sorrow.[56] The weakness of human nature, which he also assumed, is itself no obstacle to making satisfaction since the strength whereby he overcame the power of the devil is a strength of power and virtue.[57] Lastly, the satisfaction of Christ is sometimes referred to by Saint Thomas as the price paid by Christ for our sins.[58]

XX.1.1,2: Restoration through satisfaction

XX.1.1,a deals with the question whether human nature needed to be repaired at all. Two familiar Anselmian arguments are cited to support the fitting-ness of restoring human nature. The first is that divine wisdom could not allow a creature--particularly a creature such as man--to be thwarted from achieving the goal for which he had been created; yet that was precisely the result of original sin. The second states that this reaching of one's end belongs to the overall perfection of the universe, which should be preserved. The actual solution to this first section of the article shows how the reparation of human nature manifests God's wisdom, mercy and power.

The second quaestiuncula of XX.1.1 poses the more direct question: Granted that human nature ought to have been restored, should it have been restored by satisfaction? Two standard arguments attempt to expose the inappropriateness of such an approach to restoration. First, creation was accomplished simply by a word from God, and thus re-creation should have also been accomplished by a similar fiat and not by some creature's instrumentality. Second, it is certainly more merciful simply to forgive than to exact redress for an offense. On the other hand, the facts that justice must be kept intact and that there is a medicinal aspect of satisfaction are recalled in the sed contra. In the solution to XX.1.1,b the same arguments with respect to the justice of God and the preservation of the order of justice in the universe are amplified. However, a new element is introduced: Looked at from the part of man, satisfaction is really a more complete way of restoring human nature since, in a certain sense, man becomes a cause of his own reparation. A parallel with merit is invoked. He who merits an eternal reward, as opposed to simply having it given to him, can be said to have a part in what he has achieved, which otherwise would not have been the case. In a reply to the second objection (dealing with God's mercy), Saint Thomas makes a corollary point: By satisfaction man's sin is not simply taken away, but his nature is restored--"ad pristinam dignitatem humanam naturam integraliter reducere."[59]

XX.1.1,c pursues a similar argument, but in a somewhat different direction. The initial arguments repeat reasons that seem to indicate that satisfaction was not the most appropriate way for man to have been rehabilitated. Here, however, the thrust of the reasoning revolves around the axiom that God is free to do things as he likes, including restoring human nature. If God is free to do otherwise, why should he not do otherwise? Again the sed contra recalls that a fault demands punishment and the order of justice must be preserved. The solution to this part of the article addresses itself to the question of how one can consider the work of man's restoration as a necessary work. The details of this discussion are not directly relevant to this study. However, in the course of the reply, Saint Thomas does speak about the partial remission of debt without satisfaction. He insists that any satisfaction that is accomplished is related in some way to the satisfaction wrought by Christ, which in itself was powerful enough to satisfy for the sins of the whole world and to which the individual acts of satisfaction that men perform are related as the imperfect is related to the perfect in any order of things.

XX.1.2 pursues another familiar question, namely, whether a mere creature could not have been able to satisfy for human nature. The introductory arguments repeat the usual objections, e.g., that it was a mere creature who sinned and caused the need for satisfaction, that God is cruel to demand more than what man is able to perform and that an angel might possibly have saved man. The sed contra restates the principle that any creature already owes all that he has to God and therefore cannot fulfill the requirements of true satisfaction. It also underscores the point that restoration of human nature is like a new creation, a recreation, and therefore only God who created would be able to re-create man in such a way that he would enjoy his former state of perfection, his "pristine dignity."

The solution to the article introduces a new term for qualifying the satisfaction made by Christ. It is called condign satisfaction; that is, satisfaction which is made in accord with the demands of strict equivalence. Saint Thomas writes that such a condign satisfaction was necessary for two reasons. First, it was necessary so that man would be truly restored and not merely forgiven; and second, as was alluded to in the previous article, that there might be a foundation upon which all other lesser acts of satisfaction might be built. This condign satisfaction demands that the redress have a kind of infinite quality to it since the offense for which it is made touches the infinite in at least three ways. First, one must consider the infinite character of the divine majesty which is offended; second, the infinite dimension of the good from which sinful man is separated by original sin, namely, the good of God himself; and lastly, the unlimited--even infinite--potential of human nature which is being restored. Human nature enjoys a kind of infinite status in this regard, that it is able to be instanced in an unlimited number of individual beings. Thus condign satisfaction must have something of the infinite to it, but no creature is capable of effecting that kind of satisfaction since no creature can do anything that is infinite.

XX.1.3,4: Satisfaction accomplished by suffering

XX.1.3 looks to understand the relationship between this kind of satisfaction in strict equivalence and the passion of Christ. Was it really necessary that satisfaction be made in this way? The core of the difficulty is resolved in the simple declaration of Hebrews 2:10: "For it was fitting that he . . . should make the pioneer of their salvation perfect through suffering." The key word to the solution of this article is "death." Sin has made man a debtor, that is, subject to death; all sin leads to death. If one is to speak about a redress in strict equivalence for sin, then the satisfactory act must involve death. Christ's passion and death made his satisfaction eminent in two ways: First, it was an act of satisfaction

accomplished by the ultimate suffering, death, and
not merely by this or that suffering; second, this kind
of satisfaction serves as an example of outstanding
satisfaction, a true examplar of what satisfaction
should be, in which other human satisfactions can find
their ideal.

The relationship between the passion and the death
of Christ and the satisfaction which he accomplishes is
also discussed throughout the nineteenth distinction.
There, however, no new statements are made in relation
to the development of a theory of satisfaction. Some
assertions are simply restated in one context or
another, for example, that Christ satisfied for all
of human nature;[60] that it was by reason of his
conjoined humanity that Christ was able to offer
condign satisfaction;[61] that it was in his human
nature that Christ satisfied;[62] and that it was
to the Father that Christ "paid" the price for our
satisfaction.[63]

The responses to the objections posed in relation
to XX.1.3 are important. Bearing in mind what was
said about the necessity of a passion and death in
order to effect the kind of satisfaction that Christ
accomplished, one can readily see why, for example, the
lesser sufferings of Christ--his hunger, his fatigue,
the shedding of his blood at his circumcision--would
not have made sufficient satisfaction.[64] Nor did
the killing of Christ actually effect the satisfaction,
but rather the love with which he underwent this
passion and gave up his life.[65] Yet love alone was
not sufficient for satisfaction. Love could take away
the sin, but sorrow or suffering is required to make
satisfaction for it.[66] Finally, the simple fact of
the Incarnation, in which God humbles himself to become
a man, does not eliminate the need for the passion and
death of the God-man, in which he experiences bitter
sorrow. The humility of the Incarnation is an antidote
for the pride of Adam's sin, but the bitter sorrow of
the passion is a remedy for the delight which Adam took
in the sin.[66A]

XX.1.4. examines the arguments that seem to
indicate that no other way of restoring human nature
would have been possible. The first section of this
article examines the central question of Anselm's Cur
Deus homo? regarding the necessity of the Incarnation.
Thus in the first four objections various arguments are
raised which suggest that God had no choice but to save

86

the world by the passion and death of His Son. Among these is an excerpt from the Cur Deus homo? which runs as follows:

> And when the Son said that the chalice could not pass from him unless he drank of it, the reason was not that he was unable to avoid death, if that had been his will, but that . . . the world was not able to be saved otherwise.[67]

Saint Thomas allows no such necessity in God and indicates the direction his response will take with the words of Luke 1:37--"For with God nothing will be impossible."

The solution to XX.1.4 offers the following clarification: Looked at from the part of God, other means than that of satisfaction would have been possible for the restoration of human nature. However, had another means been chosen it would be more fittingly referred to as a liberation and not a redemption since no price would have been paid. Looked at, however, from the part of man, there is only one way, and that is the way that God has in fact chosen, since man cannot satisfy for himself and must accept satisfaction as a gift. Finally, all things considered, Saint Thomas endorses the present economy of salvation as one outside of which it is not easy to imagine a more fitting way of restoring the human race. As far as Anselm's remark is concerned, Saint Thomas merely explains that he was speaking from the point of view of man, supposing the present order of things. In general Saint Thomas is careful to preserve the divine freedom but anxious also to see the workings of God's wisdom in the present state of affairs.

This desire to recognize the necessity of the present economy of salvation as the most appropriate is the core of the response to the sole quaestiuncula attached to XX.1.4, namely, whether there was not a more appropriate way to have saved man. Saint Thomas says simply that there does not seem to have been a better way as far as we are concerned. If, however, there had been--and the possibility must always be left open--it would have demanded an entirely different order of things.

The response to the four objections of XX.1.4 throws some more light on the role of the passion in the work of satisfaction. For example, Christ's

violent death, as opposed to a normal one, is more
expressive of the satisfactory character of his sufferings. Christ's sufferings, too, are a clearer
expression of the Christian way of life since one
is called upon to renounce earthly attachments and
seek the joys of heaven. Then there is the devil to
consider. Like Saint Anselm, Saint Thomas consistently
refuses to give him any rights over man, but he does
acknowledge that man deserved what he got, namely,
enslavement to the devil. Thus, satisfaction, as
opposed to sheer exercise of divine force, was a more
fitting way to liberate us since we were justly bought
back. Finally, Saint Thomas sees a kind of parallel
between man sinning at the devil's instigation and
man killing Christ at his instigation. This seems to
have been a more fitting way of accomplishing the
passion than if the devil himself had been Christ's
executioner. These final two considerations reflect a
lingering medieval preoccupation with the devil's role
in man's fall.

Résumé

The discussion of this twentieth distinction
focuses sharply on the necessity of the Cross. Why was
it that the satisfaction for original sin had to be
accomplished by the physical sufferings and death of
Christ? With regard to this central question two
issues are addressed: First, why was it required that
Christ die in order that satisfaction be made, and
second, was God free to choose some other means of
satisfaction, or was he constrained to this one?

The thrust of the response to the first of these
two issues is simply that this ultimate act of destruction and suffering was required in order that the new
life, which is the result of Christ's satisfaction,
might be given to mankind. The satisfaction of Christ
is a moment of re-creation; in a sense the new life is
really the life which mankind possessed before the
Fall. There are several references to the "pristine
dignity" of man which is restored by the passion
and death of Christ. Thus, the satisfaction that is
made is condign, or accomplished according to the
rigors of a strict equivalence. It is a preeminent
satisfaction, powerful enough to bring about this kind
of re-creation. The new life given back to mankind
must be sought by each man. So the satisfaction
of Christ is preeminent also since it serves as an
exemplar for the satisfactions that the Christian must

make. These, insofar as they imitate the suffering of Christ, dispose the believer to look for the true happiness of heaven.

The second question concerning God's freedom is twofold. Was God free to satisfy for mankind in some other way or was he constrained to accomplish our satisfaction in the way he did? The fundamental response is simply that there is no necessity in God; at least there is none that would require him to act externally in a certain way. Hence the possibility of saving mankind in some other way must always be accorded him. However, in keeping with Saint Thomas's disdain for unfounded speculation, he insists that the mere possibility that God could have acted otherwise does not allow one to ignore the way in which he has in fact freely chosen to act. So, given the present order of things, Saint Thomas acknowledges that the satisfactory death of Christ is the most fitting way for God to have saved us and is the most beneficial way for man to have been saved.

What is most striking about the texts of the third book of the Scriptum super Sententias is simply that Saint Thomas chooses to emphasize the satisfactory aspect of the mystery of Christ, both in the discussion of the motive for the Incarnation and in the treatment of the passion of Christ. This is all the more significant when one considers that the theme of satisfaction is not one that figures prominently in the text of Peter Lombard. We have already had occasion to note that Abelard's "moral" interpretation of the passion and death of Christ seems to have had a heavy influence on the work of the Lombard. Indeed the word "satisfaction" does not even appear in the text of the twentieth distinction of the Sentences. The questions which Saint Thomas chooses to treat in connection with that distinction, however, indicate that for him (and his contemporaries) the notion of satisfaction, as presented by Anselm, was one that any serious theological discussion of the mystery of Christ had to take into consideration.

At the same time, as has been noted in this section, Saint Thomas did not hesitate to qualify and even to correct Anselm's theory of satisfaction. There is also a point, even in this work of the young Saint Thomas, where he completes the satisfaction theory of Anselm. At the very end of Cur Deus homo? Saint Anselm asks his interlocutor, Boso, to consider the "great" reason why the death of Christ actually accomplished the salvation of the human race. Speaking of the recompense (retributio) which God the Father owed to the Son because of the great gift (tantum donum) of his death, Anselm poses the question:

> Anselm: If the Son wished to give to another what was owed to him, could the Father justly prohibit him or deny the one to whom the Son wished to cede his rights?
>
> Boso: Indeed not! I think the Father would have to acquit the debt of the one to whom the Son wished to give his recompense. . . .
>
> Anselm: To whom would the Son more fittingly cede the fruits and the recompense which his death was worth than to those for whose salvation he became man?[68]

The reason why the satisfaction of Christ, within the horizons of Cur Deus homo?, was effective for the salvation of the human race is, in the final analysis, a mercantile one. The death of Christ is a unit of exchange with which he who owed nothing because of sin to the Father, could pay the debt owed by sinful man.

While it is true that Saint Thomas, as in XX.1.4.b, will acknowledge that the reason why our salvation is a redemption (redemptio) and not merely a liberation (liberatio) is because Christ has paid the price (per solutionem pretii) for our sins by his satisfactory death, it is equally true that the value of Christ's satisfaction is not found simply in his death. In XX.1.3 he writes:

> The passion of Christ was not satisfactory by reason of the killing of Christ but because of the way in which he underwent his sufferings. He wished to suffer with the greatest love and, because of this love, the passion was acceptable to God.[69]

This is a significant shift of emphasis in the presentation of the theory of satisfaction and one that, when fully developed in the later works, will rescue Saint Thomas's soteriology from the criticism leveled against that of Saint Anselm, namely, that Cur Deus homo?

presents the death of Christ as a barter carried on between Father and Son. Nonetheless the role that love plays in giving satisfaction its value is not as developed in the Scriptum as in the later works of Saint Thomas. In this early period Saint Thomas's reflection on satisfaction is still very much in a juridic framework in which the demands of justice are the predominant influence in his thinking on satisfaction.

Another factor reflected in Saint Thomas's discussion of the passion and death of Christ is the definition of satisfaction found in the pseudo-Augustine's Liber ecclesiasticorum dogmantum. That definition, which speaks about the curative and preventative effects of satisfaction, suggests to Saint Thomas that a dolorous passion was required, in addition to maximal love, in order to satisfy completely for man's sins. In response to the question whether satisfaction had to be accomplished by the passion of Christ, Saint Thomas writes:

> Contrition not only finds its value in love but also in sorrow. While charity wipes away the stain of sin, it is sorrow which is taken into consideration for the satisfaction of the punishment due to sin.[70]

It is the dialectic between the two definitions, that of Anselm and that of the Liber, which furnishes Saint Thomas with the tools for his analysis of the satisfaction of Christ. As a result, Saint Thomas's redemption theology avoids the one-sidedness of a simple moral interpretation of Christ's passion, which Abelard appears to have favored, as well as the mercantile description of Christ's agreement with his Father that mars the satisfaction theory of Anselm.

There is another issue concerning the satisfaction of Christ which is, at least initially, less clearly treated in the Scriptum super Sentential. That issue is the relationship between the satisfaction made by Christ and the satisfaction which men are required to make for their own sins. Thus in I.1.2 ra/6, where Saint Thomas is describing the difference between the gravity of original sin and that of actual sin, he explains that since original sin affected the good of the whole human race, satisfaction for it requires someone whose worth exceeds the good of the whole human race. Actual sin, on the other hand, affects only the good of a single individual, and so satisfaction for it

91

can be made by any man whatsoever "with human grace."
Here the lack of a critical edition of the text hampers
the investigation, since another printed edition refers
to a "divine" grace. The ambiguity is increased by a
note which Saint Thomas appends to the response:
"Certain authors are of the opinion that even for
actual sin a mere man (<u>purus homo</u>) cannot satisfy
sufficiently. . . ."[71]

The ambiguity here does not center on whether a
man is able to make satisfaction to God without his
grace. Saint Thomas consistently held that grace
was necessary to accomplish satisfaction. For example,
he says that man's satisfaction is given a kind of
infinite value by grace, which itself has a kind of
infinite value since it merits an infinite reward, in
order to compensate for the kind of infinite damage
which sin causes to God's honor.[72] Or, to cite a
text close to the one under discussion, he says that
Adam was able to satisfy "with the help of God's grace"
for the original sin insofar as it was, for him, a
personal one, but not to make satisfaction to the
extent that it affected the whole human race.[73]

The ambiguity seems rather to revolve around the
relationship between the satisfaction of Christ as it
was accomplished by his passion and death and the
satisfaction which the members of Christ make for their
sins.   In effect, Saint Thomas appears to adopt the
position of the "quidam" whose opinion he merely cited
in I.1.2 ra/6 as he continues his treatment of the
satisfaction of Christ. For example, in I.1.2 ra/7,
the same text that discusses the satisfaction which
Adam could have made for his personal sin, Saint Thomas
writes that the holy men of the Old Testament satisfied
for their sins by the various rites of the Old Law, but
they were not admitted to the vision of God because
"the corruption of nature has not yet been healed
by the satisfaction of Christ."[74] The suggestion
seems to be that the ancients, with the help of God,
performed satisfactory actions which were valid in
themselves but wihout effect as regards the reward of
eternal life because the satisfaction of Christ had not
yet opened the gates of heaven to mankind.

In the treatment of the passion of Christ the
ambiguity is resolved. There Saint Thomas clearly
states that the satisfaction accomplished by the
members is related to the satisfaction of Christ

"as anything imperfect arises from that which is perfect in its genus."[75] This is unequivocally taught in XX.1.1,c ra/3, where Saint Thomas says:

> The remission of punishment which is accomplished by all men, especially satisfactory punishments, is founded on the value of Christ's satisfaction, which more than accounted for the removal of all the punishment due to sin, considered in itself. Hence it is necessary that individual acts of satisfaction be founded on the condign satisfaction of Christ.[76]

It is the distinction between the stain of sin (culpa) and the debt of punishment to sin (poena) that permits Saint Thomas to affirm that it is not contrary to the mercy of God to demand satisfactory recompense for the punishment due to sin even after the stain of sin has been wiped away by his merciful forgiveness. It is the definition of penitential satisfaction as found in the Liber ecclesiasticorum dogmatum that allows him to integrate the medicinal role of satisfactory actions into his development of a theology of the satisfaction of Christ.

Scriptum super Sententias, Book Four: The Satisfaction of the Members

In the prologue to Book Four of his Scriptum super Sententias Saint Thomas introduces the theme by quoting from Psalm 107:20: "He sent his word, and healed them, and delivered them from destruction." We have already remarked that contrary to the conception of Peter Lombard, who viewed the last book of his Sentences as a single unit dealing with signs (of which Saint Augustine spoke), Saint Thomas's plan makes the third and fourth books of his commentary a single discussion of the return (reditus) of creatures to God. He writes:

> There is a continuity between the two books since in Book Three the mission of the Word made flesh was discussed and in this present book the effects of that mission of the Incarnate Word.[77]

The effects of Christ's mission as presented by Saint Thomas are three, namely, the sacraments, the resurrection of the dead, and the glory of those who rise.

The discussion of the sacraments and of the last things offers some additional insight into the relationship between the satisfaction of Christ and the satisfaction of the members. The sacraments are instruments of the healing which Christ's mission brought to man, as the verse of the psalm indicates --". . . and healed them." This healing is applied to that which is most frightening to man, his destruction by death, which is the third element in the thematic excerpt from the psalm. Man needs this healing because by sin he has been subjected to the penalty of death --the whole of mankind by the sin of Adam and each individual man when he ratifies that sin by his own personal sins. Saint Thomas explains how man is subjected to the penalty of death in terms of the distinction between culpa and poena:

> Because sin by its nature is something willed, punishment must be of a sort that it is contrary to our will. Sin (culpa) reduces man to a state of weakness; punishment (poena) subjects man to death. Sin is the road to punishment; weakness is the road to death.[78]

The satisfactory punishments undertaken by man and founded upon the satisfaction of Christ transform the punishment due to sin into an instrument of healing. Speaking of satisfactory punishments Saint Thomas writes:

> Satisfactory punishments heal sin in two ways. First, they are a recompense for sin, and thus sin is healed by the expiatory satisfaction of Christ. Second, they are a healing medicine by means of which a sick member is cured.[79]

Further clarification of this teaching is found in the discussion of the sacrament of baptism, whose effect, the taking away of all temporal punishment due to sin, is different from that of the sacrament of penance. In IV.2.1,b Saint Thomas discusses the effect of this sacrament of initiation. He begins by examining several objections that seem to point to the conclusion that baptism could not remove all of the temporal punishment due to sin. The core of these arguments is simply that faults are not rectified without some punishment and that either man undertakes the satisfaction himself or else he is punished by God;

this draws on a theme from Augustine's <u>Enarrationes in Psalmos</u>.[80] The response is clear and unequivocal: "Christ, by his death, satisfied sufficiently for the sins of the whole human race, even if they would have been more than they actually are."[81] When a man is baptized he is baptized into the death of Christ, as Saint Paul teaches in Romans 6, and the baptized person receives the full effects of Christ's passion and death. By "full effects" is understood that the man who is baptized is absolved not only from the sin (<u>culpa</u>) but also from all obligation to make satisfaction (<u>poena satisfactoria</u>).

Several texts suggest the reason why incorporation into Christ by baptism eliminates the need for further penitential satisfaction on the believer's part. The fundamental reason is the reality of the union between Christ and the believer. For example, in IV.2.1,b ra/1 Saint Thomas explains this special effect of baptism as a result of the believer having had the benefits of Christ's sufferings reputed to him. He cites I Corinthians 12:26: "If one member suffers, all suffer together," and Isaiah 53:4: "Surely he has borne our griefs and carried our sorrows." This exception to the need for satisfaction, based on the unique relationship between Christ and the newly-baptized, only serves to emphasize the rule that in living out the baptismal commitment subsequent sin is only fully rectified by satisfaction on the part of the one who receives the forgiveness of Christ in the other sacraments.

The final texts touch upon the concrete economy of salvation history. In II.1.4,b ra/1 Saint Thomas suggests that it was fitting that the sacraments of the New Law were not instituted immediately after man's sin so that, left to his own resources, man might recognize his need for the healing which they bring. He repeats in the following response his contention that only the perfect satisfaction of Christ could have dignified (<u>dignificavit</u>) human nature so that it would be rendered suitable to receive the graces which the sacraments bestow. Such was not the case prior to the Incarnation and so the satisfactions undertaken by the holy men of the Old Testament participated in the efficacy of Christ's passion in an imperfect way.

In XLVIII.1.2 Saint Thomas talks about the final coming of Christ in glory and he poses the question: "Will Christ, when he comes in judgment, appear in the form of a glorified body?" The arguments give reason why he should appear in the form of our infirmity. The response Saint Thomas gives is that Christ is called a mediator between God and man for two reasons: In the first place he satisfied for man and, secondly, he pleads for men before the Father, communicating to them those things which are of God. Thus Christ carries man's sins to God and God's gifts to man. In his first coming it was appropriate that he appear in the form of our lowliness since the purpose of that coming was to satisfy for our sins; in the second coming, however, he will come to manifest the justice of God. Hence the appropriateness of his appearance in glory since at that time Christ will show the glory of the divinity which was his from the beginning.

The Scriptum super Sententias is a work of the young Saint Thomas. It is generally agreed that Saint Thomas did not exhibit the kind of polished theological systematization in this work as would be the case in his Summa. Indeed he himself abandoned the Scriptum in favor of constructing a new method in teaching theology. As far as the discussion of satisfaction is concerned, one is able to discern in the Scriptum the lines that Saint Thomas's future theologizing would follow. Considered in comparison with the work of Anselm, it is a good example of the freshness of approach and the new ideas which Bernard Guy, in his early biography, attributed to the teachings of Saint Thomas. Perhaps the most noteworthy indication of this newness is the move towards the personalizing of the notion of satisfaction. Although the Summa will give it far clearer and more explicit expression, certain elements of this personalism have already emerged in the Scriptum. Among these is the way in which Saint Thomas works with the two classical definitions of satisfaction to elaborate a meaningful statement about the relations between God and man. What remains to be more clearly articulated is how the satisfactions which men undertake do, in fact, give honor to God and how this is related to the unique satisfaction accomplished by Christ on the cross.

CHAPTER 4

DEVELOPMENT OF CENTRAL IDEAS CONCERNING THE MYSTERY OF CHRIST: THE GRACE, THE LOVE AND THE HUMILITY OF THE GOD-MAN

Poena and Culpa in the De Malo

Satisfaction would have no meaning apart from sin. Saint Thomas explains his notion of satisfaction--be it the satisfaction of Christ for original and subsequent sin or the satisfaction of his members for their own personal sins--with reference to the punishment (poena) which is incurred by the disordered act of sin (culpa). This division of the evil of sin into culpa and poena was part of the theological tradition which Saint Thomas inherited. The authority of Saint Augustine, for one, undoubtedly played a role in Saint Thomas's choosing to incorporate this concept into his theological synthesis, after he had first subjected it to philosophical analysis. In the De libero arbitrio Saint Augustine wrote that there are two species of evil, that which we do, culpa, and that which we suffer, poena.[1] Peter Lombard employs the concept in his Sentences when he asks about the reality of sin.[2] The De Malo 1.4 is a detailed, philosophical analysis of this Augustinian principle that does not hesitate to qualify some of Saint Augustine's conclusions.

An initial treatment of this same issue is found in Saint Thomas's commentary on the distinction of the Sentences referred to above. In Scriptum II.35.1, Saint Thomas asks, in the context of defining sin, whether evil is sufficiently divided into malum culpae and malum poenae. His explanation is not as detailed as that of the De Malo and, because of his use of traditional terminology, somewhat less clear. In the Scriptum Saint Thomas distinguishes between defect of nature (malum naturae), which is any privation of a good which should be part of a given form, and a fault (peccatum), which is any privation of some perfection which should be part of the operations of that form. At the level of natural things or of art a defective operation is a peccatum. At the level of free will, because of the dominion which rational creatures

97

have over their actions, _peccatum_ is spoken of as voluntary and referred to as sin (_culpa_). Likewise in rational creatures a defect of nature takes on an added significance, namely, that as an evil it is contrary to one's will and is referred to as punishment (_poena_).

The exposition of De Malo 1,4 eliminates the threefold distinction and speaks simply of malum culpae and malum poenae, posing the question of whether one can speak of these two classes of evil as an exhaustive division of evil. We shall examine the reply first and then we shall consider four of the thirteen arguments and responses to the arguments that are of interest for the notion of satisfaction. Saint Thomas begins his reply by stating that rational (and intellectual) creatures are related to good and to evil in different ways than are other creatures. It is the rational creature's freedom to choose that accounts for this difference. Saint Thomas refers to a text of Fulgentius of Ruspe (though attributed at his time to Saint Augustine) which says: "Twofold is the evil of the rational creature: the one whereby he willingly turns from the highest good; the other wherewith he is punished in his life."[3]

The following explanation speaks, then, about evil with regard to rational creatures. Since evil is opposed to good it can be divided in the same way that good is divided. Any perfection can be considered either as a form or habit; that is, either as a constitutive element in the subject, or as a permanent disposition in the subject to action. Likewise evil can be regarded as something that deprives a form of whatever it needs to operate, or as the actual defective operations themselves. On the physical level one might use the example of blindness, which is deprivation of form, and the inability to see, which is a defective act. On the level of free will, however, a defective act can only be the result of man's free choice; as such it is called _culpa_. There can be deprivation of form in rational creatures as well, affecting either the good of soul, body or even that of external things. In this case the evil is that of _poena_, or punishment. That the evil which befalls man is a punishment is a conclusion to which one is less impelled by reason of philosophical analysis than from the teachings of the faith ("secundum fidei catholicae sententiam").

The second part of Saint Thomas's discussions is composed of two sections. The first section draws three conclusions from the analysis of poena; the second contrasts poena and culpa. There are three things that can be said about poena. In the first place, poena, as it affects rational creatures, is bound up with culpa. It is the tradition of the faith that all poena is the effect of either the sin of nature or man's personal sins. Secondly, poena is always contrary to man's will because the will naturally inclines to the good and shrinks from evil.[4] Thirdly, poena is related to suffering since it does not proceed from man's natural inclinations but from some external cause which results in violence to nature and therefore suffering.

In the second section Saint Thomas contrasts poena and culpa. First, as has already been explained, culpa is an evil operation whereas poena is an evil that inheres in the subject of the operation. On the level of physical things an evil disposition in the subject results in defective operation, as when a lame thoroughbred is unable to finish a race. At the level of free will the reverse is true, and thus man's culpa incurs poena for him. In this way, observes Saint Thomas, divine providence rectifies the malum culpae by means of the malum poenae. Secondly, culpa is something that is willed, but poena, precisely as an evil, cannot be willed by man. Thirdly, culpa is something that man does, but poena something that he endures, as Saint Augustine mentions in the text of the De libero arbitrio already cited.

Four of the thirteen arguments attached to this article are important because of the clarification which they provide concerning poena and satisfaction. 1.4 ag/2 cites a well-known remark from Saint Augustine's Confessions: "You have ordained it, Lord, and thus it is so, that every inordinate desire is its own punishment."[5] The objector proposes that if sin is punishment then there is no reason to regard each as a different class of evil; rather they are the same. Saint Thomas responds in ra/2 by saying that sin is not willed as something inordinate, but as an apparent good; however, the fact that it is willed accounts for the definition of culpa. It is true, as a secondary consideration, that in choosing sin man unwillingly suffers from its disorders; this touches upon the definition of poena.

If every sin is in some concomittant way a punishment for a previous sin, as ag/5 proposes, how could the original sin be said to be of such a kind, since there was no previous sin to have been a cause of punishment? Saint Thomas replies in ra/5 that punishment is related to sin more as an effect than as a cause, so that even the original sin has punishment associated with it, though original sin cannot be considered to have been precipitated by some previous disordered act or by the deprivation of grace which is the result of sin.

A definition of evil given by Augustine in the De natura boni, cc.35-37 suggests that every evil is a punishment since, according to the definition cited, evil is a corruption of some natural mode, species or order. The objection, ag/6, concludes that this is exactly what punishment is. Saint Thomas responds, in ra/6, that this is a definition of generic evil. When, however, the corruption is something suffered by a subject, one refers to a specific definition, malum poenae; when the corruption is something in an action of a subject the reference is to malum culpae.

The final argument bears directly on the notion of satisfaction. The objection, ag/9, claims that punishment should not be thought of as having anything to do with evil since it is really something good. The example given is that those who perform satisfaction are indeed praised for so doing since they willingly undertake punishment for their sins. In the response, ra/9, Saint Thomas offers a valuable distinction. He writes:

> Punishment, considered in relation to the subject, is an evil because it deprives him of something (in one way or another). However, when it is considered in relation to the one who imparts punishment, it can be considered as a good, when the punishment is a just one.[6]

In the case of the one who performs satisfaction, insofar as it is willingly undertaken or accepted (which is essential to satisfaction), he who imparts the punishment and he who suffers are one and the same person--whence its goodness.

This discussion of the two aspects of evil, the malum culpae (which we will translate as "stain of sin") and the malum poenae (the punishment due to sin) is clearly an important one for the doctrine of satisfaction. De malo 1.4 is a philosophical analysis of evil, as Saint Thomas's acknowledgement of the external authority of the faith for certain conclusions indicates.[7] In the Summa theologiae[8] he will explain how these two aspects of evil are drawn together into a single theological conception of sin. In brief, the stain of sin is related to the malum culpae because it refers to the culpable alienation from God that the Christian concept of sin means. Culpa, as implied in the metaphor of stain, and the debt of punishment (reatus poenae) refer to the abiding conditions of the sinner after sin. For the moment, however, this philosophical analysis of the De malo will suffice for an intelligible reading of the following texts dealing with the satisfaction of Christ and of his members.

The Satisfaction of Christ the Head

De Veritate: Satisfaction and the Graced
Humanity of the Word

Q.29.3: The grace of Christ

Several texts of the disputed question De Veritate offer Saint Thomas the occasion to clarify his understanding of satisfaction. The first of these texts is found in Question 29, the topic of which is the grace of Christ. The third article of the question asks, "Is the grace of Christ infinite?" It is an extremely important article since it articulates Saint Thomas's clarification, found only in summary form in the Scriptum, of an assertion based on Saint Anselm's argument, namely, that the debt incurred by Adam's sin could only be paid by the infinite merit of Christ.

Seven arguments are cited that seem to indicate that the grace of Christ is infinite. For the notion of satisfaction 29.3 ag/4 is the most important:

> Anselm in Cur Deus homo? proves that God had to be incarnated because satisfaction for human nature could not be made except through infinite merit, which could not be that of a mere man. From this it is evident that the merit of Christ as man was infinite. But the cause of merit is grace. The grace of Christ was therefore infinite, because an infinite effect cannot proceed from a finite cause.[8a]

In the reply Saint Thomas first addresses himself
to a text from Scripture, John 3:34--"For he whom God
has sent utters the words of God, for it is not by
measure that he gives the Spirit." A tradition in
medieval theology, the Glossa ordinaria, had used this
as a proof text for the thesis that the grace of
Christ is infinite.[9] Saint Thomas explains how the
interpretations of the Glossa ordinaria are untenable
when this text is read in its fuller biblical context.
He concludes that the words of the gospel seem to refer
to the habitual grace of Christ "in which the Holy
Spirit is shown to have been given to the soul of
Christ, the union by which that man was the Son of God
being presupposed."[10] The habitual grace of Christ,
as Saint Thomas has already pointed out in 29.2,
properly refers to the grace of Christ which is his as
a consequence of the union of his human nature with the
person of the Word.[11] This grace, which according to
exact theological analysis is distinguished from the
gratia unionis, is a created grace and as such is
--absolutely speaking--finite. However, there is a way
in which it can be considered infinite.

In order to explain how a finite, created grace
can be said to be infinite, Saint Thomas continues his
reply with a philosophical analysis of the finite and
the infinite. His conclusion is that it is possible to
imagine something which is infinite under one formality
and finite under another. For example, if we consider
an infinite white body, its whiteness will not on this
account be infinite in intensity, but only (indirectly)
in extension; for something whiter might be found. Or,
if one were to conceive of a sentient soul which
possessed whatever was of the perfection of sensi-
bility, such a soul would be finite essentially because
of its limited act of existence, yet as regards the
formality of sensing it would be infinite because its
sentience would not limited to any particular mode of
sensing.

This provides Saint Thomas with the necessary
concepts to explain how the grace of Christ can be said
to be essentially finite, but infinite as to the mode
of grace. He writes:

> In like manner I say of the habitual grace of
> Christ that it is essentially finite because
> its act of being is limited to a particular
> species of being, that of grace; yet it is
> infinite in the line of grace. For, although
> a person's perfection in point of grace can

102

be considered to be any one of an infinite number of modes, no one of them was wanting to Christ, but he had grace in all fullness and perfection to which the formality of this species, grace, can extend.[12]

This teaching allows Saint Thomas to respond to the objection concerning the infinite merit of Christ. The objection, as stated, claims to represent the doctrine of Saint Anselm on satisfaction, though, in fact, there is but a single reference in the Cur Deus homo? to the satisfaction of Christ as merit.[13] Saint Thomas explains in 29.3 ra/4 that it is impossible to speak about Christ's merit as infinite since it is not possible for an action infinite in intensity, which in this case is the merit of Christ, to proceed from a form whose essence is finite, namely, the grace of Christ. The merit of Christ, then, like his other operations, is not infinite. However, it is possible, in deference to Anselm's authority, to speak of a certain infinity with reference to the merit of Christ based on the uniqueness of his divine personhood. Saint Thomas writes:

> But it had a certain infinity from the circumstance of the person who was of infinite dignity; for the greater the one who humbles himself, the more praiseworthy his humility is found to be.[14]

Q.29.7: Satisfaction and merit

A second article of the De veritate, 29.7, clarifies a key question associated with Saint Thomas's notion of satisfaction. This is an important article for two reasons. In the first place, in the course of his reply to the question of whether Christ could merit for others Saint Thomas distinguishes between two aspects of a human act informed by grace. The first aspect, that of merit, is something positive: meritorious human acts dispose man for glory. The second aspect, that of satisfaction, is something negative: satisfactory human acts remove an obstacle that prohibits one from entering into glory. In turn Saint Thomas shows how these two aspects can be applied to the human work of the God-man. The second reason for the importance of this article is that in it Saint Thomas indicates why the merit and the satisfaction of Christ can spiritually affect (spiritualiter influere) the members of his Church.

The thirteen arguments suggest reasons why Christ either could not merit for others or need not merit for them. Two of these arguments touch directly upon the notion of satisfaction. The first, ag/6, suggests that if Christ could merit for others then any of his acts would have sufficed for our salvation and the passion would not have been necessary. The second, ag/7, proposes that the merit of Christ is superfluous since each individual's actions, informed by grace, merit for him eternal life.

The first of the sed contra arguments clearly shows the direction that Saint Thomas's reply will follow. I John 2:2 states that Christ satisfied for our sins: "He is the expiation for our sins." Since there can be no satisfaction without merit, Christ did merit for us. The following two arguments indicate the reason why this is possible. Christ is the head of his body, the Church. As the head in a physical body functions not simply for itself, but for all the members of its body, so Christ's work was meritorious for his members. This doctrine of the headship of Christ, Saint Thomas continues, implies some kind of union between Christ and the members of his Church. In a striking phrase, Saint Thomas says simply, "Christ and the Church are quasi one person." Therefore Christ was able to merit for others as if in their person ("Christus quasi ex persona aliorum mereri potuit").[15]

In his reply Saint Thomas elaborates on the two aspects according to which any human act can be said to have value as regards obtaining eternal glory. They correspond to the two ways in which a man could be separated from glory. The first of these ways is something negative in man, namely, the unworthiness of a man, and indeed of a sinner, to see God. To the extent that a person does not have charity there is a lack in him of the required worth or dignity for final glory. Saint Thomas writes:

> As the act of sin results in a certain deformity of the soul, so meritorious acts result in restoring a certain beauty and dignity in it.[16]

The second way is something positive in man, an impediment to his entering into glory; it is the debt of some temporal punishment due to sin. Man's actions that atone for sin are not ordered to dispose him positively for glory; rather they serve to remove an obligation to penalty that stands in the way of his receiving his ultimate reward. Saint Thomas writes:

> And so this human work is ordered to glory much like the price paid to free a man from a penalty due; in this way the human work takes on the character of a satisfaction.[17]

Saint Thomas then explains the work of Christ in terms of these two aspects of any good human act. It is possible of course, as the responses to the objections clearly indicate, to conceive of a good human act that is meritorious but not satisfactory, although the reverse is not true. The purpose of this discussion of the work of Christ in terms of merit and satisfaction is to show that from both aspects the work of the God-man was more efficacious than that of any other man.

First, with regard to merit, Saint Thomas explains that when a man performs a meritorious act, thereby disposing himself in a positive way to receive the reward of glory, such an act can only benefit him who performs it. No ordinary man can merit condignly for another. Christ, however, can merit in this way. The reason that Saint Thomas offers to explain this is not an elaborate one. He refers to the theological axiom of Saint John Damascene, which states that the humanity of Christ was an instrument of his divinity. For this reason, Christ, according to his humanity, is able spiritually to influence other men ("spiritualiter influere potuit in alios homines"). Accordingly he can merit for them and the fruit of this merit is that men receive the necessary fittingness to enter into glory ("unde et eius opus in aliis causare potuit idoneitatem ad consecutionem gloriae").

Second, with regard to satisfaction, Saint Thomas explains that it is a general rule that one man can satisfy for another, presupposing that the former be in a state of charity. Christ alone, however, is able to satisfy for the whole human race. He writes:

> Although one man can satisfy for another. . . he cannot satisfy for the whole race because the act of one mere man is not equal in value to the good of the whole race. But the action of Christ, being that of God and man,

had a dignity that made it worth as much as the good of the entire human race, and so it could satisfy for others.[18]

In defining both the meritorious and the satisfactory aspects of Christ's human actions, Saint Thomas has defined as well the double effect which Christ's actions have for man, that of merit and that of satisfaction. The choice of words with which Saint Thomas describes the effect of Christ's meritorious actions is significant. Christ's merit gives man a worthiness (dignitas) or a fitness (idoneitas) for glory. When Saint Thomas speaks about sin as leaving the soul in a deformed state ("in quamdam animae deformitatem"), merit is spoken of as effecting a contrasting result, bringing the soul into a state of splendor and worth ("in quamdam animae decorem et dignitatem").

The relationship between the meritorious and the satisfactory aspects of the work of Christ is clarified in the responses to the objections. In ra/6 Saint Thomas explains the need for a special kind of act, in this case the death of Christ, in order that a meritorious act be considered satisfactory. Saint Thomas writes:

> Although every one of Christ's acts was meritorious for us, yet to make satisfaction for the debt of human nature, which was made liable to death by the divine sentence, as is seen in Genesis 2:17, he had to undergo death in the place of all.[19]

In ra/7 the need for satisfaction, in addition to merit of Christ, is accounted for in terms of the debt of nature. This debt of nature, the result of original sin, kept the Old Testament saints from arriving at glory despite the fact that they had personal grace to merit for themselves. The question of how that grace was given (which remained ambiguous in the Scriptum) is clearly resolved, at least with regard to its mediation, in the same response when Saint Thomas writes that "personal grace was never given to anyone after the sin of the first man except through faith, either explicit or implicit, in the Mediator."[20]

This last remark touches upon the question of how the merit and satisfaction of the God-man can spiritually affect others. As indicated in the sed contra arguments, sc/2,3, the explanation for this is

106

founded upon the relationship that exists between Christ and his Church. The reason why Christ is able both to merit and to satisfy for others is because of the personal union that exists between himself as head and other men as members of the Church. This headship, as an earlier question in the De veritate points out,[21] is associated with the humanity of Christ, which, in Damascene's phrase, is an "instrument" of his divinity. This represents a considerable shift of emphasis in Saint Thomas's thought from that of the Anselmian satisfaction theory. In Saint Anselm the reason why Christ was able to satisfy for others was because of an agreement which the Son had with his Heavenly Father to transfer the fruits of his satisfaction to those who were in need of having a debt atoned for. The jurical cast of thought is clear. Saint Thomas, on the contrary, seeks a deeper, personal reason to explain why Christ's satisfaction was able to atone for others' sins. The phrase of sc/3 is especially important in this regard: "Christ and the Church are quasi one person." The reason why Christ is able spiritually to affect the members of his Church is the personal union, which Saint Thomas asserts here but does not elaborate, that exists between himself and them.

Q.29 4: The headship of Christ

The relationship, merely suggested in 29.7, between Christ the head and the satisfaction for his members is treated in somewhat more detail in 29.4. This article is devoted to the question of whether the grace of headship belongs to Christ in his human nature. In his study of Saint Thomas's teaching on the headship of Christ,[22] T. Potvin recalls that the scholastic tradition understood the term "head" as signifying a principle of order and perfection, exercising a vital influence on the body. In the present article Saint Thomas applies these concepts to Christ, affirming that he is the head of the Church in his human nature. Properly speaking, however, "the whole Christ in both of his natures together is the head of the whole Church."[23]

The text of Colossians 1:18-20 allows Saint Thomas to explain the headship of Christ in terms of the traditional threefold signification of the term "head." Christ is at the head of the Church's order and, as such, possesses the authority to govern: "He is the head of the body, the Church; he is the beginning, the first-born from the dead that in everything he might be preeminent." As a principle of perfection Christ possesses the highest dignity in the Church, "for in him all the fullness of God was pleased to dwell." Therefore, he is able to exercise a vital influence over his members, signified by the words, "and through him to reconcile to himself all things." Christ's headship, as Potvin points out, is understood by Saint Thomas, as it was by Saint Paul, not merely in the sense of one who exercises authority, but also in the sense of one who saves mankind and grants us the possibility of becoming sons in the Son.

The responses to the arguments confirm this interpretation of the headship of Christ, according to his human nature, as regards the work of satisfaction and reconciliation. In 29,4 ra/3 Saint Thomas says that Christ the head had to satisfy for the sin of nature in his visible humanity in order to heal the wound of sin that left man disinclined to submit to the invisible government of the Word. Accordingly, in ra/4, Christ could not be called head of the Church prior to the Incarnation, except if one considers the faith which the Old Testament saints had in Christ prior to his coming. Nonetheless, the fact that Christ's merit and satisfaction were not yet actual meant that there was not the fullness of grace available to such men of faith before the Incarnation as there was afterwards.

De veritate 29 is an important question for Saint Thomas's teaching on satisfaction. It includes a detailed clarification of the question as to how the merit of Christ, in itself finite, can be said to have an infinite effect. It distinguishes too, between the merit of Christ, which disposes man for glory, and the satisfaction of Christ, which atones for the punishment due to sin. In addition it shows how the satisfaction of Christ derives its value from the sacred humanity of the God-man (according to which Christ is the head of the Church) and especially from his death on the cross. Finally, Christ's ability spiritually to affect the lives of the members of the Church united to him in faith, is accounted for, but not fully explained, in terms of his humanity as an instrument of his divinity.

Q.26.6,9: The suffering of Christ

In De veritate 26, a question treating of the passions of the soul, several texts are found, which explain the satisfaction of Christ in terms of the sufferings endured in the course of his expiatory death. Recall that in 29,7 ra/6 Saint Thomas explained the need for the death of Christ, in addition to the other meritorious works of his life, because of the punishment of death which was due to man on account of Adam's sin. In 26,6 rc/4 a fuller explanation is given as to why the sufferings of Christ merited both for himself and for his members what his other works could not. First Saint Thomas speaks of the person of Christ. Christ more fittingly ("per quamdam decentiam") merited the glorification of his body by his sufferings than he did by the meritorious acts which preceded his passion, since the "splendor of the resurrection is by a certain fittingness properly a reward of the passion, as exaltation is the proper reward of humility."[24] With respect to his members, Christ also merited ("nobis autem meruit") by his passion in a way that he did not by his previous merits "inasmuch as in his passion he gave satisfaction for the sin of the whole human race."[25] Saint Thomas adds, by way of explaining this in terms of human suffering, that "retribution by way of suffering is required for satisfaction as a sort of compensation for the pleasure of sin."[26]

The very difficulty of enduring great suffering, as 26,6 rc/6 explains, can be a positive factor for merit. Of itself difficulty is calculated to reduce the willingness with which one undertakes a difficult act such as suffering, and thus it can decrease merit which is the greater as it is the more voluntary. However, as a person makes an effort against the difficulty the result is that merit is increased. More important, difficulty is essential for a meritorious act to be satisfactory since the definition of satisfaction includes the notion of punishment.[27]

Apart from explaining why the passion of Christ was necessary for satisfaction, these two texts should be seen as complementary to what was said in 29,7 as regards how the merit of Christ restores a dignity and fittingness to sinful man. Here the effects of the satisfaction of Christ as well as the satisfactory acts performed by his members are described with reference to the moral definition of satisfaction. The wounds of sin are healed by the suffering which is a kind of compensation for the pleasure of sin; the difficulty of the suffering strengthens one against future temptations.

In the course of responding to the question whether Christ was able to experience the passion of sorrow in his higher reason, 26,9, Saint Thomas offers a valuable clarification as to what constitutes the true value of Christ's satisfaction. The occasion for this clarification is Saint Thomas's appreciation for the uniqueness of the ontological constitution of the God-man. He affirms, in accord with his doctrine on the knowledge of Christ, that there could be no reason for psychic suffering or sorrow in his "higher reason" from the standpoint of the object of his "higher reason," since at every moment of his life, including that of his passion, Christ was in perfect possession of the beatific vision ("scilicet ex parte aeternorum, quibus perfectissime fruebatur"). Such contemplation precludes sadness or sorrow.

However, this seems to pose a difficulty for the doctrine on satisfaction, as 26.9 sc/2 points out:

> Satisfaction corresponds to the fault. But by his passion Christ satisfied for the fault of the first man. Now since that fault reached as far as higher reason, the passion of Christ must also have reached as far as his higher reason.[28]

The response given to this objection is an extremely important one for Saint Thomas's notion of the satisfaction of Christ. In it he points out the value of Christ's love in his making satisfaction for sin, which is a theme that will figure significantly in his discussion of satisfaction in the Summa contra gentiles. Insistence on the role of Christ's love in his satisfaction will also permit Saint Thomas to maintain his teaching on the adequacy of Christ's satisfaction and at the same time to preserve the integrity of his teaching on the ontological structure of the God-man. Saint Thomas writes in 26,9 rc/9:

> Christ's passion would not have satisfied except insofar as it was undertaken voluntarily and from charity. It is accordingly not necessary, just because the fault was in Adam through the operation of higher reason, that suffering be in the higher art of Christ's reason as regards its proper operation; for the sufferer's movement of charity, which is in the higher part of reason,

corresponds for the purpose of satisfaction to whatever fault was to be found in higher reason.[29]

The final text from the _De veritate_ on the role that charity plays in the making of satisfaction reiterates an important principle--one to which Saint Thomas will have occasion to have recourse in discussions of the efficacy of Christ's satisfaction for his members.

Summa Contra Gentiles: Satisfaction "ex dignitate personae patientis" and "ex maiori caritate procedens"

Book Three: The notion of satisfaction accomplished in love

In the third book of the _Summa contra gentiles_ Saint Thomas discusses man's need to be liberated from sin in order to reach his ultimate goal of beatitude. In the context of this tract there is a question devoted to how man is liberated from sin which discusses the role that satisfaction plays in the process. This affords an opportunity to contrast a later writing of Saint Thomas on the doctrine of satisfaction with the teaching of the _Scriptum_. The contrast touches on two points, namely, the role that love plays in satisfaction, and how it can be said that one man· can satisfy for another.

Saint Thomas opens the discussion, in 3,158 by citing several reasons why, from a psychological standpoint, the remedy for sin entails some form of punishment. For example, when one pays a price for something (in this case the punishment undergone as part of receiving pardon), one is more appreciative of what has been received than if it had been given without cost. Having observed that our sensible nature recoils from what causes suffering or pain, Saint Thomas also argues that punishment for sins of the past will lessen the attractiveness of sin in the future. Similarly, the delight which attracts one to wrong-doing will be less forceful in the future if one has undergone punishment as a result of the sinful pleasure. For these reasons, punishment does play a role in liberating man from sin. When these punishments are freely undertaken by the repentant sinner, man is said to satisfy God. When, on the other hand,

these punishments are inflicted on the sinner by
God, they are more properly referred to as purgative
(purgatoria) than as satisfaction.

This description of the psychological reasons that
make satisfaction a suitable part of the process of
man's liberation from sin is, fundamentally, in accord
with the teaching of the Scriptum on the medicinal
effects of satisfactory punishments. The following
remarks, however, on 3.158 enlarge considerably the
role that love plays in the making of satisfaction.

Recall that in De veritate 26,9, written probably
a year or less before the Summa contra gentiles,
Saint Thomas had affirmed that the love of Christ for
mankind, found in his higher reason, satisfied for
whatever there was of sin in Adam's higher reason.
Consequently, there was no need to affirm that Christ
suffered in his higher reason (which would have been
impossible given Saint Thomas's understanding of the
perfection of Christ's knowledge and beatitude). In
the present text he introduces a similar idea with
respect to the satisfaction that man can make to
God.

Saint Thomas affirms that it is possible to
conceive of a case where an individual would be so
remorseful for past sins and so moved toward loving God
that the need for satisfactory or purgative punishments
could be entirely eliminated.[30] Assuming that the
purpose of punishment is ultimately to attach the soul
more firmly to God and to lessen or obliterate its
attraction to evil, it follows that, according to the
strength of one's love for God and the corresponding
abhorrence of one's past sins, the need for punishment
is proportionately decreased. Nor is it impossible
to imagine a case, writes Saint Thomas, where the
force of one's love would be of such magnitude that it
would cancel entirely the need for undergoing any
satisfaction.

A similar case was alluded to in the Scriptum,
where Saint Thomas considered the possibility of a
sinner repeatedly confessing a past sin with the effect
that the partial remission of the temporal punishment
due to sin, achieved in each sacramental confession,
would eventually eliminate all of the punishment owed
as a result of that particular sin.[31] Viewed against
the teaching of 3,158, this theological opinion loses
the appearance of a mechanical formulation. Rather,

it is the love and repeated acts of sorrow of the repentant sinner that account for the reduction or even the elimination of the need for punishment.

This clearly represents a development in the thought of Saint Thomas on the role of a sinner's love in the making of satisfaction. In the earlier Scriptum, he had noted the difference between restitution and satisfaction. The former is the mere giving back of something--for example, property--that is owed, either voluntarily or under constraint, while the latter is a redress for an offense which one has committed against another. Accordingly satisfaction was seen as an interpersonal affair in which love played an indispensable but, at that moment, somewhat undefined role. One could not redress an offense without love and when it was present the punishment of satisfaction was made easier to bear. In general, however, Saint Thomas exhibited a certain hesitancy about drawing too many conclusions from the fact that love had a role to play in the making of a worthwhile satisfaction. In the Scriptum one is struck more by satisfaction in the reestablishment of the broken order of justice than by the role it plays in healing a broken friendship.[32]

There is evidence of this same caution when, in the Scriptum, Saint Thomas speaks about one friend making satisfaction for another. There are texts which affirm that one can make satisfaction for another, although this should not be done without some just cause since its medicinal effects would be forfeited on the part of the guilty party. As Father Lécuyer points out in his article "Prolégomènes à la théologie de la satisfaction,"[33] the emphasis is again on the demands of justice and equivalence. There is no explicit mention of the feelings that arise between the guilty party and the one who performs the satisfaction for him, nor of the guilty one's desire to satisfy himself, nor of the suffering that he undergoes seeing his friend suffer for him. Unquestionably Saint Thomas offers a more explicit and positive teaching on the role that love plays in the performance of satisfaction in the Summa contra gentiles than in his earlier Scriptum.

The developed thought of Saint Thomas on love's role in satisfaction is reflected in 3.158 when he speaks about friendship and satisfaction. Noting a remark of Aristotle's Nicomachean Ethics 3.3 that what one does through a friend is done as if by oneself,

Saint Thomas comments on the reason for this. Friendship makes out of two individuals a kind of unity (ex duobus facit unum), especially when love and not mere affection is the binding force. Citing the same scriptural passage as he did in the Scriptum, Galatians 6:2, "Bear one another's burdens, and so fulfill the law of Christ," Saint Thomas draws the same conclusion as in that work, namely, that it is possible for one man to satisfy for another. A man can satisfy for another on the condition that both are in the state of charity--Christ's satisfaction for sinners being an exception to this general rule.

Saint Thomas's description of the effects which this love of friendship has on the vicarious (although the term does not appear in the text) satisfaction is evidence of his increased appreciation of love's role in the performance of satisfaction. Saint Thomas writes:

> The punishment which a friend suffers on behalf of another does not escape entirely the one for whom the satisfaction is undertaken. It is as if he himself were undergoing the punishment, suffering as he does with the friend who is making the satisfaction. This is so much more the case as the guilty one realizes that it is because of himself that the friend is suffering. Furthermore, the charity which moves the friend to undertake the satisfaction makes the work more pleasing to God than if the guilty one had performed the satisfaction himself. The former is prompted by love while the latter would have been moved by necessity.[34]

This increased appreciation of the effect that love has in giving satisfaction will be reflected in Saint Thomas's discussion of Christ which is found in the fourth book.

Book Four: The satisfaction of Christ

The part of the fourth book of the Summa contra gentiles which is pertinent to this study is questions fifty to fifty-five, a section entitled De convenientia Incarnationis. Under this heading Saint Thomas discusses two subjects--original sin, 4.50-52, and the Incarnation itself, 4.53-55. Among the theological syntheses, the juxtaposition of the discussion of the

Incarnation with that of original sin is unique to the
Summa contra gentiles. In 4.51 an objection is posed
concerning the communicability of Adam's sin. The
objection asks why the satisfaction of Adam was not
communicable to the whole human race, although his sin
was. Saint Thomas responds in 4.52 by observing that
at the time of Adam's sin his nature possessed an
excellence lost by the fact of the sin itself. Hence
the sin of Adam was communicable to the whole race by
reason of the perfection which he possessed, but the
satisfaction which he performed after the sin was
simply a personal act, effective only for Adam since
his wounded nature was bereft of the preternatural
excellence which made communicability possible.

4.53: Objections

Chapters 4.53-55 discuss the fittingness of the
Incarnation and are the occasion for a lengthier
treatment of our subject. Twenty-six objections are
presented in 4.53 which could be used to show either
the impossibility or the incongruity of God's having
assumed a human nature. Seven of these twenty-six
objections, in contrast to the seven out of nine
presented in the _Scriptum_, bear directly on the claim
that Christ had to satisfy for our sins. The _Summa
contra gentiles_ was written for missionaries who were
obliged to respond to the objections of unbelievers,
many of whom were deeply influenced by Greek and
Arabian philosophy. Given the theme of the absolute
transcendence of God found in many such philosophical
systems, one understands why Saint Thomas would devote
considerable attention to explaining the Incarnation
against the charge that it threatened the divine
transcendence. The seven objections which discuss
satisfaction take into account the reasons that could
be posed by one who either did not understand why
Christ would have had to suffer for the sin of Adam or
why he would have needed to satisfy for man's actual
sins.

The seven objections related to the notion of
satisfaction are as follows.[35] (1) In the first place,
it seems unfair to say that Christ had to become a man
in order to die for our sins since justice demands that
the one who sinned should be the one who satisfies.
(2) Secondly, if someone greater than a pure man was
needed to satisfy, certainly an angel would have
sufficed. (3) Thirdly, one sin cannot satisfy for

another; hence Christ's death should have been a natural one and not a violent act as it was. This constitutes one group of arguments.

A second group is based on the supposition that the death of Christ could not have satisfied for man's sin. (4) The fourth argument suggests that it could not have satisfied for his personal sins, since in that case it would seem that Christ should die frequently inasmuch as man sins frequently. (5) Neither, according to the fifth argument, could it satisfy for Adam's sin, since it would be foolish to assert that the death of a single man, namely, that of Christ according to his humanity, would be able to accomplish what the combined efforts of all mankind were unable to do. (6) Sixthly, if Christ did satisfy for the sin of Adam, why is man still urged by the Christian scriptures to accept suffering as a punishment for sin? (7) And seventhly, if the death of Christ was adequate to take away the sins of mankind, why are Christians still told to seek absolution from a priest? The supposition behind the last two arguments is that both further suffering and/or sacramental absolution would seem at best superfluous if it were true that the death of Christ had paid the price for the sin of Adam. It is noteworthy that, with the exception of the argument about the angel given in the second place, none of the arguments given in the Summa contra gentiles corresponds exactly with those of the Scriptum.

4.54: Arguments in favor

Following the list of objections that one might hear from a Moslem or Jew challenging the Christian faith, Saint Thomas outlines eight arguments that might be used to show that the Incarnation, far from being incompatible with the divine goodness, was quite fitting to the notion of an all-good God. Each indication of fittingness is founded upon man's desire to achieve perfect happiness. The first seven of these arguments provide the context within which satisfaction is dealt with; they are summarized below in order to give perspective to the final argument which concerns man's need for satisfaction.

The Incarnation was a most efficacious help for man to attain beatitude because it helped to close the gap that existed between humanity and divinity. It also served as a reminder to man that his call is to live with God and that his happiness lies in God alone. It aided man to know certain truths about God in a way that was intelligible for man's mode of knowing reality. The God-man drew men to himself not only by imparting knowledge but also by love since he incarnated in a recognizable form the love God has for man. In the Incarnation God also gave man hope by establishing a ground for friendship, that is, the required equality arising from a shared nature that must exist between friends. The Incarnate Word was also able to give concrete examples of virtues which otherwise would have remained abstract ideals. Finally, lest man's knowledge of his sinfulness keep him from trusting in God's love, Christ assured us that our sins were forgiven.

When they are examined in detail these seven indications of the fittingness of the Incarnation exhibit a harmonious coherence. One can discern within the arguments, taken as a whole, an inner thrust moving toward the conclusion that the Incarnation was an eminently fitting thing for God to accomplish. The starting point of this argumentation is man's natural desire to find perfect happiness and the belief that God alone can fulfill such a desire in man. The different arguments eliminate one by one any objection that might suggest that man could not possibly realize such a union with God or, at least, that such a union would be extremely difficult to imagine. The conclusion of the argumentation is that the Incarnation is not only highly congruous with the divine goodness but also most "convenient" for man's salvation.

In the eighth and final argument the starting point which Saint Thomas chooses is a different one. Here he cites the tradition of the Church which teaches us that the whole human race was infected with sin. It is clear, based on what was said in 3.158, that God does not forgive sin without satisfaction. From this point follows the familiar outline of the argument for the need of a God-man to make adequate satisfaction for the sin of the human race. The argument is identical with that which we have already seen in the Scriptum. Mna sinned and broke the right order of justice in the world; sin, in turn, demanded satisfaction. A mere man was unable to make this satisfaction since the good of the whole human race was at stake. Nonetheless justice demanded that he who sinned should satisfy. Therefore what was needed was someone who could make the satisfaction (potest) as well as someone who ought to make satisfaction (debet). The angels are eliminated from candidacy since, although by nature higher than man, in terms of their call to beatitude they are man's equals.

Both men and angels find their happiness in God. Only a God-man was able to make the required satisfaction for the sin of the human race.

Admittedly this line of argumentation seems to follow closely that of Anselm. It is possible that the distinctive purposes of the <u>Summa contra gentiles</u> explain why Saint Thomas chose to emphasize the <u>rectus ordo</u> which is broken by sin rather than the <u>debitum</u> owed to God by the sinner. The responses to the objections in 4.55, however, do reflect Saint Thomas's personal contribution to explaining how the suffering and death of the God-man, in fact, made the satisfaction required by a sinful human race.

4.55: Responses to objections

Saint Thomas's responses to the seven objections referred to above are as follows: (1) The objection is raised that such vicarious satisfaction appears to contradict the principle that he who sinned should be the one to give satisfaction. Saint Thomas responds, by recourse to the discussion of 3.158, that one man can satisfy for another and that such satisfaction can even be more pleasing to God than if it had been made by the guilty person by reason of the love of the one satisfying for the sin of another. (2) The following response repeats the reason why an angel could not have been this kind of friend to man. In fact Saint Thomas argues that there would have been something repugnant about such an arrangement, something not in keeping with man's dignity. (3) The real worth of Christ's death, writes Saint Thomas returning to the theme of charity and satisfaction, lies not in the actual death itself, if viewed as an act of violent and sinful men, but in the charity with which Christ freely bore such a wicked death ("ex caritate ipsius, qua voluntarie mortem sustinuit"). (4) Nor should Christ be obliged to undergo such a death each time that men sin since the worth of Christ's satisfaction is founded upon the intense love with which he sustained his death. In addition, the dignity of his person makes a single death sufficient for a complete satisfaction ("tum propter eximiam caritatem qua mortem sustinuit; tum propter dignitatem personae satisfacientis").

(5) This same reason is cited by Saint Thomas when he responds to the objection that Christ's death, given that it was according to his human nature, is of no greater value than that of any other man. Yet this is not the case since his human nature is united to the

118

person of the Word. Christ's death was indeed an adequate satisfaction for the sins of the whole human race precisely because of the value which accrues to it by reason of the fact that he, being of greater dignity, willingly undertook, out of great love, a punishment for others who are of lesser worth than himself. The fact that Saint Thomas draws attention to these two points concerning the person of Christ, namely, the dignity of his person ("ex dignitate personae patientis") and the great love with which he suffered ("ex maiori caritate procedens") is very important.

In the Summa contra gentiles Saint Thomas clearly emphasizes as opposed to a mere mention in the Scriptum, that the love of Christ is the reason why his expiatory death achieved the goal of reconciliation which the Scriptures consistently attribute to it. Saint Thomas explains the relation between the dignity of the person of Christ and the love with which he undertook his sufferings by reference to an argument drawn from human experience. He says that in human affairs whatever is done by one of greater dignity, especially the undertaking of suffering, is more highly valued than what is done by one of lesser dignity. In the Summa theologiae Saint Thomas's emphasis on the love of the man Christ in explaining the efficacy and the consequences of his satisfaction will be given fuller articulation. Nonetheless in the Summa contra gentiles this emphasis on the love of Christ is important to note since it clearly separates Saint Thomas's personalist theological understanding of Christ's satisfaction from the exclusively juridical framework, with its use of mercantile language, in which the theology of Cur Deus homo? sought to explain the efficacy of Christ's death. The Summa contra gentiles also represents a much clearer statement of Saint Thomas's personalist perspective on satisfaction than one finds in the Scriptum where, although reference is made to the love of Christ, the full implications of Christ's love for the satisfaction he achieved are not developed.

The remaining responses address issues related to the satisfaction of the members. (6) Having described the sufficiency of Christ's satisfaction, Saint Thomas goes on to explain that the need for our subordinate satisfaction is still a real one. He explains that the presence in the world of certain penalties (poenalitates) attached to sin does not mean that the satisfactory work of Christ was adequate.

These penalties serve to quicken our faith, allowing us the occasion freely to seek to participate in the effects of Christ's passion and death, rather than, as otherwise might be the case, be compelled toward them. (7) The need to have the effects of Christ's death applied to each individual member requires, however, that one seek out the particular means in which the universal cause of our salvation, the death of Christ the Head, is applied; among these means are the sacraments. Responses six and seven explain, then, the necessity of satisfaction on the part of the members in addition to the fully adequate satisfaction accomplished by the death of Christ on the cross.

Book Four: Sacraments and the satisfaction of the members

The language which Saint Thomas employs in the course of responding to objections six and seven is noteworthy, especially as he refers to the relationship between Christ the Head and the members. One finds a certain clarification as to how the satisfaction of Christ the Head affects the members as they perform satisfactory works for their own sins. Recall that in the De veritate Saint Thomas employed the striking Pauline phrase, "Christ and the Church are quasi one person,"[36] to explain how Christ could merit for others. The language of the Summa contra gentiles, consistent with its emphasis on the dignity of the person of the God-man, continues this personalist emphasis in explaining how the satisfaction of Christ is related to that of his members.

In the sixth response referred to above (4.55), Saint Thomas compared the death of Christ and its effects with the sin of Adam and its effects for the human race. The death of Christ is referred to as a kind of universal cause of salvation ("quasi quaedam universalis causa salutis"), as the sin of Adam was a similar cause of damnation. Universal causes must be aplied to individual cases. The application of Adam's sin is explained, according to one traditional teaching in the Church,[37] in terms of carnal propagation. The effects of Christ's death, however, are applied to an individual by way of a spiritual regeneration (per spiritualem regenerationem), by which man is, in a certain way, joined to (conjungitur) and incorporated into (incorporatur) Christ. For this reason a believer must be born anew in Christ and seek the other things, i.e., satisfactory punishments, in which the power of the death of Christ operates.

120

The seventh response speaks of the sacraments' role in communicating the salvation of Christ (effluxus salutis) to men. Since this salvation is not passed along simply by the fact of being born, sinful man must seek to adhere to Christ by the application of a well-ordered will (studium bonae voluntatis). This reference to man's freely choosing to belong to Christ is interpreted to mean that Christ must become for each of his members a personal good (personale bonum). This being the case, Saint Thomas concludes that, although Christ has cleansed the world of original sin, it is necessary that those who are born into the world with the effects of original sin should seek the sacraments of salvation (sacramentis salutis). Although there is no explicit reference to seeking the Christian sacraments in faith, such is clearly implied since Saint Thomas makes reference to the believer adhering to Christ as a personal good.

The question of the causality exercised by the sacraments, so meticulously debated within the scholastic tradition, is outside the scope of this present study. The need of the Christian believer to adhere to the person of Christ, indeed freely to choose him as a personal good in his life in order to benefit from the efficacy of Christ's expiatory death, is a part of Saint Thomas's theology of satisfaction which clearly reflects the message of the New Testament. These texts indicate how Saint Thomas envisioned what a believer, in the actual living out of his life of faith, must do in order to profit from the benefits of Christ's death which the faith assures was suffered for him.

The heading under which Saint Thomas discusses the sacraments ex professo in 4.56-78 is "The effects of the Incarnation." The satisfaction of the members is discussed in connection with the chapters on baptism, penance and extreme unction. A final remark is found in the last section of the fourth book, which discusses the final resurrection of the dead.

In the single chapter, 4.59, devoted to the sacrament of baptism, Saint Thomas explains how the spiritual birth (spiritualem generationem), which is the proper effect of this sacrament, removes both original sin and personal sins as well as the punishment due to them. For this reason satisfaction is not demanded of the newly baptized. In the brief

<u>De articulis fidei et ecclesiae sacramentis</u>, written around the same time as the <u>Summa contra gentiles</u>,[38] he explains that should one die just after baptism he would enter immediately into eternal life.

In 4.72 Saint Thomas offers an explanation for this effect of baptism in terms of the kind of personal union with Christ that is brought about in that sacrament. He writes:

> Our union (<u>conjunctio</u>) with Christ in baptism is not a result of our operation, as if originating from within us (since nothing generates itself as such), but a result of Christ's operation, in whom we have been born anew to a living hope. The remission of sins in baptism is accomplished, then, by the power of Christ himself perfectly and fully joining us to himself. Thus not only the stain of sin is removed, but also the debt of punishment is also absolved.[39]

In this text Saint Thomas indicates the difference between baptism and penance as regards their effect on the temporal punishment due to sin. Baptism's effect is unique insofar as it removes all of the temporal punishment due to sin. Penance, on the other hand, does not, and this accounts for the fact that punishment for sin in varying degrees does remain after the healing of penance is applied to the sins committed after baptism. Yet Saint Thomas does refer to the case of one whose turning toward God and to the merits of Christ ("conversio mentis in Deum et ad meritum Christi"), along with his detestation for sin, could be so great as to cancel entirely the debt of sin. When this is not the case, however, satisfactory works are enjoined on the penitent for the temporal punishment due to the sin which he has confessed and for which he is sorry.

In 4.73, where Saint Thomas discusses the sacrament of extreme unction, he has occasion to reflect on the circumstances in which this sacrament is received. He writes that both corporeal suffering as well as virtuous acts can be counted as satisfaction for past sins; the latter, however, are more advantageous since they not only satisfy for past sins but also train man for virtue in the future. One is not counseled to delay satisfaction, however, nor is satisfaction optional. In 4,91, when speaking of the alternatives of reward or punishment that await man immediately after his death, Saint Thomas emphasizes the importance of penitential satisfaction as a means of preparing oneself for eternal glory. Since the vision of God totally exceeds man's natural faculties, no man can be admitted to glory until he is purified. Accordingly, what is not satisfied for in this life is purged in the next; if this were not the case man would be lazy about making satisfaction for his sins in the hope that they would be forgotten after death.

Résumé

These brief excerpts from the Summa contra gentiles which treat of the subordinate satisfaction made by the members of Christ indicate the integral role that satisfaction plays in the achievement of their final goal of beatitude. This Summa's discussion of the satisfaction of Christ, however, constitutes its main import for this study and is the context in which the teaching on the satisfaction of the members should be read. The emphasis of the Summa contra gentiles on the great love of Christ and the dignity of the person of the Incarnate Word moves Saint Thomas's understanding of the medicinal effects of satisfaction, especially as these were described in the Scriptum, to a new level of theological reflection.

Satisfaction for the temporal punishment due to sin is fitting (as 3.158 points out) and required (as 4.72, 73,91 reiterates), but the power of Christ's love for the sinner and the sinner's turning to the person of Christ as a "personal good" transforms the sinner's satisfaction from an act of penitence to a true act of reconciliation. Indeed, the power of love can even eliminate the need for any satisfaction whatsoever, when this conversio mentis to God and to the merits of Christ is strong enough. Such a "conversion" on the part of the repentant sinner establishes in him the attachment to God that is the goal of Christ's salvific work and the fulfillment of spiritual regeneration.

One cannot but be struck by the recourse which Saint Thomas has to the charity of Christ that recurs throughout his discussion of satisfaction in the Summa contra gentiles. The impression is given that a shift has taken place in his thinking about how it is that the God-man does in fact accomplish the work of satisfaction. In the earlier systematic work, the Scriptum super Sententias, we were struck by the juridical view taken by Saint Thomas as he explained the need for a God-man to pays a debt owed in justice to God. Because

123

of the sin of the human race it was the order of justice that was broken, and so justice demanded that it be repaired. The satisfaction made by Christ was regarded as a reparation of that broken order of justice. Although not a mercantile conception of the Incarnation, as that of Anselm's has been characterized, it nonetheless suggests the setting of a courtroom if not a marketplace.

While it is true that in the Summa contra gentiles this juridical backdrop is still present, something new appears. The sufficiency of Christ's satisfaction requires not only a juridical frame of reference but also a more personal perspective in order to explain its adequacy. It is no longer merely the God-man who could (potest) and who ought (debet) who makes valid satisfaction, but also the man Jesus Christ who, moved by an intense love, willingly gives himself over to death for our sins. Saint Thomas's emphasis is focused upon the dignity of the person of the God-man and the intensity of his love that renders the satisfaction he performed perfectly adequate and acceptable to God.

What explains this development in the thought of Saint Thomas? Two things might help contribute to an explanation, although neither can be shown to be apodictically applicable. One part of the explanation might be that some new influence began to exercise itself on the thinking of Saint Thomas. One such influence which is known to have affected him during the period when he wrote the Summa contra gentiles is that of Greek theology. Much has been written on this and it is outside the scope of this present study to do more than simply state the fact that at this moment of his career, for a variety of reasons, among which was his presence at the Papal Curia, Saint Thomas was exposed to sources of theology from the east that hitherto had been unknown to him.[40] One fruit of this exposure (and in fact a cause of it as well) was the composition of the Contra errores Graecorum, a work begun at the request of Urban IV to help with reconciliation talks between eastern and western Christianity. Father Dondaine has shown that the composition of the Contra errores Graecorum preceded the writing of the fourth book of the Summa contra gentiles.[41] This exposure to eastern theology, traditionally understood to lean more toward a spiritual, with its emphasis on divinization and mysticism, than a juridic view of the Christian faith, played a role in the shift of emphasis evidenced in the texts cited above.

124

Another part of the explanation of Saint Thomas's apparently deeper understanding of the mystery of the Incarnation that appears in the Summa contra gentiles has also to do with the sources of Christian theology. At the same time that Saint Thomas undertook the composition of the Contra errores Graecorum he also began a glossa continua on the four gospels which has come to be known as the Catena aurea. In the second part of this work, i.e., the glosses on Mark, Luke and John, completed sometime after the death of Urban IV in 1264, Saint Thomas makes the following attestation:

> That this commentary may be more complete and have more continuity, I have had many works of the Greek doctors translated into Latin, and I have added extracts of them to the commentaries of the Latins, being careful to place the names of the authors before their testimonies.[42]

The date of the composition of the Catena aurea (1262/63–1267) makes it less easy to argue that Saint Thomas was working on it at exactly the same time as the Summa contra gentiles (1259–1264). However, it does not seem rash to assume that during the time that Saint Thomas was composing the fourth book of the Summa contra gentiles he was also actively engaged in collecting and examining representative texts of the patristic tradition, especially the commentaries on the New Testament by the Fathers of both the east and the west.

Further light is thrown on the development which takes place in Saint Thomas by considering a text of the Summa contra gentiles which discusses the role that prayerful meditation on the revealed mysteries of the Christian faith plays in increasing one's understanding of those mysteries. Father Chenu has spoken of the Summa contra gentiles as a "work of contemplation of truth."[43] In this respect Chenu also points to a passage from the De Trinitate of Saint Hilary which Saint Thomas adapts somewhat in the beginning of the Summa contra gentiles. The text runs as follows:

> Undertake in faith, move ahead, be persistent. You will not reach the end, I know, but I shall congratulate myself on your progress. For he who pursues the infinite in piety of mind will always become more proficient as he goes onwards, even if, as will happen, his efforts do not always succed. But do not

betake yourself into that mystery, do not plunge yourself into the arcanum of that unending nativity, presuming to comprehend the sum total of intelligence; understand, rather, that those things are incomprehensible.[44]

Perhaps we are unable to ascertain exactly what sources were available to Saint Thomas at the time he was working on the Summa contra gentiles. But we can assume that the new emphasis evident in the discussion of charity's role in christological satisfaction and in the satisfaction of the members is the result of Saint Thomas's mature and meditative reflection upon the sources of theology, which include the patristic heritage of both the east and the west in addition to the revealed Word of God.

De Rationibus Fidei: Satisfaction and the Humility of the Suffering Servant

The emphasis on the dignity of the Incarnate Word and the charity of Christ, so marked in the Summa contra gentiles, is not the emphasis of the De rationibus fidei. This work, written in response to a request from a cantor of Antioch for theological help in answering objections posed by unbelievers and heretics against certain truths of the faith, discusses satisfaction in light of the humility of the Suffering Servant and in the juridical framework of reestablishing the balance of justice. As an intellectual in service to the apostolic needs of evangelization, Saint Thomas undoubtedly chose his theological approach with regard for the religious and intellectual positions of those to whom the arguments would be addressed. Since the De rationibus fidei was written during the same period of time as the Summa contra gentiles, there is no reason to assume that its reliance on the juridical argument for satisfaction is a regression on Saint Thomas's part. Probably Saint Thomas felt that the approach would be more persuasive to the Saracens with whom the anonymous cantor had to deal.

In effect, Saint Thomas is asked to explain the folly of the cross with respect to the wisdom of God, which is the same problem that Saint Paul responds to in I Corinthians 1:18. Saint Thomas's purpose, then, is to show that there is nothing incongruous about the Word of God having suffered and died for our salvation. The first line of argumentation, and the one to which he devotes the most space, is to explain the fittingness of the kenosis. L. Cerfaux summarizes this central element of Pauline christology as follows:

> Christ has abandoned his heavenly riches (the usual metaphor for divine glory and possessions, the state of Christ in his divine existence) and has made himself poor (as a member of the human race) in order to gain heavenly rewards and blessings for mankind.[45]

Saint Thomas's efforts in the seventh chapter are directed toward explaining how the poor, humble and obedient life of Christ is eminently suited to accomplish the work of man's salvation. The first argument of the chapter explains how the earthly life of the God-man is a witness to man concerning inordinate attachment to material riches which obstruct man's attainment of his true final goal.

Christ's poverty and sufferings are explained in terms of the example they set for man, the instruction they give to him and their confirmation of the divine character of Christ's message. Saint Thomas accounts for the poor circumstances of the life of Christ and the bodily weaknesses which he endured by noting that they provide examples for men as to how they should regard temporal fortunes and misfortunes in the light of the authentic spiritual goods in which their true happiness lies. An especially instructive example is set by the death of Christ, since by his willing acceptance of death he taught men that they should not allow any difficulty, not even the fear of death, to alter them from following a life of virtue.

The Incarnate Word also teaches men by his human words. The Incarnation is conducive to the successful accomplishment of this goal so that men could hear the message of truth announced in a concrete way. To insure that men would accept Christ's teaching not as merely another human teaching, but as a truth come from God he confirmed his teaching with miracles. The poverty of Christ meant that he had no human resources, and so the miracles he performed could only be the result of divine power. Since those who actually witnessed the miracles worked by Christ could hardly be led to think that they were the products of human ingenuity or power, they would be more disposed to listen to and accept the teaching of the poor Christ as divine truth.

Saint Thomas observes that the example set by the poor life of Christ and the credibility which his poverty gave to his teaching is reason enough to show the fittingness of the kenosis, his choice to unite human infirmity with divine power. Anyone who refuses to accept the wisdom manifest in the Incarnation, remarks Saint Thomas in an exceptional passage, must have a head harder than rock, because at the death of Christ even the rocks were split asunder.

Saint Thomas pursues the discussion by establishing a connection between the kenosis of the Word and the motive for the Incarnation. Man is redeemed by one who shares the infirmities of human nature and who unites those infirmities to divine power. In this way the power of God shines through the weakness of man. Man is liberated from the sin of pride and disobedience whereby Adam preferred himself to God, and, at the same time, he is taught, by Christ's humility, that he must not prefer himself to God. This humility also leads man to trust in God for the blessings which the Incarnate Word gains by his death. In this way, concludes Saint Thomas, the order of human justice is reestablished since man realizes that he is and must be entirely subjected to God.

There is another aspect to the order of justice that must also be considered. The balance of justice is not reestablished merely by man's being redirected to his true final goal; there is also the question of punishment for sin. This is the transition by means of which Saint Thomas links the discussion of the poverty of Christ to that of the satisfaction of Christ. He writes that the order of justice demands that a certain balance be maintained, "as when a judge takes from him who, having received the goods of another has more than he ought to have, and gives what has been taken to someone who has less."[46] When man sins he indulges his own will at the expense of reason's measure and of the divine law. The rectification of the balance requires that he be punished either by suffering an evil or giving up something good which he possesses. Sometimes this punishment is freely sought; sometimes it is imposed by another.

Given that the entire human race was under the guilt of sin, man was required to undergo the penalty that would reestablish the balance of justice. The familiar argument for the need of a God-man to perform the kind of satisfaction required of mankind follows in the text.

Saint Thomas concludes this very brief discussion by asserting that the contention of the Saracens that God should have saved man without human satisfaction, or should have preserved man from sin, is repugnant on two counts. First, it is repugnant to the order of justice which requires that satisfaction be made for an offense, and second, it is repugnant to the order of human nature which endows man with freedom of choice.

When everything is taken into consideration there is a marvelous wisdom manifested in the way God's providence has ordered the course of man's salvation history. Saint Thomas writes:

> In all of this does the wisdom of God especially make itself manifest since through the Incarnation and death of his Son God both preserved the order of justice as well as the dignity of human nature and at the same time mercifully provided a remedy for the salvation of man.[47]

The shift of emphasis to the sufferings of the poor Christ who makes satisfaction for sinful man has already been explained in terms of the purpose of the De rationibus fidei. This practical reason should not, however, obscure the fact that Saint Thomas's teaching here is consistent with the biblical understanding of the relationship between the kenosis and Christ's expiatory death. This is the position from which Saint Thomas develops his doctrine of satisfaction in the text of the De rationibus fidei. The humbling of the Word of God, which is concretely manifested in the poverty of Christ's earthly life, his susceptibility to suffering and death, is ordered to the reparation of Adam's unjust pride and disobedience. The teaching of the De rationibus fidei should also be understood as a complement to that of the De veritate and the Summa contra gentiles. It provides Saint Thomas the opportunity to consider the satisfaction of Christ, even viewed in its juridical context, as a work necessary to restore the image of God in man, a renewal that permits man to achieve his final goal of beatific union with God.

Compendium Theologiae: Résumé of
Basic Teaching

The Compendium theologiae presents itself as a summary abridgement of Christian doctrine. Given its purpose, one is not surprised to discover succinct recapitulations of Saint Thomas's teaching on christological satisfaction nor to discover that such recapitulations, by reason of their summary form, offer little by way of development in his teaching. Father Chenu insists on the importance of the ordering of the questions in the Compendium as a means toward a fuller understanding of Saint Thomas's doctrine.[48]

Chapter 200, "That only an Incarnate God ought to have restored human nature," is an example of where the position of an abbreviated exposition of man's need for the satisfaction of Christ tells something of how Saint Thomas considered satisfaction within a broader theological context. The reparation of human nature by Christ is required on two accounts, which Saint Thomas described in the previous chapter: (1) Man would not be able to arrive at perfect beatitude unless the infection of sin were removed, and, (2) given his human frailty, man needs help consistently to seek good and avoid evil. For these reasons the satisfaction of the God-man is necessary.

In Chapter 200 the recapitulation of why only a God-man could accomplish these goals is presented. Neither Adam nor any homo purus was able to restore human nature since no individual's worth is able to compensate for a sin which affects the whole of the human race; similarly, no homo purus could be a cause of grace. Even the angels, by reason of their equally gratuitous calling to perfection and beatitude, could not have repaired human nature. God alone can save man (potest). God, however, could not ignore or bypass the demands of the ordo justitiae. Hence it was fitting that God become man so that one and the same individual might be able both to satisfy the demands of justice --the obligation of man--and to restore human nature --the prerogative of God.

In Chapter 226, with the defects assumed by Christ, another concise formulation is found. Saint Thomas prefaces this discussion with the principle that a friend can suffer a penalty for a guilty party since love is a kind of unitive force which makes of two individuals a certain unity. Yet no individual man was capable of making condign satisfaction, as was explained above, nor could an angel be such a friend for man since an angel is a creature and lacks the infinite dignity required to repair an offense that has something of the infinite about it. God alone, having assumed a human nature, can save man. Because man's sins merited punishment, the human nature assumed by Christ must also be able to suffer the punishments owed by man. Only Christ can be the kind of friend that man needs.

However, there are two kinds of punishment which result from sin--those which, because of their potentially satisfactory character are able to draw men closer to God, and those which can only serve to separate men from God. The latter category of punishment, which includes additional sins--ignorance, disordered passions and the like--is not inflicted on the human nature assumed by Christ. The defects which make the endurance of satisfactory punishment possible, such as the necessity of dying and the very ability to suffer, are those which Christ assumed with his human nature. Principally it was the punishment of death that Christ suffered whereby he redeemed the human race.

In Chapter 227 Saint Thomas continues the discussion of Christ's death on the cross. It would have been insufficient merely to have assumed the defects that would have allowed the God-man to suffer; Christ actually had to undertake his passion and death. Christ intended that his death accomplish three goals, namely, satisfaction for our sins (remedium satisfactionis), the signification to the believer of the necessity of living an essentially cruciform life (salutis sacramentum) and the offering of an outstanding example of virtue, especially charity, patience, fortitude and obedience (exemplum perfectae virtutis).

In Chapter 228 Saint Thomas, as if to underscore the importance of the mystery of the cross, repeats the three ends served by Christ's death on the cross. He also includes two allegorical scriptural interpretations to emphasize two points: (1) that Christ, the friend of man, really satisfied for the sin man had committed; (2) but in so doing he paid a debt which he himself did not owe. With respect to the first point, Saint Thomas quotes the Wisdom of Solomon 11:17: "One is punished by the very things by which he sins." This refers to the death of Christ on the wood of the cross as satisfaction for the sin of Adam accomplished through the instrumentality of the wood of the tree of the knowledge of good and evil. The second point is made by reference to Psalm 69:4, where the words of the psalmist--"What I did not steal must I pay back?"--are put onto the lips of Christ. Chapter 231 describes other bodily sufferings of Christ that he endured in perfectly satisfying for the sin of Adam. These include the punishments which derive from man's wounded nature, such as hunger, thirst and weariness, and those which originate from external sources, such as wounds and beatings.

The Compendium theologiae was to have been divided into three parts dealing with faith, hope and charity, based on I Corinthians 13:13. Saint Thomas considered that this passage taught that the whole perfection of the present life consisted in these three virtues. The first part, on faith, treats all the basic truths of faith with the exception of the sacraments. The other two parts were never finished. The discussion of the satisfaction of Christ is part of the discussion of faith as it relates to the humanity of Christ. It places satisfaction in the context of original sin, the Incarnation, and the passion and death of Christ, and in so doing it corresponds to the plan of the Summa theologiae.

Some Minor Works: Satisfactory Acts of the Members

There are five texts, found in works of Saint Thomas written during the same periods of his career as those under discussion in this chapter, that treat of the satisfactory acts which are either undertaken or enjoined upon the members of the Church. The first three, taken from the De perfectione spiritualis vitae, Quaestio de quodlibet 3 and the disputed question De caritate, discuss satisfaction in the context of the three vows of religion, i.e. poverty, chastity and obedience. The fourth and fifth texts, drawn from the Quaestio de quodlibet 3 and 2 respectively, discuss satisfaction as it is a part of the sacrament of penance, either directly or in the related question of indulgences. Examination of these texts affords the opportunity to see how Saint Thomas applies the principles and insights, as worked out or gained in the course of his systematic treatment of satisfaction, to practical issues affecting Christian living.

These texts are important because they reflect the three major developments that took place in Saint Thomas's teaching on satisfaction during the middle period of his career. First, one is able to discern Saint Thomas's heightened awareness of the difference between the positive role of merit, which is the work of charity that renders man fit for the reward of eternal life, and the negative role of satisfaction, which removes the obstacle of punishment due for sin. The positive effects of satisfaction, namely its medicinal functions, are also stressed, especially in connection with the discussion of religious life. Secondly, the role that love plays in the repentant sinner's return to God, and the subsequent effects of that love on the need for satisfaction and the kind of satisfaction required are evident in these texts. Thirdly, the movement from a juridical conception of Christ's satisfaction to a personalist one, so clear in the other texts of this period, is also seen in these texts which treat of satisfaction of the individual members of the Church. Evidently this third development is dependent on the two previous points, in particular point two.

Satisfaction and the Perfection of Charity

The first text is found in the De perfectione spiritualis vitae, a treatise on the nature of the spiritual life and the life of perfection. In Chapter 12 Saint Thomas explains why religious life can be considered a supremely satisfactory work. His inspiration for this conclusion is the commentary of Gregory the Great on Ezechiel, from which he quotes directly in the course of his explanation cited below. Saint Thomas first refers to the authority of Saint Augustine and Cicero concerning the signification of the word "religion" as pertaining only to the worship of God. Sacrifice is one way in which worship is given to God, and it takes two forms, as Saint Thomas explains using the text of Gregory:

> There is a difference between sacrifices and holocaust. While every holocaust is a sacrifice, not every sacrifice is a holocaust: in a simple sacrifice it is the custom to use only a part of the animal; when it is a question of a holocaust the entire heifer is offered up. When, therefore someone vows one thing to God, but holds

133

something else back, that is a sacrifice; when, on the contrary, he vows to God everything that he has, all that with which he lives, all that he knows, that is a holocaust.[49]

Saint Thomas concludes that since those who pronounce the vows of poverty, chastity and obedience dedicate themselves to God in this total way they are fittingly referred to as religious because they have made of themselves a holocaust, which is a supreme act of the virtue of religion.

There is, however, the non-holocaust sacrifice spoken about in the Old Testament, and one form it can take is the sin-offering. The vows of religion can be considered to fulfill this command as well, namely, to satisfy for sin. Indeed, based on the notion of holocaust as a perfect sacrifice, it can be said that the vows of religion are means whereby man makes perfect satisfaction to God ("perfecte homo Deo satisfacit"). Accordingly, religious life should be spoken of not only as a state of perfect charity but also as a state of perfect penitence. Because of this perfection, concludes Saint Thomas, there is no sin so grave that it would require that one enter religious life as a satisfaction. Saint Thomas adds to this the bold comment that religious life can be viewed as transcending all satisfaction ("quasi religionis statu omnem satisfactionem transcendente"). However, one might be counseled to enter religious life for some grave sin rather than bear the heavy burden of satisfaction that would be imposed upon a grave sinner who remained in secular life. Saint Thomas is aware that, in fact, this had been a practice in the Church.[50]

This very question, whether sinners should be allowed to enter religious life, is the subject of the Quaestio de quodlibet 3.5.3. In this article Saint Thomas looks at the question from a different perspective, namely, from the point of view of the advantages of religious life for one who has sinned. His response is based upon satisfaction's twofold medicinal role, that of healing sin's wounds and that of strengthening man against sin in the future. The religious state, he concludes, is especially suited to both purposes. Given the perfect state of penitence that religious life is, there is no satisfaction that can be equated with the penances of persons in religion (it is understood that there could be no better healing for sin than religious life). Secondly, no better protection

against committing sin in the future than religious
life could be found. Those who would suggest otherwise merit one of Saint Thomas's rare expressions of
exasperation. He writes:

> It is stupid to say that someone who is
> weaker because of sins committed in the past
> should not seek out a securer life style.[51]

This particular question reflects Saint Thomas's
appreciation for the penitential side of satisfaction
as well as the potential character of his defense
of the religious state. However, in the course of
explaining why a sinner is better protected against
sin in the future if he chooses to enter religious
life, Saint Thomas offers a remark that reflects his
understanding that satisfaction's ultimate purpose is
not simply the reform of a person's moral character but
the firmer attachment of the repentant sinner to God.
In contrasting the poverty of the religious state with
the danger of riches he writes:

> It is difficult for those in the world
> not to be enticed by the world's riches.
> Chrysostom, commenting on Matthew 19:23-24,
> says that the Lord is teaching that a rich
> man who clings to his possessions with
> inordinate attachment (per amorem) will not
> enter the kingdom of heaven, and that a rich ·
> man who has many possessions will do so only
> with difficulty.[52]

The implication is that the satisfactory acts--in this
case religious poverty--are not ordered simpy to atone
for sin but to dispose one as well for the act of
charity that merits eternal life.

In the disputed question, De caritate 1.11,
Saint Thomas addresses himself to the question of the
relationship between charity and the vows of religion.
The question is asked whether all men are obliged to
have perfect charity. In the reply Saint Thomas
distinguishes four ways in which the perfection of
charity can be understood. (1) The first way is that
which is associated with the definition of charity, or
the perfection which arises from the removal of any
inclination that is opposed to charity. (2) The second
way pertains to the preservation of charity, or the
perfection that arises from the removal of worldly
preoccupations "which retard human affection from
freely progressing toward God" ("ne libere progrediatur

in Deum"). (3) The third way pertains to the perfection of charity which man will possess in eternal life; and the fourth way refers to the perfection of God himself. Saint Thomas responds to the question of the article by saying that in this life each man is bound to seek the perfection of charity understood in the first way, since that is equivalent to having the virtue itself. One is not bound, however, to have the perfection of the second way, since any charity suffices for salvation. As to the third and fourth ways, man is clearly not bound to the impossible.

In the course of responding to an objection, ra/5, Saint Thomas has the occasion to apply this teaching to the kind of perfection sought after by religious. He writes that the perfection of Christian life consists essentially in the soul's charity ("ad interiorem mentis dispositionem, et praecipue in actu caritatis"). In a secondary way, or per accidens, the perfection of Christian life consists in certain external things, such as virginity and poverty. Saint Thomas offers three reasons why such things belong to the perfection of charity. (1) First, they remove impediments to man's more spontaneous love for God ("quibus remotis mens liberius fertur in Deum"). In an important comment Saint Thomas underlines the relationship between poverty and the soul's interior attachment to God: He writes that "poverty belongs to perfection only inasmuch as it disposes one to follow Christ."[53] (2) The second reason why external things can be considered as constitutive of perfection is that they manifest the effects of charity in the soul, such that one who perfectly loves God will avoid the things that can separate him from God. (3) The third reason is the fact that the three vows of religion constitute perfect satisfaction for sin.

This is an important article because it clearly shows how Saint Thomas measures the true value of the vows of religion which he describes as supreme acts of satisfaction. By way of interference, it can be said that this doctrine on the perfection of charity is applicable as well to all kinds of satisfactory acts. Such acts are considered to belong to the perfection of Christian life in a secondary, or per accidens, way and as such they have value only to the extent that they serve the principal perfection of eternal life which is the soul's adhering to God in love. Saint Thomas writes:

Whence it does not follow that the poorer a man is the more perfect he is. Perfection in such things should be measured by reference to that in which perfection principally consists. Accordingly, a man would be said to be more perfect whose poverty drew him further away from earthly occupations and made it easier for him to serve God.[54]

It is true that the hardships of religious life, such as poverty and celibacy, serve the medicinal ends of satisfaction, as the Quaestio de quodlibet 3 pointed out, and atone for past sins. However, it must be maintained, in light of the teaching of De caritate, that these and by inference all satisfactory acts find their true perfection only insofar as they dispose man to seek and rest in that personal union with God that is properly speaking (principaliter) the perfection of charity.

Sacramental Satisfaction

Another Quaestio de quodlibet, 3.13.1, discusses the satisfaction that is enjoined on a penitent in the sacrament of penance. The article asks whether a sacramental satisfaction is constituted by the words of the priest to the penitent, namely, "and whatever good you do be the cause for the remission of your sins."[55] The difficulty centers on the fact that nothing of a determined nature is enjoined on the penitent, such as satisfactions in the sacrament of penance are required to be.

In the course of his reply Saint Thomas responds to questions such as why a penitent is bound to perform a satisfactory act (because of the sin which requires it and the injunction of the priest who imposes it); how an enjoined act of satisfaction benefits the penitent (by reason of the nature of the satisfactory punishment itself and because of the work's participation in the efficacy ex vi clavium of the sacrament); why satisfaction is beneficial in itself (because it expiates for past sins and guards against future ones) and what criteria a priest can use in deciding upon a suitable satisfaction (either his own judgment or the opinion of another).

Because the priest is free to choose any satisfaction he judges suitable for the penitent he is entitled to assign "whatever good you do" as a satisfaction for the remission of sin. Accordingly, Saint Thomas responds positively to the original question and asserts that a satisfaction of this undetermined kind is indeed sacramental.

He continues his explanation by offering some practical observations as regards the choice of a satisfactory penance. A priest should not, he writes, burden a penitent with too much penance, lest, as a small flame is smothered by too much wood, so a small amount of contrition could be extinguished by too great a penance. This could result in a sinner's despair rather than in his satisfying for his sin. Rather a confessor should indicate to a penitent the kind of satisfaction that his sins would deserve, but he should enjoin only what he judges him able to bear. In this way, Saint Thomas observes, the penitent might be freely moved to perform even more satisfaction than that enjoined by the priest. Such satisfaction would be rendered more expiative for past sins if the priest adds the words in question, since this would serve to include such additional satisfaction under the power of the keys.

The power of the keys is traditional theological language, based on Matthew 16:19, for the sacramental efficacy of penance. In the Summa contra gentiles 4.72 Saint Thomas writes that the power of the keys has its efficacy from the passion of Christ.[56] In the earlier part of the response Saint Thomas explains that satisfaction is required only for that punishment not removed by either the power of the keys or the penitent's own sorrow. If we recall the personalist emphasis of the Summa contra gentiles, which considered the possibility of an individual's repeatedly confessing a given sin and thereby repeatedly submitting himself to the mediation of Christ's passion through the power of the keys, the reason for Saint Thomas's flexibility with regard to imposing a determined penance and his counsel to impose a light one becomes clear. Saint Thomas shows greater concern to emphasize the healing effects of penance, as they are accomplished by the repentant sinner's personal union with Christ and the power of his death in the sacrament, than to insist on the juridical demands of matching a determined penance with a given sin.

This same priority of emphasis is seen in his remarks concerning the penitent's contrition. Satisfactory acts should be of such a kind that they promote the sinner's return to God rather than, by being excessive, move him to despair of ever attaining his final goal. Evidence for Saint Thomas's appreciation of the reconciliatory effects of penance is found as well in the concluding lines of the quodlibetal question. He says that priests should add the prayer "whatever good you do" to the imposition of a satisfaction because

> even though such undetermined satisfaction might not be of great efficacy (maiorem vim) for guarding against future sin, it will, as a sacramental satisfaction, expiate for past sins because of the power of the keys (virtute clavium).[57]

If the preceding text shows Saint Thomas's willingness to relax the demands of casuistry with regard to the imposition of a penitential satisfaction because of the power of Christ operative in the sacraments, the following text, Quaestio de quodlibet 2.8.2, considers the case of one unable to perform a satisfactory act at all. The case in question is the historical one of a man who has accepted the crusader's cross and received the papal indulgence of full remission of his sins which was attached to such an act. The crusader has fulfilled the requirements of the papal bull, namely, that he be truly sorry (vere poenitens) for and confess his sins. Before the man is able to leave (ante iter assumptus) on the crusade he dies. The question is posed whether such a person benefits from the papal indulgence. The case may seem of little relevance to our question; nevertheless it leads Saint Thomas to propose some very suggestive thoughts on satisfaction.

The first two arguments suggest that the crusader would receive the full benefits of the indulgence since he had fulfilled the requirements of the papal bull, which promises remission of all punishment due to sin. Against this, in the first sed contra Saint Thomas quotes Saint Augustine, who wrote that "it is one thing to take out the arrow, another to heal the wound." According to this metaphor, the taking out of the arrow refers to the remission of sin, but the healing of the wound refers to the reforming of the image (reformationem imaginis) which is progressively accomplished by satisfactory acts. Evidently a crusader who dies before he undergoes the burdens of a holy war has no opportunity for such self-reformation, with the result that he would be unable to enter immediately into glory. There is an important point made in this sed contra, namely, the identification of the purpose of satisfactory works with the restoration of the image of God in the repentant sinner. The medicinal role of satisfaction is identified with the process of man's being moulded to the image of God. The punitive requirements of vindictive justice receive no mention.

Saint Thomas's developed reply is of special interest. He begins by stating the general rule that the work of one man is able to be satisfactory for another, according to the intentions of the one who performs the satisfaction. He then immediately refers to the works of Christ and of the saints which constitute a kind of treasury (thesaurus) for the Church. He writes:

> Christ shed his blood for the Church and did and underwent many other things whose worth is of infinite value because of the dignity of his person. . . . Likewise all the other saints had the intention that those things which they did and suffered for God would be useful not only for themselves but for the whole Church.[58]

This thesaurus can be dispensed by the one who presides over the whole Church, the Pope, as he deems necessary, to anyone who through charity is a member of the Church. In this case "the passion of Christ and of the other saints is imputed (imputetur) to him as if he had suffered sufficiently for the remission of his sins."

Saint Thomas continues his reply by listing the requirements for a valid indulgence: (1) that it be given for a cause which pertains to the honor of God, or one useful for the Church; (2) that the Pope, or one with proper authority from him, confer the indulgence; and (3) that he who benefits from the indulgence be in the state of charity. These three conditions, Saint Thomas observes, are specified in the papal bull containing the indulgence for the crusade. He notes, however, that while the bull calls for contrition and confession it does not mention satisfaction. This is because the indulgence itself eliminates the need for that (cedit in locum satisfactionis). On the basis of these conditions Saint Thomas concludes that the deceased crusader would benefit from the indulgence because the reason for receiving the indulgence was simply the promise to join the Crusade and not the actual undertaking of the journey.

The response to the sed contra argument, ra/3, is another important text since it explains why the crusader--who has not had the chance to benefit from satisfaction's medicinal effects, i.e., the restoration of the image of God--could enter immediately into glory. Saint Thomas distinguishes the role of satisfaction as medicinal from its role as punitive. The indulgence satisfies for the punitive aspect of satisfaction, namely, the remission of all punishments due to sin; it does not, however, substitute for satisfaction's medicinal effects, for which the actual working out of satisfaction (labor satisfactionis) is required. Accordingly, Saint Thomas cites the custom of encouraging crusaders freely to take on satisfactory acts for their medicinal role, i.e., the work of self-reformation.

Something of an ambiguity occurs in the text at this point. Saint Thomas had referred to the healing role of satisfaction as "labor satisfactionis." In the following paragraph, after stating that crusaders should undertake such satisfactory acts as a precaution against sin in the future, he says, "Nor is any burdensome labor required for this" ("nec ad hoc requiritur aliquis labor"). The reason given for this apparently contradictory assertion is that the "labor" of Christ's passion suffices. It might be that, by appealing to the burden of Christ's sufferings, imputed by jurisdiction to the crusader, Saint Thomas exempts the latter from the normal medieval external forms of satisfaction which are directed towards the always-necessary self-reformation. This could be seen in terms of public penitential pilgrimages, etc., which a man on a boat, armed with a papal bull, need not undertake. Or it could be that Saint Thomas is simply referring to the lightening of the burden that a man who has been united to the passion of Christ by the sacrament of penance would experience as he undertook the task of self-reformation. In any case, such medicinal effects of satisfaction are unnecessary for one who is dying; it is the liberation from the debt of punishment that is important for him.

This incidental ambiguity should not obscure the fact that this text is an important one for two reasons. First it makes explicit reference to the union of the Church in charity and thereby establishes the ground for the communication of satisfaction. Saint Thomas, by recourse to what is admittedly a mercantile term, speaks of the treasury of satisfaction which is filled up ("infinitus est thesaurus"), as it were, by the sufferings and other deeds of Christ and of the saints. The members of the Church can benefit from these satisfactory acts, not only those of Christ the Head, as _De veritate_ 29.4 and 7 pointed out, but those of other members of the Church as well, according to the general rules laid down for the satisfaction made by one man for another in charity. This becomes the case when the treasury of satisfaction is imputed to them, as ra/4 says, either sacramentally, as with the sacramental absolution of penance, which remits part of the punishment due to sin, or by jurisdiction, as with the "spiritual grace of an indulgence" which remits (in the case in question) the whole punishment due to sin.

The second reason for this article's importance is the interpretation, suggested in the context of or a reference to Saint Augustine, of satisfaction's medicinal role, namely that satisfaction promotes the process of reforming the image of God in the repentant sinner. The medicinal role of satisfaction, previously emphasized in terms of healing the weaknesses which sin causes in man and of strengthening him against temptation in the future, is here spoken of as restoring the image of God in fallen man. It is interesting that in the _sed contra_ argument Saint Thomas does not refer to the definition of satisfaction in the _Liber ecclesiasticorum dogmatum_. It is possible that this omission--though caution should be exercised against reading too much into a single text--is evidence of Saint Thomas's increased appreciation of the role that satisfaction plays in the life of the Christian believer. Satisfaction, according to this developed understanding of its function, is ordered to the believer's personal union with God and therefore, as _De caritate_ pointed out, subordinated to the principal work of the growth of charity in the soul. In addition, if the second resolution of the textual ambiguity is the correct one, the penal aspects of satisfaction are transformed ("nec ad hoc requiritur aliquis labor") from being burdensome punishments and cures for sin into means whereby the individual member of the Church is personally united, in love, with Christ, who--it can be said--has infinitely satisfied for all the members of his Church.

CHAPTER FIVE

SUMMA THEOLOGIAE: THE DEVELOPED NOTION
OF SATISFACTION IN THE CONTEXT OF
IMAGE-RESTORATION ACCOMPLISHED
IN THE PERSON AND BY THE
REDEMPTIVE DEATH OF
JESUS CHRIST

Prima secundae: Punishment as Restorative

Sin and Punishment

In an exceptional essay attached to his translation of prima secundae 86-89, T. C. O'Brien has written
that "the debt to undergo punishment incurred by sin is
at the centre of the theology of a redemptive, atoning
Incarnation and of the theology of the essentially
'cruciform' Christian life."[1] Saint Thomas's understanding of sin, especially of the effect of sin,
is indispensable background material for a thorough
understanding of his teaching on the satisfaction
of Christ. For that reason a summary of the major
emphases of his discussion of the effect of sin in the
Summa theologiae is presented here. The focus for this
summary is prima secundae 87.6,7,8 which discusses
the notion of punishment (reatus poenae) as it is
afflictive and therefore potentially satisfactory.

Earlier in the prima secundae Saint Thomas discusses the reality of sin itself, and there one finds
in 72.1 ra/2 what might be considered his preferred
definition, namely, that sin is an action lacking due
order (actus debito ordine privatus). The "due order"
of which he speaks has also been discussed previously,
in 21.3,4, and characterized as a decidedly interpersonal one:

Each man's actions have the quality of merit
or demerit through being directed to another
person (considered either as an individual or
as a member of the community). In both
respects our acts, good or bad, are meritorious or otherwise in the sight of God.[2]

143

The major concern of the secunda pars is the human act; the section referred to here shows that merit and demerit are qualities necessarily related to each human act and, as such, are suggestive of the "stream of internal finality," as Father Gilby describes it,[3] that guides human activity from its origin to its end. This interpersonal order is the arena, as it were, in which man's free activity directs the overall movement of the rational creature to God. Sin is an action which breaks out of that due order--be it with regard to one's self, to one's neighbour or to God--whose final term is the creature's union with God.

The punishment that is the result of sin is similarly intrinsically connected to this broken order. It is not a mere extrinsic imposition of a penalty for a fault committed but the necessary consequence of a bad act. The sinner stands liable to punishment, first of all, because his sin violates the due order, intrinsic to the structure of created being. This due order, universally applicable to all beings, takes on an added significance in man, who is a rational being. For man the ordo debitus becomes an ordo justitiae, as justice properly applies to intelligent beings.

Saint Thomas writes at the beginning of the prima secundae:

> Things possessing intelligence set themselves in motion towards an end, for they are masters of their act through their own free decision, of which they are capable by reason and will.
> . . . .Intelligent creatures are ranked under divine providence the more nobly because they take part in providence by their own providing for themselves and others. Thus they join in and make their own the eternal reason through which they have the natural aptitudes for their due activity and purpose (ad debitum actum et finem).[4]

The evil of a disordered human act is a fault (culpa) and is liable to punishment (poena) precisely because of man's capability of apprehending his proper end and his ability freely to choose that end. "We are left with the conclusion," Saint Thomas writes, "that only in voluntary activity do good and bad constitute the reason for praise and blame and that in these, evil (malum), failure (peccatum) and culpable fault (culpa) are identical."[5]

144

Such a conception of sin is entirely consonant with Saint Thomas's understanding of the expression of the eternal law as positive statements of the same inner finality of the rational creature's movement toward the good and, ultimately, toward God. If punishment is not an arbitrary, external imposition, then still less are the precepts of the law arbitrary or imposed from without.[6] This attitude on sin and punishment, it should be remarked, is at some remove from the perspectives of casuistic "moral theology" with respect to right and wrong, commandments and precepts. According to the mind of Saint Thomas, man makes himself liable to punishment precisely because by sinning he fails to fulfill himself as one bound to a given end, an end to be attained by his own proper activity. By such a failure he fails as well to recognize himself as one related to other persons, with whom he is inescapably involved as a social being, and to God as a creature. Eternal punishment is the unavoidable result as well of such a failure. "God is not the afflictive avenger," comments O'Brien, "punishment for mortal sin is the state of separation and estrangement, of loss."[7] Or, as Saint Thomas himself writes in the treatise on charity, secunda secundae 24.10, "God does not turn further away from anyone than the person has turned away from him."

This outline provides the context for the final three articles of prima secundae 87. 87.1 discusses why liability to punishment follows necessarily as a direct effect of sin and 87.2 how one sin can be said to be the effect of another sin. From this point two further discussions ensue: the first treats, in 87.3-5, of eternal punishment, mentioned above, and the second of punishment as it is afflictive. It is at this juncture that the discussion of satisfactory punishment begins.

87.6: Reordering of the Effects of Sin

It is 87.6 which is the key article of the discussion. Saint Thomas poses the question as to whether the debt of punishment continues after sin. The three arguments suggest reasons why it is untoward that punishment be the lot of one whose sin has been taken away. The sed contra quotes II Samuel 12:13-14, where the prophet Nathan tells David that although his sin of adultery has been forgiven, the child that he has begotten will die.

The argument proceeds on two levels. First, relying on concepts of justice, it argues that divine, vindictive justice requires recompense for sin. In accord with his personalist doctrine on sin, Saint Thomas, by his emphasis on the will as the place of punishment, relates punishment as well to the human person who has sinned. This shift to an anthropological emphasis on punishment distinguishes Saint Thomas's mature discussion of the issue from that of the Scriptum super Sententias, where punishment seems to be more directly related to God's unwillingness to allow anything disordered to remain and therefore acquits fault by punishment, ("quia Deus nihil inordinatum relinquit, ideo numquam culpam sine poena dimittit").[8]

Saint Thomas writes:

A sinful act makes a person punishable in that he violates the order of divine justice. He returns to that order only by some punitive restitution that restores the balance of justice, in this way, namely that one who by acting against a divine commandment has indulged his own will beyond what was right, should, according to the order of divine justice, either voluntarily or by constraint be subjected to something not to his liking.[9]

Accordingly even after sin there still exists, by reason of justice's demands, a penal debt.

The second level of argumentation logically moves the discussion from the idea of simple poena to that of poena satisfactoria. Here, too, personal emphasis is given to the removal of the stain of sin, accomplished by man's choice to be rejoined to God and the subsequent restoration of the soul's splendor (proprii nitoris). It is precisely the sinner's willing acceptance of the divine order of justice, and the satisfactory punishments which it requires, that effects the restoration. Saint Thomas writes:

As to the taking away of the stain of sin, clearly this cannot be wiped out except by the soul being rejoined to God; it was by drawing away from him that it incurred the impairment of its own splendour which. . . is what the stain of sin is. Now the soul is joined to God through an act of the will [which] . . . embraces the order of divine justice.[10]

This act of the will is primarily an act of charity, both an act of conversion and an act of repentance, which turns the repentant sinner back to God from whom he has previously turned away by sin. This act of love, then, transforms the satisfactory punishment which the sinner undertakes.

Saint Thomas describes what it means for the sinner to "embrace the order of divine justice." This is to be willing to accept satisfactory punishment, or if one does not spontaneously take on some form of penance, then at least one must patiently bear the punishments that are imposed. In either case the punishments are satisfactory. What should be noted here is that, viewed in this light, satisfactory punishments are not simply the demands of an abstract order of justice; rather they are seen as something one willingly suffers in order to be more fully reconciled with God; the sinner embraces God's saving justice.

In point of fact, writes Saint Thomas, satisfactory punishment is punishment only in a somewhat diminished sense of the word. This is the case since punishment in its proper meaning, or abstractly considered, implies something that goes against the will and consequently something that an individual would not seek out. Satisfactory punishment, on the other hand, although when considered in the abstract would be against one's will, is voluntary in the actual instance ("simpliciter est voluntaria, secundum quid autem involuntaria"). Hence it is possible to consider a case where two individuals might look upon a given punishment in entirely different ways and with divergent dispositions. The one, with no understanding about the need for satisfactory suffering, would recoil from the suffering; another, who understood what satisfaction meant, would embrace it. Saint Thomas's conclusion to the entire argument is that the debt of punishment which exists after sin should be regarded as a satisfaction rather than as an outright punishment.

This article shows a significant development in Saint Thomas's view of poena and macula and, at the same time, is evidence that the movement towards personalism, already noted in earlier sections of his writings, has come to full term. Clearly Saint Thomas understands more profoundly the ordo justitiae when it

is applied to the God-man relation--a relation which is
eminently personal. As a result, the juridical concept
of poena is itself discovered to be purely personal,
something which is already clear for macula. The
responses to the arguments, ra/1 and ra/3, affirm that
macula concerns the will, that is, the will turned
against God, and results in the subsequent loss of the
soul's splendor. Even when the stain of sin is wiped
out, poena is required to turn back, to heal, other
powers of the soul that have been deformed by sin.
It is, then, a question of looking at the same reality
--the disruption of the whole person caused by sin--
from two sides thereby indicating a substantial link
between concepts previously understood only as juridically related.

In his earlier writings Saint Thomas described
how the love of Christ affected the value of his
satisfaction and how the love of the members affected
their satisfactory actions. Here the attitude regarding poena, namely, the desire for union with God and
the necessary self-reformation, is what makes it
satisfactory. As a result, simple poena becomes
satisfaction and, by the same token, becomes a gradual
submission of the whole person to his own supernatural
finality. It is a gradual submission because sin is
not simply a macula to be wiped clean, even by charity;
poena, as ra/3 points out, is also required to heal and
cure the soul, progressively bringing the whole person
into union with God.

It is equally significant, in support of this
interpretation, that in 87.6 ra/3, when Saint Thomas
speaks of satisfaction from the side of divine vindictive justice, remarking that "punishment is called
for as well in order to reestablish the balance of
justice," he speaks as well of a clearly personal,
human value which results from meeting the demands
of justice. Having cited the healing effects of
satisfaction, he continues by saying that punishment is
required for justice's sake "and to undo scandal,
namely that those who have been scandalized by the sin
may be edified by the repentance; this is clear from
the example given about David."[11] This linking--in the
same sentence--of divine justice and the personal good
of the community taken as a whole, as well as what has
been said in the body of the article, is a further
indication of a significant change in Saint Thomas's
understanding of satisfaction. Saint Thomas's focus on
the relation of satisfaction to the human person will

be of central importance for the interpretation of Christ's satisfaction for his members as treated in the **tertia pars**.

87.7,8: Remedial Punishments

The question is posed, in 87.7, whether in every case sin is the reason for a punishment. This is a classic locus in the Summa theologiae for Saint Thomas's teaching on the mystery of evil, the scandalum iniquitatis. In the course of the reply Saint Thomas suggests how a sinner can personally profit from some kinds of affliction. In the first place he affirms that punishment, in the simple, punitive sense, is always related to either one's own sins or the original sin. In fact, reductively, whatever there is of punitive suffering in the world is ultimately reduced to the sin of the First Parents. This is why Saint Thomas can assert, as in the De malo,[12] that human evil is divided into the malum culpae and the malum poenae. Our concern, however, is directed toward Saint Thomas's remarks in this article on satisfactory punishments.

Satisfactory punishments, however, may not be the result of an individual's own sin, as is the case when one person who has not sinned willingly undergoes punishment in place of another. The explanation given for why this is possible is love. As Saint Thomas writes: "In some cases those who are different in their purely penal obligations are one in will, through their union in love."[13] Such a teaching is in harmony with what was said in the Summa contra gentiles concerning a friend's satisfaction for one to whom punishment is due.

Another point made in this article, 87.7, concerns how something may seem punitive when in reality it does not fully have the quality of punishment. Saint Thomas refers to the loss of certain lesser human goods, such as bodily health or financial security, which can be providentially (secundum divinam providentiam) removed from an individual either in the interest of his own salvation, the salvation of others who are warned by such punishments, or the glory of God. Such adversity, which can even befall little children, as ra/1 points out, is ultimately explained in terms of man's fallen nature which needs such "bitter potions" in order to progress in virtue through adversity and to realize that the supreme values are those of the spirit. These afflictions, which in the broad sense can be considered satisfactory, as in the broad sense they are the result of original sin, are another example of the role that satisfactory punishment plays in the gradual movement of man toward God and an appreciation of divine things.

The following article, 87.8, asks whether one person is punished for the sins of another. Saint Thomas answers the question by reference to the three purposes of punishment that have been described up to this point, namely, satisfaction, penalty and healing. It has already been explained that one man can satisfy for another by reason of a bond between them, ("inquantum sunt quoddammodo unum"). On the other hand, purely penal punishments are only afflicted on an individual as a result of his own sins.

Saint Thomas's explanation of how remedial punishments can be suffered by others than those to whom they are due, especially in cases where there is an existing relationship, such as parents and children, masters and servants, is a noteworthy example of his comprehension of the psychology of human behaviour. His conclusion is that one may suffer as a result of the sins of another, as when an entire family suffers because of a profligate father, but such punishments borne by the innocent party will always be of the temporal variety and in the end will redound to his spiritual benefit. No spiritual punishment is ever inflicted on someone because of the sin of another. The importance of the article lies mainly in the description Saint Thomas gives, especially in ra/1,3, of the way remedial punishments affect the complex network of interpersonal relationships, particularly familial ones.

Remedial suffering, such as has been described in 87.7,8, is only a partial transformation of the concept of punishment. The complete transformation of punishment, as it is discussed in the Summa theologiae, comes with satisfaction. The reatus poenae interpreted in terms of justice is contrary to the will of the offender; interpreted in terms of charity it takes on a voluntary and thus satisfactory character. The manifold of acute human sufferings is not easily reconcilable with the notion of an all-powerful and loving God--indeed, as some say, they are a scandal--if the only value that could be assigned to them is that of redressing offenses against divine vindictive justice. When, however, such sufferings are understood to be satisfactory, and, more importantly, ordered to the ultimate spiritual well-being of the one who

150

undergoes them, they point to the radical significance of God's providence as a personal love. By remedial sufferings man is made cognizant of where his true happiness lies; by satisfactory punishments his whole being is progressively brought into conformity with that happiness, which is the experience of a personal union, in love and knowledge, with God.

The performance of satisfactory punishments is not all that is required, however, for man to achieve this union with God that is entirely above his natural powers and capacities. The tract on sin, from which we have been examining these texts, points to the tract on grace. The much-debated question of justification is outside the scope of this work. However, it should be noted that the transformation of punishment into a means of disposing man for personal union with God—all the while preserving suffering's natural values of healing, reforming, and so forth—at the same time points to that which is the highest perfection of the human person, his call to grace. Only in the context of sin overcome by the divine mercy can satisfaction be made, as Saint Thomas explains by reference to the works of mercy:

> The act of mercy, however, is directed against sin, either by way of satisfaction when it follows justification, or by way of preparation, for "the merciful obtain mercy," when it can precede justification. . . .[14]

Tertia pars, Q.1: Satisfaction as the Subordinate Theme of Christ's Redemptive Incarnation

Presupposition: The God-Centered Dynamism of the Human Person

Saint Thomas devotes the whole of his secunda pars to a consideration of man as he is the image of God and thus as he is responsible for his own action. The discussion of satisfactory actions and the role that they play in the re-forming of that image, which has been disfigured by sin, is an instance where the directive concept of the Summa theologiae, that of exitus-reditus, guides Saint Thomas interpretation of the various aspects of the divine economy. C. E. O'Neill describes this concept of the Summa as follows:

God as he is the goal of man's life in life everlasting, God as he is the point to which all our universe is tending, whether unconsciously and in obedience to a law of development written into its being, or consciously and in freedom, and therefore hazardously, with the possibility of eternal frustration--this is the master-concept of the Summa. [15]

It is important to understand the implications of God's final causality. God, as final cause, is not separated from creation as the finish-line of a race is separated from a runner at the sound of the starting-gun; rather he is present to creation as an active cause, even as creation tends toward him as final cause. In the prima pars 8.3 Saint Thomas explained that God is present to creation in a twofold way. [16] First, he is present to all that exists as an active cause of their being. In addition, God is present as a direct object of knowledge and love to the souls of the just through grace. Grace is required to establish the necessary proportion between knower and known, lover and beloved, that does not exist naturally for man with regard to the divine Trinity. Only in the second way does one speak of a personal relationship between man and God.

Satisfactory punishments, as they are spoken of in the Summa, are valued primarily in terms of the role they play in conditioning man for this personal relationship with God. Indeed, one could say that their exclusive value consists in this role since the very order of divine justice, which man embraces in performing them, is not distinct from the order of divine final causality immanent in the God-centered dynamism of the human person. Man comes forth from the hand of God, is endowed with intelligence and the capacity to love, and is destined to return to God; being set, as it were, between God and God, he is the image of God. The notion of image, however, is not a static concept; rather it is a dynamic one which suggests growth and movement towards a goal, as Saint Thomas remarks in another part of the Summa, "man is not only said to be an image, but to the image (ad imaginem), of God, by which is signified a certain movement toward perfection." [17]

Sin renders the image sterile and meaningless by marring its splendor and beauty since it is an act directed away from God. Satisfactory punishments, as the quodlibetal text concerning the crusader pointed out,[18] restore the image's perfection and, in the gradual working out of salvation, make it once again fruitful and operative.

This work of restoration, even taking into consideration man's efforts at satisfactory deeds, is not a work that man is able to accomplish by himself. In the prima pars 95.4 ra/1, Saint Thomas writes:

> Even before sin man needed grace for achieving eternal life, and that is what grace is principally for. But after sin man also needs grace over and above this for the remission of sin and the support of his weaknesses.[19]

In the following response, ra/2, he explains that the difficulty man encounters in the actual living out of this graced activity accounts for its satisfactory character.

Saint Thomas in his Summa and Saint Anselm in his Cur Deus homo?, whatever the difference of their perspectives, are in full agreement on the fundamental New Testament belief that man needs Jesus Christ, who, as Colossians 1:15 says, "is the image of the invisible God, the first-born of all creation." It is into a sinful world, a world of sterile, vestigial images,[20] that God sends his Word, the perfect and consubstantial image of himself, who becomes man and through his human service to the Father accomplishes the work of restoration in which all other satisfactions find their worth. Christ is the way, writes Saint Thomas, the way in which God restores man to his created image; he is the inner dynamism which bears creation toward its fulfillment in him.

The texts of the tertia pars that treat of satisfaction are primarily drawn from Saint Thomas's discussion of Christ the Saviour, which single discussion[21] he divides into two parts: one which deals with the mystery of the Incarnation, in which God becomes a man for our salvation (1-26); and a second which touches on what was done and suffered by our Saviour, that is, by God incarnate (27-59). The tract on the sacraments, only part of which was completed by Saint Thomas,[22] offers texts which relate

satisfactory deeds to the sacraments of the New Law;
these, as Saint Thomas explains in 60.6 ra/3, "are
conformed in a certain way to the incarnate Word. . .
as in the mystery of the Incarnation the Word of God is
united to sensible flesh."

Programmatic Essay: The Incarnation and
Man's Attainment of Beatitude

The very first question of the tertia pars is what
might be called a programmatic essay for the discussion
that follows; certainly this is true as regards the
question of the incarnate Word's satisfaction for sin.
In 1.1 Saint Thomas addresses himself to the question
of the fittingness of the Incarnation. A textual
comparison, as regards organization of materials,
between the discussion of this question in the Summa
and the parallel discussion in the Scriptum gives an
indication of the radical change that has taken place
in Saint Thomas's theological understanding of the
Incarnation. In the latter work a single question,
"Whether it was becoming (congruum) to God to be
incarnated,"[23] was devoted to an ex professo discussion of this issue. In the Summa the issue is divided
into the question of 1.1, "Whether it was fitting
(conveniens) for God to become incarnate," and that of
1.2, "Whether the incarnation of the Word of God was
necessary for the restoration of the human race."

1.1: Arguments for fittingness

A comparison of the parallel references, from the
point of view of doctrinal content, shows exactly
what is the nature of the change in Saint Thomas's
perspectives. In the article of the Scriptum all
nine arguments posed against the fittingness of the
Incarnation are based in one form or another on the
notion of satisfaction. The reply which Saint Thomas
gives, though it speaks of God's mercy, justice and
wisdom, as well as God's assuming a human nature in
order to draw men to a love and knowledge of himself,
subordinates the entire discussion to the supposition
of original sin and the consequent need for God himself to repair its effect ("sed ipse Deus hominem
repararet").

In the Summa Saint Thomas answers the question
with a different emphasis. In 1.1.sc/1 he mentions,
by reference to Romans 1:20, man's need to be drawn to
the invisible things of God by those things which he

can see; he also refers to the Damascene's De Fide Orthodoxa, where the goodness, wisdom, justice and power of God manifest in the Incarnation are spoken of. It will be the theme of goodness (as contrasted with the Scriptum's mercy and justice) that will guide his explanation in the reply; indeed, the central focus of the explanation is the very nature of God which is goodness ("ipsa autem natura Dei est bonitas"). Saint Thomas's choice of the goodness of God as the perspective from which to interpret the Incarnation is entirely consistent with the master-concept of the Summa. In the prima pars 5.4. ra/2, he had written that "good things are said to pour forth their being (diffusivum sui) in the same way that ends are said to move one." It is extremely important to emphasize that, for Saint Thomas, goodness implies final causality and presupposes as well efficient and formal causality.

We shall use the teaching of the programmatic essay, 1.1-6, as a guide for interpreting the texts of the tertia pars that are related to Saint Thomas's theology of satisfaction. In the Summa one can refer to a theology of satisfaction according to the proper meaning of the term. This is because in the Summa, certainly more clearly than in his earlier works, Saint Thomas uses the word satisfaction as a theo-logia, a word about our relation to God. The Incarnation, as the first question of the tertia pars clearly shows, is primarily understood as a self-communication of the divine goodness, which restores to fallen man the splendor of his God-like image through the "super-abundant" (superabundans) satisfaction of the incarnate Word. One must not, however, interpret the divine goodness as simply equivalent to the divine generosity. Rather, the stress here is on the divine goodness as it implies final causality which--being immanent in the image--leaves an opening for human freedom. God's goodness implies man's free activity; indeed it is the condition which makes it possible. The term, "bonitas divina," in the Summa is Saint Thomas's shorthand for the whole system of God-man relations as he conceived it. All of the other texts which treat of satisfaction --e.g., in relation to the physical and spiritual disabilities undertaken by Christ in his human nature (14,15), in relation to his priesthood and mediation (22,26), in relation to his passion (46-48) and the effects of his expiatory death (49,50,52) as well as to the sacraments and the satisfaction of the members (68-90 passim)--can only be correctly interpreted in terms of this fundamental teaching on the Incarnation.

155

In the reply to 1.1 Saint Thomas explains the fittingness of the Incarnation in terms of the self-communication of the divine goodness as follows:

> Whatever is truly suited to a thing is so by reason of its distinctive nature; for example, discursive reasoning befits man who is by nature rational. But the very nature of God is goodness, as Dionysius makes clear. Therefore whatever forms part of the meaning of the good befits God.
>
> But goodness implies self-communication, as Dionysius shows. Therefore it is appropriate for the highest good to communicate itself to the creature in the highest way possible. But, as Augustine teaches, this takes place above all when "he so perfectly joins human nature to himself that one person is constituted from these three: Word, soul, flesh." Clearly then, it was right for God to be incarnate.[24]

The union of the Word of God to "flesh" and to a changeable human soul is the subject of an objection, ag/3, against the fittingness of the Incarnation. It would appear, says the objector, that the supreme uncreated spirit, who is God, could not find compatibility with a body which is as distant from him as wickedness is from supreme goodness. The first part of Saint Thomas's response is as follows:

> Since God, who is uncreated, unchanging and incorporeal, brought changing and bodily creatures into being out of his goodness, all those characteristics whereby they differ from the creator are established by his wisdom and ordained towards his goodness. Likewise the evil of penalty (malum poenae) is brought in by his justice because of his glory.[25]

Saint Thomas explains that whatever incompatibility might appear in the Word's assuming a human nature with its imperfections must be understood in terms of God's wisdom (a Dei sapientia) in providing for man in the actual economy of salvation. In this regard it is very significant that Saint Thomas refers to the malum poenae as something which God allows "because of his glory." This, of course, is entirely consonant with his teaching in the prima secundae where Saint Thomas explained how punishment for sin is reordered toward satisfaction. In the present text, 1.1 ra/3, the justice of God is said to be served by the manifestation of his glory; this is the case because in the Incarnation God's goodness provides the means for making satisfaction for sin. Indeed the very bodily disabilities which are the subject of the objection are the material means, at least, whereby Christ was able to undertake and accomplish his sufferings and death. The malum poenae, then, is ordered not to the satisfaction of God's vindictive justice but for the manifestation of his goodness and glory through the restoration of the God-image in his creatures. As such, this teaching is consonant with a basic principle of the Summa, namely, that everything which God does in the world is ordered to the bonitas divina as an end. It is also noteworthy that such a conception of the divine justice alters the meaning of Saint John Damascene (as he is quoted in the sed contra) since the justice of God is shown not by dealing justly with the devil, but by the justification of a sinful human race.

The second part of the response considers an imperfection in human nature that is not a part of God's plan (recessum ab arte divinae sapientiae) and is contrary to his goodness. For this reason Christ did not assume the malum culpae with his human nature. Saint Thomas continues:

> But the evil of fault is committed by a turning aside from the plan of God's wisdom and the order set by his goodness. Accordingly God could rightly take to himself a nature created, changeable, bodily and liable to penalty, but not one subject to moral fault (malum culpae).[26]

Apart from establishing the fittingness of the Incarnation in terms of the self-communication of the divine goodness with all the human activity which this implies, in 1.1 Saint Thomas cites the two basic principles that will guide his subsequent explanation of the satisfaction of Christ and allow him to explain how that satisfaction is the superabundant one required for man's salvation. The providential character of the malum poenae (a conclusion referred to elsewhere[27] as knowable only by faith) allows Saint Thomas to explain why the Word had to assume a human nature capable of suffering punishment, especially the suffering of the passion. The absence of malum culpae in the assumed nature, though not of those involuntary evils capable of causing the soul suffering, allows him to explain the sinlessness of Christ and, more important for the question of satisfaction, the perfection of created charity possessed by the soul of Christ.

1.2: Necessity of the Incarnation

The following article, 1.2, on the necessity of the Incarnation for the restoration of man, interprets the basic principle of the divine goodness that had been established in the previous article in terms of man's salvation. The sed contra argument quotes John 3:16: "For God so loved the world that he gave his only Son, that whoever believes in him should not perish but have eternal life." The Incarnation is necessary to free man from perishing in order that he might possess eternal life. In the first half of the reply Saint Thomas distinguishes between absolute necessity, which the Incarnation was not inasmuch as God could have chosen another way to repair (reparare) human nature, and necessity as it is used to describe something required for a better and more expeditious attainment of a goal, which is the sense in which the Incarnation was necessary.

For man's furtherance in good and deliverance
from evil

In the second half of the reply Saint Thomas lists ten indications of usefulness for the Incarnation. Significantly, the first five refer to man's further-ance in good (ad promotionem hominis in bono). Only then do the following five occur with reference to man's deliverance from evil (ad remotionem mali); all then explain why apart from the Incarnation "there was no other course more fitting for healing our wretchedness." The authority of Saint Augustine is referred to without exception in each of the ten arguments. The first five are as follows:

Let us consider this, beginning with man's furtherance in good.

First, with regard to faith, greater assur-ance is guaranteed when the belief rests on God himself speaking. Thus Augustine writes: "Truth itself, the Son of God made man, established and confirmed faith that men more confidently might journey to it."

158

Second, as to hope, which is lifted to the heights, for, to quote Augustine, "nothing is so needful to build up our hope than for us to be shown how much God loves us. And what is a better sign of this than the Son of God deigning to share our nature?"

Third, as to charity, which is most greatly enkindled by the Incarnation for, as Saint Augustine asks, "What greater cause is there for the coming of the Lord than to show God's love for us?" He goes on: "If we have been slow to love, let us not be slow to love in return."

Fourth, as to right living, we are set an example. Augustine says, in a Christmas sermon: "Not man, who can be seen, should be followed, but God, who cannot be seen. So then, that we might be shown one who would be both seen and followed, God became man."

Fifth, as to the full sharing in divinity, which is true happiness and the purpose of human life. This comes to us through the humanity of Christ, for, in Augustine's phrase, "God was made man that man might become God."[28]

The second five, of which the final one refers to man's need for satisfaction, explain how the Incarnation was useful (utile) in delivering man from evil:

Moreover, the Incarnation was effective in delivering man from evil.

First, for our instruction, lest we put the devil above ourselves and go in awe of him who is the author of sin. And so Augustine writes: "When human nature is so joined to God as to become one with him in person, these proud and evil spirits no longer dare to vaunt themselves over man because they are without flesh.

Second, we are taught how great is the dignity of human nature, lest we sully it by sin. To the point Augustine writes: "God showed us the exalted place that human nature holds in creation by appearing to men as a true man." So also Pope Leo: "O Christian, acknowledge your dignity! Having been made a sharer of the divine nature, refuse to fall back into your previous worthlessness by evil conduct."

Third, to do away with human presumption "the grace of God, with no preceding merits on our part, is shown to us as in the man Christ." So writes Augustine.

Fourth, as he adds: "The pride of man, which is the greatest obstacles to our union with God, can be rebutted and cured by such great humility on the part of God."

Fifth, it rescues man from thralldom. This, as Augustine writes, "should be done in such a way that the devil is overcome by the justice of a man, Jesus Christ," which was accomplished by Christ making satisfaction for us. One who was merely a man could not make satisfaction for the entire human race, and how could God? It was fitting, then, for Jesus Christ to be both God and man. On this Pope Leo says: "Weakness is received by power, humility by majesty, that one and the same mediator between God and man might die from the one and rise from the other, and thus we were fitly restored. Unless he were truly God, he could not provide a cure; unless he were man, he could not offer an example."[29]

An analysis of the fifth reason, that which deals with the satisfaction of the incarnate Word, suggests three points that are noteworthy. In the first place, the position of this argument based on satisfaction at the end of the list of ten reasons for the utility of the Incarnation might, superficially read, suggest a truly subsidiary concern for Saint Thomas. However, the ordering of the arguments under the two headings, promotio in bono and remotio mali, indicates that the final argument in each series is related to the four which precede it as the perfection or consummation of the others. Thus, in the first series, the Incarnation is spoken of as ordered toward man's restoration: first, because the incarnate Word speaks the truth which man accepts in faith; second, because the Incarnation moves man to hope that the promise of eternal life, accepted in faith, is actually attainable; third, because the charity of the wayfarer is greatly enkindled by this show of God's love for man; fourth, because all of these virtues are more effectively communicated by concrete example than by abstract instruction; and fifth, because it is through the humanity of Christ that man receives the fruit of a God-centered life, the eternal full sharing in divinity which is "true happiness and the purpose of human life."

The same movement is seen in the arguments which lead up to the need for satisfaction. The Incarnation is ordered towards delivering man from the evil first, of believing in the power of evil; second, from the evil of despising his own nature; third, from the evil of presumption; and fourth, from the evil of pride. None of these deliverances from various kinds of spiritual evils would be of ultimate significance for man's happiness unless, as the fifth reason suggests, he were rescued from the thralldom (servitute) that prohibited him from realizing the ultimate purpose of his life, which only Christ's satisfaction for sin makes possible.

The arrangement of the ten indications of the Incarnation's usefulness also manifests a logical, indeed (theo-)logical, order consistent with Saint Thomas's emphasis on the Incarnation as a manifestation and realization in man of God's goodness, as presented in 1.1. Together the final reasons of each series express Saint Thomas's understanding of the true theological placement of the Incarnation in the mystery of God's relation with man. The God-man, through his satisfactory sufferings, restores to fallen man the full sharing in divinity which is man's final and divinely given goal. Here the order of divine final causality is expressed as it operates in the present Christ-centered economy of salvation. Coming as it does at the beginning of the tertia pars, 1.2 is the insertion point for Saint Thomas's christology into the master-concept of the whole Summa theologiae.

The absence of any direct reference to Saint Anselm is a second noteworthy feature of the final indication of usefulness for the Incarnation. There is an indirect reference to the satisfaction theory of the Cur Deus homo?, namely, the employment of the classic phrase, "homo autem purus satisfacere non poterat . . . Deus autem satisfacere non debebat." But it is to Saint Augustine that Saint Thomas turns for a reference to man's need for liberation from thralldom. One reason to explain this is that of consistency;

Saint Augustine has provided inspiration for the previous nine arguments. However, it should be noted that in making this choice Saint Thomas introduces into his *Summa* a text from Saint Augustine that reflects the latter's adoption of the ransom from the devil theory, something that the *Cur Deus homo?* had eliminated from popular currency in western theology.[30] The reference by Saint Augustine to the "justice of a man, Jesus Christ," however, could be understood by Saint Thomas as pointing to Christ's innocence and his satisfaction for the sins of others. This is a theme developed elsewhere in his writings and one which usually moves him to put on the lips of Christ the verse of Psalm 68: "What I did not steal, must I now restore?"

A third item in the final indication of usefulness concerns the other reference to patristic authority, that of Leo the Great, important in the development of christology for his *Tome*, received at the Council of Chalcedon in 451. The significance of Saint Thomas's using the excerpt from one of Leo's sermons, quoted twice in the course of the ten indications for usefulness, is twofold. First, one finds a formulation different from that of Anselm's *debet* and *potest*. It was not God who was the only one who could make the satisfaction required of man, but he was the only one who could provide the cure (*remedium*) required by man. Similarly it was not man who alone ought to have made the satisfaction, since he sinned, but man—thus Christ himself—who was able to give a concrete example of goodness. The choice of this particular text is consistent with Saint Thomas's developed understanding of satisfactory punishments as cures and, in certain circumstances, also as good examples ("ut aedificentur in poena qui sunt scandalizati culpa").

Second, with respect to Saint Leo's quotation, Christ is spoken of as the "mediator" between God and man ("unus atque idem Dei et hominum mediator"). Leo speaks of Christ the mediator as acting in a way that was befitting man's restoration ("quod nostris remediis congruebat"), for he died to weakness and rose up from humility. This pattern of activity is the same as that followed by the member of Christ when he embraces satisfactory punishments. Through the satisfaction undertaken by the member, God heals the weaknesses of soul caused by past sins and raises the soul up from its fallen earthly condition to the splendor and majesty of its God-like image. In a later article,

26.2, Saint Thomas will cite the fact that Christ satisfied as man for the sin of the human race as a ground for his being mediator of God and man.

For the satisfactory works of the members

An objection, which has been used before,[31] is posed in relation to the question of 1.2; it seems to deny the necessity of the Incarnation for the restoration of the human race on the basis of God's mercy. Joined to this objection, in ag/2, is a second traditional objection, namely, that since man is able to satisfy for his own sins the satisfaction of Christ is superfluous and therefore the Incarnation is unnecessary. A textual variation in the Piana edition of the Summa supports the presence of this objection; the Leonine edition (used here) omits the variation. The argument, ag/2, is as follows:

> Moreover, the only thing necessary for the restoration of human nature fallen through sin is that man should satisfy for his sin. For God ought not to require more than man is capable of. Now God is more inclined to show mercy than to punish; and thus, as the act of sin is charged to man, so too, it seems, the contrary act cancelling it should be credited to him. Therefore the incarnation of the Word of God was not necessary for the restoration of the human race.[32]

The Piana edition adds after the phrase "that man should satisfy for his sin" the sentence, "But a man admittedly can make satisfaction for sin."

Saint Thomas's reply is an important one for the explanation it gives of the relationship between the satisfaction of Christ and the satisfactory actions of the members. This is a subject, as the extended commentary of Cajetan on this response mentions,[33] that was not clearly expressed in the Scriptum, Saint Thomas responds:

> Satisfaction can be termed sufficient in two ways--completely or incompletely. In the first way satisfaction is condign, i.e., it is a recompense equalling the fault committed. So understood, sufficient satisfaction is beyond the power of anyone merely human, since all human nature is corrupted by sin, with the result that the goodness of any

one individual or even of many would not make adequate recompense for a disability affecting the whole nature. Further, a sin against God has a kind of infinity about it, because of God's infinite majesty; the seriousness of an offence is in proportion to the dignity of the one offended. Thus for condign satisfaction the act of the one atoning should be infinite in worth—an act, that is, of one who is both God and man.

In a second way satisfaction is termed sufficient, but incompletely so, i.e., sufficient because of the willingness of the one accepting it even though it does not equal the offence. So understood the satisfaction of one who is purely human is sufficient. Yet since whatever is incomplete presupposes something complete which supports it, every expiatory work of one who is merely human derives its value from the atoning work of Christ.[34]

The objection is answered on two levels. First, Saint Thomas considers satisfaction as it is made for the sin of nature which, by reason of its extension to all the members of the human race, requires a satisfaction by one whose goodness is adequate to compensate for the corruption of so extensive a good. This reflects the Anselmian condition for satisfaction, namely, that one does not satisfy "unless he returns a thing of greater value than that for which one ought not have sinned."[35] In the case of original sin, the good is that of the whole human race. Hence not even many, or presumably all, of the human race could make condign satisfaction for the original sin.

The second level considers sin, including actual sins, as they possess the character of a kind of infinite transgression by reason of the infinite divine dignity which sin offends. Condign satisfaction consequently requires one whose actions are of infinite value, a condition fulfilled only by one who is both God and man (Dei et hominis existens). This too reflects an interpretation, if not the actual thought, of Cur Deus homo?; Saint Thomas's phrasing of the issue reflects as well his clarifications of the problem in the De veritate.

What is significant about this response to the argument based on satisfaction as unbecoming the mercy of God is the absence of any reference to the justice of God. This, of course, is a departure from a fundamental perspective of Cur Deus homo?, namely, the need for satisfaction in order to preserve the ordo rectus and to restore to God the honor which sin has taken away from him. Saint Thomas makes no reference to the need for satisfaction in order to fulfill the demands of God's justice, nor even to avoid the possible scandal to others that could result if the Supreme Judge forgave an offense without commensurate punishment.

Even in the second half of the response, which treats of the satisfaction of the members, that is, of a pure man (puri hominis), no mention is made of the general principle of vindictive justice, namely, that he who has sinned should satisfy. On the contrary, Saint Thomas discusses the kind of satisfaction made by men that is sufficient, though only relatively so, because of the good will of another. Such sufficiency is not founded upon the conditions for condign satisfaction but upon the principle of the "willingness of the one accepting it"[36] to count the satisfaction as sufficient.

To avoid the implication that such simple acceptance, even on the part of God, is, in the actual economy of salvation, sufficient for the kind of satisfaction required of the members, Saint Thomas immediately refers to the condign satisfaction of Christ. All the satisfactory actions of the members derive their worth as atonement for sin from the perfect satisfaction of Christ. The reason for this, as well as the reason for the requirements of justice being of no expressed concern, is that the satisfaction of the members is ordained to their "full sharing in divinity"--something only made possible by the incarnate Word. The notion that the justice of God is satisfied in the accomplishment of image-restoration will be given fuller explanation in later sections, especially 22.1-6 on the priesthood of Christ.

1.3: Motive of the Incarnation

The remaining articles of the first question of the tertia pars complete Saint Thomas's programmatic essay. In 1.3 the celebrated question of the motive of the Incarnation is found. "If man had not sinned, would God nevertheless have become incarnate?" Saint

165

Thomas expresses preference for the opinion of those who respond negatively. The basis for his preference is the data of revelation, since "everywhere in the sacred Scripture the sin of the first man is given as the reason for the Incarnation."[37]

Saint Thomas's preference for a negative response to the question cannot be interpreted to mean that he teaches that man's sin caused the Incarnation. In the prima pars 19.2 Saint Thomas expressly rules out anything being a cause of God's willing other than himself: "Since God wills nothing apart from himself, unless it be for an end which is his goodness. . . it follows that nothing else moves his will except his goodness."[38] The consistency of his teaching on the fittingness of the Incarnation as self-communication of the divine goodness with this teaching is clear. However, in the actual economy of salvation, as Saint Thomas's recourse to the Scriptural evidence underlines, the communication of God's goodness cannot be separated from the actual, sinful condition of man. The "recapitulation" of all things in Christ, of which Colossians speaks, and of which beatitude in the souls of the just is the principal effect, is impossible apart from the satisfaction of Christ: "And through him to reconcile to himself all things, whether on earth or in heaven, making peace by the blood of his cross."[39] In somewhat crude scholastic language sin is sometimes referred to as a material cause of the Incarnation, but better put it is the inescapable condition into which God sent his Son propter gloriam Dei.

A correct understanding of how Saint Thomas conceived the reality of sin in the world as a motive for the Incarnation is very important. It is abundantly clear from the programmatic essay that, according to Saint Thomas, the primary purpose of the Incarnation is the furtherance of man in good. The answer to the question of why God became man is, for Saint Thomas, so that man might attain his ultimate goal of beatitude. It is by reason of the actual, sinful situation in which man must pursue this ultimate goal that the Incarnation has a remedial or satisfactory purpose as well. The satisfactory purpose (or motive), however, remains for Saint Thomas a subordinate one relative to the Incarnation. The two purposes, promotio in bono and remotio mali, nonetheless are intrinsically related because of the supremacy of God's loving providence which accomplishes in the Incarnation of the Word both the satisfaction of the divine urge to love and the

166

reparation of man's sin against that love. God's purpose is not thwarted by man's sin, which, after all, is possible only because of God's having endowed man with real freedom, but neither is the divine will determined by some act of created being. Thus Saint Thomas's position on the question of the motive for the Incarnation does not imply that the sinful abuse of human freedom placed some necessity on God to initiate a new means to accomplish his eternal plan for salvation.

Tertia pars, Qq. 2-26: Presuppositions for Understanding the Satisfaction of Christ: The Perfections and Disabilities of the God-man

It is clearly evident that no attempt to understand what it is that God has done in Jesus Christ--and certainly this is true of systematic theology's effort to aid in that understanding--can be successful apart from the New Testament's account of what Christ did and said and suffered, together with his exaltation and his sending of the Holy Spirit on his Church. Yet a purely functional christology, as the Church learned as early as Nicea, is not only incomplete but calculated to betray the true meaning of Christ's life-bringing message of salvation. It is because Christ is both divine Word and a man that what he did and said has the power to bring the words of everlasting life to men.

Qq. 2-15: The Ontological Structure of the God-man

The following fourteen questions of the tertia pars are devoted to Saint Thomas's meditation on the ontological structure of the God-man (2-6) and the endowments, both natural and supernatural, of his humanity (7-15). An apologetic for the necessity of an ontological christology is beyond the scope of this work. Suffice it to observe that Saint Thomas's efforts in this regard are not directed towards drawing a metaphysical blueprint, as it were, of Christ, but, as is proper to the task of systematic theology, towards correlating the human features of Christ which emerge from the pages of the New Testament and from the interpretive tradition of the Church with the inward structure of the God-man.

A study of the general outlines of Saint Thomas's christology as well as one of any of its specific details is in itself a subject for scholarly investigation. A study of Saint Thomas's understanding of Christ's satisfaction, based on texts from all his works in which he actually refers to the satisfaction of Christ, must take into account (without reproducing the results of such scholarship) the methodology, main lines and significant details of the _Summa_'s discussion of the person and the life of Christ. To proceed any other way would be something like undertaking a study of analytic geometry which would take algebra into account but completely ignore the principles of plane geometry.

The setting for the pertinent texts of this section of the _tertia pars_ (2-15), texts largely drawn from the treatment of the disabilities assumed by Christ with his human nature, can be outlined as follows:[40]

> How are we to understand the revealed truth that the Word is incarnate?
>
> > Understanding the actual union of God and man in the light of the Church's teaching and with the aid of philosophical principles (2).
> >
> > Considering the mystery from the point of view of the divine person who assumes a human nature (3).
> >
> > Considering the mystery from the point of view of what was assumed (14-15):
> >
> > > The human nature and its parts assumed by the Word (4-6).
> > >
> > > The qualities characterizing this assumed nature:
> > >
> > > > its perfections: grace (considered as personal and as capital) (7,8); knowledge (9-12); power (13),
> > > >
> > > > its weaknesses, accepted in view of the redemptive mission (14, 15).

The human nature of Jesus Christ

Central to the understanding of the revealed truth that God is incarnate is the actual union that exists in the person of the Word and his humanity. An article of key importance for Saint Thomas's teaching on the hypostatic mode of union ("de modo unionis Verbi incarnati quantum ad ipsam unionem") is 2.2. In that article Saint Thomas analyzes the hypostatic union in the light of the Church's teaching and with the aid of a philosophical examination of created personhood. Such a discussion is indispensable for his theology of satisfaction. The value of the satisfaction accomplished in the humanity of Christ, as we have already had the occasion to note, derives from the dignity of his divine person. No other explanation is offered to explain how the satisfaction of a man could atone for a sin whose extension leaves no creature unsullied,[41] and whose gravity approaches the infinite inasmuch as it is an offense against the infinite dignity of God himself.

Saint Thomas's meditation on the mystery of the person of Christ--aided considerably by the then recent availability of texts from the great christological councils as well as by the philosophical reflection on created personhood which those texts inspired (of which the work of Boethius is an important example)[42] --resulted in the fact that the _Summa_'s tract on the mystery of the Incarnation is an innovative one as compared with the scholastic tradition that preceded.

United to the person of the Word

The conclusion of 2.2 presents in cryptic form the main points of Saint Thomas's teaching on the relationship of the person of the Word with the human nature which he assumed. It also indicates the importance of such an ontological statement on the God-man for the members' belief in his salvific work (function). Saint Thomas writes:

> Consequently, all that is present in any person, whether belonging to his nature or not, is united to him in person. If, then, the human nature is not united to the Word in person, it would not be united at all. To hold that would be to abolish belief in the Incarnation and to undermine the entire Christian faith. Since, therefore, the Word has a human nature united to himself, even

though it does not form part of his divine nature, it follows that this union was effected in the person of the Word, not in the nature.[43]

Three points relative to the relationship of the divine person and his human nature can be extracted from this article. First, the person of the Word is preexistent. As such Christ's created human nature is not constitutive of his person but comes to or is joined to it. Second, this infinite person possesses the divine nature and is identical with it. Third, the human nature hypostatically united to the person of the Word is a concrete, individual one, not merely a formal act. The merit of Saint Thomas's formulations on the hypostatic union lie principally in the emphasis on the unity of the incarnate Word, a unity of being --though the limits of reason to explain this mystery need be especially borne in mind in this regard-- and therefore of his human and divine operations. Consequently it is impossible to conceive of Christ or any aspect of him apart from the unity communicable by the divine person, in whom and through whom all that is assumed finds its being.

That a human nature was assumed by the person of the Word and not by any other divine person is a revealed truth that offers Saint Thomas the occasion to reflect on the reasons for its fittingness. These reasons found in 3.8 are important to note since they reiterate and in a way summarize his teaching on the purposes behind the redemptive Incarnation. The inspiration for his remarks comes from the trinitarian theology where he explains the personal signification, as regards the divine essence, of the names "Son" and "Word." In the prima pars he explains how "Word" can be understood as the proper name of that divine person whose intra-trinitarian procession comes about after the fashion of intellectual emanation. He writes,

> In the divinity "Word" as a literal term refers to a person and is a name proper to the Son. The reason is that a word denotes a kind of coming forth from the mind; but in the Godhead the person proceeding on the basis of such an emanation of mind is called the Son, and . . . such a procession is a begetting. Therefore it must be that in the divinity the Son alone properly has "Word" as his name.[44]

The reasons of fittingness which Saint Thomas describes for the Word-Son becoming incarnate are arranged under three headings. The first of these is founded on the Word of God as the exemplar of all creation and the means, through the personal participation of the Word with creation in the Incarnation, for creation's final perfection. Rational creatures are the special beneficiaries of this re-creation by reason of their capacity to participate in the Incarnate Word as, by appropriation, he is the Wisdom of God.

The second and third reasons consider Christ as, according to his divinity, Son and Word. The second of the three reasons, that based on the divine person as Son, suggests the fittingness of the Son's becoming incarnate in terms of man's achieving his final goal of beatitude:

> A further reason can be taken from the purpose of the union, the accomplishment of the predestination of those who are preordained for a heavenly inheritance. To this sons alone have a right: "If sons heirs also." Appropriately, then, through him who is Son by nature men share by adoption in a likeness to his sonship: "Those whom he foreknew he predestined to share the image of his Son."[45]

There is a striking parallel between these texts, along with the doctrine which they contain, and those found at the beginning of the tertia pars. The two series of indications of usefulness for the Incarnation, those pertaining to the promotio in bonum and those to the remotio mali, express Saint Thomas's teaching on the goodness of God as final cause, which the Incarnation manifests. Through Christ, the Son of God, man reaches his predestined goal of beatitude by means of sharing in the image of God's son.[47] In Christ, the word of God's true wisdom, the evil of fault committed by turning aside from the plan of God's wisdom, is remedied.

It is these two aspects of God's providential care for his creation, especially man, that summarize Saint Thomas's theology of satisfaction. God's self-communication of goodness is not thwarted by man's disorders because God transforms the very effect of those disorders, punishment, into satisfactory punishments for the "manifestation of his glory." Satisfaction heals the disorder of sin and restores the tarnished image to its intended splendor. Such a divine work is unimaginable apart from a divine worker. It is the satisfaction of Christ, in which all of man's satisfactions find their efficacy, that opens up the way to man's salvation. "Our Saviour, the Lord Jesus Christ," Saint Thomas writes in the prologue to the tertia pars, "showed in his own person that way of truth which, in rising again, we can follow to the blessedness of eternal life."

Taken from Adam's stock

The previous text, 3.8, explained the fittingness which Saint Thomas sees in the person of the Word assuming a human nature; the present, 4.6, explains the fittingness of the kind of human nature assumed, namely, one from the stock of Adam. Although the article makes no explicit reference to the Pauline typological antithesis of Adam and Christ, the juxtaposition of this text with that of 3.8 clearly suggests the parallel of which Saint Paul makes such fruitful use. The interpretation, indeed subtle correction of Saint Augustine's argument for the fittingness of Christ's having conquered the devil in the flesh of the very race which the devil had conquered, betrays Saint Thomas's understanding of this biblical theme (one used by Saint Paul against the Judaizers) and its ramifications for an authentic understanding of Christian salvation.

Saint Thomas begins his reply by quoting Saint Augustine's De Trinitate,[48] which affirms the fittingness of Christ's having assumed a human nature from Adam's stock rather than one, presumably created for the Incarnation, that would have been sinless. Saint Thomas writes:

> As Augustine teaches, "God could have taken on human nature from another source and not from the race of that Adam who by sin enthralled the human race. Yet he judged it better to take up a man of that conquered race and through him to conquer its enemy."[49]

Further on in the De Trinitate Saint Augustine explains the reason why God "judged it better" to assume a human nature stemming from Adam. He emphasized the manifestation of justice, indeed ironic justice, that Christ's conquering of the devil in Adam's flesh manifests:

172

(Satan), conqueror of the first Adam and holding in his power the human race, has been conquered by the second Adam, [thus] losing his grasp on the Christian race, [which] has been set free out of the human race and from human fault, through him who was not in the fault, although he was of the race.[50]

In the three reasons which Saint Thomas posits in 4.6 he clearly modifies the emphasis found in Saint Augustine. This is especially evident in the final reason where Saint Thomas speaks about the new dignity to which man is raised as a result of the Incarnation. Saint Thomas writes:

Three reasons can be adduced. First of all, it seems to be a matter of justice that he who committed the sin should pay the price. Thus, that whereby satisfaction was to be paid for the entire human race was rightly assumed from that nature corrupted by sin.

Secondly, it forms part of the enhanced dignity of man that the conqueror of the devil should be born of the race the devil had vanquished.

Thirdly, it more clearly manifests the power of God that from a nature abased and weakened he raised one exalted to such virtue and dignity.[51]

As can be seen, Saint Thomas's reason for Christ having assumed a human nature from Adam's race lies not in the "justice" of his having liberated man from the thralldom of the devil, but in the justification of a sinful race. The satisfaction of Christ moves the fallen sons of Adam to a new dignity. Is not this the antithetical comparison that Saint Paul suggests in Romans 5:10-21? It begins with one man's sin, that of Adam, and finishes with the justice of one man, that of Christ. It begins with the condemnation of all men of Adam's race and finishes with justification and life for all men.

The assumption of a human nature by the Word of God entails the assumption of the parts of that nature, body and soul. In 5.1 Saint Thomas describes two reasons why the human body assumed by Christ had to be a real one. Leaving aside the implications of this question as regards certain gnostic heresies,52 it is serviceable as a terse introduction to the following discussion of the disabilities of body and of soul that were undertaken by Christ in his human nature. The question posed is whether the Son of God assumed a true body. The second reason that Saint Thomas gives for answering in the affirmative is as follows:

> A second reason can be taken from what the mystery of the Incarnation accomplished. If Christ's body had not been real but imaginary he would not have undergone real death; the events narrated by the Evangelists would not be factual but a kind of pretense. From that it follows that no real human salvation resulted, since the effect must correspond to its cause.53

The bodily weaknesses assumed in view of Christ's redemptive mission

Detailed explanation of what Saint Thomas meant by the "effect must correspond to its cause" is found in 14.1,4 which discuss why the Word should have assumed a body that carried with it bodily disabilities. The question itself is posed in 14.1: whether the Son of God ought to have taken a human nature that carried bodily disabilities. The arguments suggest difficulties about accepting Christ's bodily disabilities, since to have taken upon himself such disabilities seems to betray the principle of perfection that has dominated the theological treatment of Christ's human condition up to this point in the tertia pars (7-13). Saint Thomas's responses will explain why the principle of perfection has to be modified by other principles, especially in the light of the facts about which the Gospels leave no room for doubt. These principles are, as has already been suggested in 5.1, that of the credibility of the Incarnation, and—more pertinent to the discussion at hand—the requirement that Christ satisfy for sin.

The reply of 14.1 lists three reasons for the fittingness of an affirmative answer to the question as posed. The second reason is that of credibility, to build up faith in the Incarnation; and the third is because of the example of patience which Christ gave in bearing suffering, as already indicated in 1.2. The first reason, and presumably the principal one for Christ's body being imperfect and therefore capable of undergoing suffering, is as follows:

The Son of God took flesh and came into the
world to make reparation for the sin of the
human race. Now one person atones for the
sin of another by taking on himself the
punishment due to the sin of the other.
These bodily disabilities--death, hunger and
thirst and the like--are punishments for the
sin that was brought into the world by Adam,
according to Romans: "Therefore as sin came
into the world through one man and death
through sin." Hence it was fitting, given
.the purpose of the Incarnation, that he
should take these penalties on in the flesh,
in place of us. As Isaiah says: "Surely he
hath borne our infirmities."[54]

An objection, ag/1, was posed that cited the
incongruity of Christ's having had a perfect soul and
an imperfect body. The response, ra/1, offers Saint
Thomas the occasion to present the complementary side
of his theology of satisfaction. It is not simply the
undergoing of punishments--they are but the materials
(materias) of satisfaction--but the attitude of the
sufferer that accounts for punishment's satisfactory
character. Christ's soul is perfect so that his
satisfaction would be perfect and have the perfect
effects that it does. Saint Thomas writes:

The punishments which one person suffers for
the sins of another are, as it were, the
material of reparation. But the principle
of it is the attitude of soul which makes
someone want to atone for another. It is
from this that reparation gets its effectiveness; it would have no effect if it did not
spring from charity. . . . Therefore the
soul of Christ had to be perfectly endowed
with knowledge and virtue so that he would
have the power to make reparation; and his
body had to be liable to suffering so that he
would not lack the material for reparation.[55]

A similar argument, 14.4 ag/2, is drawn from the
contrast between the perfection of Christ's soul and
the imperfection of his body. The argument, however,
concludes with a different proposal: If Christ's soul
was perfect should he not have assumed all of the
disabilities possible? In the reply Saint Thomas
distinguishes between which imperfections were fittingly undertaken--always from the perspective of Christ's
need to satisfy for the sins of all humanity, as ra/2

points out--and those which would have detracted from Christ's salvific purpose and therefore have been unfittingly embraced. Saint Thomas writes in 14.4/co, that Christ was exempt from the human disabilities which are irreconcilable with perfect knowledge and grace; for example, ignorance, proneness to evil and difficulty in doing good. He was likewise spared those kinds of disabilities that befall individuals who have some genetic defect or which result from damage caused by some form of unhealthy activity. Those disabilities which Christ did assume are described as follows:

> There is a third set of disabilities that are shared by all men as a result of the sin of the first parent--death, hunger, thirst and the like. These are the disabilities that Christ assumed. They are what Damascene calls "the natural and unembarrassing afflictions"--natural because they are common to all humanity, unembarrassing because they do not imply any lack of knowledge and grace.[56]

The clarification which these texts give to Saint Thomas's teaching on the satisfaction of Christ is clear: Christ undertook those physical disabilities that were required for him to suffer satisfactory punishments, but only those that would contribute to and not detract from the positive, salvific work of the Incarnation. The brevity and clarity of this principle should not be construed as a facile move on the part of Saint Thomas, nor a kind of theological sleight-of-hand for there is another characteristic of 14.1-4 that must be noted, and that is the frequent recourse which Saint Thomas has to Scripture.

In the De rationibus fidei Saint Thomas was posed with the problem of explaining to non-believers, presumably Saracens, the reason for the Christian belief in a "suffering God." In the course of that response he drew in fine detail a theological picture of the Suffering Servant of Isaiah. It is unquestionably the same biblical theme--extended to include pertinent New Testament references cited below--that lies behind his analysis of the bodily disabilities of Christ.

In the course of question 14.1.2, Isaiah 53 2-5,7 is referred to. This is the scriptural reference that inspires Saint Thomas to theologize on Christ's weaknesses:

Surely he has borne our griefs and carried
  our sorrows;
yet we esteemed him stricken, smitten by God,
  and afflicted.
But he was wounded for our transgressions,
he was bruised for our inequities;
upon him was the chastisement that made us
  whole,
and with his stripes we are healed.

This is the work of Saint Thomas the theologian, exercising the true function of theology, namely, to correlate the isolated data of the documents of revelation--in this case those that treat of the servant born in the likeness of men (Philippians 2.7) who is the merciful and faithful high priest (Hebrews 2:17-18), who suffers the hostility of sinners (Hebrews 12:3), yet shares their sinful flesh (Romans 8:3)--into a coherent body of truth, at once faithful to the revealed word and intelligible as a unified doctrine of salvation.

The disabilities and perfections of Christ's soul

Christ's sinlessness

The discussion of 14.1 introduces the principles that Saint Thomas follows in explaining the disabilities of the soul of Christ in 15.1-10, specifically in regard to the fundamental exemption of his soul from the disability of sin. In the initial articles, 15.1-2, the fact of Christ's thorough sinlessness, that is, as regards sin itself and the fomes peccati,[57] is explained. This has already been implied in 14.1 ra/1, which spoke of the perfection of charity in the soul of Christ, required for his perfect satisfaction. Sin occurs on the same level of reality as does charity, namely, on the level of the soul's relation to God; the perfection of charity is incompatible with the presence of any sin. When in 15.1 Saint Thomas asks whether there was any sin in Christ he continues his explanation by applying the principles of the previous question to Christ's sinlessness and its relation to his satisfaction.

It is likewise significant, in terms of the function of systematic theology, that in the course of establishing the fact of Christ's sinlessness--the question of impeccability not being raised here--Saint

Thomas responds to no fewer than five objections from Scripture which seem to indicate the contrary. In the reply Saint Thomas writes:

> It has been remarked already that Christ undertook our disabilities to make reparation for us, to prove the truth of his human nature and to become for us an example of virtue. On each of these counts it is clear that he ought not to have taken on sin.
>
> Firstly, sin contributes nothing toward satisfaction. In fact it rather obstructs the ability to make satisfaction because, as Ecclesiasticus puts it, "the Most High does not approve the gifts of the wicked." Likewise sin does nothing to authenticate human nature. For sin forms no part of human nature, a nature which has God for its cause; rather it is contrary to nature, having been introduced, as Damascene puts it, "from a seed sown by the devil." Thirdly, by sinning Christ could not give an example of virtue because sin is the opposite of virtue. Therefore in no sense did he take on the disability of sin, either original or actual. This is what is in I Peter: "He committed no sin; no guile was found on his lips."[58]

The objections posed to this article are aimed at clarifying the effect of the sinful condition into which God sent his Son in the person of Christ himself. Four of these arguments rely on Scriptural texts that sometimes employ a forceful use of language--e.g., Psalm 22:1, Romans 5:12, and even pointed phrasing, e.g., II Corinthians 5:21, ("He [God] made Him [Christ] to be sin")--to speak of this sinful condition and its effect on Christ. Saint Thomas's consistent purpose, in keeping with his general principles regarding the Incarnation, is to explain how this sinful condition does not detract from the positive work of the Incarnation. The basic principles for this resolution have already been established in the Summa contra gentiles as regards one man satisfying for another and in the De veritate as regards the universal effect that the satisfaction of Christ the Head has on his members.

The question of the sinful condition into which God sent his Son is undoubtedly most forcefully expressed, as has been suggested, in the text of II Corinthians 5:21. Saint Thomas addresses himself to this text, as presented in 15,1 ag/4, in terms of the overall purpose of the Incarnation as satisfaction, although in the response ra/4, the reference is a veiled one.[59] Saint Thomas speaks of Christ as a "victim" for sin and, in that sense, made to be sin. A second explanation offered to interpret the text, however, speaks more directly in terms of satisfaction. Saint Thomas suggests that II Corinthians 5:21 refers to the vulnerability of Christ's body which was required for satisfaction. He writes in 15.4 ra/4:

> God "made Christ to be sin" not by making him a sinner but by making him a victim for sin. There is a parallel in Hosea, where the priests are said to "feed on the sin of my people," because according to the Law they would eat the victims offered for sin. In the same sense we have in Isaiah: "The Lord has laid on him the iniquity of us all," meaning that he gave him up to be a victim for the sins of all men. Or "made him to be sin" could mean "in the likeness of sinful flesh," as in Romans. And this would be because of the vulnerable and mortal body which he took on.[60]

Christ's capital grace and his members

The question of Christ's identification with his members, both in their sin (in the sense qualified above) and as a cause (implied) of their healing, is discussed in relation to Christ's words from the cross--"My God, my God, why hast thou forsaken me?" Saint Thomas has recourse in 15.1 ra/1 to the principles of allegorical interpretation to explain this cry--originally found in Psalm 22--as Christ speaking for the members, though not for himself personally, even as he is the head of the members. This single, cryptic reference to the doctrine of the body of Christ, discussed in the De veritate specifically with reference to the satisfaction of Christ for the members,[61] refers to the discussion of the grace of Christ, both personal and capital, in 7 and 8. In 8.1, speaking about the grace of Christ as head of the Church, Saint Thomas teaches that Christ "has the power to infuse grace into every member of the Church."[62] He writes in 8.1 ra/1:

Christ as God can give grace (or the Holy Spirit) in his own right. As man he can also give it, but instrumentally. For his humanity was "the instrument of his divinity." And so his actions brought salvation to us through the power of the divinity. They caused grace in us both by meriting it and by some kind of efficient causality. What Augustine denies is that Christ as man gives the Holy Spirit in his own right. But in the role of instrument, or minister, even other saints are said to give the Holy Spirit, as in Galatians--"Does he who supplies the Spirit to you. . . ."[63]

The phrase St. Thomas quotes from Saint Augustine 15.1 ra/1, "Christ and his Body are taken as one person" ("Christi et Ecclesiae una persona aestimatur"), is the equivalent of the striking phrase he employed in the De veritate 29.7 sc/3, "Christ and the Church are one Body" ("Christus et Ecclesia sunt quasi una persona"). This personal relationship between Christ and his members is the reason why the perfection of grace, which is a personal quality of Christ, can spiritually affect the members who do not possess that perfection in their own persons. The principle employed to explain this power to infuse is a favorite one for Saint Thomas and central to his christology.[64] It is a properly theological principle, based on John 1:14,16 but drawn from principles of Aristotelian and Platonic philosophy, namely, that the most perfect representative of any kind exercises a causal influence on all the participants in that kind. Explaining why Christ had the fulness of grace, Saint Thomas writes in 7.9 that

> Christ received the fulness of grace so that it could be passed on (transfunderetur), as it were, from him to others. Hence he required the maximum grace; just as fire, which is what makes things hot, is itself the hottest thing of all.[64a]

The doctrine that the humanity of Christ is used instrumentally by the entire Trinity as "first cause" of man's redemption[65] and of the grace that affects it means that the connection between Christ and his members must be a direct, physical one. It is direct since no other self-sufficient (perfectus) mediator of God and men exists[66] other than Christ himself. It is physical because the fact of Christ's being an intermediary and performing the function of a mediator, to bring together (officium conjungendi), are two functions which Christ as man performs.67 The nature of this physical causality—the phrase itself is not found in the text of Saint Thomas—of the humanity of Christ, as regards spiritually affecting other men, is not easily analyzed. Saint Thomas has frequent recourse to metaphor when he speaks of the exercise of this causality. For example, some form of the verb "to pour" is used, either "to pour onto" (transfundere), "to pour into" (infundere) or "to overflow" (redundare), to express the transmission of grace from Christ to the members.68

The use of a figure of speech to explain how instrumental causality works is reason for caution with respect to drawing too many conclusions from the doctrine of Christ's mediatorship being a physical one. "Reality need not correspond to figure in every detail," Saint Thomas writes in 48.3 ra/1, "but only in some regard, since reality surpasses figure."69 Unquestionably the aspect in which the figurative use of some form of the verb "to pour" corresponds to Christ's spiritually affecting his members lies in the fact that the members are truly ontologically affected by the grace of Christ as it is a principle of merit or of satisfaction for them. It need not, however, and seemingly does not indicate the presence of a physical inclusion of all men in Christ. The phrase in 48.2 ra/1—"The head and the members form as it were a single mystical person"70—argues against such an interpretation by the use of "quasi" to modify "single person" (una persona). Apparently Saint Thomas's use of the quasi indicates his awareness that to have spoken simply in this matter would have been to have spoken loosely and therefore inaccurately about divine things. The quasi is also a way of pointing out the analogical gulf that exists between the biblical notion of the Body of Christ—itself a metaphor used to express a judgment of faith—and the empirical notion of the human person, which is a concept borrowed from philosophy.

Nevertheless, it must be emphasized that Saint Thomas never envisages the mystical body of Christ in purely juridical terms. As regards a discussion of satisfaction this is perhaps best substantiated by his rejection of the theory of "transfer of merit" in Cur Deus homo?, whereby Saint Anselm explains how man benefited from Christ's satisfaction.71 To speak of the rights Christ has won and of the imputation of

these rights to those who believe in him, as would be
the case if the union between Christ and his members
were merely a moral one, would be to consider merit
under only one of its aspects--and a quite restricted
one at that. It is true that man has no claim on
beatitude, but the merit of Christ must do more than
merely establish such a claim for man. The New Testament metaphor of the vine and the branches simply does
not permit such a restricted interpretation of the work
of Christ.

Neither is Saint Thomas's theological analysis
of what merit and satisfaction accomplish in man
intelligible in terms of doctrine of imputation of
grace. In this regard the text of De veritate 29.7 is
an extremely important one.[72] The positive perfection
of the image of God in man and the gradual restoration
of his soul to the dignity and splendor that makes
it fit to be united with God, as suggested in that
article, cannot be explained by simple imputation to
man either of Christ's satisfaction or of his merit.
The text of the De veritate, in fact, speaks about this
intrinsic perfecting of the image in terms of an
interplay between merit and satisfaction. The merit
shared in by man by reason of his being "quasi" one
person with Christ bestows on man the worth (dignitas)
and the fitness (idoneitas) required for glory; satisfaction removes the penalty of sin that keeps man from
entering into that glory. The "crusader text"[73]
suggested an even closer interplay between the mode of
merit and the mode of satisfaction; both operative in
view of the gradual restoration of the God-image in the
whole person.

Qq. 16-26: Some implications of the
Hypostatic Union

The following questions, 16-26, which complete
the first half of Saint Thomas's discussion of the
mystery of the Incarnation, are introduced under the
heading De his quae consequuntur unionem--on the
implications of the union. It should be noted that
these implications do not refer to properties or
functions of Christ objectively deriving from what has
been said of his ontological structure in questions
2-15 but to logical deductions which may be made from
what has already been established.[74] An outline of the
subjects treated in these questions is as follows:[75]

182

De his quae consequuntur unionem, on the implications of the union. Those that affect--
    Christ himself:
    statements relating him as existing and coming into existence; (16).
    as regards his unity;
        (dealt with elsewhere--questions regarding unity or plurality as to knowledge and nativity; cf Question 17, Introduction).
        of existence (17),
        in volition (18),
        in activity (19),
    his relations with his Father:
    Christ as related to the Father;
        subjection (20),
        prayer (21),
        priesthood (22),
    the Father considered as related to Christ;
        problem of adoption (23),
        predestination (24),
    in relation to us;
        our adoration of him (25),
        his mediation (26).

Christ as related to the Father: his priesthood

The question of the priesthood of Christ, 22.1-6, is an important one--indeed, from one perspective, a central one--for Saint Thomas's theology of satisfaction. The office of the priest is to give worship to God, which is an act of the virtue of religion; Christ the priest is the eminently religious man. Another function of the priesthood is to communicate God's goodness to man through the "gifts and sacrifices for sins," as Hebrews 5:1 says, by which the priest satisfies to God on behalf of man. In 22.1 Saint Thomas establishes Christ's eminent fulfillment of these tasks:

> Now these functions are carried out by Christ in an eminent degree. For through him divine gifts are brought to men--"by whom Christ he hath given us most great and precious promises: that by these you may be made partakers of the divine nature." It was he also who reconciled the human race to God --"In him [Christ] it hath well pleased the

Father that all fulness should dwell, and through him to reconcile all things unto himself." Consequently Christ was a priest in the fullest sense of the word.[76]

The twofold purpose of the Incarnation is immediately evident from this interpretation of the work of Christ the priest which is based on the scriptural description of the Levitical priesthood's functions in Hebrews. Note that Saint Thomas qualifies the effect that the Levite's sacrifices had as regards satisfaction--in some degree (aliqualiter) such sacrifices make reparation to God. The description of Christ's full salvific sacrifice, in 22.2, in which Christ is both victim and priest, highlights the fullness of the reconciliation which it accomplishes, namely, "perfect union with God." Saint Thomas explains:

Man must make use of sacrifice for three reasons. Firstly, to obtain remission of sin, by which he is turned away from God. It is, accordingly, the office of a priest "to offer up gifts and sacrifices for sins." Secondly, in order that man may be preserved in the state of grace, united at all times with God in whom are found his peace and salvation. It was for this reason that, under the Old Law, the peace victim was immolated for the salvation of the offerers. Thirdly, to win for man's spirit perfect union with God, something which will be realized fully only in heaven. This was why, under the Old Law, the holocaust was offered, that is, a sacrifice wholly consumed by fire.

Not all of these benefits have been made over to us by Christ's own humanity. For, in the first place, our sins have been blotted out--"He was delivered up for our sins." In addition we have received through him that grace which saves us--"He became to all that obey him the cause of eternal salvation." Finally, through him we have laid hold on the consummation of glory--"We have confidence in the entering into the Holies [that is, into heavenly glory] by the blood of Christ." We may conclude therefore that Christ as man was not only priest but likewise victim and,

184

indeed, the supreme victim, for he was at once a victim for sin, a peace victim and a holocaust.[77]

It seems that the central concern of 22.2 is the sacrifice of Christ. There are three elements which comprise the benefits which are derived from this sacrifice. The first is, as it were, a negative aspect of the benefits, namely the remission of sins. This, of course, is the work of satisfaction. The second element is the positive aspect of sacrifice, preservation in grace. The third is the eschatological element, perfect union with God. Christ himself, unlike the Levitical priests, as 22.4 ra/3 explains, did not need to share in these benefits inasmuch as he was sinless.[78] Though the work of the priestly Christ according to his humanity, the satisfactory element of his sacrifice is inseparable from the divine nature of the Godman "whose human actions draw their efficacy from his divinity."[79] In 22.3 Saint Thomas explains the fullness of Christ's satisfaction by reference to the macula culpae and the reatus poenae. The stain of guilt is removed by grace, granted to men by virtue of the priesthood of Christ, which turns the sinner's heart back to God; and liability to punishment, the reatus poenae, is satisfied for by the reparation of Christ who, according to Isaiah 53:4, "has borne our griefs and carried our sorrows." The priesthood of Christ, concludes Saint Thomas, has full power to satisfy for sins.[80]

Consistent with previous teaching,[81] Christ's satisfaction finds its value not in suffering but in love. It is, as 22.4 ra/2 states, "in virtue of that act of worship of his by which, under the influence of his love, he submitted with humility to his passion" that the sacrifice of Christ was a true one for the satisfaction of sin. It is, as the same reply points out, this personal devotion of Christ that makes his real sufferings efficacious--his executioners certainly did not consider themselves as doing something for God--and won for him the glory of resurrection. Christ's love, then, makes of his sacrifice both true worship and authentic satisfaction. Although Saint Thomas never loses sight of the intimate connection between the sufferings of Christ and the satisfactory aspect of his sacrifice, it is the priestly sacrifice of Christ, motivated by love and undertaken with humility, that brings together justice and satisfaction.

It is this final consideration in which the main import for Saint Thomas's understanding of the priesthood of Christ lies. The pages of the New Testament leave no doubt as to the centrality of the passion in the life of Christ. Saint Thomas reflects this concern --as the frequent references to Scripture testify-- in clearly making satisfaction for sin a primary task imposed on Christ the priest. It has already been remarked that Saint Thomas frequently casts new light on the traditional ways of speaking about the Incarnation as satisfying God's justice. Both Saint Augustine's way of speaking about the justice of the incarnate Word destroying, in the flesh of Adam's stock, the power of the devil over fallen man and Saint Anselm's view of Christ's satisfaction restoring the broken order of divine justice in the world are incorporated into Saint Thomas's discussion of the priesthood and passion of Christ in such wise as to interpret them inlight of the threefold benefit which results from his charity-infused sacrifice.

In his programmatic essay Saint Thomas spoke of God's justice as introducing satisfactory punishment for his glory, namely, the restoratin of fallen man. The requirements of vindictive justice are of con- siderably less concern for Saint Thomas in the Summa than they were in the Scriptum. It is at this point that the question of the priesthood of Christ takes on import and significance. Christ is the just man, the one who offers to God the sacrifice that is his due; it is he who pays the debt of true priestly worship. This Christ does for all humankind and through it for all creation. It is by an act of justice, not of retributive justice, but of religion, the worship of sacrifice, that men are reconciled to God. This explains, as well, why the discussion of Christ's priesthood is something which must (logically) be spoken about in terms of the God-man's relation to his Father--though, as we have noted, Saint Thomas relates its effects to the members of Christ.

Christ, then, is the priest of mankind. As 22.3 shows, "a priest is constituted an intermediary between God and man, . . . but the only person who stands in need of an intermediary with God is one who is unable to approach God for himself." By his satisfaction Christ restores the order of justice in man's relation to God. The order of personal relationships with God and his fellows--into which man by his very finality is drawn--is restored from the disruption of sin by the satisfaction which Christ accomplished in love. It is, then, by an act of worship, the religious expression of justice, that Christ opens the way to love. The satisfaction of Christ the Priest is not ordered to appease God's vindictive justice, rather, according to this profound understanding of the redemptive work of Christ, it makes possible the communication of the divine goodness.

Christ as related to the members: his mediation

The work of the satisfaction of Christ, as it wins for man the possibiltiy of reaching his final goal of beatitude, is more properly spoken of as the work of Christ the mediator of God and man. It is Christ's function as mediator that concerns his relation to men rather than his relation to God, and in this it is distinguished from his priesthood.

The brief question devoted to the mediatorship of Christ explains Christ's function as mediator by his satisfaction in terms practically identical with those used in describing his work as priest. For example in 26.2 ra/3 Saint Thomas writes:

> It is quite true that the power of taking away sins with personal authority belongs to Christ as God. But it is as man that he satisfies for the sin of the human race; and it is on this ground that he is called the mediator of God and men.[82]

The same question explains the New Testament teaching on the uniqueness of Christ's self-sufficient mediatorship in the face of the apparent contradiction posed by certain scriptural texts which attribute the function of mediation to many men, e.g., Romans 8:6. Christ, of course, shares his mediation in a participative way with other men--for example, with the priests of the New Testament--but their efficacy is sterile apart from the one self-sufficient mediation of Christ. Question 26 is a prefatory one as well since it serves to introduce the remaining discussion of Christ's mediation as it is exercised in the mysteries of his life and death, together with the sacraments of the Church.

Tertia pars, Qq. 46-59: Satisfaction
"To Win for Man's Spirit Perfect
Union with God" as the
Key-Notion of Christ's
Redemptive Death

Saint Thomas distributes his examination of the mystery of Christ's life, death and exaltation under four headings, as he explains in the preface to questions 27-59:[83]

Having gone through the matters relating to the union of God and man and the corollaries that follow from that union, we turn now to the things which the incarnate Son of God actually did and suffered in the human nature united to him. We shall examine under four headings the things involved:

first, in his coming into the world;
second, in the regular course of his life;
third, in his departing from the world;
fourth, in his exaltation after his life on earth.

The subjects of direct interest to this study which are treated under these headings can be summarized in the following way:[84]

How are we to understand Christ's passion and death, whereby "he departed from this world"?

Christian reflection on the mystery of the passion, from the perspective of what Christ suffered (46), as well as the causes (47), modes of efficacy (48) and effects (49) of the passion.

Christian reflection on the death of Christ (50); his burial (51); and his descent into hell (52).

How are we to understand the exaltation of Christ?

The resurrection, considered from the point of view of its relation to the passion (53); as it affected Christ himself (54) and how the resurrection of Christ was manifested (55); the causality of the resurrection (56).

The mystery of Christ's ascension (57),
and his sitting at the right hand of God
in majesty (58) and in power (59).

The Method of Investigation Employed
by Saint Thomas

The methodology that Saint Thomas employs to
undertake his investigation of Christ's passion and
death is important to note. This is true not only
because this methodology is used by Saint Thomas
in those texts which discuss the satisfaction of
Christ (found primarily in the discussion of Christ's
passion and death) but also because to understand Saint
Thomas's method is to understand how he went about
doing the work of theology. The casual or uninformed
reader could read this section of the Summa and come to
Harnack's conclusion about Saint Thomas's soteriology
--"multa sed non multum."[85]

On the contrary, an understanding of Saint
Thomas's intention to relate the entire mystery of
Christ's life and death to the central theological
truth of God's relation to men, and ultimately to the
very nature of God himself, results in being able to
appreciate that for Saint Thomas christology is a
true theo-logia, a "word about God." Apart from
the coherence of this perspective with that of the
documents of revelation it also avoids the unhappy
results that stem from making christology the central
focus of theological investigation, not the least of
which is theology's sometimes rapid degeneration into
being primarily a statement about men rather than about
God.

Saint Thomas's methodology, then, can be described
in terms of the three principal ways in which he
interprets the fruit of the Church's meditative reflection on the mystery of Christ's life. The abundance of
patristic citations in this section of the Summa is
evidence that Saint Thomas addresses himself to the
Church's meditation on her Saviour. However, Saint
Thomas's personal contribution to that meditation
is a real and valuable one; it certainly is not one
of merely organizing, after the fashion of a gloss,
pertinent texts under the proper headings. Saint
Thomas's method of proceeding is, rather, truly meditative, drawing the reader to reflect on the mysteries of
Christ as they have been understood in the life of the
Church. As an indispensable aid for this meditation

Saint Thomas unifies the rich and varied details
of the Christian economy of salvation into a single
theological statement about what it is that God has
done in Jesus Christ.

The three methodological principles used by
Saint Thomas are: (1) application of the principles,
established in 2-26, concerning the ontological structure of the God-man to the various aspects of his life,
death and exaltation; (2) accounting for the benefits
that derive to men by reason of God's choice to save
them through the concrete, visible humanity of Christ;
(One example of this is Saint Thomas's practice of
citing the instructive value of the mysteries of
Christ's life, as they, in addition to what Christ
taught, communicate divine truth) and (3) relating the
individual events of Christ's life to the central event
of his ministry, the commencement of the New Law of
grace.[86] Saint Thomas's concern, then is not to
collect the details of Christ's life simply for the
purpose of presenting them. Rather his concern is to
interpret those details in the light of the Christian
gospel's message of salvation. This is Saint Thomas
doing the work of the theologian--not simply multiply-
ing data, but drawing meaning from it.

46. 1-6: Programmatic Essay: Redemption
with all the Human Values of
Satisfaction

The initial question, 46, which treats the passion
of Christ serves a twofold purpose. The first three
articles serve as a kind of programmatic essay (as the
first question of the tertia pars) did for Saint
Thomas's entire christology) for the discussion that
follows (49-52). The remaining articles, following the
methodology outlined above, serve to put before our
minds the reality of Christ's suffering, looked at from
many different aspects, (e.g., the mental and physical
pain of Christ, the time, the place of the passion,
etc.). These articles are intended to recall to our
minds and focus our attention upon what exactly it is
that the God-man suffered for our salvation.

In the programmatic essay, 46.1-3, Saint Thomas
relates the passion of Christ to our salvation in much
the same way that he related the Incarnation to the
self-communication of the divine goodness in 1.1-6.
First he affirms that there is no absolute necessity,
either on the part of God or of man, for Christ to have

190

suffered. There is an intrinsic necessity, however, one which exists once a given end has been determined to be accomplished. Under this consideration, Christ's sufferings were necessary for man's liberation, for his own exaltation and for the fulfillment of Old Testament prophecies, which manifested God's decree concerning them. Nor does such an obligation for Christ to suffer violate the principle that God is merciful, as Saint Thomas explains in 46.1 ra/3:

> The liberation of man through the passion of Christ was consonant with both his mercy and his justice. It is consonant with his justice because by his passion Christ made satisfaction for the sin of the human race, and man was freed through the justice of Christ. It is consonant with his mercy because, since man was by himself unable to satisfy for the sin of all human nature, God gave him his Son to do so. According to Paul: "They are justified freely by his grace through the redemption which is in Christ Jesus, whom God has set forth as a propitiation by his blood, through faith." In so acting God manifested greater mercy than if he had forgiven sins without requiring satisfaction. Paul therefore writes: "God, who is rich in mercy, by reason of his great love with which he loved us, even when we were dead by reason of our sins, brought us to life together with Christ."[87]

This thought is pursued in the following article, 46.2, which asks whether other ways were possible for God to save man. Again, absolutely speaking, others were possible, but given the hypothesis (ex suppositione) that the present order of salvation history was foreknown, no other way was possible. An argument is posed, ag/3, that since God's justice required satisfaction, and since Christ is the faithful servant of God, then his passion must have been the only way, absolutely speaking, of saving man. It is the response to this argument, ra/3, that shows a development in Saint Thomas's understanding of satisfaction as a requirement for the divine justice:

> Even this justice depends upon the divine will which requires satisfaction for sin from the human race. For if God had wanted to free man from sin without any satisfaction at all, he would not have been acting against

justice. Justice cannot be safeguarded by the judge whose duty it is to punish crimes committed against others, e.g., against a fellow man, or the government, or the head of the government, should he dismiss a crime without punishment. But God has no one above him, for he is himself the supreme and common good of the entire universe. If then he forgives sin, which is a crime in that it is committed against him, he violates no one's rights. The one who waives satisfaction and forgives an offense done to himself acts mercifully, not unjustly.[88]

There is a shift of emphasis in this response from that given to the same objection by Saint Anselm and, for that matter, by Saint Thomas himself in his earlier works. For Anselm and the early Saint Thomas the thought of God forgiving sin without punishment implied a disorder--even when his mercy, which was said to be served by his justly demanding satisfaction and providing it in Christ, was taken into consideration. Furthermore the possibility of bad example to human judges, who are required to punish offenses justly, was cited as a reason for satisfaction. Here, however, in ra/3, the supremacy of God's goodness in invoked to explain why God could have chosen to liberate men without demanding satisfaction by the sufferings of Christ. It could be argued that the implications drawn from other kinds of human experience, e.g., the man who waives satisfaction and simply forgives an offense being called merciful and not unjust, contributed to the alteration of Saint Thomas's previous hesitancy in this matter. A better explanation, however, might be found by considering that Saint Thomas better understands the transcendence of God and, therefore, is less hesitant to speak about God in terms other than those suggested by the experience of human behavior.

The use of the term "liberate" (pro liberatione, modus liberationis, ad liberationem) throughout these three articles represents an important choice by Saint Thomas. His concern is to preserve the absolute freedom of divine love to communicate itself and yet to give due value to the actual way in which God does manifest his love. This leads Saint Thomas to conclude[89] that although God could have freed man from his sins in some other way than by the sufferings of Christ, such a freeing would not have been a redemption with all the (human) values of satisfaction, but simply a liberation.

The following article, 46.3, offers the indications of fittingness that suggest why, in effect, such a simple liberation from sin would not have been as useful as the way chosen by God; man's salvation is best served by the passion of Christ. Saint Thomas indicates five reasons which specify the benefits that accrue to man by reason of redemption by satisfaction as opposed to simple liberation from sin:

> First, man could thus see how much God loved him, and so would be aroused to love him. The perfection of his salvation consists in this. Paul therefore writes: "God shows his love for us, in that while we were yet sinners, Christ died for us."

> Second, he gave us an example of obedience, humility, constancy, justice and other virtues which his passion revealed and which are necessary for man's salvation. Peter notes that "Christ has suffered for us, leaving you an example that you may follow in his footsteps."

> Third, by his passion Christ not only freed man from sin but merited for him the grace of justification and the glory of beatitude.

> Fourth, man thus feels a greater obligation to refrain from sin, as Paul says: "You were bought with a great price, so glorify and bear God in your body."

> Fifth, in this way a greater dignity accrues to man. Man has been overcome and deceived by the devil. But it is a man also who overcomes the devil. Man has merited death; a man by dying would conquer death. "Thanks be to God," Paul writes, "who has given us the victory through our Lord Jesus Christ."

> It was therefore better for us to have been delivered by Christ's passion than by God's will alone.[90]

It is important to realize that Saint Thomas in representing these five reasons is in fact spelling out some of the human values entailed in satisfaction. In 46.1 ra/3 he affirmed that God actually showed greater mercy in saving man by the satisfaction of Christ than if he had simply dismissed the guilt of man's sin. The five values he puts forth here are ways of supporting that contention. This, then, is a key article in the programmatic essay because it points to the centrality of satisfaction in any attempt to explain the full dimensions of Christ's salvific death and "the greater dignity which accrues to man" from it.

The remaining articles of 46, as has already been remarked, serve to put the reality of the passion before our mind. The first of these articles, 46.4, accomplishes his purpose. The primary image of Christ's passion is the cross; 46.4, asks why Christ had to be crucified. Seven indications of fittingness are given for the cross and Christ's having suffered upon it. They take into account a broad range of meanings to which one might have recourse in explaining the mystery of salvation--Old Testament figures of salvation; the cosmic dimensions of Christ's salvation and its universal effects for all men; the call to an ordered, virtuous life and the fortitude necessary to follow such a call. The second of these indications of fittingness explains Christ's death as a satisfaction for the sin of Adam:

> Death by crucifixion was suited in every way to atone for the sin of our first parent, who in violation of God's command sinned by taking the fruit of a forbidden tree. It was fitting, in order to satisfy for that sin, that Christ should allow himself to be fixed to the tree of the cross, thus restoring as it were what Adam had stolen. "Then did I pay," the psalmist says, "what I did not take away." Augustine says that "Adam scorned the precept and plucked the fruit from the tree; but what Adam lost, Christ found again on the cross."[91]

The question of Christ's actual physical and mental sufferings, experienced in the course of undergoing his passion, is the subject of 46.5-7. Saint Thomas describes the sufferings of Christ in the light of the principles established concerning the disabilities of body and soul assumed by Christ in his humanity. The concern of the articles is to describe the supreme character of Christ's physical and spiritual sufferings, the sensitivity of the one suffering and the magnitude of the sufferings themselves. Christ's internal suffering, for example, was especially affected by the realization that he was

194

satisfying for the sins of the world, as in 46.6, as well as by the knowledge of his own innocence, as in 46.6 ra/5. An especially balanced remark is made by Saint Thomas as he describes how Christ suffered sadness in the course of making satisfaction. In 46.6 ra/2 he writes:

> The Stoics saw no utility in sadness and, looking upon it as completely contrary to reason, taught that a wise man should avoid it completely. Actually, however, some sadness is praiseworthy, . . . when, for example, it proceeds from a holy love; this occurs when a man is saddened over his own or another's sin. Sadness can also be useful when it is aimed at satisfying for sin, for "the sorrow that is according to God produces repentance that tends to salvation." Christ, then, in order to satisfy for the sins of all men, suffered the most profound sadness, absolutely speaking, but not so great that it exceeded the rule of reason.[92]

47.1-3: Christ's Loving Obedience to his Father's Will

In 46.2 Saint Thomas indicated the reason why man could not have been liberated from sin by any other means than the satisfaction of Christ, accomplished on the cross. "Given a certain hypothesis (ex suppositione facta)," he wrote, "there was no other way. It is impossible that God's foreknowledge should be erroneous and that his will or plan be frustrated."[93] The first three articles of the following question, 47.1-3, clarify the nature of this hypothesis in terms of the interplay between the free, salvific will of God and the human response of Christ. In what way can God be said to be the cause of Christ's sufferings and in what way is Christ himself the cause of his own death? The urgency of this clarification is indicated in the remaining articles, 4-6, where Saint Thomas, in the course of attempting to determine the responsibility of those who actually executed Christ, describes the killing of Christ as "a most grievous sin" in itself (ex genere peccati).

There is a parallel structure to Saint Thomas's explanation of God's role and Christ's participation in his killing. It centers on three points--command and obedience, love given and love received and, finally,

the absolute power of God and of the God-man to have
restrained those who slew Christ. The following texts,
the first of which looks at God's role and the second
at Christ's, explain Saint Thomas's thought. First,
speaking of the Father in 47.3 co/, Saint Thomas
writes:

> God the Father delivered Christ to his
> passion in three ways.
>
> First, by his eternal will, he ordained our
> Lord's sufferings in advance for the libera-
> tion of the human race. "The Lord laid upon
> him the guilt of us all," and, "The Lord was
> pleased to crush him in his infirmity."
>
> Second, by filling him with charity he
> inspired in him the will to suffer for us.
> "He was offered because it was his own
> will."
>
> Third, he did not shield him from suffering
> but abandoned him to his persecutors. Hence
> as he hung on the cross Jesus said: "My God,
> my God, why have you abandoned me," that is,
> God delivered him into the power of those who
> persecuted him.[94]

The second series of texts, drawn from 47.2,3
passim, describes Christ's response to his Father's
will: First, Christ received a command from his Father
to suffer.

> Although obedience conveys the idea of having
> to do what has been commanded, it also
> implies the will to carry out that command.
> Such was Christ's obedience.
>
> [Second], the same response prompted Christ's
> sufferings out of charity and out of obedi-
> ence. He fulfilled the precepts of charity
> out of obedience and was obedient because of
> his love for the Father who had given him the
> command.
>
> [Third], Christ suffered the violence that
> caused his death and at the same time died by
> his own will, for he had the power to prevent
> it.[95]

This is an extremely important discussion for Saint Thomas's theology of Christ's satisfaction for three reasons. The first reason is its merit in terms of a theological analysis of why Christ's death made satisfaction to God, as compared with the explanation given in Cur Deus homo? Saint Thomas situates this reason in the mystery of Christ's loving obedience to his Father's plan to bring about the salvation of man by the establishment of the new covenant of grace. Saint Anselm was satisfied with a simple explanation, but one that was less faithful to scriptural revelation, which spoke in terms of an agreement between Christ and his Father concerning the transfer of Christ's satisfaction to man. A somewhat untoward anthropomorphizing takes place when Saint Anselm describes God as unable not to accept such an agreement when proposed by Christ, his Son. Saint Thomas's understanding of satisfaction, already supplied with a fully personalized interpretation of poena, as discussed in the secunda pars,[96] need have no recourse to such a theory of penal substitution. The satisfaction of Christ is applied to his members as they, united with him, freely undertake the performance of satisfactory deeds and thereby progressively perfect the salvific work of divine grace within them.[97]

Secondly, throughout his works Saint Thomas regularly insists on the charity of Christ as that which gives value to his undertaking of satisfactory punishments. In the Scriptum Saint Thomas distinguished between restitution and satisfaction on the basis of the attitudes which the latter required --either regret or humble respect--whereas restitution demanded the mere return of ill-gotten goods. In the Summa contra gentiles this distinction was elaborated upon considerably in the light of Saint Thomas's reflection on the nature of the attitudes that are found in two men when one satisfied for the other. Indeed the love of the one making the satisfaction increased its acceptability to the extent that the actual punishments required could be mitigated.[98] In the Summa itself Saint Thomas explained Christ's sinlessness as a marked exception to the various disabilities of soul that he assumed with his human nature. This was a consequence of the grace of union and the perfection of created charity which it effected in the soul of Christ. In 47.1-3 all of these developments are drawn together in the explanation of how Christ's love and obedience actually brings about the inauguration of the New Law. Nor is it far-fetched to suggest that Saint Thomas's meditation on the mystery of Christ's satisfaction was itself a cause for change that is discernible in the discussion of one man's satisfying for another as it is initially presented in the Scriptum and, subsequently, in the Summa contra gentiles and in the Summa theologiae.

Thirdly, in point of fact all of the themes that Saint Thomas uses to describe the satisfaction of Christ, especially those inspired by the New Testament, converge in these articles to present a single doctrine on the salvation of man as willed by God and accomplished by Christ. The obedience of Christ to his Father's plan recalls the disobedience of the first man who by sinning departed from the wisdom of God's plan. This is the theme of the New Adam so consistently referred to by Saint Thomas, not only with respect to Christ's obedience but also to his humility as contrasted with Adam's pride, to the wood of the Cross as contrasted with the wood of the tree of knowledge of good and evil, and in other examples where the satisfaction of Christ is spoken of as chiefly to take away original sin.

A second biblical theme that is incorporated into the mystery of salvation is that of the Suffering Servant. As early as the postil on Isaiah this theme captured Saint Thomas's attention as an important one for understanding the mystery of Christ.[99] The theological picture of the suffering God in the De rationibus fidei, drawn for apologetic purposes, is a fine example of the rich use Saint Thomas makes of this theme that spans both Testaments. The analysis of the disabilities of Christ's body and soul in the Summa is ordered to explain, in terms of the ontological structure of the God-man, why it is that Christ could suffer and fulfill the role of Suffering Servant as found in Isaiah and Saint Paul's writings. The biblical texts of the Suffering Servant, which oftentimes, especially in preaching, have inspired an unbalanced and highly untheological presentation of Christ and his work,[100] are harmonized when Saint Thomas places them in the mystery of Christ's obedience to his Father's plan of salvation. Seen in such a perspective these texts lose all suggestion of a vengeful God who exacts a terrible punishment from an innocent victim.

The third theme, suggested especially by the fact that Christ rendered to God a loving submission to his will out of obedience, is that of the priesthood of Christ. The connection is already made in Hebrews

10:5,7: "Sacrifices and offerings thou hast not desired. . . . 'Lo, I have come to do thy will, O God.'" Christ as priest offers to God the ultimate worship that is his due. Yet it is not the sacrifice of his body on the altar of the cross that constitutes this perfect worship, but his offering of obedience and love to God that eminently fulfills this obligation of the virtue of justice which is latria.

There is, however, a deeper mystery here, namely, that the sacrifice of Christ, as was suggested in 22.3, while offered to God is nonetheless something from which man benefits. Christ's satisfactory offering opens the way to man's realization of his final goal of beatitude. It must not be forgotten that the divine will to which Christ is obedient--even to suffering and death--is the salvific will of God for man's salvation. It is, then, the charity of Christ, for he "was obedient because of his love for the Father," that inaugurates the New Law of love which provides for man the way to final union with God in knowledge and love. Likewise it is the divinely-bestowed gift of charity to the members of Christ (just as Christ's own charity was God-given) that gives to their satisfactory deeds the power to bring about, ad promotionem in bono, that very union. In 46.4 ra/1, Saint Thomas explains in terms of fittingness why Christ should not have been put to death by fire in imitation of the Old Testament holocausts. The wood of the cross, he explains, is prefigured in the wooden altar used for such sacrifices, but "in the holocaust of Christ the material fire was replaced by the fire of charity."[101]

48.1-6: Satisfaction: Key-Notion for Interpreting Christ's Redemptive Death

Having visualized the concrete details of the passion and situated its causality in the eternal plan of God to save all men in Christ and in the will of Christ himself, Saint Thomas devotes 48.1-6 to a discussion of the efficacy of the passion, i.e., how it accomplishes its results. The five modes which Saint Thomas describes in these articles are his method of analyzing the way in which the passion of Christ actually brings about the salvation for man which the Gospels and the entire New Testament insist is the result of Christ having obediently surrendered himself to his Father's will.

There is a certain aspect under which 48.1-6 can be considered a summary question in the Summa theologiae. Materially speaking, one does not find new doctrine presented nor marked change of nuance in Saint Thomas's manner of presenting what he does. Saint Thomas speaks of the passion of Christ working by way (per modum) of merit (48.1), of satisfaction (48.2), of sacrifice (48.3) and of redemption (48.4) by way of divine (48.5) instrumental causality (48.6). All of these subjects have been presented before in the course of the tertia pars and given detailed explanation in the light of the principles previously established in other sections of the Summa and repeating them at this point in his treatment of Christ's passion.

The very structure of the Summa itself, which is an articulated and coherent synthesis of theology, suggests that such an explanation is inadequate. In addition, the way in which Saint Thomas organized his discussion of the Incarnate Word in the tertia pars argues against regarding question 48 as a mere summary, and still less as a repetition. Recall that Saint Thomas chose to organize (though not divide) his discussion of the Incarnation under two main headings, namely, the mystery of the Incarnation itself and those things which Christ did and suffered. Question 48 makes a statement about the death of Christ. The relationship of Saint Thomas's theology of the passion to his entire theological synthesis is suggested in the texts of 48 themselves. There are, for example, the references that Saint Thomas himself makes to other sections of his work, such as to the personal and capital grace of Christ, which is a principle of his merit, (7.1,9: 8.1,5), or that he intended to make but did not complete, as is the case with satisfaction in the context of the sacrament of penance. There are, as well, obvious relationships between the modes discussed in 48 and earlier treatises in the Summa; for example, between the mode of merit and the treatise on the priesthood of Christ (22.3,4) and between the mode of efficient cause and the relationship of Christ's human nature to his divine person as discussed from various standpoints in 2.6, 13.2 and 19.1.

Thus it is apparent that 48.1-6, like any question in the Summa, must be read in the light of the entire work in order to understand fully what it is that Saint Thomas is teaching about the passion of Christ. It is highly unlikely that these articles, whose very brevity suggests previous acquaintance with the different topics discussed therein, could be understood apart from the references cited above or—much less—apart from the context of the two programmatic essays, 1.1-3 and 46.1-3, that Saint Thomas places respectively at the head of his entire discussion of the Incarnation and at the beginning of his treatment of the passion.

The first four modes consider the mystery of the effect of the passion which the God-man suffered in his humanity. It is as a man that Christ merited, satisfied, offered sacrifice and redeemed other men, but as God that he saved us through his human sufferings. The final mode, that of efficient causality, examines the humanity of Christ as an instrument of his divinity in terms consistent with Saint Thomas's teaching on the unity of the nature of Christ in the person of the Word. Saint Thomas seeks to outline the various levels of comprehension from which one might consider the single revealed truth that God saved man by the expiatory death of Jesus Christ. To accomplish this he separates, in light of the main themes that have already been mentioned and analyzed, the different aspects of the passion in order better to present a single, coherent picture of its efficacy.

Accordingly, it is clear that no sharp, formal distinctions are able to be drawn between the different modes which Saint Thomas describes in 49. Nevertheless, there is a question that is clearly answered in examining these modes and which is undoubtedly among the chief reasons for Saint Thomas having included them at this point. It should be noted that the effects themselves of the passion, as opposed to how these effects are accomplished, will be the topic of the following question. The question posed and answered by these articles concerns the key-notion which Saint Thomas uses to explain the passion and death of Christ. The question is not what the key-notion or fundamental purpose of the Incarnation is—since that has already been explained in the programmatic essay, 1.1-3—but rather what the key-notion or the fundamental purpose is, as Saint Thomas envisions it, of Christ's suffering and death in accord with the plan of God's salvation for man.

The thesis that will be outlined and defended in the following pages is that the key-notion in Saint Thomas's theology of the redemptive death of Christ is satisfaction. The procedure for defending this thesis is as follows: First, an examination of texts, drawn from question 48, that seem to suport the view that satisfaction is simply one of several good analogies which aid in understanding why the human act of the Savior involved a penal aspect. Second, a review of the argument that the capital merit of Christ is, of the four modes which Saint Thomas analyzes in the same question, the one which has the best claim for being the key-notion. Third, defense of the thesis that satisfaction is the key-notion for explaining how the work of image-restoration in Christ is accomplished in the actual economy of salvation. The notion of satisfaction is interpreted, of course, in light of Saint Thomas's entire theology, especially as it is presented in his Summa theologiae. The remainder of the chapter is devoted to an exposition of 49.1-6 which discuss the effects of Christ's passion in terms of the efficacy of satisfaction and its central position in Saint Thomas's entire theological reflection on, and clarification of, the mystery of Christ's redemptive death.

Alternative interpretations of Q.48

B. Catão: No key-notion

B. Catão in his study of Saint Thomas's notion of salvation and redemption has concluded that the satisfaction of Christ is certainly not the key-notion ("notion maîtresse") which allows us to understand in what the redemptive value of the cross consists. It is simply, writes Catão, "a good analogy which, among others, aids in understanding why the human act of the Saviour was one of humiliation, suffering and death on the cross."[102]

The very suppleness with which Saint Thomas speaks of the various modes might at first glance suggest that in fact there is no key-notion, that no single one of the modes is the one which can truly be said to be the chief mode under which the other four are ordered and by which they are given their intelligibility in the overall explanation of the efficacy of Christ's death. For example, in terms of the headship of Christ, merit and satisfaction are spoken of in practically identical terms. In 48.1/co Saint Thomas speaks of the merit of Christ:

> We have pointed out that Christ was given grace not only as an individual but insofar as he is head of the Church, so that grace might pour out from him upon his members.

Thus there is the same relation between what another man does in the state of grace and himself.[103]

In 48.2 ra/1 the efficacy of Christ's passion as regards satisfaction is thus explained:

The head and members form as it were a single mystical person. Christ's satisfaction therefore extends to all the faithful as to his members. When two men are united in charity one can satisfy for the other.[104]

In 48.2 co/ Saint Thomas explains why the satisfaction of Christ emimently fulfills the requirement specified by the very definition of satisfaction itself. It should be noted here that the definition of the Cur Deus homo? is modified by Saint Thomas to include a satisfaction that is not only the equivalent of the offense but even one that outweighs the offense. This will enable him to speak of Christ's passion as a "superabundant" satisfaction to God:

A man effectively satisfies for an offense when he offers to the one who has been offended something which he accepts as matching or outweighing the former offense. Christ, suffering in a loving and obedient spirit, offered more to God than was demanded in recompense for all the sins of mankind because, first, the love which led him to suffer was a great love; second, the life he laid down in satisfaction was of great dignity, since it was the life of God and of man; and third, his suffering was all-embracing and his pain so great. . . . Christ's passion, then, was not only sufficient but superabundant satisfaction for the sins of mankind.[105]

The explanation that Saint Thomas offers of the sacrifice of Christ accomplished in his passion is given in strikingly similar terms. In 48.3 co/ Saint Thomas writes:

This gesture, this voluntary enduring of the passion, motivated as it was by the greatest love, pleased God. It is clear then that Christ's passion was a true sacrifice.[106]

In 48.4 ra/1:

> Christ's flesh is the most perfect sacri-
> fice. . . since being sinless, it was
> efficacious for the cleansing of sin.[107]

The mode of redemption is itself described in
terms similar to those that described the mode of
satisfaction and of sacrifice. In 48.4 co/ Saint
Thomas writes of redemption:

> Christ offered satisfaction . . . by giving
> the greatest of all things, namely himself,
> for us. For that reason the passion of
> Christ is said to be our ransom (redemp-
> tio).[108]

In the sed contra, 48.4 sc/, Saint Thomas quotes I
Peter 2,19, which speaks of our redemption as the
result of Christ's having been offered up as a victim,
"a lamb without blemish and without spot."

> On the other hand Peter write: "You were not
> redeemed with perishable things, with silver
> or gold, from the vain manner of life handed
> down from your fathers, but with the precious
> blood of Christ, as a lamb without blemish
> and without spot."[109]

This text suggests as well the theme of justice
which, according to the significant modifications
already noted both with respect to God and to the
devil, links the mode of redemption with that of
satisfaction, as it is the payment of something owed.
"He does not pay, however, who does not perfectly
satisfy," Saint Thomas explains in 48.2 sc/, although
in the case of the satisfaction of Christ, which is
something owed by other men not by Christ, "it is said
of Christ: 'Must I restore what I did not steal?'"[110]
This same text also links the modes of redemption,
satisfaction and sacrifice with that of merit. In 48.1
co/ Saint Thomas writes of merit:

> It is clear that if anyone in the state of
> grace suffers for justice's sake, by that
> very fact he merits salvation for himself,
> for it is written: "Blessed are they who
> suffer persecution for justice's sake."[111]

From a purely textual comparison all of the four modes that refer to the passion of Christ as he suffered it according to his human nature seem to be interchangeable, or at least closely related to one another. Such a conclusion is further suggested by the relationship that Saint Thomas establishes, in what is clearly an important text (48.6 ra/3), between Christ's passion viewed in relation to his divinity and the mode of instrumental causality which is exercised in each of the four previously described modes. Saint Thomas writes:

> When Christ's passion is viewed in relation to his divinity it can be seen to act in an efficient way; in relation to the will which is rooted in Christ's soul, by way of merit; in relation to the very flesh of Christ, by way of satisfaction, since we are freed by it from the guilt of punishment; by way of redemption, inasmuch as we are thereby freed from the slavery of sin; and finally, by way of sacrifice, thanks to which we are reconciled by God.[112]

G. Lafont: The capital merit of Christ

The truly summary character of the above text, placed at the very end of 48, suggests that the key to Saint Thomas's explanation of the meaning of the efficacy of Christ's passion lies in his doctrine of the instrumental causality of the humanity of Christ. It has already been remarked that the notion of instrumental efficient causality is a key one for Saint Thomas's entire theological synthesis in the Summa.[113] Relative to Saint Thomas's christology it is crucial for establishing the reason why the meritorious and satisfactory deeds of Christ could "spiritually affect" the members. Father O'Neill writes of instrumental causality that it

> . . . is not, consequently, the peripheral element in the Thomist system which it is sometimes represented as being. It is an essential element of the synthesis. It is the means by which Saint Thomas introduced into western theology the richly suggestive intuition of the Greek Fathers that the very union of God with human nature brought redemption to all that is human. The sacred humanity of Christ, because it is united to the person of the divine Son, is the source

from which salvation merited by Christ
is physically communicated (that is, by
efficient causality) to all who are united in
the one mystical person of Christ.[114]

It has already been noted in the discussion of
De veritate 29.7 that Saint Thomas had immediate
recourse to this principle in order to explain the
universality of Christ's merit and satisfaction. His
careful analysis of Christ's human and divine activity
in the *Summa*[115] altered somewhat his interpretation
of the effects of that activity. In the *Summa* he
prefers to assign Christ's merit to his human activity,
as in 19.3, although communication of that merit is
explained in terms of the headship of Christ and the
ability of a head to influence its members, as in 19.4.
In the articles of the summary question, 48.1,6, merit,
headship and instrumental causality are reunited to
explain the full meaning of Christ's salvific actions
for man.

The implications of this in terms of a search for
the key-notion of the passion's efficacy are plain. It
is the capital meritorious grace of Christ, as it is
transmitted to the members, that ultimately explains
why Christ's passion accomplished the salvific, predestined plan of God. The reason for this conclusion
is considerably enhanced when one recalls the doctrine
of man as God's image, which is a thematic one for the
entire *Summa*. The theme of the restoration of the
image of God in creation, along with the role that
merit and satisfaction play in that restoration of the
God-image in man, the rational creature, has already
been described as a central one for interpreting Saint
Thomas's doctrine on the movement of the creatures
toward their final goal of beatitude. The passion of
Christ stands at the center of that movement. The
linking of merit and instrumental causality seems to be
the center of Saint Thomas's explanation of how that
passion, along with faith and the sacraments of faith,
effect the recapitulation of all things in Christ of
which Saint Paul speaks in Ephesian 3:21,22, where he
specifically refers to Christ's headship over his
church--"Christ Jesus himself being the cornerstone, in
whom the whole structure is joined together and grows
into a holy temple in the Lord."

Such an understanding of the recapitulatory nature
of Christ's work, entirely consonant with Saint Thomas's announced program in composing the *Summa*, would
seem to indicate that the capital meritorious grace of

Christ, and therefore the modus meriti, is, in fact, the key-notion that explains the full efficacy of Christ's passion. Father G. Lafont favors this conclusion when he writes that it is the capital merit of Christ which gives the works of Christ their efficacy for us. He cites 49.1 co/ to summarize and support his suggestion. At the same time he acknowledges that certain "aspects complémentaires" are added by Saint Thomas, namely, the modes of satisfaction, sacrifice and redemption, to bring out the full intelligibility of the merit of Christ. The text of 49.1 co/ is as follows:

> Christ's passion causes the forgiveness of sins by way of ransom. He is our head and has, by his passion--endured out of love and obedience--freed us, his members, from our sins, the passion being as it were the ransom. It is as if, by performing some meritorious work with his hands, a man might redeem himself from a sin he had committed with his feet. For the natural body, though made up of different members, is one, and the whole Church which is Christ's mystical body is deemed to be one person with its head, Christ.[116]

Satisfaction: Required for the work of image-restoration

Can the notion of capital merit alone, however, be the key to understanding the efficacy of Christ's passion? Not if one considers the eternally predestined plan of God as the supposition actually given. "Once, however, a certain hypothesis is granted (ex aliqua suppositione facta) there was no other way," writes Saint Thomas in 46.2 co/, "for the passion of Christ to bring about man's salvation;" that is, to accomplish the work of image-perfection and, it must be emphasized, image-restoration. It is this actual order of salvation, which includes the divine permission for sin, that demands not only capital merit but also capital satisfaction. This is what Saint Thomas explains in 48.1 ra/2 in which he expresses what must be the clearest indication of the centrality of satisfaction for Christ's passion, and in so doing suggests that it is the key-notion for explaining the other modes according to which the passion of Christ accomplishes its effect:

From the moment of his conception Christ
merited eternal salvation for us. On our
part, however, there were certain obstacles
which prevented us from enjoying the result
of his previously acquired merits. In order
to remove these obstacles, then, it was
necessary that Christ suffer.[117]

It is the profound reality of God's plan as willed,
which includes the permission to sin, that ultimately
explains satisfaction's key role in answering the
question of why Christ had to suffer for us.[118]

It would seem that no other conclusion is possible
in order to interpret question 49, which Saint Thomas
devotes to the actual results themselves of Christ's
passion, 49.1-6. The very ordering of the articles
within the question parallel the two fundamental
reasons that Saint Thomas gives in 1.2 for the fittingness of the Incarnation. These are, first, that the
Incarnation was effective for man's furtherance in good
because by it man is brought to "the full sharing in
divinity, which is true happiness and the purpose of
human life," and second, that the Incarnation was able
to deliver man from evil, that is, "to rescue man from
thralldom . . . which was accomplished by Christ making
satisfaction for us."

In 49.1-6 the results of Christ's passion are
discussed in the reverse order. First, with respect to
remotio mali, the passion of Christ is said to free us
from sin (49.1), from the power of the devil (49.2) and
from the debt of punishment (49.3); consequently the
passion rescues man from the thralldom of sin. By
being placed in the third position, satisfaction is
presented as the capstone to Christ's full salvific
work, or as the necessary theological clarification for
understanding the Pauline metaphor of redemption. The
second series of articles, 49.4-5 (49.6 being devoted
to a discussion of the exaltation of Christ), discusses
the results of Christ's passion as they relate to the
primary reason for the necessity of the Incarnation,
promotio in bono. In 49.4 Saint Thomas describes the
reconciliation with God that is effected by Christ's
sacrifice and, finally, in 49.5, the meaning of the
metaphor "to open the gates of heaven."

It has already been remarked, in connection with
Father Lafont's use of this text, that 49.1 unites the
notion of merit and instrumental causality in explaining the passion of Christ as freeing man from sin.

Indeed, all of the various modes in which Christ's passion is said to operate are referred to in the course of Saint Thomas's sed contra and reply in this article. These include (1) merit: "It is as if, by performing some meritorious work . . ."; (2) satisfaction: "The passion being as it were the ransom (pretium). . ."; (3) sacrifice: "He has loved us and washed us from our sins in his own blood"; (4) redemption: "Christ's passion causes the forgiveness of sins by way of redemption. . ."; (5) efficient causality: "The flesh in which Christ endured his passion is the instrument of his Godhead."[119] This article should be seen as a summary presentation of Saint Thomas's global perspective on the result of Christ's passion viewed through the four modes (discussed in the previous question) by which the passion's effect was accomplished.

The efficacy of Christ's passion considered in light of the presence of evil in the world

The arguments posed against this article, 49.1 ag/1-5, are aimed at either denying that the passion which Christ suffered in his humanity is able to bring about the forgiveness of man's sins. The existence of other means to receive forgiveness of sins as well as the fact that sins were committed after Christ's passion seem to indicate that the passion is not the sufficient cause of the forgiveness of sins. Saint Thomas responds to the first objection in ra/1,2 by recourse to the principle of instrument causality. His response to the second line of argumentation, apart from asserting the sufficiency of Christ's passion "somewhat as if a doctor were able to make up a medicine by which any kind of future ill could be treated,"[120] recalls the place of faith and sacraments in the Church, whereby the effects of Christ's passion are concretely and subjectively applied to the members.

The subject of 49.2 is an important one for understanding why Christ's satisfaction is of central significance for understanding Saint Thomas's explanation of the mystery of the passion. In asking whether Christ's passion freed us from the power of the devil Saint Thomas addresses himself to the question of the objective effect of the passion of Christ, as explained in the previous article, and its subjective effect on individual men as well as on the condition of mankind at any given moment in salvation history. The arguments posed at the beginning of this article are representative of the classical ones, in one form or another, which try to show that Christ's passion has not really changed the world. Reference is made to the experience of temptation by just men in ag/1,2 and to the existence of widespread unevangelization in ag/3.

In the reply Saint Thomas simply affirms the objective reality of Christ's victory over the devil in terms of the passion's effects of remission of sin and reconciliation to God. He also addresses himself in a third point to the theme of the injustice of the devil's work as contrasted with the justice of that of Christ, which is a theme drawn from Saint Augustine's De Trinitate. The same modification, noted above with regard to 46.3 ra/3, is present in the particular text chosen from Saint Augustine. The justice of Christ's passion is viewed not in contrast to the devil's unjust usurpation of power--even to plotting the death of Christ--but in the justice of Christ freeing those who believed in him from that power.[121]

The responses to the arguments, however, are of primary importance. It is here that Saint Thomas establishes the fact that "in accordance with the hidden plan of his judgments" God's actual salvific plan for reconciling all men with himself includes the permission to sin. The permission to sin not only accounts for the original sin, and therefore the "chief" reason for Christ's passion, but also the continuation of sin in the world. Saint Thomas's perspective on this confrontation of the power of evil with man's desire to find happiness in God is a simple one: "The remedy prepared by Christ's passion is always available to man. . . . The fact that some prefer not to use this remedy in no way detracts from the efficacy of Christ's passion."[122]

The full meaning and explanation of the mysterium iniquitatis are not quite so simply discovered. Two points seem crucial in terms of the present discussion. The first is the fact that evil is present in the world before and after the passion of Christ. This fact is consistently explained by Saint Thomas, in keeping with his fundamentally Christian belief in a supreme God, as opposed to any form of dualism, by reference to God's permissive will: "The devil was not so strong that he could harm men without God's permission." "Even now God allows the devil to try men's souls, . . ." "God permits the devil to deceive men. . . ."[123] The eternal plan of God includes the permission for men to sin and, according to God's wisdom, this must work for man's salvation and not against it. Secondly, it is the notion of satisfactory punishments, especially as seen in prima secundae 87.6-8, that offers the explanation as to how the mysterium iniquitatis, which Saint Thomas insisted has no reason for existence apart from man's sin, is incorporated into God's plan of salvation for all men.

The programmatic essay offers the best summary of Saint Thomas's understanding of the relationship between man's actual sinful condition and the passion of Christ. An objection is formulated in one of the arguments, 1.3 ag/3, that is attached to the question whether God would have become incarnate had man not sinned. This objection argues that since human nature is not made more capable of grace through sin, though even after sin it is capable of the grace of union, God would have become incarnate even if man had not sinned in order to fulfill this obediential potency in man. Saint Thomas responds simply that man's nature has no claim to realizing its capacity to be united with God. This is something beyond the range of nature's power in itself and can only be fulfilled by God's always free bestowal of grace. Then Saint Thomas adds in 1.3 ra/3:

> Nothing, however, stands in the way of human nature's being lifted to something greater, even after sin. God permits evil that he might draw forth some good. Thus the text in Romans reads: "Where wickedness abounded, grace abounded yet more," and in the blessing of the Paschal Candle: "O happy fault that merited so great a redeemer."[124]

It is the role of Christ the Redeemer, as he makes satisfaction for sin, that is the fulfillment of his promise that God draw forth some good from evil. This is the reason for the keystone position of article 49.3 which treats of the effect of the passion as freeing man from the punishment of sin. Saint Thomas's explanation is brief in the reply:

> Christ's passion delivered us from the debt of punishment in two ways. First of all, directly, for the passion of Christ was adequate, and more than adequate, to satisfy for the sins of all mankind. Once sufficient satisfaction has been made, the debt of punishment ceases. Second, indirectly, for

211

Christ's passion is the cause of the forgiveness of sin, and sin is the basis for the
debt of punishment.[125]

It is the satisfaction of Christ for man's sins
that completes his work as Redeemer in the actual order
of creation, which includes human nature, capable both
of sin and of repenting for sin. It is here that a
comparison with angelic nature is significant. In 4.1
ag/3 an argument is made for the greater fittingness of
God's having assumed an angelic nature than a human
one. Saint Thomas responds, in ra/3, that although God
could have chosen this alternative, "the fittingness on
the point of need would be missing, however. . . .
Even though angelic nature in some way is burdened with
sin, that sin is irremediable."[126] In man, because
of his inability to grasp in a single intuition all
of the effects of any given action, sin is not irremediable. For this reason human nature has need of a
redeemer, and the Word of God, because of that need,
fittingly became flesh and not angelic spirit.

The meaning of Christ's satisfaction for
those who suffer in the world

The response to the arguments attached to 49.3
explain how that remedial work of Christ's satisfaction
is applied to the members in the ongoing process of
image-restoration. The principle which underlines each
of the three responses is that the suffering, which
man incurs as a result of sin, becomes a means of
redemption when it is united with the satisfaction of
Christ.

There is a parallel between these responses,
evident even in their numerical ordering, and the
responses to the previous article which described the
providential role of the evil which God permits in the
world. In 49.2 ra/1,2,3 Saint Thomas explains first
that God, in addition to permitting the devil to try
men's souls, also permits him to justly punish or harm
those who succumb to his temptations; second, that
temptation is always considered a call to believe in
the power of Christ's passion, either implicitly, prior
to the passion, or explicitly, after it; third, that
this permitted presence of evil is a permanent part of
God's saving plan and will continue even to the last
days.

In the responses to 49.3, Saint Thomas first explains, in ra/1, that Christ's passion can have no effect on those condemned to hell since they are not able to have contact with it either through faith, love or the sacraments. In ra/2, Saint Thomas describes how an individual member answers the call to believe in and benefit from the power of Christ's passion. He contrasts the unique means, baptism, which completely configures (configurari) the member to Christ and consequently requires no subsequent satisfactory punishments, which are required for the sins committed after baptism. Significantly for the doctrine of satisfaction, such punishments are also said to configure man (configurentur Christo) to Christ. In ra/2 Saint Thomas writes:

> In order to benefit from Christ's passion one must be likened to him. We are sacramentally conformed to him in baptism, for "we were buried with him by means of baptism into death." Hence no atoning punishment is imposed upon men at baptism, for they are then completely freed by the satisfaction offered by Christ. And since "Christ died once and for all for our sins," man cannot be conformed to Christ by being baptized a second time. It is therefore right that those who commit sin after baptism should be made to conform to the suffering Christ by experiencing some penalty or suffering in their own persons. This punishment, which is much less than man's sin deserves, does nevertheless suffice because Christ's satisfaction works along with it.[127]

The final response, ra/3, presents a miniature outline of the entire program of Christian living as it is ordered to reverse the effects of the permanent presence of evil in the world. The essentially cruciform pattern of Christian life as it opens for man the way to his final goal emerges in this brief paragraph, harmonizing in the process the themes of adoptive sonship and suffering wherein the members are united to the Son and Suffering Servant for their eternal glory. The mysterium inequitatis is truly a "happy fault" because of the satisfaction of Christ. In ra/3 Saint Thomas explains:

> Christ's satisfaction brings about its effect in us insofar as we are incorporated into him as members are into the head. But members

213

should be conformed to their head. Hence
just as Christ, who besides having grace in
his soul also had a body that could suffer,
attained through his passion to a glorious
immortality, we who are his members are freed
by his passion from the debt of any punishment whatsoever. But we must first have
received into our souls "the spirit of adoption as sons" by which we are marked out for
the inheritance of a glorious immortality,
while yet retaining a body subject to suffering and death. Later, when we have "become
like Christ through suffering and death," we
will be led into eternal glory, according to
the Apostle who says: "If we are sons, we
are heirs also; heirs indeed of God and joint
heirs with Christ, provided that we suffer
with him, so that we may also be glorified
with him."[128]

Reconciliation: Effect of Christ's
satisfaction

The work of satisfaction is the work of reconciliation; the last half of the response serves as a
transition to the following article, 49.4, in which
Saint Thomas addresses himself to the issue of man's
actual reconciliation with God which the passion of
Christ has effected. Satisfaction is the work of
reconciliation because it is the complementary work of
image-perfection, properly spoken of as an effect of
charity and merit; the complement which satisfaction
accomplishes is the work of image-restoration. For
fallen man no other way than that of satisfaction could
make it possible for him to achieve union with God.
This as well is the fulfillment of God's plan, "the
mystery of his will according to his purpose which he
set forth in Christ, as a plan for the fullness of
time, to unite all things in him . . . ."[129] The
perfection of the order of created reality, as it was
established in the Word, is brought to realization in
the Word-Son, of whom Saint Paul writes in Colossians
1:21,22:

He is the image of the invisible God, the
first-born of all creation; for in him all
things were created. . . . He is the head of
the body, the church; he is the beginning,
the first-born from the dead, that in everything he might be preeminent. For in him all
the fullness of God was pleased to dwell, and

through him to reconcile to himself all things, . . . making peace by the blood of his cross.

In 49.4 Saint Thomas continues his meditation on the passion. He writes that "Christ's passion is the cause of our being reconciled with God in two ways, first because it removes sin which makes man God's enemy."[130] Colossians 1:21-22 continues:

And you, who once were estranged and hostile in mind, doing evil deeds he has now reconciled in his body of flesh by his death, in order to present you holy and blameless and irreproachable before him.

The second reason given by Saint Thomas for the reconciliatory effect of Christ's passion is that:

. . . it is a most acceptable sacrifice to God. It is a property of sacrifice that it appease God; man also forgives an offence committed against him when some mark of respect is tendered him. Hence we read: "If the Lord stirs you up against me, may he accept an offering." Similarly, the fact that Christ suffered voluntarily was so great a good that, on account of seeing this good accomplished in human nature, God was appeased in regard to all the offences of the human race. This applies of course to those who are united in the way we have said to the suffering Christ.[131]

It is this reconciliation accomplished by the satisfaction of Christ and achieved in the individual member as he is united with Christ that allows the primary purpose of the Incarnation, the communication of the divine goodness, to be achieved. In the responses to the arguments of 49.4, two of which suggest that the passion of Christ could not be a cause of God's loving us, since he is said to have always loved us, Saint Thomas answers in ra/1: "God loves in all men the nature which he has made; what he hates in man is the sins which men commit against him."[132]

The following response, ra/2, even more clearly expresses how the satisfaction of Christ—which removes the block that sin placed between God and man—fulfills the purpose for which God, as Saint Thomas announced in

215

the opening lines of the tertia pars, saw fit to become man, namely, that he might communicate himself to others (ut se aliis communicet). Saint Thomas writes:

> When we say that Christ's passion reconciled us to God we do not mean that God has begun anew to love us, for it is written that "with age-old love I have loved you." Thanks to Christ's passion the cause for hatred has been removed, both because sin has been wiped away and because compensation has been made in the form of a more agreeable offering.[133]

The work of Christ's passion, as it is said to open for us the gates of heaven, is the subject of 49.5. The metaphorical image, as Saint Thomas explains, refers to the removal of the obstacle to man's achieving his final goal. Christ's passion has removed both the obstacle of Adam's sin, the original sin, and those sins which find their origin in it. The priesthood of Christ is invoked since his satisfaction is primarily offered to God, as a sacrifice of latria, but the change which it effects takes place in man as he is called to share in the fruits of Christ's passion by faith, love and the sacraments. Saint Thomas develops this idea in 49.5/co:

> A closed gate prevents entrance. Men were prevented by sin from entering the heavenly kingdom. Two kinds of sin prevent us from entering the heavenly kingdom. The first is the sin common to the whole human race, namely, that of our first parent, which deprived man of entry into the heavenly kingdom. Thus, after Adam's sin, "God placed the cherubim and the flaming sword which turned every way, to guard the way to the tree of life."
>
> Through Christ's passion, however, we are delivered not only from the sin of the entire human race both as regards the sin and the debt of punishment (for Christ paid the price of our ransom), but also from our own sins, provided we share in his passion by faith, love and the sacraments of faith. Thus through Christ's passion we find the door of the heavenly kingdom open. It was this that the Apostle had in mind when he wrote: "Christ as high priest of the good things to

come entered once for all by virtue of his
own blood into the Holies, having obtained
eternal redemption."[134]

The place of Christ's satisfaction in relation
to merit is very well summarized in the response to
one of the arguments attached to this article. An
objection is posed in ag/1 that the passion of Christ
could not have opened the Kingdom of Heaven to men
since the saints of the Old Testament clearly merited
union with God.

It seems the holy patriarchs who performed
works of justice (opera justitiae) would have
fitly gained entry into the heavenly kingdom
even apart from Christ's passion.[135]

Saint Thomas's response is a concise summary, in terms
of the actual order of salvation history, as to why the
present economy of salvation required the satisfaction
of Christ. In ra/1 he explains:

By the performance of good works the patriarchs merited entry into the heavenly kingdom
through faith in Christ's passion: "Holy
men by faith conquered kingdoms, wrought
justice." Thanks to their faith, each of
them was cleansed from sin as far as his own
personal purification was concerned. Yet
neither the faith nor the righteousness of
any of the patriarchs sufficed to remove the
obstacle of guilt for the whole human race;
that impediment was removed at the price of
Christ's blood. Hence before Christ's
passion no one could enter the kingdom of
heaven and attain that everlasting beatitude
which consists in the full enjoyment of
God.[136]

The final article, 49.6, looks to the effect which
Christ's passion had on his own person. Saint Thomas
is careful to distinguish between the exaltation of
Christ's body, which Christ is said to merit by his
passion, and the exaltation of his soul, "which did not
have to be acquired by him by way of merit."[137] It is
the innocence and humility of Christ that make his
having undergone the passion a fitting reason for him
to have received the exaltation of his body. "When a
man of upright will deprives himself of something he
ought to have, he deserves to have something additional

given him as a reward (quasi merces) for his upright intention."[138]   The exaltation of the body of Christ is the reward for his upright intention.   It is the same upright intention that Saint Thomas describes in the opening lines of 50.1, on whether "it was fitting that Christ should die":

> One way of satisfying for another is to submit to the penalty that the other deserved.   Christ wished to die so that he might make satisfaction for us by his death. I Peter says: "Christ died once for our sins."[139]

CHAPTER SIX

THE SATISFACTION OF CHRIST MEDIATED TO THE MEMBERS IN THE CHURCH OF FAITH AND SACRAMENTS

Sons in the Image of the Son

Adoptive Sonship as the Model for Understanding the Union of Head and Members in the Church

Father G. Lafond, in his study of the Summa,[1] suggests that Saint Thomas's understanding of the nature of the union that exists between Christ and his members in the Mystical Body can be clarified in terms of his doctrine on the mystery of the Incarnation itself. Saint Thomas's insistence on the true hypostatic union of the human nature of Christ to the transcendent person of the Word and on the authentically human ("from Adam's stock") nature assumed by the divine person; in addition, his teaching on the instrumental character of Christ's human activities as they are united with his divinity ("It is one and the same saving action," writes Saint Thomas in 19.1 ra/2, "by which his humanity and his divinity save us") is the framework for understanding the kind of unity all men have in Christ. It is important to realize that Saint Thomas harmonizes this doctrine concerning the mystery of Christ's ontological constitution with that of God's predestined plan of salvation for all men which is accomplished in the man Jesus Christ.

The situating of the divine plan of salvation in the human actions of Christ, who is at once hypostatically united with divinity and genetically related to all those who share his human nature, is the key to explaining, as much as any mystery can be explained, the Mystical Body without espousing the extreme interpretations of physical[2] inclusion or merely moral union. Father Lafont writes:

The Saviour realizes the perfection of the
Image of God in the order of grace and merit
because of his being that Image in the order
of the hypostatic union. Hence he includes
really in himself, at the moment of his
passion, all men inasmuch as they are to be
saved, which is the equivalent of saying that
he restores the fullness of the Image of God
to all creation.[3]

Such a perspective on the efficacy of the passion
and the union which it effects between Christ and his
members focuses on the grace of union which belongs to
Christ alone as he is Son by nature and the grace of
adoption whereby we are made sons in the Son. Saint
Thomas's doctrine of the Mystical Body, then, is a
doctrine which rests upon the definition, found in
Romans 8:15-17, of adoptive sonship as a relationship
to God which results from man's being established by
divine grace in Christ's work of image-perfection and
image-restoration accomplished at the moment of his
passion. Such a work, as 48.5 clearly teaches, is the
work of the whole Trinity which alone can effect, as
first cause, such a perfection in man and effect, as
well, the final term of that perfection which is the
union of man with the triune God. The establishment of
man in such a personal relationship of knowledge and
love with God can only be effected by the whole trinity
of Persons operating in the unity of the divine nature,
just as the created image in man, which the passion of
Christ restores and perfects, is modelled upon the
tripersonal divine nature.[4]

Such is man's ultimate reconciliation with God.
Adoptive sonship makes the members of Christ one in him
as he is one, as the person of the Word, with the
Father and the Holy Spirit. Certain texts in Saint
Paul which seem to suggest that adoptive sonship is a
participation in the natural sonship of Christ do not
appear to contradict this conclusion. Saint Thomas
explains that the second person, as regards his intra-
trinitarian procession, is Son precisely because he is
Word. He makes use of this theological insight to
explain why it was fitting that the Son, rather than
the Father or the Holy Spirit, become incarnate. In
3.8 he writes:

The Son's becoming incarnate was altogether
appropriate, and first of all from the
meaning of the union. Like is fittingly
joined to the like. We can look to one sort

of general affinity between the Son, the Word of God, and all creatures; the craftman's mental word, i.e., his idea, is a pattern for whatever he fashions; so too the Word, God's eternal conception, is the exemplar for all creation. Creatures are first established, though changeably, in their proper kinds by a sharing in that likeness; similarly it is fitting that creatures be restored to their eternal and changeless perfection through the Word's being united, not participatively, but in the person with the creature. The craftsman repairs his own work when it has been damaged on the same mental model he used in making it.

A second reason can be taken from the purpose of the union, the accomplishment of the predestination of those who are preordained for a heavenly inheritance. To this sons alone have a right; "If sons, heirs also." Appropriately, then, through him who is Son by nature men share by adoption in a likeness to his sonship: "Those whom he foreknew he predestined to share the image of his Son."[5]

As the Word, the second person of the Trinity, is one with the Father by reason of a common nature and a common spiration of the Spirit, so the member of Christ is one with the triune God by reason of grace, which is a creature's participation in the divine nature, and by the bond of faith and charity in which man attaches himself to God in love. The adopted son, who participates in the sonship of Christ, manifests the goodness of the whole Trinity in creation, as Christ, Son by nature and not adoption, perfectly represents the wisdom and the goodness of God in the order of created being.

The Sacraments of the Church: Instruments for Restoring the Image of God in Man

It is the biblical theme of adoptive sonship which stands at the center of Saint Thomas's sacramental theology. This is certainly true insofar as the sacraments are described as "instruments" of the humanity of Christ, as he himself is the incarnate Word-Son. The tertia pars, as we have seen, clearly teaches that it is in Christ, the Son by nature, that his members are adopted by the Father. The notion of adoptive sonship, centered as it is on the notion of man as the image of God, is the basis for the continuity of Saint Thomas's treatment of the sacraments not only with his christology in the tertia pars, but also with the principles of his entire Summa theologiae. The image of God, together with its philosophical explanation in terms of exemplar, efficient and final causality, is at once central to Saint Thomas's theological anthropology and a leitmotiv of his Summa.

The theology of merit and of satisfaction, as explained by Saint Thomas, is a doctrine on image-perfection and image-restoration respectively. The notion of God as the final cause of all creation is accomplished in the concrete historical economy of salvation by the passion of his Son and communicated to man through faith and the created things or acts combined with words which are the sacraments. The necessary role of the sacraments in applying the fruits of Christ's passion is clearly described at the beginning of Saint Thomas's discussion of the notion of what the sacraments of the New Law are in themselves. In 61.1 ra/3 he writes:

> The passion of Christ is the sufficient cause of man's salvation. Yet it does not follow on this account that the sacraments are not necessary for man's salvation, for they produce their effects in virtue of the passion of Christ, and it is the passion of Christ which is, in a certain manner, applied to men through the sacraments, as is borne out by the following saying of Saint Paul: "All of us who have been baptized into Christ Jesus were baptized into his death."[6]

It should be noted, as regards the notion of adoptive sonship, that the same text from Romans 6 is employed in this response as it was used by Saint Thomas in responding to a similar objection posed against the self-sufficiency of the passion in 49.3. At that point he explained the need for the members to be "configured" (configurentur) to Christ through the image-restorative work of suffering and through a similar kind of configuring that occurs in the sacraments.

Adoptive sonship is primarily an eschatological reality, as Saint Paul indicates when he remarks in Romans 8:15: "And if sons, heirs also; indeed of

222

God...." As such, adoptive sonship does not consist so much in a state of being as in a tendency toward beatitude. Saint Thomas's comment on the Eucharist is especially significant in terms of its reference to the place of the sacraments in the life of the wayfarer and in terms of the Pauline doctrine of the gradual perfection of adoptive sonship in the believer. In 79.2 ra/1, he writes:

> Christ's passion, in virtue of which this sacrament works, is indeed the sufficient cause of glory, not, nevertheless, that we are at once brought thereby into heaven, for beforehand we must, as Saint Paul states, "suffer with him" that afterwards we may be "glorified with him." And so the sacrament does not immediately usher us in, but gives us the strength to journey to heaven. That is why it is called the viaticum.[7]

Saint Thomas's theology of the sacraments is warp and woof of the Summa's master-concept of man set between God and God, and of the notion of final causality which controls the gradual progression of all created reality to its Maker. At the very start of the tertia pars Saint Thomas establishes this connection by referring to the sacraments as those things "by which we attain salvation" (quibus salutem consequimur).

The Harmony of Doctrine in the Summa's Teaching on the Work of Image-Restoration with Reference to the History of Salvation

The Work of Satisfaction before and after the Coming of Christ

The harmony of Saint Thomas's sacramental theology with the method and doctrine of the whole Summa can be demonstrated by an examination of texts in which he speaks explicitly about the notion of satisfaction. The texts are drawn from each of the three major parts of his systematic analysis of the rational creature's origin and movement towards God.

The Old Law

In his discussion of the creation of man in God's image in the prima pars, Saint Thomas considers the characteristics of man in the state of original justice, that is, as he came forth from the creative hand of God. In 95.4 the particular aspect under consideration is whether man was better able to merit in the state of original justice than after sin. Saint Thomas's conclusion is that man's deeds would have been more effective for meriting in the state of innocence than after sin, since grace would have been more plentiful then, "finding no hindrance to its entry in human nature," and consequently the meritorious deeds, of which grace is the principle, would have been greater as well.

However, explains Saint Thomas in ra/2, there is a perspective from which fallen man is in a better position to merit than he was before sin. Human nature is enfeebled by sin and as a result it encounters difficulty in performing meritorious deeds. This difficulty can be considered an advantage, not in terms, perhaps, of the actual deed accomplished, but in terms of its proportional value. There is a "proportional quantity" to merit that it reckoned according to the capacity of the one performing the meritorious deed and not according to the absolute value of the deed done. Man, enfeebled by sin, merits more proportionally ("secundum quantitatem operis proportionalem") than he would have in the state of original justice. In addition, insofar as there is something of a penal character to difficulty, such good deeds are also considered as satisfaction for sin.[8]

The sacramental system belongs to the present order of salvation in which, as we have seen, the permission to sin is a providential datum. The sacraments of the New Law, like the passion of Christ itself of which they are extensions, are prefigured in certain realities of Israel's religious experiences. In his discussion of the period of the Old Law in the prima secundae, Saint Thomas posits the principle that "the reasons for the figurative sacrifices of the Old Law are to be drawn from the true sacrifice of Christ."[9] In 102.3 ra/8 he explains the meaning of the sin-offering, which under certain circumstances was offered in the manner of a holocaust, as prefiguring the perfect satisfaction made by the immolation of Christ for the sins of all the people.[10] The sacraments of the Old Law, though more numerous, were ineffective since they, being mere figures, were separated from the New Law of grace.

The New Law

The true work of image-perfection and image-restoration is one of the gospel of grace. In the following tract, that of the New Law of grace in the prima secundae, Saint Thomas explains the principle of grace as it is a cause for merit, and the relationship of merit's work to that of satisfaction as the latter is ordained to remove the impediment of sin and its punishment with which fallen man is encumbered. The following text, 114.2 co/, clearly expresses how man, through merit and satisfaction, is disposed for his final goal of beatitude:

The state of man without grace may be thought of in two ways. The first is the state of intact nature, as it was in Adam before sin; the other is the state of spoiled nature, as it is in us before our restoration by grace. If, then, we have in mind man in the first of these states, there is only one ground on which he cannot merit eternal life by his purely natural gifts without grace. This is because man's merit depends on the divine preordination. Now in no case is a creature's act ordained by God to something surpassing the proportionate order of the power which is the principle and source of the act; for it is by an institution of divine Providence that nothing should act beyond its own power. But eternal life is a good which surpasses the proportionate order of created nature, since it even surpasses its knowledge and desire, according to the text of I Corinthians: "Eye has not seen, nor ear heard, nor has it entered into the heart of man." Thus it is that no created nature is a sufficient principle and source of an act which merits eternal life, unless there is provided in addition a supernatural gift, and this is called grace.

But if we have in mind man under sin, over and above this, there is a second ground, owing to the impediment of sin. For since sin is an offence to God which excludes the sinner from eternal life . . . no one in the

state of sin can merit eternal life without
first being reconciled to God and having his
sin forgiven, and this takes place through
grace. For it is not life but death that is
due to the sinner, according to the text of
Romans: "The wages of sin is death."[11]

In one of the responses, ra/3, Saint Thomas specifically adds that, given the impediment of sin, no one
can merit anything from God "without being reconciled
to him by making satisfaction" ("nisi ei satisfaciens
reconcilietur").

In the secunda secundae, where Saint Thomas
analyzes the particular steps that man takes in returning to God (as well as the misguided ones that turn
him away from him), the three traditional works of
satisfaction--almsgiving, fasting and prayer--are
discussed in connection with the respective virtues of
which they are a part. Prayer is an act of religion
and as such a potential part of justice. Fasting
is an act of abstemiousness and thereby attached to
temperance. Almsgiving is an act of charity through
the medium of mercy. In 32.1 ag/2, an objection is
posed that argues against almsgiving as an act of
charity since, as a work that accomplishes satisfaction, it should be considered a work of justice.
Saint Thomas's response in ra/2 resolves the objection
by recourse to the distinction between an act being
elicited by one virtue and commanded by another. He
also shows why each of the three traditional penitential practices, when employed as a means of satisfaction for sin, are incorporated into the worship of God
which is latria. Saint Thomas explains:

> There is no reason why an act which properly
> speaking belongs to the virtue which im-
> mediately elicits it should not also be
> attributed to another virtue, in the sense of
> being commanded by it and directed to that
> virtue's own end. And it is in this way that
> giving alms can be counted as a work of
> satisfaction, in the sense that our compas-
> sion for the wretched is directed towards
> satisfying for our sins. As well as this,
> the same act, when directed to appeasing God,
> assumes the character of sacrifice and so is
> commanded by the virtue of latria.[12]

The above texts of the Summa, taken from those places in the prima pars and the secunda pars where Saint Thomas speaks explicitly of satisfaction, include, at least indirectly, references to the stages of the Heilsgeschichte--from creation and fall through the old dispensation of figures and works to the New Law of grace and efficacious works. It is possible, as well, to discern in these texts traces of the exitus-reditus theme as it is employed by Saint Thomas to describe the Christian Heilseconomie. First, Saint Thomas points out what advantage--the disadvantages being all too clear--human nature, enfeebled by sin, possesses with respect to man's seeking his final goal of beatitude. The fact that the performance of good deeds is more difficult for sinful man is interpreted as an advantage precisely because of the potentially satisfactory character of activity which is difficult. Secondly, in the period of the old dispensation man's efforts at attaining his final goal are thwarted because they lack the perfect and efficacious mediation of Christ's satisfaction, merely prefigured in the rites of the Old Law. Thirdly, full image-restoration is possible only under the New Law of grace which is founded upon the perfect merit and satisfaction of the Redeemer. The satisfactory works of the members are shown to be related to the virtue of justice through its religious expression, latria. The restoration of the image of God in man is accomplished by the sacrifice of Christ the Priest to which the satisfactory works of the members, like prayer, fasting and almsgiving, are joined. It is in this sense that the theological clarification of Saint Thomas throws some light onto how the sacrifice of the cross satisfies the divine justice. God's justice is satisfied precisely by giving to him the worship, i.e., the works of satisfaction that are his due. Likewise these works of satisfaction are ordered to the accomplishment of God's salvific purpose, the restoration of all things in Christ, because they bring about in the life of the members who perform them in union with Christ, that progressive configuration to him which is the work of image-restoration.

In the following pages two groups of texts will be examined which explain more fully how Saint Thomas conceives of this work of image-restoration (and image-perfection) in each of the stages of salvation history. The first group, drawn from various sections of the Summa, describes the image of God in man at the various stages, i.e., creation, fall, old law and new law. Our attention is drawn to how Saint Thomas describes the inner dynamism of the image as it seeks to reach its perfection in beatitude. The second group of texts, drawn mostly from the <u>tertia pars,</u> sets forth the role of the sacraments as separated instruments of Christ's saving action under the new dispensation and as they are prefigured in the rites of the old dispensation.

The Image of God in Man at the Major Moments of the <u>Heilsgeschichte</u>

Creation

Creation is after the image of God.

There is found in Genesis 1:27: "God created man to his own image." Now it is by the soul that man is after God's image.[13]

Fall

Original sin reduces this image, by which man is made capable of knowing and loving God, to a mere vestige, to a state of enfeeblement and consequent frustration since, while fallen man retains his natural capacity to know and love God, he does so only with difficulty and without the possibility of achieving the full union in knowledge and love to which his rational nature, by reason of its very structure, draws him.

The unity of faith in the two covenants attests the unity of the end; for it has been said already that the object of the theological virtues, among which faith is included, is the last end. And yet the state of faith differs in the Old and in the New Law; for what they believed was going to happen, we believe has happened.[14]

All the differences which are proposed between the New Law and the Old rest on the difference between what is perfect and what is imperfect. For the precepts of any law are given in view of the active exercise of moral virtues. Now imperfect men, who do not yet have the stable habit of virtue, are drawn to the exercise of the virtues in a different way from those who are perfect in virtue. For those who do not yet have the stable habit of virtue are drawn to the

exercise of virtue by some extrinsic motive,
e.g., the threat of penalties, or the promise
of external rewards such as honour or riches
and so on. And therefore the Old Law, which
was given to the imperfect, i.e., to those
who had not yet obtained spiritual grace, was
called "the law of fear" inasmuch as it
induced men to observe its precepts by the
threat of various penalties; and it is said
to contain various temporal promises. Those
on the other hand who have moral virtue are
drawn to the exercise of virtuous actions for
the love of virtue, not on account of some
external penalty or reward. And so the New
Law, consisting primarily in spiritual grace
itself implanted in men's hearts, is called
"the law of love"; and it is said to contain
spiritual and eternal promises which are the
objects of virtue, especially charity. And
so men are drawn to them intrinsically, not
as to what is external to them but as to what
is their very own.[15]

Old Law

This Old Law period of preparation, ordered to
bring man to a personal awareness of his enfeeblement
and to appreciate the full implications of his frustrated natural desire for God, is a period of signs and
figures, mere shadows of the reality promised and
ineffective in terms of actually achieving it. Yet
because of the "unity of faith in the two covenants"
the Old Law was good, although imperfect.

There is no doubt that the Old Law was
good, for just as a doctrine is shown to
be true from the fact that it is in conformity with right reason, so too a law is
shown to be good from the fact that it is
in conformity with reason. The Old Law was
so conformed. . . .

The end to which divine law is directed is to
bring man to the attainment of his goal of
eternal happiness. Now any kind of sin
--not only acts performed in the external
sphere but internal ones too--constitutes an
obstacle to this end. This is why that which
is adequate for the completeness of human
law, namely, the prohibiting of offences and
the apportionment of penalties, is not

adequate for the completeness of the divine law. This latter is required to make man totally equipped to share in eternal happiness—something which can be achieved only by the grace of the Holy Spirit, for it is by this that "charity is poured into our hearts," which fulfills the requirements of the law. For, "the grace of God is eternal life." Now the Old Law was not able to confer this grace; that was reserved to Christ. This is why we find it stated: "The law was given through Moses, grace and truth come through Jesus Christ." It is for this reason, then, that the Old Law is indeed good, but, incompletely so: "The law made nothing perfect."[16]

New Law

The whole power of the New Law of grace perfects, by meritorious grace, the image of God in fallen man and restores it as well to a state of fitness for seeing God, by the grace-infused satisfactory actions which man performs:

> Now it is the grace of the Holy Spirit, given through faith in Christ, which is predominant in the law of the New Covenant and in which its whole power consists. So before all else the New Law is the very grace of the Holy Spirit, given to those who believe in Christ.[17]

> The Gospel Law involves two things. Primarily, it is the very grace of the Holy Spirit given inwardly. And in this respect the New Law does justify. As Augustine says: "There"—in the Old Covenant—"a law was set up externally, with which the unjust might be threatened; here"—in the New Covenant—"it is given internally, so that they may be justified by it." The other secondary aspect of the Gospel Law is found in the testimonies of the faith and the commandments which order human attachments and human actions. In this respect the New Law does not justify. So Paul says: "The letter kills, but the spirit gives life."[18]

> Thus even the Gospel letter kills unless the healing grace of faith is present within.[19]

Satisfactory works are healing only insofar as they are performed in accordance with the spirit of the New Law, that is to say, as they are performed in the course of living out a charity-directed life. They produce their effect of image-restoration, however, only because of God's gratuitous gift of justification and not because of the human effort involved.

> What falls under the merit of equivalence is that to which the motion of grace extends. Now the motion of any mover does not only extend to the final term of the movement but also to the whole development of the movement. Now the end-term of the movement of grace is eternal life, while the development of this movement takes place by growth in charity or grace. . . .[20]

> The desire with which one desires restoration after falling, and likewise the prayer for it, are called just because they tend towards justice. But this is not because they depend on justice by way of merit, but only on mercy.[21]

Satisfaction is a pleasing sacrifice offered to God in worship; it makes man pleasing to God in Christ. God's justice is appeased because the hidden plan of his wisdom to unite all things to himself in Christ is manifested in the community of Christ's members who are made just through satisfaction.

> What God seeks from our good works is not profit but glory, that is, the manifestation of his own goodness; this is what he seeks from his own works too. The reverence we show him is of advantage not to him but to us. And so we merit something from God, not as though he gained any advantage from our works but inasmuch as we work with a view to his glory.[22]

The Nature of Sacramental Mediation throughout the Heilsgeschichte

The role that Saint Thomas assigns to the sacramental system in each phase of the Heilsgeschichte is determined by his understanding of how man in the various "states" of redemption is able to move toward his final goal of beatitude.

State of original justice

In the state of original justice the sacraments played no role since man, prior to the original sin, had no need to be redeemed. The unsullied God-image in man was perfectly ordered toward its perfection in God ("ex rectitudine status illius"). Man's natural desire for God, of course, was unable to fulfill itself and thus

> in the state of innocence man had need of grace, although he did not need to attain to this grace through any visible signs but rather did so in a spiritual and invisible manner.[23]

The sacraments, inasmuch as they are sensible signs, were accordingly inappropriate. This is the case, explains Saint Thomas in 61.2 co/, not only as the sacraments are ordered to remedy sin, "but also inasmuch as they are designed for the perfecting of man's soul."

Original sin

The rectitude characteristic of the state of original justice is shattered by sin. Man is reduced to a state of enfeeblement that affects his ability, although not his capacity, to know God in faith; as well as his readiness, although not his capability to accomplish meritorious actions of justification. The movement towards God for fallen man, as he is encumbered by sin, is a difficult one; the aids that are given him in the sacraments of the Old Law, while more numerous than those of the New Law, are less expressive than the latter of the saving power of Christ to which they, in an indirect way, point.

> The state of the human race after sin and before Christ can be considered under two aspects, first from the point of view of the essential meaning of faith, and in relation to this it has always remained the same in the sense that it has always been through faith in the future coming of Christ that men have been justified.

> But we can consider the state of the human race under a different aspect, that namely of the greater or lesser intensity of sinfulness, and also of explicit knowledge of

Christ prevailing within it. For as the
years passed sin began to gain an increasing
hold upon man in virtue of the fact that as
human reason was darkened by sin the precepts
of the natural law were no longer adequate
to enable him to live aright, making it
necessary to define the precepts in the form
of a written law, and together with these to
institute certain sacraments of faith. It
was also necessary that as the years passed
the knowledge of faith should become increasingly explicit. For, as Gregory says, with
the passing of the years knowledge about God
grew and increased. Hence it was also
necessary under the Old Law to define certain
specific sacraments of the faith which men
had concerning the Christ who was to come.
And in fact these sacraments are related to
those which existed before the Law as that
which is determinate is related to that which
is indeterminate. For prior to the Law it
was not specifically laid down for man which
sacraments he should use, as it was laid down
by the Law. This was necessary both because
of the obscuring of the natural law and in
order that the signs in which the faith was
expressed might be more specific.[24]

Old dispensation

The sacraments of the Old Law, like the Law itself, served a useful and good purpose inasmuch as they
indicated to man the perfection of the Law that was to
be accomplished by Christ. There was a unity of faith
in Christ, as Saint Thomas observed, that united the
Old and the New Laws and accounted for the justification of the Old Testament saints. Indeed, one of the
Old Testament rites, circumcision, could be considered
as a sign of justifying faith, as Saint Thomas explains
in 62.6 ra/3, inasmuch as it specifically directed the
recipient toward the future redeemer. In 70.4 co/
Saint Thomas contrasts the efficacy and effects of
baptism with those of circumcision:

> We must say that in circumcision grace was
> bestowed, with all the effects of grace, but
> not in the same way as in baptism. In
> baptism grace is conferred by the power of
> the sacrament itself which it has insofar as
> it is an instrument of the already realized
> passion of Christ. Circumcision, on the

other hand, conferred grace insofar as it was a sign of faith in the coming passion of Christ in such a way that a man who accepted circumcision made profession of such a faith, an adult for himself and someone else for an infant. For this reason Saint Paul also says that "Abraham received the sign of circumcision, the seal of his justification by faith," because justification came from the faith signified and not from its sign, circumcision. Further, because it operates as an instrument of the power of the passion of Christ, baptism, but not circumcision, imprints a character which incorporates a person into Christ and bestows grace more abundantly than circumcision; a reality already present is more effective than a mere hope.[25]

However, despite their value as more or less representing that faith in the passion of Christ through which men are justified, "it is clear that the sacraments of the Old Law did not contain within themselves any power by which they could actively contribute to the conferring of justifying grace."[26] Saint Thomas again explains in 62.6 co/ how the sacraments of the Old Law played a role in the justification of the Old Testament saints:

The Fathers of old were justified by faith in the passion of Christ as we ourselves are. For the sacraments of the Old Law constituted a special kind of protestation of that faith inasmuch as they pointed to the passion of Christ and its effects.[27]

New law of grace

Sacraments and image-restoration

The sacraments of the New Law possess the full power to effect the saving work of God in man because they are instruments of the passion of Christ and consequently are ordained to the work of image-perfection, but primarily image-restoration, since they are subsequent to Christ's "having suffered" and not signs that he was "destined to suffer." Saint Thomas writes in 61.4/co:

234

Just as the fathers of old were saved through
faith in the Christ who was to come, so we
too are saved through faith in the Christ who
has already been born and suffered. Now
sacraments are the sort of signs in which the
faith by which man is justified is explicitly
attested, and it is right to have different
signs for what belongs to the past, the
present, or the future. For, as Augustine
says, the same reality is proclaimed in one
way when it is still to be achieved and in
another when it has already been so. So
too the very words _passurus_, "destined to
suffer," and _passus_, "having suffered," sound
different to our ears. Hence it is right
that in addition to the sacraments of the Old
Law which foretold realities that lay in the
future there are certain other sacraments in
the New Law to stand for realities which have
taken place in Christ in the past.[28]

Instruments of grace

The sacraments of the New Law are instruments of
the freely-given grace of the New Law. It is the grace
of God which ultimately accomplishes in man the work of
image-restoration, as it infuses the satisfactory
works, which the members of Christ undertake, with the
charity required to make such works of self-reformation
efficacious for disposing man for ultimate union with
God in knowledge and love.

Now it belongs to God alone to produce grace
in this way as its principal cause. For
grace is nothing else than a certain shared
similitude to the divine nature. This is
confirmed by the passage in II Peter which
runs: "He has given us most great and
precious promises, that by these you may be
made partakers of the divine nature."

An instrumental cause, on the other hand,
acts not in virtue of its own form, but
solely in virtue of the impetus imparted to
it by the principal agent. Hence the effect
has a likeness not to the instrument but
rather to that principal agent, as a bed does
not resemble the axe which carves it but
rather the design in the mind of the carpen-
ter. And this is the way in which the
sacraments of the New Law cause grace. For

235

it is by divine institution that they are
conferred upon man for the precise purpose of
causing grace in and through them. [29]

The sacraments are distinguished from the instrumental nature of the humanity of Christ insofar as
they, unlike it, are separated, not conjoined, to the
"principal efficient cause of grace."

Now there are two kinds of instruments, one a
separate instrument such as a staff, the
other a united instrument conjoined to the
principal agent such as a hand. And it is by
the conjoined instrument that the separate
instrument is moved as a staff is moved by
the hand. Moreover the principal efficient
cause of grace is God himself, and the
humanity of Christ stands to him in the
relation of a conjoined instrument, whereas a
sacrament stands in the relation of a separate one. Thus it is right that the power
to bestow salvation should flow from the
divinity of Christ through his humanity into
the actual sacraments. [30]

Expressions of worship

The significance which Saint Thomas attaches to
the efficacy of the grace of the sacraments is twofold.
It is ordered, especially in the case of baptism and
penance, to the accomplishment of the work of satisfaction, namely, image-restoration, and to the perfection
of the soul for the worship of God. There is a comple-
mentarity presented in the following text which insists
on the sacraments as instruments of the satisfactory
passion of Christ--granted that in the Eucharist this
is a secondary purpose--and at the same time placing
them in the larger and more complete plan of God's
saving work. There is, as has been noted, a theological reason which is the basis for asserting the
complementary relation between the two effects of
sacramental grace. The satisfactory works of the
members, as they are commanded by the virtue of latria,
become themselves the pleasing sacrifice of worship
which is offered to God in and through the efficacy of
Christ's passion. Thus Saint Thomas has no difficulty
in describing the effects of the sacramental system
in the pattern of Christian life as satisfactory and,
at the same time, expressive, both within formal
liturgical structures and outside of them, of the
worship owed by man to God.

Furthermore sacramental grace seems to be designed chiefly to produce two effects: First, it removes the defects of past sins inasmuch as the guilt of these endures even though the sinful acts are transitory. Second, sacramental grace is designed to perfect the soul in all that pertains to the worship of God in terms of the religion of the Christian life. Now from the arguments set forth above it is manifest that Christ delivered us from our sins chiefly through his passion, and that not merely by way of efficient causality or merit, but by way of satisfaction as well. Similarly through his passion he also inaugurated the rites of the Christian religion by "offering himself as an oblation and sacrifice to God." From this it is manifest that in a special way the sacraments of the Church derive their power from the passion of Christ and that it is through the reception of the sacraments that the power flowing from this becomes, in a certain way, conjoined to us. This is signified by the fact that from the side of Christ hanging on the Cross there flowed water and blood, the first of which pertains to baptism and the second to the Eucharist, these two being the greatest of the sacraments.[31]

The sacraments, then, derive their power from the passion of Christ, apart from whom neither the sacraments of the Old Law, which simply pointed out to men the faith that they must have in the future redeemer in order to be saved, nor those of the New Law, which actually are instruments of justification, have Christological meaning. "It is fitting," writes Saint Thomas in 62.5 co/, "that the power to bestow salvation (virtus salutifera) should flow from the divinity of Christ through his humanity into the actual sacraments."[32] Christ is the Ursakrament, the primary instrument which God uses to accomplish his saving plan. Accordingly the sacraments are modelled upon Christ--even their very structure of word-visible sign is suggestive of the ontological structure of the Word-man. Their operation, both in the period of the Old Law and in that of the New, is determined not only by the "state" of redemption in which, because of his sin, man was found to be, but by the way in which God, according to the dictates of his wisdom and his desire to remedy sin, was acting through Christ to accomplish his eternal plan to bring all men through faith and sacraments to their final goal of beatitude.

Tertia Pars: The Sacraments of Baptism and Penance

Saint Thomas's discussion of the sacraments of baptism and confirmation, of the Eucharist and penance, applies the principles established in his presentation of the general theology of the sacraments as these, in turn, are based upon his theological interpretation of the efficacy of Christ's satisfactory passion. This discussion, then, is one of the economy of salvation, not as it is realized chiefly in the moment of Christ's passion but in its extension of the work of the passion throughout time. As such, the treatment of the individual sacraments belongs to and is inserted into the speculative framework of the exitus-reditus in the same way that Saint Thomas's treatise on the mystery of Christ in the tertia pars belongs to and is inserted into that directive theological concept. In the final section of his chef-d'oeuvre Saint Thomas describes how the eternal plan of God to save all men, perfectly and sufficiently accomplished in the passion of Christ, extends to all those who are members of his Body.

The brief outline of the various stages of the historical exitus-reditus, presented above from the perspective of man's need for and ability to perform satisfactory works, is the precise perspective from which Saint Thomas's sacramental theology must be read in terms of its relationship to the general discussion of the Summa. Saint Thomas emphasizes this in 62.2 ra/2:

> Vices and sins are eliminated adequately so far as the present and the future are concerned in that through the virtues and gifts man is restrained from sinning. But with regard to sins of the past, the guilt of which remains even though the sinful acts are transitory, a special remedy is applied to man through the sacraments.[33]

Such is especially the case with baptism and penance. Therefore an examination of these sacraments, as treated by Saint Thomas, completes a study of his theology of satisfaction as it is ordered to explain the complete restoration of the God-image in man through the period of the New Law of grace.

The Sacrament of Baptism: Incorporation into Christ as Adopted Sons

The questions of the tertia pars which treat of baptism (66.-69.) and the preparation for baptism (70., 71.) discuss the special effect of this sacrament in terms of the sinful condition of man, in which it is administered, and with respect to the penalty due man for his sin. Significantly, the theme of Romans 6, that of adoptive sonship, is the biblical inspiration of Saint Thomas's theologizing in this treatise. It serves as well as a principle of coherence between the discussion of baptism (and the other sacraments as they are possible for man as a result of baptism) and the leitmotiv of the tertia pars and, inasmuch as the doctrine of adoptive sonship and that of the image of God are intrinsically related, the entire Summa.[34] Saint Thomas writes in 69.1 co/:

> As St Paul says: "All of us who have been baptized into Christ Jesus were baptized into his death." And later he concludes: "So you also must consider yourselves dead to sin and alive to God in Christ Jesus our Lord." It is evident from this that by baptism a man dies to the old life of sin and begins to live the newness of grace. But every sin pertains to the former old life. It follows then that every sin is taken away by baptism.[35]

There is, however, an effect of baptism which is unique to this sacrament, in contrast with those of the others; this is its effect with regard to the penalty due to sin. The sacraments of the New Law are said by Saint Thomas to "effect what they signify."[36] The sacramental washing of baptism is suggestive of the twofold effect that a physical washing has on the body—elimination of bodily stain (read: macula peccati) and bodily refreshment. The special effect of baptism is the removal of the entire debt to undergo punishment (reatus poenas) or, to complete the metaphor, to give refreshment to one's soul which results from its being absolved from punishment. Such a teaching does not stand in opposition to Saint Thomas's basic principle of satisfaction, namely that by it the work of image-restoration is accomplished in man. (It should be noted that the sacramental water of baptism is said to refresh [refrigerat] as well as wash away [abluit].) Satisfaction as image-restoration is, as we have seen, at the heart of Saint Thomas's theology of satisfaction and at the core of his explanation as to why God allows suffering in the world as the necessary material, so to speak, for satisfactory works. The theological reason given by Saint Thomas to explain the special effect of baptism is perfectly consistent with his doctrine of image-restoration since it is based on his understanding of the "quasi" one person that is constituted by Christ and his members.

Against the background of the doctrine of the Mystical Body, the text of 69.2 (especially ra/1) must be read as a very important one. It not only relates the special effect of baptism, as to the full remission of the punishment due to sin, to the sufferings of Christ the Head but also dispels all suspicions that Saint Thomas interprets the nature of that relationship in a minimal way. The existential effects of satisfaction, that is, the ever-necessary work of self-reformation that must go on in the believer as his soul is gradually configured to that of Christ and thus to God, are de facto accomplished by baptism precisely because of that union of the member with the perfectly-formed image of the suffering Christ. Saint Thomas writes in 69.2 ra/1:

> Since the one baptized, inasmuch as he becomes a member of Christ, participates in the pain of the passion of Christ just as if he himself suffered that pain, his sins are thus set in order by the pain of Christ's passion.[37]

No mere moral union between Christ and his members, nor a theory of imputation of the effects of Christ's merits to those who of themselves would be unable to lay claim to beatitude, would be adequate to explain this kind of participation by the members in the passion of Christ. It is such a participation--and the cause is always known from its effects--that accounts for the special effect of baptism as Saint Thomas describes in the reply to the same article, 62.2:

> A person is incorporated into the passion and death of Christ through baptism: "If we have died with Christ we believe that we shall also live with him." It is clear from this

that to everyone baptized the passion of
Christ is communicated for his healing just
as if he himself had suffered and died. But
the passion of Christ is sufficient satisfaction for all the sins of all men. Therefore
the one who is baptized is freed from the
debt of all punishment due to him for his
sins, just as if he himself had sufficiently
made satisfaction for all his sins.[38]

Although the newly-baptized member is himself
freed from the debt of penalty for sin he is, as was
explained above,[39] inescapably involved with those who,
by reason of their post-baptismal sins, are so burdened
with penalty for sin. In addition, the special effect
of baptism does not fully extend to the body of the
believer in Christ (except insofar as the state of the
soul's innocence is communicated to the body of which
it is the form). The special effect would, however, be
fully manifest in the believer's body should such a one
die immediately after baptism, in which case, as Saint
Paul teaches, "the mortal puts on immortality."[40]
Saint Thomas explains this particular ordination of
divine providence as reasonable in the light of the
untoward consequences which would result if baptism
actually effected a premature exaltation of the member's body as well as the purification of his soul.
One such consequence would be the obvious attraction
that such an effect would be for a falsely motivated
reception of the sacrament. Another such consequence,
a positive reason for God's ordination of baptism's
effects, is that man is made aware of the need for
continual spiritual training (spirituale exercitium) by
the presence of the inclinations to sin within himself.
It must be observed, however, that the invitation to
perform spiritual exercises is a result of, and not a
means to, the attainment of the full benefits of
Christ's passion which the soul receives in baptism.
It is because of God's love for the creature, manifested in the passion of Christ, that man is moved
to perform spiritual works of any kind and not the
creature's spiritual exercises which obtain for him the
love of God.[41]

The principal reason, however, why the penalties
of the present life are not entirely removed by baptism
is explained by Saint Thomas in 69.3 co/ in terms
of the process of configuration to Christ which it
accomplishes in the member. Saint Thomas explains this
in the first of the three reasons given in the text:

> Because by baptism a man is incorporated into
> Christ and becomes one of his members, . . .
> it is therefore fitting that what took place
> in the head should also take place in the
> member incorporated with the head. But
> Christ, although from the first moment of his
> conception he was full of grace and truth,
> nevertheless had a body subject to suffering
> which through suffering and death was raised
> to a life of glory. So also a Christian in
> baptism acquires grace in his soul and yet
> has a body subject to suffering in which he
> may be able to suffer for Christ; but he will
> finally be raised to a life without suffer-
> ing. In this regard, St Paul says: "He who
> raised Christ Jesus from the dead will give
> life to your mortal bodies also through his
> Spirit which dwells in you." Later he adds:
> "Heirs indeed of God and fellow heirs with
> Christ, provided we suffer with him in order
> that we may also be glorified with him."[42]

This is an extremely significant text because of its
ramifications for the full understanding of Saint
Thomas's doctrine of the Mystical Body and because of
the parallel that is drawn between the life of Christ
and the life of the members. Christ the Head, who
possesses the fulness of grace by nature, is the model
for the baptized member who possesses the grace of
adoptive sonship yet is capable as well, of suffering
by reason of his human condition and his presence in
the world. The sinless Christ's ability to suffer
allowed him to make the perfect satisfaction; the
member's suffering--even that of the newly-baptized
members--allows him to maintain in himself the fruit
of that satisfaction which is the perfect restoration
of his God-image and the right of such a person so
perfected to attain beatitude. The baptized Christian
possesses, to the extent that he preserves his baptismal innocence, the full life of "the grace of the
Holy Spirit and [of the] abundance of gifts and virtues
which are given in baptism"[43] just as Christ his
head possessed from the moment of his conception a life
filled with grace and with truth.

This parallel between the Son and the adopted
sons is at the center of the mystery that explains why
the members must follow in the path of Christ from
suffering to exaltation. The Christian's life of
spiritual exercises is his movement, under the God-
centered impulses of final causality, from the origin

of that movement, which is God, to the term of the movement, which is God. The adage of Saint Theresa of Avila reflects Saint Thomas's doctrine in this regard: "To be on the way to heaven is heaven itself."[44] To know the reason why suffering is still a part of the sinless baptized soul is to approach the mystery of why the sinless Christ suffered for our sins. The reason and the result are perhaps the same mystery: suffering in Christ and in his members is no longer punishment but the manifestation of God's wisdom and justice in the recapitulation of the entire created order (of which the infra-human part, as Saint Paul teaches, "groans" too)[45] in Christ.

The text of 69.5 co/ is a clear summary of the work of image-perfection, looked at from its global perspective, which baptism accomplishes. Incorporation of the member into Christ results in the _illuminatio_ of the soul, as contrasted with the sinful soul's deprivation of that divine splendor, and in the _fecundatio_ of the soul, as contrasted with the sterility of the vestigial image left in man by sin. Saint Thomas develops this point in his reply:

> By baptism a person is reborn in the life of the spirit which is proper to the faithful of Christ, as St Paul says: "The life I now live in the flesh I live by faith in the Son of God." But there is no life if the members are not united to the head from which they receive feeling and motion. Thus it is necessary that a person be incorporated by baptism into Christ as a member of him. But as feeling and motion flow from the natural head to the members, so from the spiritual head, which is Christ, there flow to his members spiritual feeling, which is the knowledge of truth, and spiritual motion, which results from the impulse of grace. Thus John says: "We have beheld him full of grace and truth, and of his fullness we have all received." It follows that the baptized are enlightened by Christ in the knowledge of truth and made fruitful by him in the fruitfulness of good works by the infusion of grace.[46]

The full realization of this state of image-perfection, as it is possessed by the baptized member of Christ, is not possible, however, as was pointed out above,[47] apart from the properly satisfactory effect

of Christ's passion which is image-restoration.
"Baptism causes the opening of the gates of heaven,"
writes Saint Thomas in 69.7, "because the obstacle to
that opening is removed by the passion of Christ."[48]
This is the same obstacle that would have prevented the
member from beholding the full vision of God's grace
and truth in the beatific vision, had not Christ
made satisfaction for sin. It is unquestionably a
key-notion of Saint Thomas's sacramental theology that
the sacraments are participations in the satisfactory
character of Christ's passion, as satisfaction is the
key-notion of the passion itself. Saint Thomas's
discussion of the place of each of the seven sacraments
in the various dimensions of the Christian's life, as
they perfect those dimensions, is not a reason for
judging otherwise. The perfect effect of the passion
of Christ, as regards the work of image-perfection,
is only possible in the actual order of salvation,
because of the satisfaction which that passion accomplished. It is the satisfaction of Christ which opens
the gates of heaven and admits those who even before
Christ "had charity and the grace of the Holy Spirit"[49]
along with all who are made perfect in Christ to the
spiritual and eternal promise of beatitude.

The Sacrament of Penance: Spiritual Medicine for Prodigal Sons

The full development of the sacramental theology
of Saint Thomas as a theology of satisfaction appears
in his unfinished treatise on the sacrament of penance.
The role of penance in the life of the baptized member
of the Body of Christ is, as is the case with all of
the sacraments, a manifestation of God's providence
which, in the case of penance, provides not only for
spiritual rebirth through baptism but also for the
contingency that a baptized member would require
a remedy for sin committed after baptism. This contingency arises as a result of man's radical freedom of
choice that is never obliterated by divine grace and
from the post-baptismal condition of human nature from
which, as we have seen,[50] concupiscence is not entirely
eradicated.

Penance is described as a medicine inasmuch as it
provides a sacramental remedy for a prodigal son, one
who has turned away from God by sin, rather than, under
the impulse of the virtues and the gifts (spiritual
exercises), maintained the perfected image of sonship
received in baptism. Penance, then, is ordained to

restore the dignity of soul, lost by sin, in which adoptive sonship principally consists. Saint Thomas explains this in 89.3 co/:

> Through sin a man loses before God a double dignity. The first and principal one is that by which "he is numbered among the children of God" through grace. This dignity is recovered through repentance, as is indicated when the father commanded the restoration of the "best robe, ring and shoes" to his prodigal son.[51]

Accordingly the purposes of baptism and penance are different ones in the single plan of God's salvation for men. Saint Thomas explains this difference in terms of the number of times that each sacrament may be received in 84.10 ra/5:

> Baptism has its power from Christ's passion as a kind of spiritual rebirth from the spiritual death of a previous life. Moreover, "it is appointed unto men once to die" and to be born once. And, therefore, man ought to be baptized but once. But penance has its power from Christ's passion as a spiritual medicine, which can frequently be repeated.[52]

The efficacy of penance, as that of each of the sacraments, is derived from the passion of Christ; its necessity, however, unlike baptism's, is a conditional one, namely, given the supposition of mortal sin. It is mortal sin, the prime analogue of sin for Saint Thomas,[53] that destroys the bond of charity and friendship with God which baptismal grace had established in the soul of the member. Mortal sin, and the tarnished God-image which it produces in man's soul, is simply man's free choice to break off the personal relationship with God that his saving initiative made possible and accomplished in the free gift of baptism. As such, it makes penance necessary to restore the image, as Saint Thomas explains in 84.5, summarizing in the process the res et sacramentum of this sacrament:

> A thing is necessary for salvation in two ways, first, absolutely; second, conditionally. That is absolutely necessary without which no one can obtain salvation; examples are the grace of Christ, and the sacrament of baptism through which one is born again in

Christ. The sacrament of penance, in turn, is necessary conditionally: indeed, it is needed, not by all, but by those in sin.

Now as James says: "Sin, when it is completed, begets death." And therefore it is necessary for the salvation of the sinner that his sin be taken away. This, indeed, cannot take place without the sacrament of penance, in which the power of Christ's passion works through the absolution of the priest, together with the action of the penitent who cooperates with grace for the destruction of sin. As St. Augustine says: "He who has created you without yourself will not make you just without yourself." So then it is clear that the sacrament of penance is necessary for salvation after sin just as bodily medicine is needed should a man have fallen seriously ill.[54]

Penance is a sacrament which properly belongs to the New Law of grace since the effect (<u>res tantum</u>) of penance is only possible because of the passion of Christ, and also because the power to forgive sins, the power of the keys, is one conferred through the mediation of the hierarchical, institutional Church. It is the suffering of Christ's passion, however, which primarily accounts for the fact that the natural impulse in man to be sorry for culpable fault, penitence, can be drawn up into and transformed by the grace of a sacrament of the New Law. Saint Thomas relies upon the New Testament account of the institution of this sacrament to explain the place of penance in the life of the believer. He writes in 84.7 co/:

From natural reason man is prompted to repent of the evils which he has done. It is of divine institution, however, that a man should do penance in this or that way. Hence, in the beginning of his own preaching, Our Lord commanded men not only to repent but also "to do penance," signifying definite kinds of acts required for this sacrament. But he determined that which belongs to the office of the ministers when he said to Peter: "And I will give to you the keys of the kingdom of heaven," etc. Then he manifested the efficacy of this sacrament and the origin of its power after the resurrection, when he said, "It behoved . . . that penance and remission of sins be preached in his name unto all nations." He prefaced this by speaking of his passion and resurrection; for, by reason of the name of the suffering and risen Christ, this sacrament had its effectiveness for the forgiveness of sins. And so it is clear that this sacrament was properly instituted in the New Law.[55]

Penance, unlike baptism, imposes a satisfaction (a determined one) for sin. This satisfaction undertaken by the penitent is not his way of cooperating with the grace of the sacrament, as a cart cooperates with a donkey to pull a load. Rather it is the actual living-out of the image-restorative work that has been accomplished in the sacrament and which man is able to perform meritoriously precisely because of, and not in addition to, God's grace. Saint Thomas contrasts, in 86.4 ra/3, the effects of baptism and penance in terms of how each sacrament effects the remission of punishment due to sin:

> Christ's passion is sufficient of itself to remove all debt of punishment, not only eternal but also temporal. And according to the way a man shares in the power of Christ's passion he also receives absolution from the debt of punishment. Now in baptism man shares wholly in the power of Christ's passion, in that through water and the Spirit he becomes one dead to sin with Christ and in Christ born again unto a new life. So then in baptism a person finds release from the debt of all punishment. In the sacrament of penance, however, one benefits by the power of Christ's passion according to the measure of the personal acts which are the matter of penance as water is the matter of baptism . . . And therefore the debt of all punishment is not taken away at once with the first act of repentance by which sin is pardoned but only with the fulfillment of all the penitential acts.[56]

While satisfactory acts are the ordinary way in which man "cooperates" with the sacramental grace of penance, God is not thereby restricted by the ordinations of his own providence. The all-sufficient satisfaction of Christ's passion, as Saint Thomas explains in 86.5 ra/1, is able to effect an immediate healing in man:

God heals the whole man completely. Sometimes he does this all at once, as he restored the mother-in-law of Peter to perfect health, so that "rising up she ministered to him." But sometimes he does this little by little, as was said of the blind man whose sight was restored. So also spiritually, sometimes he converts the heart of man with such great force that in an instant he attains perfect spiritual health, with not only pardon for sin but also with the eradication of all sin's remnants, as was the case with Mary Magdalene. Sometimes, however, he first forgives sin through operating grace; and afterwards, through cooperating grace, he takes away sin's after-effects little by little.[57]

The importance of this text is to indicate that, while justification is never bestowed on man apart from his free choice to accept it,[58] the perfecting of the initial grace of justification can be and sometimes is accomplished apart from man's "cooperative" efforts, though never apart from his continued attention to the kind of life that is required--one of "spiritual exercises"--in order to maintain the perfect God-image of the justified soul.

In the ordinary way of divine providence the actual living out of a grace-filled life (gratia co-operans), realized through the sacramental satisfactions of penance, is in effect the same way of life for the prodigal member as that described as necessary for the newly-incorporated member in terms of the practice of "spiritual exercises." Both ways, that of satisfaction and that of "spiritual exercise," are ordered to maintain, and--in the case of satisfaction--to restore, the image of God in the soul of the member of Christ. The significant difference between the two is that the personal satisfactory acts that are attached to penance are the transformations of punishment justly owed by the prodigal member, whereas the newly-baptized member's sufferings are explained only in terms of a more direct reference to the mystery of suffering and sonship, since such a person, through baptism's special effect, is more closely configured to the innocent suffering Son.

The healing and restorative effects of penance and satisfaction ordinarily extend throughout a life-time of personal salvation history although, as explained above, God could restore a tarnished image in a single instant. Saint Thomas describes, in 86.4, the process of the living-out of a charity-ordered life in terms of the different ways which grace works in the interplay of divine causality and human free agency. Grace is the principle of charity in man and, according to a traditional division, can be spoken of as "operating grace" (gratia operans) and "co-operating grace" (gratia co-operans). Saint Thomas employs this distinction to distinguish the two moments in the justification of a sinner, as that act of divine grace removes the debt of punishment incurred by the sinner's willful turning from him. He writes in 86.4 ra/2:

> Grace in man is operating with regard to his justification and co-operating with regard to his living rightly. Therefore, pardon for sin and guilt of eternal punishment is the work of operating grace; but the release of the burden of temporal punishment, that of co-operating grace, in the sense, namely, that with the help of divine grace a person is absolved from the debt of temporal punishment also because of bearing suffering patiently. Therefore, just as the effect of operating grace comes before the effect of co-operating grace, so also the remission of sin and of eternal punishment comes before the full release from temporal punishment. Each is from grace, but the first is from grace alone, the other from grace and free will.[59]

This is an important text for its emphasis on the personal destructiveness of sin and the subsequent personal restoration accomplished by satisfaction. The fruit of man's freely choosing the disorder of sin is the temporal punishment which he incurs (the debt of eternal punishment having been removed by the sacrament itself). In the sacramental satisfactions which are attached to penance the penitent freely chooses to unite himself with Christ's satisfaction and to live out the ever-necessary work of self-reformation, all of which is accomplished under the continued impulse of grace. The fruit of satisfaction is the healing in his very person of the disorders that arise from an untoward attachment to some created good.

Such a personal interpretation of satisfaction is unequivocally supported by Saint Thomas's description, in 90.1-4, of the integral parts of penance, that is,

those things which are required for a complete act of
penitence and its subsequent sacramentalization in
penance. Saint Thomas writes of satisfaction which,
along with contrition and confession, makes up the
whole of the sacrament of penance: "For here in
penance not only is the restoration of the balance of
justice sought, as in retributive justice, but above
all (magis) the reconciliation of friendship."[60]
This is the work of image-restoration as it is carried
out in the works of satisfaction, which the priest,
possessor of the power of the keys, assigns to the
penitent who has confessed with his lips the sins
for which he is sorry in his heart. Because the
performance of the satisfaction forms an integral part
of the sacrament, the interior acceptance of the
satisfaction imposed and the performance of it is a
channel of sacramental grace. The sacrament of penance
(sacramentum tantum) is the union of the priest's words
of absolution with the acts of a penitent, contrite,
confessing and willing to make satisfaction.

It is possible to conceive of the work of image-
restoration from the perspective of the one who accepts
the New Testament's call to believe and repent as
passing through a threefold stage of development. This
development is measured by the changes of heart,
conversion in the ordinary English sense of the term,
immutatio, or a change within man in Saint Thomas's
terminology, that may occur in one who is on the way to
salvation. Saint Thomas describes these steps in
reference to the virtue of penitence, which is the
predisposition for a faith-filled reception of penance
(or in the case of an adult, of baptism as well) whose
fruit is the justification (res tantum) of the member.
Saint Thomas describes the three major moments in the
ordinary course of an individual's personal salvation
history in 90.4:

> This change of heart is threefold. The first
> is by rebirth to a new life. This is the
> concern of the repentance preceding baptism.
> The second is by reforming after a life
> that has been ruined by sin. This is the
> objective of repentance for mortal sins
> committed after baptism. The third change is
> towards living a more holy life. This
> engages the repentance for venial sins, which
> are pardoned through any fervent act of
> charity.[61]

The virtue of penitence, even when elevated into the sacramental order and consequently endowed with the power of the sacramental application of Christ's passion, as described above, remains a virtue attached to justice "because the penitent grieves over sin committed as it is an offense against God and because he has the purpose of amendment."[62] As such it belongs to the species of justice which is commutative justice since it governs relations between non-equals, in this case between God and man. The fact that penitence is a virtue which gives to God the justice which is his due does not imply that it is a theological virtue; penitence has for its matter and objective that which is just and not God himself. Satisfactory works as they are the fruit of penitence and as they are joined to the sacramental efficacy of penance are, then, properly speaking, works of justice.

Nonetheless, there is a wider significance to penitence and the satisfactory works which it elicits by reason of the fact that these works play a directive role in man's relationship to other men and to God. The fruits of penitence are, as it were, brought into contact with all of the other theological and moral virtues, as Saint Thomas explains in 85.3 ra/4:

> Although penitence is directly a species of justice, nevertheless in a fashion it includes what belongs to all virtues. For inasmuch as it is a kind of justice governing man's relationship with God it must join with the theological virtues which have God for their object. Hence penance is associated with faith in Christ's passion through which we are justified from sins, with hope of pardon and with hatred of sin which belongs to charity.

> Inasmuch as it is a moral virtue it shares in prudence which directs all moral virtues. From its very nature, being a kind of justice, its concern is not only with what belongs directly to justice, but also with what belongs to temperance and to fortitude, namely, inasmuch as the pleasurable things for temperance to deal with or the frightening things for fortitude to moderate become matters required in justice. In this way, both to abstain from delights according to temperance and to sustain hardships according to fortitude, belong to justice.[63]

The Satisfaction of Divine Justice:
Restoration of all Things
in Christ

It is not an exaggeration to say that, according to Saint Thomas's conception, satisfactory works play a central role in the life of the Christian and especially in the life of the prodigal member of Christ's body. Satisfaction is the offering to God of something that is his due, and thus it is worship, as Saint Thomas indicates in his treatise on the priesthood of Christ. The member who shares in that priesthood by his configuration to the person of Christ offers such a pleasing sacrifice as well by uniting his sufferings, whereby they become satisfactory, to those of the head. It is this notion of satisfaction as pleasing sacrifice which is, in a certain aspect, the consummation of Saint Thomas's theology of satisfaction.

It is highly significant, then, that in his discussion of the Eucharist, to which he assigns a primacy among the other sacraments of the New Law, the notion of satisfaction appears as an effect of that sacrament. The Eucharist as sacrament was not primarily instituted for the remission of sins but for the member's spiritual nourishment through union with Christ and his members. The faith with which the Eucharist is celebrated and received is a measure of the faith of the members in the passion of Christ and a sign, as well, of the charity produced by the sacrament in their souls. Charity and sin are incompatible and thus Saint Thomas speaks of a concomitant principal effect of the Eucharist as the partial remission of sin in the member proportionate to the fervor and devotion, that is, the faith, with which it is received.

However, if one considers the Eucharist as a sacrifice, subordinated to the sacrificing Christ, it does have the power, shared by all sacrifices, of making satisfaction for sin, as Saint Thomas explains in 79.5 co/:

> Considered as a sacrifice, however, it has the power of rendering satisfaction. In this the affection of the offerer is counted more than the size of the offering, as our Lord said of the widow who offered two coins that "she has put in more than all." Although the offering of the Eucharist suffices of its own quantity to satisfy for all punishment,

> nevertheless, it renders satisfaction for those for whom it is offered, and also for those who offer it, according to the amount of their devotion, and not for the whole penalty.[64]

The fact that a part and not the whole of the punishment due to sin is pardoned is explained, in ra/3, in terms of a defect in man's devotion and not in Christ's power. This is the work of Christ the Priest as he offers himself for the satisfaction of man's sins and as he communicates that satisfaction, in the primary sacramental representation of his passion, to his members.

There is undoubtedly a juridical aspect to the theology of redemption. In the Sentences, as has been seen, this perspective is more prominent in Saint Thomas's understanding of the satisfaction of Christ. The theological tradition launched by the Cur Deus homo? is unquestionably a large part of the explanation for this early emphasis on justice in Saint Thomas's theology. It is true, however, that in the Summa, despite the radical change of theological perspective, as evidenced in the entire theological synthesis of image-perfection and image-restoration, that is, the directive-concept of exitus-reditus, there remain references to satisfaction that are decidedly juridical. The very mode of salvation as redemption, as a "buying back," with satisfaction referred to as a "price" paid, is but one indication of this; another is the numerous references to Christ's having justly ransomed his members from servitude, even from a servitude to the devil. Are these references to be considered as so many untidy bits remaining from an earlier theological period which Saint Thomas has failed to integrate into the new and superior synthesis of the Summa?

It seems that such is not the case. The treatise on the priesthood of Christ together with its emphasis on the justice of the act of worship, latria, that Christ the priest offers to his Father is a key treatise for Saint Thomas's incorporation of whatever there is of justice in the theology of redemption into his general theological scheme based on divine final causality. Saint Thomas, then, draws up the juridical notion of redemption--and continuity with the Old Testament revelation concerning the wrath of God must be considered as a motive for this as well--into a harmonious understanding of God's justice as a manifestation of, and not separated from, the divine goodness. The very notion of commutative justice, that which exists between members of a family, is quite central to this synthesis, as Saint Thomas explains in 85.3. One is struck by the emphasis on familial relationships which Saint Thomas, in imitation of the New Testament, employs to speak of God, who wants not so much to punish (vindictive justice) his prodigal children as to bring them into union with himself through the means of sacramental satisfaction and the power of Christ's passion which lies behind it. In 85.3 he writes of penitence:

> It is this sort of being that enters into penitence, and it is thus that the penitent turns to God, with the purpose of amendment, . . . as the son to his father according to Luke: "Father, I have sinned against heaven, and before you."[65]

In all of this the priesthood of Christ is of central import since it is by reason of God's only Son and his perfect worship of the Father that such a union with God is possible for all of God's prodigal, adoptive sons.

> For all alike have sinned, and are deprived of the divine splendour, and all are jus-tified by God's free grace alone, through his act of liberation in the person of Christ Jesus. For God designated him to be the means of expiating sin by his sacrificial death, effective through faith. God meant by this to demonstrate his justice, because in his forbearance he had overlooked the sins of the past—to demonstrate his justice now in the present, showing that he is himself just and also justifies any man who puts his faith in Jesus.[66]

CONCLUSION

The present study has been an exercise in historical theology. In such an exercise, careful attention must be paid to both terms of the phrase "historical theology." If this work has succeeded in illuminating the historical fact of development in Saint Thomas's soteriological teaching on Christ's satisfaction, its purpose has not been simply to ascertain and interpret a body of historical data. Rather, beyond the rendering of judgments of historical fact, the author has been mindful of a larger and properly theological aim: to render valuable and distinctive elements of Saint Thomas's teaching in this regard available to contemporary discussion of Christ's saving work.

Materially speaking, the study has traced an arc of development from a juridically construed understanding of Christ's satisfactory work in Saint Thomas's Scriptum super Sententias to a thoroughly personalist understanding established in the Summa theologiae. Indeed, as Chapter Two argued, a personalist inspiration was never utterly absent from Saint Thomas's reflection on Christ's saving work, as the biblical commentaries surveyed in that chapter witnessed. However, this inspiration does not actually or predominantly determine the account of satisfaction which Saint Thomas renders in his earliest work of theological synthesis, the Scriptum. For there, as indicated in Chapter Three, the Aristotelian understanding of virtue and the definitions of Anselm and pseudo-Augustine prevail, with the result that the notion of satisfaction is largely construed as an act of penitence. Only once Saint Thomas freed himself from the limitations of theological method and of the Auctoritates of Peter Lombard in works of original systematization such as the Summa contra gentiles did personalist categories (and above all, the pivotal role of the surpassing charity informing Christ's human will) begin to emerge. This trajectory is closely associated with a broader theological understanding of justice as it figures in the account Saint Thomas gives of satisfaction. For alongside the Aristotelian model of justice is set an "evangelical" understanding of justice, one which Saint Thomas never fully succeeded in relating to the Aristotelian model. Both share the

255

ratio of rectus ordo or rectitudo, but the latter more
clearly indicates that the performance of the just deed
proceeds on a prior divine initiative and that it
consists formally in the subordination of the human
person and his destiny to God in love. It is this same
evangelical justice which is the inner motive of
Christ's satisfactory work and to the restoration of
which that work is directed. What is an emerging trend
in Saint Thomas's first original works of synthesis is
consolidated in his account of Christ's satisfactory
work in the Summa theologiae, as examined in some
detail in Chapter Five, and that determines the several
personalist relevances of satisfaction to individual
destiny and communal salvation-history, as suggested in
Chapter Six.

Beyond the historical ascertainment of the fact of
development in Saint Thomas's satisfaction-model,
however, the author is convinced that this development
constitutes a significant enrichment of the soteriological tradition and a precious legacy for the ongoing
work of theological revision as well. Indeed, this
enrichment consists preeminently in a systematic
employment of a style of thinking that may rightly be
called "personalist" and one that also exhibits the
rudiments of a sense of human historicity. The results
of the present study suggest that Saint Thomas's
overall theological vision as expressed in the Summa
theologiae can illuminate certain issues of moment for
contemporary soteriology in such wise that, if the term
"satisfaction" cannot be restored to current usage,
then certainly the substance of Saint Thomas's understanding of satisfaction can and should be.

In the first place, the central elements of
explanation which Saint Thomas employed in his account
of Christ's satisfactory work are those which are at
the heart of the whole enterprise of theology as he
understood and practiced it in the Summa theologiae and
which provide that enterprise with remarkable systematic unity. For, as we noted earlier in this work, it
is to an account of salvation-history as enacted in
Christ in the tertia pars that Saint Thomas's theological exercise is directed as to an end. Once that goal
has been attained, its intelligibility should be
allowed to cast its light back upon the preceding
moments of explanation—as it were, retroactively
determining prior intelligibilities.

In Saint Thomas's view, the divine reality is distinguished as sheer subsistent _esse_, which is identically subsistent understanding and loving. The persons of the Father, the Son, and the Holy Spirit communing in the divine nature are both distinguished and constituted by relations of mutual opposition within acts of knowing and loving. Yet some of the richness and originality of Saint Thomas's trinitarian theology is lost if their communion is regarded as being only at the ontic level, at the level of the intelligibility of the common divine nature. For their communion is personal as well, insofar as each of the subsistent relations constitutive of the persons is also a subject of the notional acts of knowledge and love. The three persons communing in the divine nature do so in that nature as distinct subjects of an identical consciousness and love.

By divine condenscension, human reality has been created in order to enter into communion with the fellowship of the divine persons—a destiny that is strictly supernatural. The openendedness of the human intellect and of human love is, as it were, the negative condition for the achievement of this supernatural destiny. This basic human constitution aptitudinally images the personal communion of Father, Son and Holy Spirit in knowledge and love. What is only a trajectory impressed upon human nature is terminated and fulfilled by the gracious conferral of resources proportionate to a supernatural destiny of communion: habitual grace and the theological virtues. By the former, the human person is transformed so as to share in the divine nature; by the latter, a share in the divine knowing and loving is conferred. Thus, the merely aptitudinal imaging of the three divine persons coincident with human nature itself is achieved as and elevated to be an actual imaging of the three divine persons as regards both their communion in the divine nature and their personal communion in knowledge and love. It should be noted, then, that the image of the three divine persons is actualized in precisely those dimensions of consciousness and free self-determination through love that also constitute the _ratio_ of human historicity.

When Saint Thomas places basic human constitution in the context of history, he enters upon his account of salvation-history—the history of the original conferral, loss through sin, and restoration of the actual imaging of the personal communion of the Father, the Son, and the Holy Spirit. To Adam personally were given habitual grace and supernatural endowments of knowledge and love; to human nature as it existed in Adam was accorded the gift of original justice, consisting in an integration of human energies as focused upon God. The sin of Adam resulted in the loss of the resources for supernatural communion with the divine persons (and thus, for actually imaging their communion in fellowship with them) and incurred as well objective guilt and proportionate punishment for human nature as generated by Adam. To this fault of nature, personal moral fault has been added by human historical agencies, attended by guilt and punishment on its own account. Thus, in Saint Thomas's view, the human need for salvation requires both a dealing with sin and its attendant guilt and punishment as the cloture of a destiny of personal communion as well as a restoration of those supernatural endowments in whose acts the perfect imaging of the fellowship of and with the Trinity consists.

Copresent with the tragedy of human history in the divine intelligence is its merciful remedy. Before all time the human history of Jesus Christ as head and salvific focus of historical humanity has been predestined; in that human history and destiny all human histories have been actively saved. The termination of that election of Christ's human history in the plenitude of grace and of all supernatural gifts constitutes Christ as historical head of humankind. Christ's is to be the first human history, the first consistent deployment of supernatural knowing and loving to perfectly image divine personal communion within God. What in Adam was to be the endowment of human nature upon the supposition of his personal obedience to God becomes in an excelling mode a gift made to that nature insofar as it is the human nature assumed by the Word and rendered obedient through his human freedom. He who in the depths of the divine reality is the perfect image expressed by the Father and together with the Father breathes forth personal love as the bond of fellowship replicates this divine communion within the medium of his humanity and his human history for our sakes.

In Saint Thomas's view, a particular expression of divine love and justice is showing mercy, and it is this condescension that accounts for the incarnation and actively shapes all that transpires in the human intellect and will of Christ. To the human will of Christ God communicates the fullness of supernatural love as a capital endowment, such that his love for the

Father should be both abounding love for us and the love of the Father on behalf of the members of his Body. Thus rectified by charity, the human will of Christ fulfills the divine justice--that is, performs the substance of Adam's original establishment in justice: a complete submission and subjection of all human energies and interests to God. It is this "evangelical" justice, suffused by excelling charity, that forms the inner core of Christ's salvific work under its satisfactory aspects. For, in this attitude of subjection and obedience, Christ ratifies the Father's salvific plan within the ambit of his human will and free self-disposal of his human history and destiny. What is salvifically determinative and satisfactory about Christ's human destiny, therefore, is not simply the physical event of his passion, the exaction of a penalty of death, but the inner attitudes of love, obedience, and self-disposal in the Father's favor that animate Christ's suffering. The perfect mesh of the Father's loving initiative to save human-kind and of Christ's human response is a crucial feature of Christ's satisfactory work according to Saint Thomas. For in that communion of loves our own imaging communion with the Trinity is restored.

Of course, Saint Thomas's account of Christ's salvific work in its satisfactory character addresses not merely the achievement of this sort of personal communion between Head and members and of the whole Body through its Head with triune fellowship. It equally confronts the historical situation of such communion and that which has rendered such communion historically impossible: the reality of human sin, historical sin as a concrete determinant of universal human history. The "economy" of sin is by no means an ultimate nor even equiparent with the economy of salvation in Saint Thomas's view. Indeed, inasmuch as human moral fault is that which lacks due order and is characterized by deficient causality and unintelligi-bility, its historical shape is parasitic upon God's governance of his creation. Likewise, medicinal punishment as an effect of human moral fault shows that God's loving intentions retain the upper hand in guiding human history to its true destiny. It is the incarnation of the Word, radically, and Christ's consequent disposal of his historical freedom in loving response to the Father which show that what is uppermost and triumphant is the Father's love. In that perfect response to the Father's saving will, Christ has freely and lovingly chosen solidarity with human history as a history of suffering (imposed as a punishment).   In virtue of Christ's solidarity with suffering humanity, penal suffering becomes "once and for all" truly restorative and rectifies human willing. For, in truth, Christ "learned obedience through suffering," inasmuch as the full range of Christ's subjection of himself to the Father's saving will include the acceptance of the experience of suffering as the historical locale for obedient and loving acceptance of that will.   The supernatural gifts which the Body have from their Head are such as to effect a personal solidarity with him in the historically unavoidable situation of human suffering.   The grace and charity which Christ's members have from and in him are the grace and the love of his cross.   These conform Christ's Body to Christ's own obedience and love.   This conformity urges Christ's members to "make up what is lacking in the sufferings of Christ"--that is, to supply their own free ratification of the experience of the Cross as the definitive historical shape of communion with the Father and the Holy Spirit in and through their Head.

APPENDIX

The Satisfaction of Christ in Saint Anselm's Cur Deus homo?

The name of Anselm of Canterbury is as closely linked to the doctrine of the redemption as that of Athanasius is to the dogma of the Trinity or that of Augustine to the teaching on grace. This is the opinion of the German scholar, F.-R. Hasse, whose work, De ontologico Anselmi pro existentia Dei argumento, written in the middle of the 19th century, remains a noteworthy study on Saint Anselm.[1] The Cur Deus homo?, written towards the end of the 11th century, remains one of the great monuments in the history of theological literature and is clearly of paramount interest for a study of Saint Thomas's satisfaction-model. For Anselm's brief work brought the notion of satisfaction into full theological currency and established it as a permanent element in Christian soteriological discussion. One historian of theology has remarked that after Anselm a treatment of the redemption could only with difficulty avoid taking some position with regard to the thesis of Cur Deus homo?; one would be obliged to either adopt it, criticize it, or reject it out of hand.[2]

Anselm has rightly been called the "Father of Scholasticism." His employment of a rational methodology in the service of the theological task foreshadowed the achievement of the theologians in the later middle ages who in turn contributed, in various ways and with different import, to the construction of a theological science out of the faith-received data of revelation. Anselm's attachment to reason may appear untoward, especially in contrast to later, better balanced models for the relationship between faith and reason. Moreover it could be argued that, in Anselm's own case, the desire to find the "necessary reasons" for things resulted in a somewhat limited perspective on and use of the sources of theology. Accordingly some biblical themes, as well as notions prevalent in earlier patristic thought, are missing from Anselm's theological reflection on the saving work of Christ. One is also struck by the prevalence of commercial metaphors and images in the Cur Deus homo?; a fact which has earned for Anselm's theological enterprise the some-what doubtful evaluation of being a "théologie de comptoir."[3]

Anselm's work is not, however, without its posi-tive contributions to the development of Christian soteriology. Significant among these is that his Cur Deus homo? seems to have eliminated the "rights of the devil" theory as a predominant theme in soteriology; an explanation which up until the time of Anselm had monopolized much of theological discussion on the redemption.[4] Promoted by a number of patristic authors, the "rights of the devil" theory advanced the view that the devil did in fact enjoy certain rights over fallen man--rights which accrued to him as a result of having successfully persuaded man to sin. Within this perspective the death of Christ is viewed as a price that had to be paid in justice to the devil in order to deliver man from bondage to sin. Anselm's explicit rejection of this theory and his shift of emphasis to the absolute rights of God, who is master of his creations, ultimately eliminated this crypti-cally dualistic understanding of the conflict between good and evil and the subsequent distortions which it introduced into Christian soteriology.

Prior to an exposition of some of the central points of Anselm's satisfaction theory, a brief word about his methodology is necessary in order to de-fine the context of this discussion. His adage, "neque enim quaero intelligere ut credam, sed credo ut intelligam,"[5] is well known. E. Gilson has made the following comment on what Anselm means by this:

> The order to be observed in the search for truth is therefore the following: first, to believe the mysteries of faith before discussing them through reason; next, to endeavor to understand what one believes. Not to put faith first is presumption; not to appeal to reason next is negligence. Both of those faults must therefore be avoided.[6]

Clearly, to seek to understand the "necessity" attaching to mystery in the way in which Anselm sought to establish that necessity is one thing; to want to understand a mystery in order to dissolve it is another. Anselm's method, however enthusiastic about reason's powers, is not a kind of rationalism. He was a man of faith, a monk whose meditation on the Word of God brought him to see a fittingness--an interior harmony--to what God had accomplished in the world; and this is what he meant by "necessity." It could be suggested that such "necessity" is understandably less apparent to those whose meditation on or attention to the Bible is less fervent than Anselm's.

In the Cur Deus homo? Anselm describes two kinds of necessity, one which diminishes or even removes the voluntary character of an action and another which makes an action all the more voluntary. It is the latter kind of necessity which is intended with respect to God's actions as, for example, when it is said that it is necessary that the goodness of God must complete what it has begun in creation, especially man. This is true even if such a completion of the whole work could be effected only through grace. He writes, "Yet we may say, although the whole work which God does for man is of grace, that it is necessary for God, on account of his unchangeable goodness to complete the work which he has begun."[7] Consequently, it is the immutability of God's goodness that explains why he could not allow the whole of humankind to remain locked out of the possibility of attaining its end. Yet sin, into which man is born and to which each individual contributes does, in fact, keep him from being united with God.

What is sin for Anselm? Quite simply, it is a theft. Sin steals from God that which belongs to him, namely, the honor that man should pay him. Nothing is less tolerable in the order of things (ordo universitatis) than that creatures take away from the Creator his due honor. There is a certain static perspective to Anselm's view of the created order and its relation to God. The peace and harmony of divine governance is reflected in the world except in those instances when man chooses to disrupt that harmony by sin, that is, by failing to be submissive to the order of things as it has been established by God.

While sin is possible because of human freedom, Anselm does not entertain the possibility that God would allow the disorder of sin and the loss of his honor, which is its consequence, to perdure. Anselm's purpose in asserting God's claim on his honor, as for example, when he writes that "the honor taken away must be repaid, or punishment must follow,"[8] reflects his concern for avoiding the misconception that the transcendent love of God is indifferent toward the weight of man's sins. Thus, either the sinner freely acquits himself of his sin and the resulting debt, or God must take some form of retributive action.

Hence he writes, "It is impossible for God to lose his honor; for either the sinner pays his debt of his own accord, or, if he refuses, God takes it from him."[9] Anselm's concern here, however, is not so much to address the question of whether man is able to have some effect on a transcendent God, but rather to assert his principle concerning the maintenance of the _ordo universitatis_ as he envisions it. Hence a necessary alternative: either inflicted punishment or voluntary satisfaction, since God takes sin seriously and demands either one or the other by way of recompense. However there is another factor in the argument which is introduced at this point: what man has taken from God by sinning, i.e., his honor, he is unable to pay back, "for a sinner cannot justify a sinner."[10] It is extremely important to know why Anselm makes this claim since it will eventually lead to opening up his argument to the need for a God-man.

It is impossible for sinful man to make satisfaction to God because everything that he might offer to God he already owes to him. For example, man's penance, contrition, humility, abstinence, work, obedience, mercy and so forth are already God's due. Yet man can only satisfy by offering a work of super-erogation, i.e., something greater than the amount of that obligation, which should have restrained one from committing the sin.[11] This is Anselm's basic concep-tion of what satisfaction is. Yet how can man offer to God something greater than his honor which is precisely what should have restrained him from sinning in the first place?

The impression is given at this point that the argument, if one excludes the alternative of punishment as an acceptable one, has reached something of an impasse. Man is unable to make satisfaction to God for his sin since he is unable to repair the total disorder which sin has introduced into the order of the universe. It is this disorder which has robbed God of his honor. Thus, it would appear that man is unable to avail himself of the alternative of satisfaction because satisfaction requires, according to Anselm's conception, that something greater than the offense be offered and man is unable to offer to God something which is greater than the entire created order-- "greater than all the universe besides God,"[12] to use Anselm's own words.

Nonetheless it remains true that it is man's responsibility to make the satisfaction because it was man who sinned. Thus, as if to accentuate the apparent impasse to which the argument is leading, Anselm states that only God is able to produce the "something greater" which is required to make satisfaction, yet only man should produce it since, as the culpable one, he alone is responsible for making good the debt of sin. Thus Anselm has brought the argument to the point where, to avoid an ultimate impasse, he is required to speak about the God-man. He proposes that for such a satisfaction "which none but God can make and none but man ought to make, it is necessary for the God-man to make it."[13] There is a certain characteristic simplicity to the way in which Anselm concludes his argument: "necesse est fieri per Christum," that is, salvation "must necessarily be by Christ."[14] The necessity, in the way in which Anselm conceives of it, derives from the infallible character of God's plan for bringing man to beatitude. The argument has come full turn: God necessarily, but freely, accomplishes that which he had intended from the beginning--to bring man to himself in spite of sin.

There are several other themes which are developed in the course of the brief treatise, Cur Deus homo?. For example, Anselm digresses at one point to discuss the nature of the beatitude which God has willed for man; he elaborates as well on the metaphysical constitution of the God-man and on the ontological structure of the person of Jesus Christ. Certain other more properly soteriological notions are also discussed: for example, Anselm notes that the effects of Christ's death were such that even those who were his executioners benefited from them. These issues, however, are of peripheral concern to the matter at hand.

It is important, however, to examine the reason that Cur Deus homo? gives to explain why the death of Christ and the satisfaction which it accomplishes does in fact restore the honor which sin had taken away from God and why man is able to share in the benefits of Christ's adequate satisfaction. The fundamental reason why the death of Christ both pays the debt owed by man to God and at the same time renders homage to him, is the freedom with which Christ offered himself up. Anselm writes, "If he allowed himself to be slain for the sake of justice, did he not give his life for the honor of God?"[15] Implicit in this resolution is the notion of an agreement, worked out, as it were, between Christ and his heavenly Father, which settles the terms under which Christ's death will be accepted. There is, admittedly, something of the notion of a barter--with all of its mercentile connotations--associated with this simple, but also somewhat naive, conceptuality.

Why is it that man is the beneficiary of this agreement? Anselm responds: To whom else should the Son have more suitably ceded the fruits and the recompense that his death was worth than to those for whose salvation he came? Could God have refused him this request since he--being innocent--could have no need of any such recompense?[16] Admittedly this description of how the merits of Christ's death are mediated to his members is succinct and hardly rich in nuance. On the other hand, it could also be that Anselm's stated purpose is to answer the question of why God became man, and was not, therefore, under any direct constraint to clarify related questions. There are, nonetheless, elements of Christian sotieriology which, as a result of Cur Deus homo?, became the focus of attention for theologians after Anselm. Prominent among these are: the affirmation of the absolute primacy of the divine honor; insistence on and reflection about man's destiny for beatitude; the nature of the relationship between Christ and his Father; and, finally, the central issue of sin and the need for satisfaction.

NOTES

INTRODUCTION

[1]The alien perspective is well-captured by the
19th century American preacher Phillips Brooks (1835-
1893), Sermons (7th Series): "You say that it (sc. the
death of Christ) appeased His (sc. God's) wrath. I am
not sure there may not be some meaning of those words
which does not include the truth which they try to
express, but in their natural sense which men gather
from them out of their ordinary human uses, I do
not believe that they are true." Cited in Gerald
O'Collins, S.J., The Calvary Christ (Philadelphia:
Westminster, 1977), p. 92. A contemporary exponent of
Reformation theology's objection to the satisfaction-
model is Wolfhart Pannenberg, Jesus--God and Man,
translated by L.L. Wilkins and D.A. Priebe, (Philadelphia: Westminster, 1968), p. 277ff., who describes the
deficiencies of the satisfaction theory (primarily as
presented by Anselm) in comparison to "the meaning
that can be seen in the event of the cross within
the context in which it happened in the light of
Jesus' resurrection." Catholic theologians tend to
place the notion of satisfaction on the periphery of
christological discussion either by reinterpreting it,
as in the case of Christian Duquoc, O.P., Christologie:
Le Messie (Paris: Cerf, 1972), pp. 213-216 ("Tel est
le sens de la satisfaction: réintégrer dans l'amour
divin des actes qui furent des échecs à la gloire de
Dieu . . . . La condition humaine, qui est actuelle-
ment une condition 'pénale', le Christ, par sa lutte
pour la justice et son amour de Dieu, la transforme
de telle sorte que l'homme puisse y réécrire son
histoire."), or by simply failing to give the issue
full-dressed treatment, as in Edward Schillebeeckx,
Jesus: An Experiment in Christology, translated by
H. Hoskins, (New York: Seabury, 1979). Writers from
within the school of Liberation Theology also tend to
ignore the notion of satisfaction, for example, Juan
Luis Segundo, S.J., A Theology for Artisans of a New
Humanity, Vols. 1-5, translated by John Drury, (New
York: Orbis, 1974).

[2]A good representative of penal substitution theorists is John Calvin, _Institutes_, II.16, translated by J. Allen, (Grand Rapids: Erdemans, 1949), I, p. 553: "Christ . . . has taken upon himself and suffered the punishment which by the righteous judgment of God impended over all sinners . . . by this expiation God the Father has been satisfied and . . . his wrath appeased." Curiously Wolfhart Pannenberg, despite his critical evaluation of other aspects of christological thought, accepts the concept of inclusive substitution (see _Jesus-God and Man_, pp. 258 ff.). Dorothee Sölle, _Christ the Representative_, translated by D. Lewis, (Philadelphia: SCM Press, 1967), p. 150, offers a different view of Christ's substitutional role: "Christ took over God's role in the world, but in the process it was changed into the role of the helpless God. The absent God whom Christ represents is the God who is helpless in this world . . . ." The work of Philippe de la Trinité, O.C.D., _La Rédemption par le sang_ (Paris: Fayard, 1959) is an excellent study of how theories of penal substitution distort the notion of satisfaction.

[3]See I.T. Eschmann, O.P., "A Catalogue of St. Thomas's Works" published in Gilson's _The Christian Philosophy of St. Thomas Aquinas_ (New York: Random House, 1956), p. 381: "The following Catalogue of St. Thomas's works consists of ninety-eight items. This counting should not be considered as definitive; indeed it is debatable. With regard to not a few titles . . . it is as yet impossible to know whether they comprise one or several works."

[4]The _Index_ documents the vocabulary used in 179 Latin works from the ninth to sixteenth centuries: in all 1,700,000 lines of text for a total of 10,600,000 words. One hundred of these are undoubtedly the works of St. Thomas Aquinas, the _In Quattuor Libros Sententiarum_ and the _Summa Theologiae_ each having been considered as four works. The compilers of the _Index_ have used whatever critical texts were available to them at the time of the _Index_'s preparation. Since for many of Saint Thomas's works no critical editions exist, the compilers chose for such works the most recent edition. For the present thesis the edition used by the _Index_ has been employed and the abbreviations adopted by the _Index_ have been used for referring to Saint Thomas's works. In some cases the manner of citing the works of Saint Thomas represents a slight change from the traditional system. A complete

explanation of these matters will be found in the yet
to be published introductory volume of the Index;
nonetheless, an excerpt of this volume containing
necessary information is found in Vol. 1, pp. ix-xiii.
The more important abbreviations are as follows: ag,
argument or objection; sc, sed contra; co, the body of
the article or question; ra, response to an argument or
objection; rc, response to a sed contra. The symbol
for number (#) is used for those works whose divisions
are so large as to require further precision for
easily locating a reference; in these cases the number
reference is to the divisions of the text introduced by
the modern editor. In those cases, e.g., some of the
biblical commentaries, where the Leonine edition was
used, the line numbers have been given after a slash
(/) in the reference. Translations are those of the
author, except for the De veritate when On Truth,
3 vols., translated by Mulligan-McGlynn-Schmidt,
(Chicago: Regnery, 1952-1954) was used. The bilingual
edition of the Summa theologiae, 60 vol., (New York:
McGraw-Hill, 1964-1975) was used for both the Latin
text (which nearly always follows the Leonine edition)
and the English translation (which was sometimes
altered to more clearly bring out the meaning of a
given passage). All citations from Scripture (apart
from those which occur within a text of Saint Thomas)
are from the Revised Standard Version as contained in
The New Oxford Annotated Bible with the Apocrypha (New
York: Oxford University Press, 1973).

[5]See Walter Brugger, S.J., "Index Thomisticus,"
Theologie und Philosophie 52 (1977), pp. 435-444.

[6]Only a small portion of Saint Thomas's uses of
the word "satisfaction" is not covered by the already
published Concordances of the Index, namely, when the
word appears in a quotation ad literram. According
to the present plan these occurrences will be tabulated
in the Fifth Concordance. This omission does not,
however, seriously affect the present research as
pointed out below with reference to the Catena aurea,
p. 125, n. 42.

[7]For example in Summa theologiae II-II, 119.2
ra/1 the following text is found: "Alii vero dicunt
quod loquitur de cupiditate generali respectu cuius-
cumque boni. Et sic manifestum est quod etiam prodiga-
litas ex cupiditate oritur: prodigus enim aliquod bonum
temporale cupit consequi inordinate; vel placere aliis
vel saltem satisfacere suae voluntati in dando." Such
a use of the word "satisfaction" is not of concern to

the present thesis and has been set aside. Note, however, that since the word occurs within an indirect quotation as opposed to one ad litteram it is included in the presently published Concordances.

[8]Gustaf Aulén, Christus Victor, translated by A.G. Hebert, (New York: Macmillan, 1969), p. 93.

[9]II Corinthians 5:19. Two recent articles by Jean-Hervé Nicolas, O.P. offer a theological perspective, in the light of Saint Thomas's teaching, on the relationship between suffering (satisfaction) and reconciliation. "La seconde mort du pécheur et la fidélité de Dieu," Revue Thomiste 79 (1979), pp. 25-49: ". . . car la réconciliation, c'est l'amour, et l'amour de Dieu même est vain si l'homme refuse de se laisser aimer. Dire 'oui' à l'amour et à la souffrance dans laquelle il se dissimule, c'est entrer personnellement dans le dessein de Dieu, c'est faire sien le salut accompli par le Christ, se préparant ainsi à faire sienne 'la gloire qui doit être manifestée en nous,' avec laquelle, proclame Saint Paul, 'les souffrances du temps présent sont sans proportion' (Rom. viii, 18)." Father Nicolas responds to those theologians who posit some kind of suffering within the Godhead as a necessary supposition for finding meaning in the cross of Christ in "Aimante et bienheureuse Trinité." Revue Thomiste 78 (1978), pp. 271-292.

[10]On this point John A.T. Robinson, Wrestling with Romans (Philadelphia: Westminster, 1979) can be read with profit, especially pp. 37-48: "The hilastērion does something not to God but to the sin which distorts and sours the relationship."

[11]James A. Weisheipl, O.P., Friar Thomas D'Aquino: His Life, Thought, and Work (New York: Doubleday, 1974).

[12]For example the Expositio et lectura super Epistolas Pauli Apostoli are the subject of considerable debate as to their date of composition. See Weisheipl, Friar Thomas, pp. 247-249.

[13]Colossians 1: 19-20.

CHAPTER I

[1]Bernard Gui, Legenda Sancti Thomae Aquinatis in S. Thomae Aquinatis Vitae Fontes Praecipuae edited by Angelico Ferrua, O.P. (Alba: Edizione Domenicane, 1968), p. 142. "Erat enim in legendo novos articulos adinveniens novumque modum determinandi inveniens et novas producens in determinationibus rationes, ut nemo audiens ipsum dubitaret quin ipsum Deus novi luminis radiis illustrasset."

[2]Weisheipl, Friar Thomas, p. 70.

[3]For examle, Juan Martinez de Ripalda, Brevis Expositio Magistri Sententiarum published in 1635.

[4]Petrus Lombardus, Sententiae in IV Libris Distinctae Lib.1,d.1,c.1, edited by PP. Collegii S. Bonaventurae ad Claras Aquas (Grottaferrata: Spicilegium Bonaventurianum, 1971), p. 55: "Ut enim egregius doctor Augustinus ait in libro De doctrina christiana Lib.1,c.2,n.2 , 'omnis doctrina vel rerum est vel signorum. Sed res etiam per signa discuntur. Proprie autem hic res appellantur, quae non ad significandum aliquid adhibentur; signa vero, quorum usu est in significando.'"

[5]Alexander of Hales, Glossa in Quattuor Libros Sententiarum edited by PP. Collegii S. Bonaventurae (Quaracchi: Bibliotheca Franciscana Scholastica, 1951), p. 4. "Sed quaeri potest quare ordine praepostero in praedicta auctoritate librorum fit distinctio. Respondeo: duplex est ordo. Este ordo rerum prout exeunt a Creatore vel Recreatore vel Reparatore, et sic proceditur in hoc opere. Et est ordo rerum prout reducuntur ad Creatorem . . . ."

[6]Tolomeo di Lucca, Historia ecclesiastica nova in Vitae Fontes, pp. 356-357. "XXV autem annorum erat, cum primo Parisius venit, ubi infra XXX annum Sententias legit, et conventum in theologia, sive licentiam recepit. Infra autem magisterium quattuor libros fecit super Sententias, videlicet primum, secundum, tertium et quartum."

[7]The threefold function of a regent-master in theology was described by Peter Cantor in his _Verbum abbreviatum_, c.1 as follows: "In tribus igitur consistit exercitium sacrae Scripturae: circa lectionem, disputationem et praedicationem . . . . Praedicatio vero, cui subserviunt priora, quasi tectum est tegens fideles ab aestu, et a turbine vitiorum. Post lectionem igitur sacrae Scripturae, et dubitabilium, per disputationem, inquisitionem, et non prius, praedicandus est."

[8]C.H. Haskins, _The Rise of Universities_ (Ithaca: Cornell University Press, 1957) includes an updated bibliography on the most important topics discussed by Haskins as well as some of the essential books or articles published since 1923 when this brief work was originally published. Hastings Rashdall, _The Universities of Europe in the Middle Ages_, a new edition in three volumes by F.M. Powicke and A.B. Emden (Oxford: Clarendon Press, 1936) is a classical source.

[9]Weisheipl, _Friar Thomas_, p. 110. Cf. M.-D. Chenu, O.P., _La Théologie comme Science au XIIIe siècle_ (Paris: J. Vrin, 1957) for a study of the relationship between biblical and systematic theology in certain 13th century theologians.

[10]The commentary on Matthew 5:11 to 6:8 and 6:14-19 found in the printed editions is spurious and attributed to Peter de Scala, O.P. (d. 1295). See Weisheipl, _Friar Thomas_, pp. 371-372.

[11]St. Thomas Aquinas, _Opera Omnia_, cura et studio Fratrum Praedicatorum, tomus XXVIII: _Expositio super Isaiam ad litteram_ (Rome: Editori di San Tommaso, 1974), p. 20. See Weisheipl, _Friar Thomas_, pp. 120-121.

[12]Peter Cantor, _Verbum_, c.1. "Lectio autem est quasi fundamentum, et substratorium sequentium. . . ."

[13]The basis for this tradition in the Dominican Order is the _Chronicle of the King of Aragon, James II_, written by Friar Peter Marsilio. See Weisheipl, _Friar Thomas_, pp. 130-131. Another suggestion is made by Peter Marc, "Introduction" to _Liber de Veritate Catholicae Fidei_ (Torino: Marietti, 1967).

[14]M.-D. Chenu, O.P., <u>Toward Understanding Saint Thomas</u>, translated by A.-M. Landry and D. Hughes, (Chicago: Henry Regnery Company, 1964), p. 292.

[15]Weisheipl, <u>Friar Thomas</u>, pp. 130-134; 144-145.

[16]<u>Ibid.</u>, p. 142.

[17]Tolomeo di Lucca, <u>Historia</u>, p. 357. "Post tres annos qui magisterii redit in Italiam, tempore videlicet Urbani IV, de quo nunc est agendum, cuius tempore multa fructuosa scripsit."

[18]Chenu, <u>Understanding</u>, p. 294. He quotes Saint Thomas's <u>Summa contra gentiles</u>, 2.4.nr6, ". . . post ea quae de Deo in se in primo libro sunt dicta, de his quae ab ipso sunt restat prosequendum."

[19]<u>De rationibus fidei</u> 2: "Ad hoc igitur debet tendere christiani disputatoris intentio in articulis fidei, non ut fidem probet, sed ut fidem defendat; unde et beatus Petrus non dicit 'parati semper ad probationem' sed 'ad satisfactionem,' ut scilicet rationabiliter ostendatur non esse falsum quod fides catholica confitetur."

[20]<u>Ibid.</u>, 7: "Si quis ergo convenientiam passionis et mortis Christi pia intentione consideret, tantam sapientiae profunditatem inveniet ut semper aliqua cogitanti plura et maiora occurrant, ita quod experiri possit verum esse quod Apostolus dicit 'Nos praedicamus Christum crucifixum, Iudaeis quidem scandalum, Gentibus autem stultitiam; nobis autem Christum Dei virtutem et Dei sapientiam.' Et iterum 'Quod stultum est Dei sapientius est hominibus.'"

[21]See Weisheipl, <u>Friar Thomas</u>, pp. 169-171.

[22]See the "Prefatio" to the Leonine edition, tomus XXVI, especially pp. 25*-26*: "l'<u>Expositio super Iob</u>, à sa mesure et en son domaine propres, peut soutenir la comparaison avec un ouvrage comme la <u>Somme contre les Gentils</u>. . . ."

[23]<u>Summa theologiae</u>, Prologue: "Consideravimus namque hujus doctrinae novitios in his quae a diversis scripta sunt plurimum impediri, partim quidem propter multiplicationem inutilium quaestionum, articulorum, et argumentorum, partim etiam quia ea quae sunt necessaria talibus ad sciendum non traduntur secundum ordinem

disciplinae, sed secundum quod requirebat librorum expositio, vel secundum quod se praebebat occasio disputandi, partim quidem quia frequens eorumdem repetitio et fastidium et confusionem generabat in animis auditorum."

[24]Among the important studies on this question are Chenu, Understanding; André Hayen, S.J., Saint Thomas d'Aquin et la vie de l'Eglise (Paris-Louvain: Desclée de Brouwer, 1952); Per Erik Persson, Sacra Doctrina: Reason and Revelation in Aquinas, translated by Ross Mackenzie, (Philadelphia: Fortress Ghislain Lafont, O.S.B., Structures et Méthode dans la Somme théologique de Saint Thomas D'Aquin (Paris-Louvain: Desclée de Brouwer, 1961), pp. 15-34. The most recent study on this subject is that of Michel Corbin, Le Chemin de la Théologie chez Thomas d'Aquin (Paris: Beauchesne, 1974), c. iv.

[25]Thomas Gilby, O.P., Purpose and Happiness, translation of Summa theologiae (1a2ae. 1-5), Vol. 16 (New York: McGraw-Hill, 1969), p. xiii. See idem, Christian Theology, Vol. 1 of the same series, especially Appendix 4.

[26]Summa theologiae, Prologue to the prima pars: "Quia igitur principalis intentio hujus sacrae doctrinae est Dei cognitionem tradere, et non solum secundum quod in se est sed secundum quod est principium rerum et finis earum et specialiter rationalis creaturae, ut ex dictis est manifestum, ad hujus doctrinae expositionem intendentes, primo tractabimus de Deo, secundo de motu rationalis creaturae in Deum, tertio de Christo, qui secundum quod homo via est nobis tendendi in Deum."

[27]Chenu, Understanding, p. 304.

[28]Weisheipl, Friar Thomas, pp. 232-234; 361.

[29]Summa theologiae, Prologue to the prima pars: "Consideratio autem de Deo tripartita erit: primo namque considerabimus ea quae pertinent ad essentiam divinam, secundo ea quae pertinent ad distinctionem personarum, tertio ea quae pertinent ad processum creaturarum ab ipso."

30Since the twelfth century and the progressive introduction of the works of Aristotle comprising the logica nova (above all, the two Analytica), the issue of theological methodology acquired new importance and self-consciousness. The question was: in what respect does theology measure up to the Aristotelian canon of scientific knowing as that canon is expressed in the Analytica Posteriora? For scientific knowing involves universality and necessity (cf. Thomas Aquinas, In I Anal. Post., lect. 4, 5); it is a knowledge of what cannot be other than the case and of the necessary conection between cause and effect. Christian theology, by contrast, centers upon a God who is utterly free in his address to human freedom and tries to render an account of the intersection and dialogue of divine and human freedoms, which is salvation-history. The methodological question for theology can be posed more precisely, therefore: how can there be a scientific account (one that matches up to Aristotle's scientific ideal) about what is contingent, free, gracious, and historical? The genius of a solution to this question of theological methodology is to find a course between theology as "sacred history," where the intelligible connection betwen the mysteries is simply narrative chronology as in Hugh of St. Victor's De sacramentis, and theology as necessitarian emanationism as in Plotinus' Enneads. Aquinas himself confronted this issue in two ways: in actu signato in the methodological treatment of ST I, q. 1 and in actu exercito in the structure of the Summa theologiae itself as he planned it. He adopted the exitus-reditus scheme from Dionysian neo-Platonism, but "fine tunes" it, building the nuance of analogical understanding into the scheme. In fact, as Fr. Colman O'Neill and others have suggested, it is perhaps more accurate to view the exitus-reditus in the pattern of the Summa not as a single circular movement (thus, Chenu) but rather in terms of concentric circles, each possessed of its own degree of necessity. Thus, one may see in ST I qq. 2-43 one cycle, an entirely intra-Trinitarian coming-forth in the Word and recoil in Personal Love; here the movement enjoys a certain necessity--i.e., that God cannot be other than a Father speaking a Word and together with that Word breathing forth the personal Bond of Love. Broadly speaking, the material in the remainder of the prima pars and in the secunda pars is considered under the aspect of nature. The necessity here is hypothetical (i.e., given that God has freely chosen to create as he has). Nevertheless, given the divine will to create, there is a certain intelligibility and consistency, certain intrinsic requirements, to the natures that have been freely posited: man cannot be other than man, given that God has freely willed to create man for beatific communion. The final scheme of coming-forth and return would be represented in the tertia pars, which is expressive of the content of concrete history. Jesus Christ comes forth and returns as the perfect and consummate historical agent in a personal history; he realizes human nature in its historically unsurpassable concrete shape; he enacts human nature as a perfect history. The necessity here is even more tenuous, in one respect; for there is no necessity that God accomplish the consummation of human destiny and human salvation from sin by the incarnation of the Son. Nevertheless, God's election of this mode of accomplishing his loving design for human history and the excellence of a human history that is hypostatically that of the Second Person of the Divine Trinity confers the necessity of an unsurpassable exemplar and final causality upon salvation-history as enacted in the personal history of Jesus of Nazareth. These necessities--that of salvation-history, that of natures as constituted by God, and that of the divine triune reality itself--are interlocking: the former two being grafted on to and deriving consistency and intelligibility from the divine "necessity" that God be a Father uttering a Word with whom he breathes forth the force of loving recoil. I am grateful to Larz Pearson, O.P. for his fraternal help in formulating this footnote.

[31]It is interesting to note that even Saint Bonaventure in his commentary on the Sentences referred to the opinion that God became incarnate in order to take away human sinfulness as "more consonant with the piety of faith" than that he did so in order to complete the work of creation. See Commentaria in Quattuor Libros Sententiarum, tomus III (Quaracchi: Collegii S. Bonaventurae, 1887) d.1, a.2, q.2.

[32]Summa theologiae III, 1.2.,co/: "Deum incarnari non fuit necessarium ad reparationem humanae naturae: Deus enim per suam omnipotentem virtutem poterat humanam naturam multis aliis modis reparare."

[33]Weisheipl, Friar Thomas, pp. 241-244.

[34]R.A. Gauthier, O.P., "La date du Commentaire de Saint Thomas sur l'Ethique à Nicomaque," Recherches de théologie ancienne et médiévale 18 (1951), p. 103, n. 91.

[35]Weisheipl, Friar Thomas, p. 245.

[36]William of Tocco, Hystoria beati Thomae de Aquino in Ferrua, Vitae Fontes, p. 56: "Scripsit super Epistolas Pauli omnes, quarum Scripturam praeter Evangelicam super omnes commendabat, in quarum expositione Parisius visionem praefati Apostoli dicitur habuisse."

[37]Weisheipl, Friar Thomas, pp. 247-249; 372-373.

[38]The edited text written or dictated by Saint Thomas (expositio) covers Romans to 1 Corinthians 7:9.

[39]Weisheipl, Friar Thomas, pp. 246-247.

[40]Ibid., pp. 254-255.

[41]Compendium theologiae, 1: "Ut igitur tibi, fili carissime Reginalde, compendiosam doctrinam de christiana religione tradam, quam semper prae oculis possis habere, circa haec tria in presenti opere tota nostra versatur intentio. Primum de fide, secundo de spe, tertio vero de caritate agemus."

[42]Weisheipl, Friar Thomas, p. 361.

[43]Ibid., p. 256. See also Gilby, Purpose and Happiness, pp. xiii-xv.

[44]Summa theologiae, Prologue to the prima secundae: "Quia, sicut Damascenus dicit, homo factus ad imaginem Dei dicitur, secundum quod per imaginem significatur intellectuale et arbitrio liberum et per se potestativum, postquam praedictum est de exemplari, scilicet de Deo, et de his quae processerunt ex divina potestate secundum ejus voluntatem, restat ut consideremus de ejus imagine, idest de homine secundum quod et ipse est suorum operum principium, quasi liberum arbitrium habens et suorum operum potestatem."

[45]Gilby, Purpose and Happiness, p. xiii.

[46]Summa theologiae, I-II, 3.8.co/: "Dicendum quod ultima et perfecta beatitudo non potest esse nisi in visione divinae essentiae."

[47]Thomas Gilby, O.P., Creation, Variety and Evil, translation of Summa theologiae (Ia. 44-49), Vol. 8 (New York: McGraw-Hill, 1967), see especially the Introduction.

[48]See Jaroslav Pelikan, "_Imago Dei_: An Explication of _Summa theologiae_, Part 1, Question 93" in _Calgary Aquinas Studies_, edited by Anthony Parel (Toronto: PIMS, 1978), pp. 27-48.

[49]_Summa theologiae_, Prologue to the _secunda secundae_: "Post communem considerationem de virtutibus et vitiis et aliis ad materiam moralem pertinentibus, necesse est considerare singula in speciali . . . ."

[50]Gauthier, "Commentaire," pp. 66-105.

[51]_Summa theologiae_, Prologue to the _secunda secundae_: "Erit igitur compendiosior et expeditior considerationis via si simul sub eodem tractatu consideratio procedit de virtute et dono sibi correspondente, et vitiis oppositis, et praeceptis affirmativis vel negativis."

[52]"Processus canonizationis sancti Thomae Aquinatis, Neapoli," n. 77 in Ferrua, _Vitae Fontes_, p. 314: "semper vacantem ad studium et lectiones et scribendum pro illuminatione fidelium . . . ."

[53]Psalms 52-54 were discovered by Uccelli in Naples (Regio Archivio 25) and published by him in Rome in 1880. See Palmeron Glorieux, "Essais sur les commentaires scripturaires de Saint Thomas et leur chronologie," _Recherches de théologie ancienne et médiévale_ 17 (1950), 237-266.

[54]"Processus," n. 79 in Ferrua, _Vitae Fontes_, p. 319: "Raynalde, non possum quia omnia que scripsi videntur mihi palee." This report comes from the testimony of Bartholomew of Capua, who in all probability, was informed by Reginald of Piperno himself.

[55]_Summa theologiae_, Prologue to the _tertia pars_: "Quia salvator noster dominus Jesus Christus, teste angelo, 'Populum suum salvum faciens a peccatis eorum,' viam veritatis nobis in seipso demonstravit, per quam ad beatitudinem immortalis vitae resurgendo pervenire possimus, necesse est ut ad consummationem totius theologici negotii, post considerationem ultimi finis humanae vitae et virtutum et vitiorum, de ipso omnium Salvatore et beneficiis ejus humano generi praestitis nostra consideratio subsequatur."

[56]Lafont, _Structures_, pp. 305-309.

[57]_Summa theologiae_, Prologue to the _tertia pars_:
"Circa quam, primo, considerandum occurrit: de ipso
Salvatore; secundo, de sacramentis ejus, quibus salutem
consequimur; tertio, de fine immortalis vitae, ad quam
per ipsum resurgendo pervenimus."

[58]Colman E. O'Neill, O.P. _The One Mediator_,
translation of _Summa theologiae_ (3a. 16-26), Vol. 50
(New York: McGraw-Hill, 1965), p. xxiv.

[59]Matthew 2:20-22.

CHAPTER II

[1]The fact was established by H. Denifle, "Quel livre servait de base à l'enseignement des maîtres en théologie dans l'Université de Paris," Revue Thomiste 2 (189), pp. 149-161. Two works of special interest on this subject are C. Spicq, O.P., Esquisse d'une histoire de l'exégèse latine au moyen âge (Paris: J. Vrin, 1944) and B. Smalley, The Study of the Bible in the Middle Ages (Oxford: Clarendon Press, 1952).

[2]Edmund Hill, O.P., Man Made to God's Image, translation of Summa theologiae (1a. 90-102), Vol. 13 (New York: McGraw-Hill, 1964), p. xxviii.

[3]Erasmus wrote in his Annotationes in Novum Testamentum, 1515, Basileae, fol. 228 v: "Et quid aliud potuisset Thomas, alioqui vir bono ingenio, qui ea temporum natus est, in quibus bonae litterae omnes et Latinae et Graecae et Hebraicae tamquam sepultae et emortuae ignotate jacebant . . . ." I am indebted to Guy-Th. Bedouelle, O.P. for this reference.

[4]Quaestiones Quodlibetales 7.6.1.co/: "Dicendum, quod sacra Scriptura ad hoc divinitus est ordinata ut per eam nobis veritas manifestetur necessaria ad salutem. Manifestatio autem vel expressio alicuius veritatis potest fieri de aliquo rebus et verbis; in quantum scilicet verba significant res, et una res potest esse figura alterius. Auctor autem rerum non solum potest verba accommodare ad aliquid significandum, sed etiam res potest disponere in figuram alterius. Et secundum hoc in sacra Scriptura manifestatur veritas dupliciter. Uno modo secundum quod res significantur per verba: et in hoc consistit sensus litteralis. Alio modo secundum quod res sunt figurae aliarum rerum: et in hoc consistit sensus spiritualis. Et sic sacrae Scripturae plures sensus competunt."

[5]De potentia 4.1.co/: "Unde si etiam aliqua vera ab expositoribus sacrae Scripturae litterae aptentur, quae auctor non intelligit, non est dubium quin Spiritus sanctus intellexerit, qui est principalis

auctor divinae Scripturae. Unde omnis veritas quae, salva litterae circumstantia, potest divinae Scripturae aptari, est eius sensus."

[6]Beryl Smalley, for one, emphasizes Saint Thomas's apreciation for the literal sense of Scripture. In Study of the Bible, pp. 269-270, she writes: "Then Aristotle, in his new role as a doctor of Christendom, integrated letter and spirit as he integrated the human personality. St. Albert and St. Thomas achieved for the literal interpretation what poor Andrew (of St. Victor), no philosopher, entangled in out-of-date philosophic clichés, had instinctively wanted to do."

[7]Spicq, Esquisse, p. 288. Fr. Spicq devotes chapter seven of his work to an extended study of Saint Thomas's use of the literal sense.

[8]Questiones quodlibetales 7.6.1.ra/3: "nihil est quod occulte in aliquo loco sacrae Scripturae tradatur quod non alibi manifeste exponatur; unde spiritualis expositio semper debet habere fulcimentum ab aliqua litterali expositione sacrae Scripturae; et ita vitatur omnis erroris occasio."

[9]See above n. 1. In addition to the works of Father Spicq and Miss Smalley, mention should be made of Henri de Lubac, S.J., Exégèse médiévale; les quatre sens de l'Ecriture. 4 Vols. (Paris: Aubier, 1959-1964), which provides a different appreciation of the spiritual interpretation of Scripture than that of Father Spicq, for example.

[10]Expositio super Isaiam 9.1: "Notandum super illo uerbo 'Paruulus natus est,' quod Christus dicitur paruulus primo in natiuitate propter etatem, Matth. II 'Intrantes domum, inuenerunt puerum cum Maria matre eius'; secundo possessione propter paupertatem, II Cor. VIII;' Scitis gratiam Domini nostri Ihesu Christi, quoniam propter uos egenus factus est cum esset diues;' tertio corde propter humilitatem, Matth. XI 'Discite a me quia mitis sum et humilis corde;' quarto morte propter mortis uilitatem, Sap. II 'Morte turpissima condemnemus eum.'"

[11]Ibid., "Notandum super illo uerbo 'datus est nobis,' quod Christus datus est nobis primo in fratrem, Cant. VIII 'Quis michi det te fratrem meum sugentem ubera matris me?;' letamini in Domino Deo uestro, quia dedit uobis doctorem iustitie;' tertio in speculatorem, Ez. III 'Fili hominis, speculatorem dedi te domui

Israel;' quarto in propugnatorem, Ys. XIX "Mittet eis saluatorem et propugnatorem qui liberet pastorem unum qui pascet eas;' sexto in exemplum operationis, Io. XIII 'Exemplum enim dedi uobis, ut quemadmodum ego feci, ita et uos faciatis'; septimo in cibum peregrinationis, Io. VI 'Panis quem ego dabo, caro mea est pro mundi uita;' octauo in pretium redemptionis, Matth. XX 'Filius hominis non uenit ministrari sed ministrare, et dare animam suam redemptionem pro multis;' nono in premium remunerationis, Apoc. II 'Vincenti dabo edere manna absconditum.'"

[12]Ibid., "Item notandum super illo uerbo 'super humerum Christi primo peccata, sicut supra satisfactorem, Ys. LIII 'Dominus posuit super eum iniquitatem omnium nostrum;' secundo clauem, sicut supra sacerdotem, Ys. XXII 'Et dabo clauem domus Dauid super humerum eius, et aperiet et non erit qui claudat;' tertio principatum, sicut supra dominatorem, Ys. IX 'Factus est principatus super humerum eius;' quarto gloriam, sicut supra triumphatorem, Ys. XXII 'Et suspendam super eum omnem gloriam domus patris eius.'"

[13]The correct reading of the Hebrew in this text, Joel 2:23, is a subject of debate among scholars. Modern commentators, however, seem to prefer to read "rain" instead of "doctor" for the disputed term. For a discussion of this see La Sainte Bible, tome VIII (1ère partie), Les petits prophètes, translation and commentary by A. Deissler and M. Delcor (Paris, Letouzey, 1961), p. 165, fn. 23.

[14]Summa theologiae I, 1.9 and 10. See Spicq, Esquisse, pp. 281-288.

[15]Summa theologiae I, 1.10.co/: "Secundum ergo quod ea quae sunt veteris legis significant ea quae sunt novae legis est sensus allegoricus . . . ." The threefold division of the spiritual sense--allegorical, moral and anagogical or eschatological--goes back at least as far as the Venerable Bede. See Gilby, Christian Theology, Appendix 12.

[16]Super Matthaeum 27.2: "Item competebat redemptioni, quia ad satisfactionem pro peccato primi hominis. Sed primus homo peccavit in ligno; ideo Dominus in ligno pati voluit; Sap. XIV,7: 'Benedictum lignum, per quod fit justitia.'"

[17]*Ibid.*, "Item competit transgressioni primi hominis; quia Adam post meridiem peccavit, Gen. III,8, ideo Christus satisfacere voluit illa hora."

[18]*Super Joannem* 19.6.4: "Locus sepulturae designatur consequenter cum dicit: Erat autem in loco ubi crucifixus est, hortus etc. Ubi notandum, quod Christus in horto captus, et in horto passus, et in horto sepultus fuit; ad designandum quod per suae passionis virtutem liberamur a peccato quod Adam in horto deliciarum commisit, et quod per eum Ecclesia consecratur, quae est sicut hortus conclusus."

[19]*Summa theologiae* I,1.10.co/: "Prout vero significant ea quae sunt in aeterna gloria est sensus anagogicus." Cf. *Questiones quodlibetales* 7.6.2.co/: "Sensus ergo spiritualis, ordinatus ad recte credendum, potest fundari . . . in illo modo figurationis quo novum simul et vetus significant Ecclesiam triumphantem; et sic sensus anagogicus."

[20]*Super Joannem* 19.6.4.: "Ecclesia . . . quae est sicut hortus conclusus." See above, n. 18.

[21]*Super Joannem* 18.1.1: "Erat autem congruus locus proditioni: unde dicit Ubi erat hortus, in quem introivit ipse, et discipuli eius. Et hoc convenienter, quia ipse satisfaciebat pro peccato primi hominis in horto commisso. Paradisus enim hortus deliciarum interpretatur. Item quia per passionem nos in hortum et paradisum coronandos introducit; Lc. XXIII, 43: 'Hodie mecum eris in paradiso.'"

[22]Chenu, *Understanding*, p. 253.

[23]*Super Matthaeum* 26.5: "Notate quod dicit, 'usque ad mortem,' per quam satisfaciam pro isto scandalo et pro aliis."

[24]C. H. Dodd, *The Apostolic Preaching and its Developments* (New York: Harper & Row, 1964), pp. 10ff.

[25]*Super ad Romanos* 3.3: "Sicut si aliquis ob culpam commissam obnoxius esset regi ad solvendam pecuniam, ille eum redimere diceretur a noxa, qui pro eo pecuniam solveret. Haec autem noxa ad totum homanum genus pertinebat, quod erat infectum per peccatum primi parentis. Unde nullus alius pro peccato totius humani generis satisfacere poterat, nisi solus Christus qui ab omni peccato erat immunis."

[26]Ibid., "Secundo ostendit unde ista redemptio efficaciam habuit cum dicit 'quem proposuit Deus propitiatorem.' Ex hoc enim Christi satisfactio efficaciam ad justificandum habuit, et ad redimendum. . ."

[27]Ibid., " . . . quia eum Deus ad hoc ordinaverat secundum suum propositum, quod designat cum dicit 'quem proposuit, Deus propitatorem'--Eph. c. 1. 11: 'Qui operatur omnia secundum consilium voluntatis suae.'"

[28]Ibid., "Et sic, dum satisfaciendo, nos redemit a noxa peccati, Deum peccatis nostris propitium facit, quod petebat Psalmista dicens: 'Propitius esto peccatis nostris' . . . ."

[29]Ibid., ". . . et ideo dicit eum propitiationem. I Jo. c.II,2: 'Propitiatio'"

[30]Ibid., "In cuius figura, Ex. xxv, v.17, mandatur quod fiat propitiatorium, id est quod Christus ponatur super arcum, id est, Ecclesiam."

[31]Ibid., "Solum autem per sanguinem Christi potuerunt remitti peccata non solum praesentia, sed praeterita, quia virtus sanguinis Christi operatur per fidem hominis, quam quidem fidem habuerunt illi qui praecesserunt Christi passionem, sicut et nos habemus. II Cor. IV, 13: 'Habentes eumdem spiritum fidei credimus.'"

[32]Ibid., "Haec autem mors Christi nobis applicatur per fidem, qua credimus per suam mortem mundum redemisse. Gal. II, 20: 'In fide vivo filii Dei, qui dilexit me,' etc. Nam et apud homines satisfactio unius alteri non valeret, nisi eam ratam haberet. Et sic patet quomodo sit iustitia per fidem Iesu Christi, ut supra dictum est."

[33]Super ad Hebraeos 1.2: "Tertio est reatus poenae cui homo addicitur ex culpa, et ad satisfaciendum per hanc obtulit semetipsum Dei hostiam in ara crucis."

[34]Ibid., 5.1: "'Et sacrificia pro peccatis,' id est quae sibi offeruntur pro satisfactione peccatorum. Lev. IV,26: 'Pro eis rogabit sacerdos, et pro peccatis eius, et dimittentur ei'"

35Ibid., 7.1: "'Omnis pontifex ad hoc constitui-
tur, ut offerat munera et hostias,' et secundum hoc
dicitur Minister sanctorum.   Christus autem est pontifex . . . .   Ergo necesse est ipsum habere aliqua, quae
offerat."

36This theme is developed by Gustaf Aulén's
Christus Victor, in a fashion typical of some Prot-
estant theologians, namely, to draw too sharp an
opposition betwen the expiatory and recapitulatory
aspects of Christ's saving death.

37Super II ad Timotheum 1.3:   "Dicit ergo 'Christus,' propter hoc, quod pro nobis passus est, 'destru-
xit mortem,' id est, satisfecit Deo pro peccatis
nostris.   I Petr. III, v. 18:   'Christus semel pro
peccatis nostris mortuus est,' etc.   Et peccatum erat
causa nostrae mortis corporalis."   It is characteristic
of Saint Thomas's understanding of Christ's salvific
work to view his conquest of the powers of death and
his satisfaction for sin as different aspects of a
single victory.

38Super ad Hebraeos 2.4.

39Super ad Philippenses 2.2:   ". . . quod 'ar-
bitratus est non esse rapinam,' scilicet 'se esse
aequalem Deo,' quia est in forma Dei, et cognoscit bene
naturam suam.   Et quia cognoscit hoc, ideo dicitur Io.
v. 18:   'Aequalem se Deo facit;' sed hoc non fuit
rapina: sicut quando diabolus et homo volebat ei
aequari.   Is. XIV, 14:   'Ero similis Altissimo,'
et Gen. c. II, 5:   'Eritis sicut dii.'   Haec autem fuit
rapina;   ideo pro hac Christus venit satisfacere.
Ps. LXVIII, 5:   'Quae non rapui, tunc exsolvebam.'"

40Super ad Ephesios 1.2:   "Secundo dicimur redempti, quia a servitute, qua propter peccatum detinebamur,
nec per nos plene satisfacere poteramus, per Christum
liberati sumus, quia moriendo pro nobis satisfecit Deo
Patri, et sic abolita est noxa culpae."

41Ibid., "Hoc quod redempti sumus et gratificati
sumus per satisfactionem Filii eius, fuit ex abundanti
gratia et misericordia, prout immeritis tribuitur
misericordia et miseratio."

42Ibid., ". . . sed Filium suum dedit, qui pro
nobis satisfecit.   Et hoc fuit ex superabundanti
gratia, qua voluit per hoc honorem humanae naturae

286

conservare, dum, quasi per justitiam, homines a servitute peccati et mortis voluit liberare per mortem Filii sui."

[43]Ibid., 2.5: "Quia ergo Christus satisfecit sufficienter pro peccatis nostris, consequens fuit ut soluto pretio fieret reconciliatio."

[44]Super ad Romanos 5.2: "Ipsa autem mors Christi pro nobis charitatem ostendit Dei, quia dedit Filium suum, ut pro nobis satisfaciens moreretur."

[45]Ibid., "Et ideo mors Christi, ex communi mortis ratione, non fuit sic Deo accepta, ut per ipsam reconciliaretur, quia 'Deus non laetatur in perditione vivorum,' ut dicitur Sap. I, 13."

[46]Ibid., "Et ex hoc mors Christi fuit meritoria et satisfactoria pro peccatis nostris, et intantum Deo accepta, quod sufficit ad reconciliationem omnium hominum, etiam occidentium Christum, ex quibus aliqui sunt salvati ipso orante, quando dixit Lc. XXIII, v. 34: 'Ignosce illis quia nesciunt quid faciunt.'"

[47]Ibid., ". . . id est in hoc quod sumus etiam nunc Deo coniuncti per fidem et charitatem."

[48]Super ad Galatas 6.1: "Tertio modo pro poena sibi debita satisfaciendo, orationibus et bonis operibus."

[49]Super II ad Corinthios 5.5: "Homines enim erant inimici Dei propter peccatum, Christus autem hanc inimicitiam abstulit de medio, satisfaciens pro peccato."

[50]Ibid., "Et fecit concordiam."

[51]Super ad Hebraeos 8.2: "Fuit autem talis oblatio munda, quia caro eius nullam maculam peccati habuit. Ex. XII, v. 5: 'Erit agnus sine macula, masculus, anniculus.' Item fuit congrua, quia congruum est, quod homo pro homine satisfaciat. Infra IX, v. 14: 'Obtulit semetipsum immaculatum Deo.' Item apta ad immolandum, quia caro eius mortalis erat. Rom. VIII, 3: 'Mittens Deus Filium suum in similitudinem carnis peccati.' Item est idem ei cui offertur. Io. X, 30: 'Ego et Pater unum sumus.' Item unit Deo illos pro quibus offertur. Io. XVII, 21: 'Ut omnes unum sint, sicut tu, Pater, in me, et ego in te, ut et ipsi in nobis unum sint.'"

[52]Super II ad Corinthios 5.5:   "Speciale autem beneficium est Apostolis collatum, scilicet quod ipsi sint ministri huius reconciliationis."

[53]Super Job, Prologus: "Intendimus enim compendiose secundum nostram possibilitatem, de divino auxilio fiduciam habentes, librum istum qui intitulatur Beati Job secundum litteralem sensum exponere; eius enim mysteria tam subtiliter et diserte beatus papa Gregorius nobis aperuit ut his nihil ultra addendum videatur."

[54]Epistola anonymi ad Hugonem amicum, ed. Martène and Durand, Thesaurum Novum Anecdotum, I, pp. 487-88. I owe this reference to Smalley, Study of the Bible, pp. 63-64.

[55]Super Job, Prologus 148-57:   "Unde eorum qui divino spiritu sapientiam consecuti sunt ad aliorum eruditionem, primum et praecipuum studium fuit hanc opinionem a cordibus hominum amovere; et ideo post Legem datam et Prophetas, in numero hagiographorum, idest librorum per Spiritum Dei sapienter ad eruditionem hominum conscriptorum, primus ponitur liber Iob, cujus tota intentio circa hoc versatur ut per probabiles rationes ostendatur res humanas divina providentia regi."

[56]Smalley, Study of the Bible, p. 236.

[57]Ibid., p. 235.   Smalley writes: "This particular book will serve as a measure for the distance between the Victorines, Hugh of St. Cher, St. Albert, and St. Thomas."

[58]Chenu, Understanding, p. 257.

[59]Summa theologiae I, 1.10.co/:   "secundum vero quod ea quae in Christo sunt facta vel in his quae Christum significant sunt signa eorum quae nos agere debemus est sensus moralis."

[60]Super Job 1/185:   ". . . singula enim peccata convenientibus satisfactionibus sunt expianda."

[61]Ibid., 7/449:   "Homo enim nihil condignum facere potest propriis viribus ad recompensandum offensam quam contra Deum commisit."

[62]Ibid., 8/97-99: ". . . secundum est ut homo pro peccatis satisfaciat, et quantum ad hoc dicit 'et Omnipotentem fueris deprecatus; 'inter satisfactionis enim opera quasi praecipuum videtur esse oratio."

[63]Ibid., 42/41-44: "Quanto autem aliquis magis Dei justitiam considerat tanto plenius culpam suam recognoscit, unde subdit 'Idcirco ipse me reprehendo,' propiam scilicet culpam considerando."

[64]Ibid., 42/44-49: "Et quia non sufficit culpam confiteri nisi sequatur satisfactio, ideo subdit 'et ago paenitentiam in favilla et cincere,' in signum scilicet fragilitatis naturae corporeae: convenit enim humilis satisfactio ad expiandam superbiam cogitationis."

[65]Weisheipl, Friar Thomas, pp. 189-195.

[66]De regno 1.11: "Tales insuper raro poenitent, vento inflati superbiae, merito peccatorum a Deo deserti, et adulationibus hominum delibuti, rarius digne satisfacere possunt."

[67]The style, language, and situation of the folktale (1.1-2.13) reappear abruptly in 42.7-17 of Job.

[68]Super Job 42/71-83: "Sed quia infideles per fideles Deo reconciliari debent, subdit 'et ite ad servum meum Iob,' ut scilicet eo mediante mihi reconciliemini, 'et offerte pro vobis holocaustum,' ut scilicet vos satisfaciatis qui peccastis. Sed vestra satisfactio indiget fidelis viri patrocinio, unde subdit 'Iob autem, servus meus, orabit pro vobis,' qui scilicet dignus est exaudiri propter suam fidem, unde subdit 'Faciem eius,' scilicet deprecantis, 'suscipiam,' scilicet exaudiendo eius orationem, 'ut non imputetur vobis stultitia,' scilicet infidelis dogmatis; et hoc exponit subdens 'Neque enim locuti estis coram me rectum sicut servus meus Iob.'"

[69]Super ad Romanos 11.4: "Exterior vero poenitentia consistit in exteriori satisfactione quae a baptizato non requiritur, quia per gratiam baptismalem liberatur homo non solum a culpa sed etiam a tota poena per virtutem passionis Christi, qui pro peccatis omnium satisfecit . . . ."

[70]Super II ad Corinthios 7.2:   "Dicendum est,
quod poenitentia habet tres partes, quarum pars prima
est tristitia, scilicet dolor et compunctio de peccatis; aliae duae sunt confessio et satisfactio.   Cum
ergo dicit, quod tristitia operatur poenitentiam,
intelligendum est, quod compunctio, seu dolor de
peccato operetur in nobis poenitentiam, id est, alias
partes poenitentiae, scilicet confessionem et satisfactionem."

[71]Super I ad Corinthios 11.7:   "Tertio modo
dicitur aliquis indignus ex eo quod cum voluntate
peccandi mortaliter, accedit ad Eucharistiam.   Dicitur
enim Levit. XXI, 23:   'Non accedat ad altare qui
maculam habet.'   Intelligitur aliquis maculam peccati
habere, quamdiu est in voluntate peccandi, quae tamen
tollitur per poenitentiam.   Per contritionem quidem,
quae tollit voluntatem peccandi, cum proposito confi-
tendi et satisfaciendi, quantum ad remissionem culpae
et poenae aeternae;   per confessionem autem et satisfactionem quantum ad totalem remissionem poenae et
reconciliationem ad membra Ecclesiae.   Et ideo in
necessitate quidem, puta quando aliquis copiam con-
fessionis habere non potest, sufficit contritio ad
sumptionem huius sacramenti.   Regulariter autem debet
confessio praecedere cum aliqua satisfactione."

[72]In psalmos (50) 6/1-6:   "Hic petit recupera-
tionem innocentiae.   Et quia considerat in se malum
culpae esse, et bonum gratiae: petit primo removeri
malum sive peccatum; secundo petit removeri effectum
peccati, ibi, 'Cor mundum crea in me Deus.'"

[73]Super Matthaeum 9.1:   "Tria habebat infirmus:
iacebat in lecto, portabatur ab aliis, ire non poterat.
Quia ergo iacebat dixit 'Surge;' quia portabatur,
praecepit ut portaret 'Tolle lectum tuum;' quia ire non
poterat, dixit 'Et ambula.'"

[74]Ibid., "Similiter peccatori in peccato iacenti
dicitur Surge, a peccato per contritionem; tolle
lectum, per satisfactionem; Michaeae VII,9:   'Iram
Domini portabo, quia peccavi ei.'   Et vade in domum
tuam, in domum aeternitatis, vel in conscientiam
propriam; Sap. VIII, 16: 'Intrans in domum meam con-
quiescam in illa.'"

[75]Super Johannem 5.5:   "Nihilominus tamen haec
tria in iustificatione Dominus praecipit.   Primo quod
surgat recedendo a peccato; Eph. v 14:   'Surge qui

dormis, et exurge a mortuis.'--Secundo praecipitur 'Tolle grabatum,' satisfaciendo de commissis. Per grabatum enim, in quo homo requiescit, significatur peccatum. Tollit ergo homo grabatum suum, quando fert onus poenitentiae sibi pro peccato impositum; Mich. c. VII, 9: 'Iram Domini portabo, quoniam peccavi ei.' --Tertio ut ambulet proficiendo in bono, secundum illud Ps. LXXXIII, 8: 'Ibunt de virtute in virtutem.'"

76"Psalmus David L. Quando venit ad eum Nathan propheta cum intravit ad Bersabee."

77The Vulgate enumeration of the psalms differs from that of modern editions of the Bible; the "Miserere" in these latter is Psalm 51. In psalmos (50) 1/7-12: "Primum, quod in ordine Psalmorum hic Psalmus est quinquagesimus, et hic est numerus jubilaeus, ut dicitur Levit. XXVII, in quo fiebat remissio omnium debitorum."

78Ibid., /22-27: "Hic autem quartus pertinet ad effectum poenitentiae. In quo ostenditur quomodo poenitentia restaurat hominem ad perfectum: et ideo inter omnes alios Psalmus iste magis frequentatur in Ecclesia. . . ."

79Ibid., Proemium: "Beatus ergo Hieronymus super Ezech. tradidit nobis eam regulam quam servabimus in Psalmis: scilicet quod sic sunt exponendi de rebus gestis, ut figurantibus aliquid de Christo vel ecclesia."

80In psalmos (37) 2: "Quantum ad tertium dicit, propter recidivum: 'Putruerunt et corruptae sunt cicatrices meae.' Cicatrix ex vulnere relinquitur: ita etiam quando quis peccavit, et dimissum est ei peccatum, sed adhuc est pronitas ad peccandum, est quasi cicatrix ex vulnere. Quandoque autem Deus sanat eam per satisfactionem et exercitium bonorum operum."

81In psalmos (50) 1: "Homo qui habet mentem bene dispositam, plus abhorret immunditiam culpae, quam austeritatem poenae; et ideo dicit, 'Amplius lava me;' quasi dicta, peto ut deleas poenam; sed amplius peto quod mundes maculam."

82Ibid., 3: "'Ecce enim veritatem dilexisti.' 'Qui vult satisfacere debet diligere ea quae Deus diligit, Deus autem diligit veritatem fidei: Joan, XVIII, 37: 'Omnis qui est ex veritate, audit vocem mean.' Item justitiam: Psal. LXXXVIII, 15:

'Misericordia et veritas praecedent faciem tuam.' Et haec necessaria est in poenitente, ut in se puniat quod deliquit. Item est necessaria confessio, ut confiteatur peccata."

[83]Super Matthaeum 5.2: "Et potest iste luctus tripliciter exponi. Primo pro peccatis non solum propriis, sed etiam alienis: quia si lugemus mortuos carnaliter, multo magis spiritualiter . . . Ponitur autem satis congrue ista beatitudo post praemissam. Posset enim quis dicere: Sufficit non facere malum: et verum est a principio ante peccatum; sed post commissum peccatum non sufficit nisi satisfacias."

[84]In psalmos (50) 5: ". . . nam per tristitiam poenitentiae cor hominis conteritur: et ideo quando sunt homines laeti, est signum quod ossa quae sunt contrita et afflicta, participant gaudium."

[85]Ibid., 6: "Hoc gaudium perdiderat Psalmista; et ideo petit restitui sibi, cum dicit, 'Redde mihi laetitiam;' non de mundanis, sed, 'Salutaris tui' idest de tua salvatione. Alia littera habet 'Laetitiam Jesu,' scilicet Salvatoris, per quem fit remissio peccatorum: Habac ult, 18: 'Exultabo in Deo Jesu meo.'"

[86]Ibid., Proemium: "Unde signatur materia in hoc quod dicit: 'In omni opere,' quia de omni opere Dei tractat."

[87]Ibid., "Omnia enim quae ad finem Incarnationis pertinent, sic dilucide traduntur in hoc opere, ut fere videatur evangelium, et non prophetia."

[88]Aulén, Christus Victor, p. 95: "In Thomas, also, certain of the characteristic points of the classic view (Christus Victor) appear, such as deliverance of men from the power of the devil, which he seeks to reconcile with the idea of satisfaction (Latin view)." Apart from this concession, Aulén classifies both Anselm and Saint Thomas (along with the Middle Ages, in general) as proponents of the Latin type of doctrine which he summarizes as follows: "The payment of satisfaction is treated as the essential element in Atonement and as accomplished by the death of Christ; the payment is primarily the work of Christ's human nature, but it gains increased meritorious value on account of the union of human nature with the Divine nature in Christ." (P. 93).

CHAPTER III

¹See Chenu, <u>Understanding</u>, pp. 273-275 for some examples of the areas where these differences occur.

²See his <u>Defensiones Theologiae Divi Thomae Aquinatis</u>, edited by Ceslaus Paban and Thomas Pègues, (Tours: A. Cartier, 1900-1907), Vols. 1-7. For biographical information see T.M. Pègues, "La Biographie de Jean Capreolus," <u>Revue Thomiste</u> 7 (1899), pp. 317-334.

³<u>Scriptum</u>, Book Four, XIV-XXII.

⁴In his commentary on the <u>Sentences</u>, Saint Thomas is still very much influenced by the Victorine perspective on sacramental theology about which David Schaff, "The Sacramental Theory of the Medieval Church," <u>The Princeton Theological Review</u> 4 (1906), pp. 206-235 writes: "Beginning with Hugh of St. Victor, the Schoolmen in unmistakeable language assert that the sacraments contain and confer grace. They have value in themselves. . . . The favorite illustration for the operation of the sacraments is medicine. Hugh of St. Victor (<u>Summa</u> IV, 1) said God is the physician, man the invalid, the priest the minister, grace the antidote, the sacraments the vase."

⁵<u>Scriptum</u>, Book Four, XIV (<u>divisio textus</u>): "Hic incipit determinare de poenitentia, quae ordinatur ad amotionem mali, quod per actum procedentium in vita ista provenit . . ."

⁶<u>Ibid</u>., XV.1: "Hic est quaerendum de satisfactione et de partibus eius; unde quatuor his quaeruntur. Primo de ipsa satisfactione."

⁷Weisheipl, <u>Friar Thomas</u>, pp. 435-436, n. 31. The study of C.H. Turner, "The <u>Liber Ecclesiasticorum Dogmatum</u> attributed to Gennadius," <u>The Journal of Theological Studies</u> 7 (1906), pp. 78-99, makes a more modest assertion: "But an alternative explanation of the name of Gennadius is perhaps rather suggested by the evidence of the MSS--namely that to Gennadius of

Marseilles is due a recension of the tract which gave it the form it bears. . . ." For our purposes we shall simply refer to the author of this work as "pseudo-Augustine".

[8]In the text published by Turner, _ibid._, p. 94, the chapter of the _Liber_ which contains the definition of satisfaction is XXIII and reads as follows: "Paenitentia uera est paenitenda non admittere sed amissa deflere, satisfactio paenitentiae est causas peccatorum excidere nec earum suggestionibus additum indulgere."

[9]Anselm of Canterbury, _Cur Deus homo?_, I, 11, edited by René Roques, (Paris: Les Éditions du Cerf, 1963), p. 266. "Sic ergo debet omnis qui peccat, honorem Deo quam rapuit solvere; et haec est satisfactio, quam omnis peccator Deo debet facere." See the Appendix for an extended treatment of Anselm's satisfaction-theory.

[10]_Scriptum_, Book Four, XV.1.1a co/: "Et quia aequalis medium est, quod suo nomine satisfactio importat (non enim dicitur aliquid satisfactum nisi secundum proportionem aequalitatis ad aliquid), constat quod satisfactio etiam formaliter est actus virtutis."

[11]_Ibid._, XV.1.1a ra/1: "Ad primum ergo dicendum, quod quamvis satisfacere in se sit debitum, tamen inquantum satisfaciens voluntarie hoc opus exequitur, rationem gratuiti accipit ex parte operantis. . . ."

[12]_Ibid._, XV.1.1a ra/2: "Ad secundum dicendum quod actus virtutis non requirit voluntarium in eo qui patitur, sed in eo qui facit, quia illius actus est; et ideo, cum ille in quem judex vindictam exercet, se habeat ut patiens ad satisfactionem, non ut agens, non oportet quod in eo voluntaria sit satisfactio, sed in judice faciente."

[13]_Ibid._, XV.1.1b ag/1: "Videtur quod non sit actus justitiae. Quia satisfactio fit ad hoc quod reconcilietur ei quem offendit. Sed reconciliatio, cum sit amoris, ad caritatem pertinet. Ergo satisfactio est actus caritatis, et non justitiae."

[14]_Ibid._, XV.1.1b ag/3: "Praeterea, cavere in futurum non est actus justitiae, sed magis prudentiae, cuius pars ponitur cautela. . . . Sed hoc pertinet ad satisfactionem; quia ipsius est suggestionibus peccatorum aditum non indulgere."

[15]Aristotle, Nicomachean Ethics, Book V, c.3, translated by W. D. Ross, in The Basic Works of Aristotle, edited by Richard McKeon, (New York: Random House, 1941), p. 1007.

[16]See Chenu, Understanding, pp. 134-135.

[17]Aristotle, Nicomachean Ethics Book II, c. 3, p. 954.

[18]Scriptum, Book Four, XV.1.1c co/: ". . . unde et satisfactio, quae est justitiae actus poenam inferentis, est medicina, curans peccata praeterita, et praeservans a futuris. . . ."

[19]Ibid., "Et secundum hoc dupliciter potest satisfactio definiri. Uno modo respectu culpae praeteritae, quam recompensando curat; et sic dicitur, quod satisfactio est injuriae illatae recompensatio secundum justitiae aequalitatem; et in idem dicitur redire definitio Anselmi, qui dicit, quod satisfacere est Deo debitum honorem impendere, ut consideretur debitum ratione culpae commissae. Alio modo potest definiri secundum quod praeservat a culpa futura. . . ."

[20]Ibid., XV.1.1c ra/4: "Nihilominus tamen ex cautela futurorum cognosci potest recompensatio praeteritorum, quia fit circa aedem converso modo. In praeterita enim respicientes, causas peccatorum propter peccata detestamur, a peccatis incipientes detestationis motum; sed in cautela a causis incipimus, ut causis subtractis facilius peccata vitemus."

[21]Ibid., XV.1.2 co/: "In his autem honoribus qui sunt ad parentes et deos, etiam secundum Philosophum, impossibile est aequivalens reddere secundum quantitatem; sed sufficit ut homo reddat quod potest: quia amicitia non exigit aequivalens nisi secundum quod possibile est. . . ."

[22]Ibid., XV.1.2 ra/1: ". . . sicut offensa habuit quamdam infinitatem ex infinitate divinae majestatis, ita et satisfactio accipit quamdam infinitatem ex infinitate divinae misericordiae. . . ."

[23]Ibid., ". . . prout est gratis informata, per quam acceptum redditur quod homo reddere potest."

[24]Ibid., "Alii vero dicunt, quod etiam quantum ad aversionem pro peccato satisfieri potest virtute meriti Christi, quod quodammodo infinitum fuit, ut in 3 lib., dist. 18, qu. 1, art. 6, quaestiunc. 1, dictum est; et hoc in idem redit quod prius dictum est; quia per fidem mediatoris gratia data est credentibus. Si tamen alio modo gratiam daret, sufficeret satisfactio per modum praedictum."

[25]Ibid., XV.1.3a co/: "Offensae autem ablatio est amicitiae restitutio; et ideo si aliquid sit quod amicitiae restitutionem impediat, etiam apud homines satisfactio esse non potest."

[26]Ibid., XV.1.3d co/: "Cum autem in omnibus illis quae gratis dantur, prima ratio dandi sit amor, impossibile est quod aliquis tale sibi debitum faciat, quia amicitia caret; et ideo cum omnia bona et temporalia et aeterna ex divina liberalitate nobis donentur, nullus acquirere potest debitum recipiendi aliquod illorum, nisi per caritatem ad Deum; et ideo opera extra caritatem facta, non sunt meritoria ex condigno neque aeterni neque temporalis alicujus boni apud Deum. Sed quia divinam bonitatem decet ut ubicumque dispositionem invenit, perfectionem adjiciat; ideo ex merito congrui dicitur aliquis mereri aliquod bonum per opera extra caritatem facta."

[27]Ibid., I.1.5a ag/5: "Impossible est sine gratia satisfacere. Sed sacramenta veteris legis erant satisfactoria; unde pro diversis peccatis diversa sacrificia injungebantur in lege. . . ." Ibid., ra/5: ". . . quamvis illa sacramenta peccata non diluerent quantum ad maculam, quia gratiam non conferebant, diminuebant tamen reatum, inquantum onerosa erant; et ideo satisfactoria esse poterant, praesupposita gratia ex fide mediatoris ei collata."

[28]Ibid., I.1.5a co/. Although Saint Thomas sides with those who did not hold that the sacraments of the Old Law confer grace, "Et ideo alii dicunt, et melius, quod nullo modo sacramenta ipsa veteris legis . . . gratiam conferebant . . . ," he excepted circumcision, holding that it conferred grace necessary to resist the urgings to sin. This is one opinion which he changed before composing the Summa theologiae III, 62.6 ra/3.

[29]Anselm, Cur Deus homo? I.11, p. 264: "Hunc honorem debitum qui Deo non reddit, aufert Deo quod suum est, et Deum exhonorat; et hoc est peccare."

[30]See ibid., n. 1 for a discussion of the notions of "rectitude" and "justice" in Saint Anselm's thought.

[31]Scriptum, Book Four, XV.1.4a ra/3: "Ad tertium dicendum quod debitum pro peccato est recompensatio offensae, quae sine poena peccantis non fit; et de tali debito Anselmus intelligit.

[32]Ibid., XV.1.4b ra/2. Saint Thomas refers to a work of Gregory the Great. In fact the reference is from Saint Augustine, De Civitate Dei, Book I, c. 8.

[33]Ibid., XV.1.1: ". . . unde quatuor hic quaeruntur. Primo de ipsa satisfactione. Secundo de eleemosyna. Tertio de jejunio. Quarto de oratione. His enim tribus homo satisfacit."

[34]Scriptum, Book Four, XV.1.4c ra/1. See also XV.4.7a.

[35]The New Testament foundation for this is the teaching of Matthew 6: 2-18. See P. Galtier, S.J., "Satisfaction" in Dict. théol. cath. XIV (Paris: Letouzey, 1939), cols. 1129-1210, for a discussion of the historical development of satisfactory works within the context of the sacrament of penance.

[36]Scriptum, Book Four, XV.1.4c ra/5: "Quod quidquid ad afflictionem corporis pertinet, totum ad jejunium refertur; et quidquid ad proximi utilitatem expenditur, totum eleemosynae rationem habet; et similiter quaecumque latria exhibeatur Deo, orationis accipit rationem. . . ."

[37]Ibid., XV.2-4.

[38]Ibid., XV.1.1c ra/3: "Nec iterum satisfactio sine Dei auxilio fit, quia sine caritate esse non potest. . . ."

[39]Ibid., XX.1.2c co/: "quia ex jejunio unius caro alterius non domatur . . ."

[40]Ibid., "Sed quantum ad satisfactionem debiti unus potest pro alio satisfacere, dummodo sit in caritate, ut opera ejus satisfactoria esse possint. Nec oportet quod major poena imponatur ei qui pro altero satisfacit, quam principali imponeretur, ut quidam dicunt, hac ratione moti, quia poena propria magis satisfacit quam aliena, quia habet vim satisfaciendi,

maxime ratione caritatis qua homo ipsam sustinet. Et quia major caritas apparet in hoc quod aliquis pro altero satisfacit quam si ipse satisfaceret; ideo minor poena requiritur in eo qui pro altero satisfacit, quam in principali requireretur. Unde dicitur in vitis Patrum, quod propter caritatem unius, qui alterius fratris sui caritate ductus, poenitentiam fecit pro peccato quod non commiserat, alteri peccatum quod commiserat, dimissum est. Nec exigitur etiam quantum ad solutionem debiti, quod ille pro quo fit satisfactio, sit impotens ad satisfaciendum; quia etiam si esset potens, alio satisfaciente pro ipso, ipse a debito immunis esset. Sed hoc requiritur inquantum poena satisfactoria est in remedium; unde non est permittendum ut aliquis pro alio poenitentiam faciat, nisi defectus aliquis appareat in poenitente; vel corporalis, per quem sit impotens ad sustinendum; vel spiritualis, per quem non sit promptus ad portandum poenam."

[41]See Ibid., XLV.2.1d; 2b; 3a ra/1.

[42]Scriptum, Book Three, Prologue: "Montes enim supremi sunt nobilissimae creaturae. . . . "

[43]See above, p. 2.

[44]Scriptum, Book Three, I.1.2 ag/1-9: "Sicut enim bonitati opponitur malitia, ita majestati opponitur infirmitas. Sed summam bonitatem non decet assumere aliquam malitiam. Ergo summae majestati indecens est omnis infirmitas. Omnis autem sapiens vitat indecentiam. Ergo cum Deus sit sapientissimus, nullo modo nostram naturam, quae infirma est, assumere debuit.
2. Praeterea, peccatum hominis et peccatum angeli fuerunt ejusdem generis, quia uterque per superbiam peccavit. Sed Deus angelorum peccato non subvenit per alicujus naturae assumptionem. Ergo nec peccato hominis subvenire debuit per incarnationem.
3. Praeterea, creatio recreationi respondet. Sed Deus ad creationem hominis nullam creaturam assumpsit. Ergo nec ad ejus recreationem incarnari eum congruum fuit.
4. Praeterea, ut in Psalm. 144, 9, dicitur, 'miserationes ejus super omnia opera ejus.' Ergo plus decuit quod Deus ostenderet immensitatem suae misericordiae quam severitatem suae justitiae. Sed ad magnitudinem miseriocordiae pertinet ut peccata sine satisfactione remittantur: unde et a Deo nobis praecipitur ut debitoribus nostris gratis dimittamus.

Ergo et Deus naturam humanam gratis reparare debuit, non expetendo satisfactionem: et ita non fuit opportunum ut Deus homo fieret ad satisfaciendum pro hominibus.

5. Praeterea, nulla crudelitas Deo est attribuenda, quia summe est misericors. Sed exigere ab aliquo plus quam potest, est crudele. Ergo Deus non exigit satisfactionem ab homine quam homo non potest implere; et ita homo per se potest satisfacere: et sic non fuit necessarium quod Deus incarnaretur.

6. Praeterea, quicumque potest satisfacere pro majori peccato, potest satisfacere pro minori. Sed mortale peccatum actuale est majus quam originale, quia habet plus de voluntario. Ergo cum homo possit pro mortali satisfacere, potest pro originalimulti fortius satisfacere; et sic idem quod prius.

7. Praeterea, in primo parente idem fuit peccatum originale et actuale. Sed ipse per poenitentiam de peccato actuali satisfecit. Ergo et de originali potuit satisfacere; et sic idem quod prius.

8. Praeterea, secundum Dionysium, lex Divinitatis est ultima per media reducere. Sed homo per peccatum a Deo abjectus erat. Ergo cum natura angelica inter naturam divinam et humanam sit media, ut in 4 cap. cael. Hierar. ostenditur, videtur quod etsi homo sufficienter satisfacere non poterat, per Angelum hoc fieri debuerit, et non per Deum incarnatum.

9. Praeterea, quodlibet bonum creatum finitum est. Sed bonum totius humanae naturae est creatum; quolibet autem finito potest Deus facere aliquid majus. Ergo Deus potest facere unam creaturam, cujus bonitas praeponderet bonitati totius naturae humanae. Ergo per illam posset recompensari corruptio totius humanae naturae: et ita videtur quod non oportuit ad reparationem humani generis Deum incarnari."

[45]Ibid., I.1.2 sc/4: "Item Jacob 4,6: 'Deus superbis resistit.' Sed per superbiam diabolus homini invidens eum servum suum constituit, et injuste in servitute detinuit, cum ad servitium Dei creatus sit. Ergo decuit ut summe potens Deus nequitiae diaboli resisteret, ut non solum hominem de ejus potestate eriperet, sed etiam e converso hominem dominum diaboli constitueret."

[46]Ibid., 1.1.2 sc/1: "Sed contra, non erat conveniens ut una nobilissimarum creaturarum suo fine totaliter frustraretur. Sed humana natura est inter nobilissimas naturas. Cum ergo tota corrupta fuerit per peccatum in primo parente, et ita beatitudine privata, ad quam instituta erat, congruum fuit ipsam

reparari. Sed reparatio humani generis non potest
fieri nisi peccatum dimittatur; nec justum est ut
peccatum sine satisfactione dimittatur."

[47]Ibid., "Sed satisfactio decenter fieri non
potest nisi ab eo qui debet satisfacere et potest.
Ergo sic debuit fieri. Sed non debet nisi homo qui
peccavit, et non potest nisi Deus: quia quaelibet
creatura totum suum esse Deo debet, nedum ut pro alio
satisfacere possit: et sic aliqua creatura pro homine
non potest satisfacere, nec ipse pro se, cum peccato
indignus reddatur."

[48]Chenu, Understanding, p. 186.

[49]Scriptum, Book Three, I.1.2. co/: "Ergo cum
humana natura lapsa esset, et nihilominus reparabilis
erat, decuit ut eam repararet."

[50]Ibid., "Similiter ut esset facilis modus ascen-
dendi in Deum, decuit ut homo ex his quae sibi cognita
sunt tam secundum intellectum quam affectum, in Deum
consurgeret; et quia homini connaturale est secundum
statum praesentis miseriae ut a visibilibus cognitionem
accipiat, et circa ea afficiatur; ideo Deus congruenter
visibilis factus est, humanam naturam assumendo, ut ex
visibilibus in invisibilium amorem et cognitionem
rapiamur."

[51]Anselm, Cur Deus homo? II.14, p. 404; 11.15,
p. 406; II.18, p. 440.

[52]Scriptum, Book Three, I.1.2 ra/6: ". . . principium autem originalis in isto, est origo ejus vitiata;
unde originale quodammodo est necessarium. . . ."

[53]Lafont, Structures, p. 305 makes the point that
Alexander of Hales in his Summa was the first to
incorporate the argument of Cur Deus homo? into the
medieval discussion of the necessity for the Incarnation. See his Summa theologica Book III, studio et
cura III PP. Collegii S. Bonaventurae, (Quaracchi,
1948), I.5.1&2 for Alexander's discussion, "Utrum
humana natura possit reparari per se an per alium."

[54]Scriptum, Book Three, II.1.2c; III.4.1 co/.
Especially II.1.2b co/: "Ad secundam quaestionem
dicendum, quod non fuit decens ut aliunde quam de
stirpe Adae Filius Dei humanam naturam assumeret,
praecipue propter tria. Primo ad servandum justitiam
satisfactionis. Si enim de genere Adae non fuisset,

ad eum non pertineret pro peccato Adae satisfacere. Secundo ad perfectam reintegrationem dignitatis Adae, qui hoc habuit ut ipse et suum genus nulla alia creatura indigeret, quasi sustentante et salvante: et hoc generi ejus redditum non fuisset, si redemptus fuisset per aliquem qui ad genus ejus non pertineret. Tertio ad servandum dignitatem specialiter ipsius Adae, qui in hoc quodam modi imaginem Dei singulariter habuit, ut sicut Deus, cum sit ens primum, omnium entium principium est per creationem; ita etiam Adam, cum sit primus homo, est principium omnium hominum per generationem; quod sibi deperiret, si Christus non de ejus genere homo fieret."

55Ibid., V.1.3s c/3: "Praeterea, ad hoc quod fiat redemptio humani generis, oportet quod sit agens satisfactionem unus Deus qui potest, et homo qui debet, ut patet ex dictis in 1 dist., quaest. 1, art. 2. Sed nullo modo duae personae possunt esse unum agens. Ergo si sunt duae personae, nondum facta est satisfactio; et ita adhuc sumus in servitute peccati, quod est contra sacram Scripturam novi Testamenti."

56Ibid., XV.2.3c co/: "Tertio ex voluntate patientis quia enim voluntarie patiebatur, ut satisfaceret pro peccato totius humani generis, ideo dolorem excedentem omnes alios dolores assumpsit."

57Ibid., XV.1.1 ra/4: "Ad quartum dicendum, quod venerat vincere fortem per justitiam, satisfaciendo; et ideo oportuit quod haberet defectus, secundum quod satisfaceret. Et praeterea per fortitudinem oppositam istis defectibus non vincitur diabolus, sed per fortitudinem virtutis et gratiae."

58Ibid., XIX.1.4 ra/2: "Ad secundum dicendum, quod pretium sanguinis sui non diabolo, sed Deo obtulit, ut pro nobis satisfaceret."; XIX.1.4b co/: "Sed quia ille proprie dicitur emere qui emptionis pretium solvit, magis quam ille qui emptorem mittit; ideo proprie loquendo dicitur Christus tantum redemptor . . ." Undoubtedly the use of this imagery derives in some part from the text of Peter Lombard, Distinction XX, "Christus ergo est sacerdos, idemque hostia, et pretium nostrae reconciliationis."

59Ibid., XX.1.1b ra/2: "Ad secundum dicendum, quod in hoc quod Deus per satisfactionem hominem reparari voluit, maxime manifestatur ejus misericordia: quia non tantum culpam ab eo voluit removere, sed etiam ad pristinam dignitatem humanam naturam integraliter reducere: quae quidem dignitas perpetuo in natura manet, sed poena ad modicum transit; unde magis manifestatur misericordia in perducendo ad aeternam dignitatem, quam in dimittendo temporalem culpam."

60Ibid., XIX.1.1a co/: "Solus autem Christus aliis potest sufficienter mereri: quia potest in naturam, inquantum Deus est, et caritas sua quodammodo est infinita, sicut et gratia, ut supra dictum est, dist. 13, qu. 1, art. 2, quaestiunc. 2. In hoc autem pro tota natura meruit, in quo debitum naturae, scilicet mortis, quae pro peccato ei debebatur, exsolvit ipse peccatum non habens; ut sic non pro se mortem solvere teneretur, sed pro natura solveret; unde satisfaciendo pro tota natura, sufficienter meruit peccatorum remissionem allis qui peccata habebant."

61Ibid., XIX.1.1b co/: "Christi autem qui nobis meruit deletionem peccatorum, invenitur sufficientia ad delendum omnia peccata nostra ex duobus; scilicet ex actione, in qua meritum consistit, quae agit ut divina, eo quod est actio Dei et hominis, ut dictum est; et ex hoc habet infinitam in merendo efficaciam; et iterum ex eo quod passio abstulit, scilicet animam Deo unitam, quae etiam habebat infinitum valorem ex hoc quod est Deo unita; et ex hoc est infinita efficacia in satisfaciendo."

62Ibid., XIX.1.5b co/: "Ipse (Christus) enim secundum humanam naturam pro hominibus satisfaciens, homines Deo conjunxit. . . ." Also, ibid., ra/3: "Ad tertium dicendum, quod quamvis nos Deo conjungere non potuisset nis Deus fuisset, quia humana natura ex divina sibi c njuncta in persona majorem efficaciam habebat, tamer satisfactionem, qua Deo reconciliati et conjuncti sumus, non exhibuit nisi per humanam naturam; et ideo secundum ipsam est proxima causa conjunctionis."

63Ibid., XIX.1.4a co/: "Et ideo per suam passionem Christus duo fecit: liberavit enim nos a potestate hostis, vincendo ipsum per contraria eorum quibus hominem vincerat, scilicet humilitatem, obedientiam, et austeritatem poenae, quae delectationi cibi vetiti opponitur; et iterum, satisfaciendo pro culpa, Deo conjunxit, et domesticos Dei et filios fecit. Unde ista liberatio duas rationes habuit emptionis: inquantum enim a potestate diaboli eripuit, dicitur nos redemisse, sicut Rex regnum occupatum ab adversario, per laborem certaminis redimit; inquantum vero Deum nobis placavit, dicitur nos redemisse, sicut pretium solvens suae satisfactionis pro nobis, ut a poena et a peccato liberemur."

64Ibid., XX.1.3 ra/4: "Ad quartum dicendum, quod quamvis gutta sanguinis quam in circumcisione fudit, esset sufficiens ad omnem satisfactionem, considerata conditione personae, non tamen quantum ad genus poenae: quia pro morte ad quam humanum genus obligatum erat, oportebat quod mortem exsolveret."

65Ibid., ra/1: "Ad primum ergo dicendum, quod passio Christi non fuit satisfactoria ex parte occidentium Christum, sed ex parte ipsius patientis, qui ex maxima caritate pati voluit; et secundum hoc fuit Deo accepta."

66Ibid., ra/5: "Ad quintum dicendum, quod contritio non tantum habet vim ex caritate, sed etiam ex dolore; et ideo ratione caritatis delet culpam, ratione autem doloris computatur in satisfactionem poenae."

66aIbid., ra/3: "Ad tertium dicendum, quod in peccato Adae non solum fuit superbia, sed delectatio: et ideo in satisfactione non solum debuit esse humilitas, quod in incarnatione factum est, sed etiam acerbitas doloris, quod in passione accidit."

67Ibid., XX.1.4a ag/2 quotes Anselm, Cur Deus homo? I, 10: "Non autem potuisse calicem transire, nisi biberet illum, dixit, non quia non posset mortem vitare si vellet, sed quoniam . . . mundum erat aliter impossible salvari. . . ."

68Anselm, Cur Deus homo? II, 19.

69Scriptum, Book Three, XX.1.3 ra/1: ". . . passio Christi non fuit satisfactoria ex parte occidentium Christum, sed ex parte ipsius patientis, qui ex maxima caritate pati voluit; et secundum hoc fuit Deo accepta."

70Ibid., XX.1.3 ra/5: ". . . contritio non tantum habet vim ex caritate, sed etiam ex dolore; et ideo ratione caritatis delet culpam, ratione autem doloris computatur in satisactione poenae."

71M.F. Moos, O.P. in his edition of the Scriptum, Book Three (Paris: Lethielleux, 1933), p. 18 notes that many codices have "humana" but strike it and put "divina" in the text of I.1.2 ra/6. See above, n. 53.

[72]Ibid., I.1.2 ra/5: "Ad quintum dicendum, quod quantitas peccati ex duobus potest pensari; scilicet ex parte Dei, in quem peccatur; et sic infinitatem quamdam habet, prout offensa Dei est, quia quanto major est qui offenditur, tanto culpa est gravior: vel ex parte boni quod corrumpitur per peccatum; et sic quantitas culpae finita est, scilicet inquantum est corruptio naturae; et ideo ad satisfactionem debitam requiritur actio hominis quae proportionetur quantitati culpae, inquantum corruptio quaedam est; et gratia, cujus virtus quodammodo infinita est, cum sufficiat at merendum praemium infinitum, per quam satisfactio proportionatur quantitati culpae, prout offensa Dei est; et ideo ex se non sufficit homo ad satisfaciendum, quia ex se gratiam habere non potest. Nec tamen Deus crudelis est hanc satisfactionem exigens: quia quamvis gratiam habere non possit ex se, et ita nec satisfacere; potest tamen satisfacere per id quod Deus paratus est dare, scilicet per gratiam."

[73]Ibid., ra/7: ". . . et sic primus homo pro eo satisfecit adjutorio gratiae Dei: vel inquantum fuit corruptio naturae, et sic pro eo Adam satisfacere non potuit. . ."

[74]Ibid., ". . . nec aliquis antiquorum patrum, nisi solum inquantum corruptio naturae in personam redunbadat; ex hac enim parte originale peccatum in antiquis patribus per fidem, decimas, circumcisionem et sacrificia solvebatur; et ideo decendentes nondum ad visionem Dei admittebantur, nisi prius per satisfactionem Christi, naturae corruptio sanaretur."

[75]Ibid., XX.1.1c ra/3: ". . . sicut imperfectum in quolibet genere oritur ex perfecto." See also ibid., XX.1.2 co/: ". . . oportebat quod pro peccato humanae naturae fieret condigna satisfactio: tum quia aliter homo non restitueretur pristinae dignitati: tum quia est conveniens esse unum primum in genere satisfactionis perfectum, supra quod omnes aliae imperfectae satisfactiones fundentur."

[76]Ibid., XX.1.1c ra/3: "Secundo, quia remissio poenae quae fit aliis hominibus, praecipue poenae satisfactoriae, fundatur supra virtutem satisfactoriam Christi, quae superabundavit ad amovendas omnes poenas quantum in se fuit; unde oportet quod particulata satisfactio fundetur supra satisfactionem Christi condignam. . . ."

[77]Ibid., Book Four, Prologue: "Item continuationem ad tertium librum: quia in tertio agebatur de missione Verbi in carnem, in hoc autem libro de effectibus Verbi incarnati. . . ."

[78]Ibid., ". . . quia ratio poenae est ut contra voluntatem sit, sicut ratio culpae ut sit voluntaria; et ideo culpa ad infirmitatem reducitur, poena ad mortem: quia via ad poenam est culpa, sicut infirmitas ad mortem."

[79]Ibid., IV.2.1b ra/2: ". . . poena ordinat culpam dupliciter. Uno modo ut satisfaciens; et sic culpa remanet ordinata per satisfactionem Christi. Alio modo ut medicina sanans, vel repraesentans membrum sanabile. . . ."

[80]Augustine, Enarrationes in Psalmos, In Psalmum LVIII, n. 13: "Iniquitas omnis, parva magnave sit, puniatur necesse est, aut ab ipso homine poenitente, aut a Deo vindicante."

[81]Scriptum, Book Four, IV.2.1b co/: ". . . Christus per mortem suam sufficienter satisfecit pro peccatis totius humani generis, etiam si essent multo plura."

CHAPTER IV

[1]Augustine, <u>De libero arbitrio</u>, Book I, I.1
(<u>Corpus Christianorum</u>, Series Latina, Vol. 29, p. 212):
"Duobus enim modis appellare malum solemus: uno, cum
male quemque fecisse dicimus, alio, cum mali aliquid
esse perpessum."

[2]Peter Lombard, <u>Sententiae</u>, Lib. 2,d.35,c.6,
p. 536: "Quaeri autem solet utrum et poena sit privatio vel corruptio boni. Ad quod facile responderi
potest, si praedicta ad memoriam revocentur. Diximus
enim supra privationem vel corruptionem boni accipi
active vel passive, id est secundum efficientiam
vel effectum. Ideoque privatio vel corruptio boni
dicitur et peccatum et poena; sed peccatum secundum
efficientiam, quia privat vel corrumpit bonum; poena
autem secundum effectum, id est secundum passionem quae
est effectus peccati. Aliud est enim culpa, aliud
poena. Alterum est Dei, id est poena; alterum diaboli
vel hominis est, id est culpa."

[3]<u>De malo</u>, 1.4 sc/: "SED CONTRA, est quod Augustinus (Fulgentius) dicit in lib. <u>De Fide ad Petrum</u>
(cap. XXI): 'Geminum est creaturae rationalis malum;
unum quo voluntarie deficit a summo bono; alterum quo
in vita punitur;' per quae duo exprimitur poena et
culpa. Ergo malum dividitur per poenam et culpam."

[4]<u>Ibid</u>., co/: St. Thomas clarifies this in the
actual argument by specifying how this principle is
true in various concrete circumstances, i.e., man's
will naturally inclines to the good and shrinks from
evil either actually as he confronts it, potentially if
he realized that an evil were overtaking him, or
according to the will's natural inclination, as in the
case of a man who may not in fact be inclined to virtue
but should be so inclined if he wished to respect his
nature.

[5]Augustine, <u>Confessionum</u>, Book I, c. 13 (PL 32:
670): "Jussisti enim, et sic est, ut poena sua sibi
sit omnis inordinatus animus."

[6]De malo, 1.4 ra/9: ". . . poena, secundum quod
comparatur ad subjectum, est malum in quantum privat
illud aliquo modo; sed secundum quod comparatur ad
agens quod infert poenam, sic interdum habet rationem
boni, quando puniens propter justitiam punit."

[7]Ibid., co/: "Est autem et in creatura intellec-
tuali invenire malum secundum privationem formae aut
habitus . . . secundum fidei catholicae sententiam,
necesse est quod poena dicitur," The emphasis has been
added because Saint Thomas only rarely and in the most
difficult problems so explicitly invokes such formulas.

[8]See Summa theologiae I-II, 86-87. See below,
pp. 143 ff.

[8a]De veritate 29.3 ag/4: "Praeterea, Anselmus in
libro Cur Deus homo probat quod oportuit Deum incarnari
quia satisfactio pro natura humana non poterat fieri
nisi per meritum infinitum, quod non potest esse
hominis puri; ex quo patet quod meritum hominis Christi
fuit infinitum; sed causa meriti est gratia; ergo
gratia Christi est infinita, quia a causa finita non
potest egredi effectus infinitus."

[9]Glossa ordinaria (PL 114:370): "Hominibus dat ad
mensuram, filio non dat ad mensuram, sed sicut totum ex
seipso toto genuit Filium suum, ita incarnato Filio suo
totum spiritum suum dedit, non particulatim, non per
subdivisones, sed generaliter et universaliter. . . ."
The history of the biblical Glossa ordinaria is imper-
fectly known; it is not the work of Walafrid Strabo, as
was once thought. See Smalley, Study of the Bible,
pp. 31-45.

[10]De veritate 29.3 co/: ". . . in qua Spiritus Sanctus animae Christi datus esse ostenditur,
praesupposita unione per quam ille homo erat Filius
Dei. . . ."

[11]Ibid., 29.2 co/: ". . . unde gratia habitualis
in Christo magis intelligitur ut effectus quam ut
praeparatio ad unionem."

[12]Ibid., 29.3 co/: "Et similiter dico de gratia
habituali Christi quod est finita secundum essentiam,
quia esse suum est limitatum ad aliquam speciem entis,
scilicet ad rationem gratiae; est tamen infinita
secundum rationem gratiae, quia cum infinitis modis
possit considerari perfectio alicuius quantum ad

gratiam, nullus eorum defuit Christo, sed habuit in se
gratiam secundum omnem plenitudinem et perfectionem ad
quam ratio huius speciei quod est gratis potest se
extendere."

[13]Anselm, Cur Deus homo? II.19: "Frustra quippe
imitatores ejus erunt, si meriti ejus participes non
erunt."

[14]De veritate 29.3 ra/4: "Unde et meritum Christi
non fuit infinitum secundum intensionem actus, finite
enim diligebat et cognoscebat; sed habuit quandam
infinitatem ex circumstantia personae, quae erat
dignitatis infinitae; quanto enim major est qui se
humiliat tanto eius humilitas laudabilior invenitur."

[15]Ibid., 29.7 sc/3: "Praeterea, Christus et
Ecclesia sunt quasi una persona; sed ratione unitatis
praedictae ex persona Ecclesiae loquitur, ut patet in
glossa super Psal. 'Deus, Deus meus, respice in me;'
ergo et similiter ratione unitatis praedictae Christum
quasi ex persona aliorum mereri potuit."

[16]Ibid., co/: "Sicut enim actus peccati cedit in
quandam animae deformitatem, ita et actus meritorius in
quendam animi decorem et dignitatem. . . ."

[17]Ibid., ". . . et sic opus humanum ordinatur
ad gloriam quasi per modum cuiusdam pretii, quo a
reatu poenae absolvitur; et ex hoc habet opus humanum
rationem satisfactionis."

[18]Ibid., ". . . licet alius homo possit pro
alio satisfacere, . . . non tamen potest satisfacere
pro tota natura, quia opus unius puri hominis non
aequivalet bono totius naturae. Sed opus Christi, in
quantum erat Dei et hominis, habuit quandam dignitatem
ut valeret bonum totius naturae; et ideo pro natura
satisfacere potuit."

[19]Ibid., ra/6: ". . . licet quilibet actus
Christi esset nobis meritorius, tamen ad satisfaciendum
pro reatu naturae humanae quae erat morti ex sententia
divina obligata, ut patet Gen. II, opportuit quod loco
omnium mortem sustineret."

[20]Ibid., ra/7: "Gratia etiam personalis nulli
umquam post peccatum primi hominis data fuit nisi per
fidem mediatoris explicitam vel implicitam."

[21]Ibid., 29.4.

[22]Thomas Potvin, *The Theology of the Primacy of Christ according to Saint Thomas and its Scriptural Foundations* (Fribourg, Suisse: Editions Universitaires, 1973).

[23]*De veritate* 29.4 co/: "Ut ergo proprie loquamur, Christus totus secundum utramque naturam simul est caput totius Ecclesiae. . . ."

[24]*Ibid.*, 26.6 rc/4: ". . . proprie claritas resurrectionis est praemium passionis, quia exaltatio est proprium humilitatis praemium."

[25]*Ibid.*, ". . . in quantum in sua passione pro peccato totius humani generis satisfecit . . ."

[26]*Ibid.*, "Poenalitas enim ad satisfactionem requiritur per modum cuiusdam recompensationis contra delectationem peccati."

[27]*Ibid.*, rc/6: "Ad sextum dicendum quod difficultas per se impedit voluntarium, sed per accidens auget, in quantum aliquis difficultati contra conatur; ipsa tamen difficultas ad satisfactionem facit ratione poenalitatis."

[28]*Ibid.*, 26.9 sc/2: "Praeterea, satisfactio respondet culpae; sed Christus sua passione satisfecit pro culpa primi hominis; cum ergo culpa illa pervenerit usque ad superiorem rationem, et passio Christi usque ad superiorem rationem debuit pervenire."

[29]*Ibid.*, rc/2: "Ad secundum dicendum quod passio Christi non esset satisfactoria nisi in quantum est voluntarie et ex caritate suscepta. Et sic non oportet quod dolor sit in superiori parte rationis Christi respectu propriae operationis, sicut in Adam fuit culpa per operationem superioris rationis, quia ipse motus caritatis patientis, qui est in superiori parte rationis, respondet in satisfactione ad id quod fuit in culpa secundum superiorem rationem."

[30]*Summa contra gentiles* 3.158: "Considerandum tamen quod, cum mens a peccato avertitur, tam vehemens potest esse peccati displicentia, et inhaesio mentis ad Deum, quod non remanebit obligatio ad aliquam poenam."

[31]Scriptum, Book Four, XVII.3.5b co/: "Alio modo (confessio) diminuit poenam ex ipsa natura actus confitentis, qui habet poenam erubescentiae annexam; et ideo quanto aliquis pluries de eisdem peccatis confitetur, tanto magis poena diminuitur."

[32]See above pp. 88-93.

[33]Joseph Lécuyer, C.S.Sp., "Prolégomènes thomistes à la théologie de la satisfaction," in Studi Tomistici (Rome: Città Nuova Ed., 1974), pp. 82-103.

[34]Summa contra gentiles 3.158: "Nam et poenam quam amicus propter ipsum patitur, reputat aliquis ac si ipse pateretur: et sic poena ei non deest, dum patienti amico compatitur; et tanto amplius, quanto ipse est ei causa patiendi. Et iterum affectio caritatis in eo quo pro amico patitur, facit magis satisfactionem Deo acceptam quam si pro se pateretur: hoc enim est promptae caritatis, illud autem est necessitatis."

[35]In the printed edition there are, in fact, 27 objections. The final one (number seven in our enumeration), however, is supplied by the editors, as their note indicates: "Hic ratio 27 deest, quae tamen solvitur circa finem cap. 55 (3960). Forte deleta est ex p.A." See Vol. III, p. 348.

[36]See above pp. 107-108.

[37]For an excellent presentation of St. Thomas's teaching on this element of Catholic doctrine see T. C. O'Brien, Original Sin, translation of Summa theologiae (1a2ae. 81-85), Vol. 26 (New York: McGraw-Hill, 1965), especially appendices 1.7; 3.4 and 7.1-12.

[38]De articulis fidei 2 (616): "Effectus autem Baptismi est remissio culpae originalis et actualis, et etiam totius culpae et poenae, ita quod baptizatis non est aliqua satisfactio iniungenda pro peccatis praeteritis, sed statim morientes post baptismum introducuntur ad gloriam Dei. Unde effectus Baptismi ponitur apertio ianuae paradisi." See Weisheipl, Friar Thomas, pp. 392-393 for dating of this work.

[39]Summa contra gentiles 4.72: "Quia igitur coniunctio nostri ad Christum in baptismo non est secundum operationem nostram, quasi ab interiori, quia nulla res seipsam generat ut sit; sed a Christo, qui

'nos' regenerat 'in spem vivam' remissio peccatorum in baptismo fit secundum potestatem ipsius Christi nos sibi coniungentis perfecte et integre, ut non solum impuritas peccati tollatur, sed etiam solvatur penitur omnis poenae reatus; . . ."

[40]I.T. Eschmann writes: "It seems that in the first part of his Italian sojourn, in the years of Urban IV, Thomas, in a way, discovered Greek theology, the part it played in theology, and the consequences which would ensue, if it were neglected, as indeed it was neglected, in a theology that was nourished merely by Latin thought." This reference is found in Weisheipl, Friar Thomas, p. 173. A classical study on the influence of Greek theology on the christological thought of Saint Thomas is I. Backes, Die Christologie des hl. Thomas v. Aquin und die griechischen Kirchen- väter (Paderborn, 1931). Note however the reservation expressed by Lafont, Structures, pp. 242-243, concern- ing some of Backes' conclusions. See also the review of H.-D. Simonin in Bulletin Thomiste 3 (1930-1933), pp. 941-947. Another study of Saint Thomas's acquaint- ance with Greek theology is Gottfried Geenen, O.P., "The Council of Chalcedon in the Theology of Saint Thomas," in From an Abundant Spring (New York: P.J. Kenedy & Sons, 1952), pp. 172-217.

[41]H. Dondaine, O.P., "Le Contra Errores Grecorum de S. Thomas et le IVe livre du Contra Gentiles," Revue des Sciences Philosophiques et Théologiques 30 (1941- 1942), pp. 156-158.

[42]Catena aurea, Expositio in Marcum, introduction: "Et ut magis integra et continua sanctorum expositio redderetur, quasdam expositiones Doctorum graecorum in latinum feci transferri, ex quibus plura expositionibus latinorum Doctorum interserui, auctorum nominibus praenotatis." Eschmann, "A Catalogue of St. Thomas's Works," in Etienne Gilson, The Christian Philosophy of St. Thomas Aquinas, translated by L.K. Shook, (New York: Random House, 1956), p. 397 writes: "Beginning with the Glossa in Marcum, St. Thomas's research in Greek Patristic sources becomes more and more intense. For the purpose of broadening the range of his informa- tion, he procured new translations of certain Greek Fathers. Because of this research into Greek theo- logical sources, the Catena marks a turning point in the development of Aquinas's theology as well as in the history of Catholic dogma." The contents of the Catena Aurea will be included in future Concordances of the Index Thomisticus that will contain citations

"ad litteram" made by St. Thomas throughout his works. The word "satisfaction" appears always to be used in a sense other than that of our study, e.g. on Mark 6:26-32 (#5): ". . . voluit eorum satisfacere voluntati. . ."; 8:35-39 (#5): ". . . erubescimus priores satisfacere. . ."; 15:11-20 (#2): "volebat quidem satisfacere populo. . ."; 10:3-12 (#1): ". . . tamquam ex praedictis non plene fuerit satisfactum. . ."; 12:27-36 (#4): ". . . quomodo satisfecit Scribae quaerenti. . ."; 15:11-20 (#2): "Judaei vero insaniae suae satisfacientes. . .".

43Chenu, _Understanding_, p. 295.

44_Summa contra gentiles_ 1.8: "Cui quidem sententiae auctoritas Hilarii concordat, qui sic dicit in libro de Trin. loquens de huiusmodi veritate: 'Haec credendo incipe, procurre, persiste: etsi non perventurum sciam, gratulabor tamen profecturum. Qui enim pie infinita prosequitur, etsi non contingat aliquando, semper tamen proficiet produendo. Sed ne te inferas in illud secretum, et arcano interminabilis nativitatis non te immergas, summam intelligentiae comprendere praesumens: sed intellige incomprehensibilia esse.'" See Hilary of Poitiers, _De Trinitate_, II, 10.

45Lucien Cerfaux, _Christ in the Theology of St. Paul_, translated by G. Webb and A. Walker, (New York: Herder & Herder, 1966), pp. 165-166.

46_De rationibus fidei_ 7/160-164: "Apparet enim in humanis iudiciis quod ea quae iniuste sunt facta ad justitiam reducuntur, dum iudex ab eo qui aliena accipiens plus habet quam debet, subtrahit quod plus habet et dat ei qui minus habebat."

47_Ibid._, /224-228: "In hoc ergo maxime sapientia Dei apparuit quod et ordinem servavit tam iustitiae quam naturae, et tamen misericorditer providit homini salutis remedium per Filii sui incarnationem et mortem."

48Chenu, _Understanding_, p. 332.

49_De perfectione spiritualis vitae_ 12/36-49: "Sed sciendum quod, sicut Gregorius _Super Ezechielem_ dicit, 'hoc inter sacrificium ac holocaustum distat, quod omne holocaustum sacrificium est, et non omne sacrificium holocaustum: in sacrificio enim pars pecudis, in holocausto vero totum pecus offerri consueverat.

Cum ergo aliquis suum aliquid Deo vovet, et aliquid non vovet, sacrificium est; cum vero omne quod habet, omne quod vivit, omne quod sapit omnipotenti Deo voverit, holocaustum est.' Quod quidem impletur per tria vota praedicta; unde manifestum est eos qui huiusmodi vota Deo emittunt, quasi propter holocausti excellentiam antonomastice religioso vocari."

[50]Ibid., 168-172. See also Quaestiones quodlibetales 3.5.3 co/: ". . . Stephanus Papa quemdam qui uxorem interfecerat, inducit ut ingrediatur monasterium, et humiliatus sub manu Abbatis cuncta observet quae sibi fuerint imperata, alioquin iniungit ei gravissimam poenitentiam, si eligit in saeculo remanere."

[51]Quaestiones quodlibetales 3.5.3 ra/1: "Stultum est autem dicere, quod alicui qui debilior est, propter peccata quae commisit, non sit ad securiorem vitam fugiendum"

[52]Ibid., co/: "Difficile enim quod in saeculo commorantes a rebus mundi non alliciantur; propter quod Matth., XIX, (23-24), secundum expositionem Chrysostomi, Dominus hoc dicit esse impossibile, quod dives, qui scilicet divitiis inhaeret per amorem, intret in regnum caelorum; sed quod dives qui habet divitias, intret, est valde difficile." See Ambrose, De Abraham 1.3.12 (CSEL 32.1, 510 ff.) for a similar teaching expounded in the context of explaining the wealth of the patriarchs. I am endebted to Boniface Ramsey, O.P. for this reference. In Contra impugnantes 1 co/188ff. Saint Thomas also defends religious life on the grounds that the greater austerities of such a life accomplishes more satisfaction.

[53]De caritate 1.11 ra/5: ". . . paupertas ad perfectionem non pertineret, nisi in quantum disponit ad sequendum Christum."

[54]Ibid., "Unde non sequitur quod magis pauper sit magis perfectus; sed mensuranda est in talibus perfectio per comparationem ad illa in quibus consistit perfectio simpliciter; ut scilicet ille dicatur perfectior, cuius paupertas magis sequestrat hominem a terrenis occupationibus, et facit liberius Deo vacare."

[55]Quaestiones quodlibetales 3.13.1: "Utrum si aliquis sacerdos poenitenti dicat: 'Quidquid boni feceris, sit tibi in remissionem peccatorum,' sit satisfactio sacramentalis."

[56]Summa contra gentiles 4.72: "Huiusmodi autem claves a passione Christi efficaciam habent, per quam scilicet Christus nobis aperuit ianuam regni caelestis."

[57]Quaestiones quodlibetales 3.13.1 co/: "Unde laudabiliter consuevit hoc a multis sacerdotibus dici, licet non habeant maiorem vim ad praebendum remedium contra culpam futuram; et quantum ad hoc talis satisfactio est sacramentalis, in quantum virtute clavium est culpae commissae expiativa."

[58]Ibid., 2.8.2 co/: "Christus autem pro Ecclesia sua sanguinem suum fudit, et multa alia fecit et sustinuit, quorum aestimatio est infiniti valoris, propter dignitatem personae: . . . Similiter etiam et omnes alii sancti intentionem habuerunt in his quae passi sunt et fecerunt propter Deum, ut hoc esset ad utilitatem non solum sui, sed etiam totius Ecclesiae." Ibid., ". . . passio Christi et aliorum sanctorum ei imputetur ac si ipse passus esset quantum sufficeret ad remissionem sui peccati . . ." This reference in Saint Thomas to satisfaction within the context of the intercession of the saints, i.e., the "thesaurus," suggests an interesting parallel with some early liturgical uses of the term "satisfaction." J. Rivière, "Sur les premières applications du terme 'satisfactio' à l'oeuvre du Christ," Bulletin de Littérature Ecclésiastique 25 (1924), pp. 285-297; 353-369, points out that the earliest applications to the work of Christ of the term "satisfaction" are found within liturgical formulations. In tracing the development of this usage h points to the prior practice of the liturgy to associate satisfaction with the communion of saints. "A l'époque où nous transporte le Sacramentaire (Veronèse), ce terme n'est rien moins qu'un néologisme. Sans parler des acceptations communes qu'il garde encore, à l'occasion, par la vertu persistante de l'étymologie, il est devenu classique dans la langue latine, depuis Tertullien, pour signifier l'ensemble des actes pénitentiels qui s'imposent au pécheur en expiation de son péché. Or la pénitence est toujours conçue comme une obligation strictement personnelle au pénitent. Sans doute, les suffrages de l'Eglise peuvent lui venir en aide, car la communio sanctorum se réalise dès ici-bas. Mais cette intervention secourable n'est jamais appelée 'satisfactio'. La nouveauté du Sacramentaire (Veronese, dit) léonien est précisément d'appliquer à la médiation des saints un terme jusque-là réservé à la réparation douloureuse

des coupables." (p. 356). One example of the usage to which Rivière refers is found in the _Sacramentum Veronese_ VIII.35, edited by L.C. Mohlberg (Rome: Herder, 1966), p. 17: "Uere dignum: prostrato corde poscentes, ut quamuis tanta sint nostra facinora, quibus etiam cum innumeribus santorum suffragiis laboremus, tu tamen inmensa pietate concedas, ne scelera magis nostra praeualeant quam satisfactio pro nobis copiosa justorum: . . ."

CHAPTER V

[1]T.C. O'Brien, <u>Effects of Sin, Stain and Guilt</u>, translation of <u>Summa theologiae</u> (1a2ae, 86-89), Vol. 27 (New York: McGraw-Hill, 1974), pp. xiii-xviii; appendix 1, p. 99.

[2]<u>Summa theologiae</u>, I-II, 21.4 co/: "Dicendum quod, sicut dictum est actus alicujus hominis habet rationem meriti vel demeriti, secundum quod ordinatur ad alterum, vel ratione ejus vel ratione communitatis. Utroque autem modo actus nostri boni vel mali habent rationem meriti vel demeriti apud Deum."

[3]Thomas Gilby, O.P., <u>Principles of Morality</u>, translation of <u>Summa theologiae</u> (1a2ae, 18-21), Vol. 18 (New York: McGraw-Hill, 1966), p. 188; see also appendices 10 and 18.

[4]<u>Summa theologiae</u>, I-II, 1.2 co/: "Illa ergo quae rationem habent, seipsa movent ad finem: quia habent dominium suorum actuum per liberum arbitrium, quod est facultas voluntatis et rationis."
<u>Ibid.</u>, 91.2 co/: "Inter caetera autem rationalis creatura excellentiori quodam modo divinae providentiae subjacet, inquantum et ipsa fit providentiae particeps, sibi ipsi et aliis providens. Unde et in ipsa participatur ratio aeterna per quam habet naturalem inclinationem ad debitum actum et finem."

[5]<u>Ibid.</u>, 21.2 co/: "Unde reliquitur quod bonum vel malum in solis actibus voluntariis constituit rationem laudis vel culpae, in quibus idem est malum, peccatum et culpa."

[6]O'Brien, <u>Stain and Guilt</u>, p. 101: "Reason and eternal law are introduced into the explanation of sin, not to substitute external obligation for inner finality, but because of the proper and formal way in which man is subject to his own inner finalization."

[7]<u>Ibid.</u>, p. 106. Cf. <u>Summa theologiae</u>, II-II, 25.10 co/: "Deus enim non plus se avertit ab homine quam homo se avertit ab ipso."

[8]Scriptum, Book Four, XXI.1.2c co/: ". . . quod culpa non potest ordinari nisi per poenam; et quia Deus nihil inordinatum relinquit, ideo numquam culpam sine poena dimittit." There are many texts in the Scriptum which suggest this juridical perspective on sin and punishment, for example, Ibid., Book Two, XLII.1.2. ra/5: "quia oportet ut quantum voluntati suae obedivit praeter legem Dei, tantum etiam in contrarium recompenset, ut sic justitiae servetur aequalitas; et ideo post gratiam recuperatam injungitur satisfactio, et est adhuc homo reus temporalis poenae." Ibid., Book Four, XV.1.4a co/: "Recompensatio enim offensae importat adaequationem, quam oportet esse eius qui offendit ad eum in quam offensa commissa est."

[9]Summa theologiae, I-II, 87.6 co/: "Actus enim peccati facit hominem reum poenae inquantum transgreditur ordinem divinae justitiae; ad quem non redit nisi per quamdam recompensationem poenae; quae ad aequalitatem justitiae reducit, ut scilicet qui plus voluntati suae indulsit quam debuit, contra mandatum Dei agens, secundum ordinem divinae justitiae aliquid contra illud quod vellet, spontaneus vel invitus patiatur."

[10]Ibid.: "Sed si loquamur de ablatione peccati quantum ad maculam, sic manifestum est quod macula peccati ab anima auferri non potest, nisi per hoc quod anima Deo conjungitur per cujus distantiam detrimentum proprii nitoris incurrebat, quod est macula. . . . Conjungitur autem Deo homo per voluntatem. Unde macula peccati ab homine tolli non potest, nisi voluntas hominis ordinem divinae justitiae acceptet. . . ."

[11]Summa theologiae, I-II, 87.6 ra/3: "Requiritur etiam ad restituendum aequalitatem justitiae et ad amovendum scandalum aliorum, ut aedificentur in poena qui sunt scandalizati culpa, ut papet ex exemplo de David inducto."

[12]See above, pp. 142-148. Se also C. Journet, "La peine temporelle du péché," Revue Thomiste (1927), pp. 20-39; 89-103.

[13]Summa theologiae, I-II, 87.7 co/: "Et quia contingit eos qui differunt in reatu poenae, esse unum secundum voluntatem unione amoris. . . ."

[14]Ibid., 113.4 ra/1: "Actus autem misericordiae vel operatur contra peccatum per modum satisfactionis, et sic sequitur justificationem; vel per modum praeparationis inquantum 'misericordes misericordiam consequuntur;' et sic etiam potest praecedere justificationem. . . ."

[15]Colman E. O'Neill, O.P., The One Mediator, translation of Summa theologiae (3a. 16-26), (New York: McGraw-Hill, 1965), p. xxi.

[16]Summa theologiae I, 8.3 co/: "Dicendum quod Deus dicitur esse in re aliqua dupliciter. Uno modo per modum causae agentis et sic est in omnibus rebus creatis ab ipso. Alio modo sicut objectum operationis est in operante, quod proprium est in operationibus animae secundum quod cognitum est in cognoscente et desideratum in desiderante." See also ibid., 43.1-8 (especially article 3) on the missions of the divine persons and ibid., 93.1-9 on the image of God in man for other texts in which Saint Thomas addresses himself to the question of the special mode of the divine presence to rational creatures.

[17]Summa theologiae I, 35.2 ra/3: "Et ideo ad designandum in homine imperfectionem imaginis, homo non solum dicitur imago, sed ad imaginem, per quod motus quidam tendentis in perfectionem designatur."

[18]See above pp. 139-142.

[19]Summa theologiae I, 95.4 ra/1: "Quia homo etiam ante peccatum indigebat gratia ad vitam aeternam consequendam, quae est principalis necessitas gratiae. Sed homo post peccatum super hoc indiget gratia etiam ad peccati remissionem, et infirmitatis sustentationem."

[20]The term is found in Augustine, for example, De libero arbitrio, Book II, XV.41 (CCSL 29, p. 265): "Quomodo enim te uerteris, uestigiis quibusdam quae operibus suis inpressit loquitur tibi et te in exteriora relabentem ipsis exteriorum formis intro revocat. . . ." The vestige is a confused and imperfect likeness of the exemplar and thus is contrasted with the image which represents the examplar more determinately and according to all of its parts. Saint Thomas clarifies the distinction in Summa theologiae I, 45.7. See also J.E. Sullivan, O.P., The Image of God (Dubuque: Priory Press, 1963), pp. 220-231 passim.

[21]See O'Neill, _Mediator_, pp. xxiii-xxiv.

[22]The final article is III, 90.4; the remainder of Saint Thomas's schema was completed by his followers using, for the most part, material from the earlier _Scriptum_.

[23]See above pp. 72-82.

[24]_Summa theologiae_ III, 1.1 co/: "Dicendum quod unicuique rei conveniens est illud quod competit sibi secundum rationem propriae naturae; sicut homini conveniens est ratiocinari quia hoc convenit sibi inquantum est rationalis secundum suam naturam. Ipsa autem natura Dei est bonitas, ut patet per Dionysium. Unde quidquid pertinet ad rationem boni, conveniens est Deo. Pertinet autem ad rationem boni ut se aliis communicet, ut patet per Dionysium. Unde ad rationem summi boni pertinet quod summo modo se creaturae communicet. Quod quidem maxime fit per hoc quod 'naturam creatam sic sibi conjungit ut una persona fiat ex tribus, Verbo, anima et carne,' sicut dicit Augustinus. Unde manifestum est quod conveniens fuit Deum incarnari."

[25]_Ibid._, ra/3: "Quaelibet alia conditio secundum quam quaecumque creatura differt a creatore a Dei sapientia est instituta et ad Dei bonitatem ordinata. Deus enim propter suam bonitatem, cum sit increatus, immobilis, incorporeus, produxit creaturas mobiles et corporeas; et similiter malum poenae a Dei justitia est introductum propter gloriam Dei."

[26]_Ibid._, "Malum vero culpae committitur per recessum ab arte divinae sapientiae et ab ordine divinae bonitatis. Et ideo conveniens esse potuit assumere naturam creatam, mutabilem, corpoream et poenalitati subjectam; non autem fuit conveniens ei assumere malum culpae."

[27]See above pp. 99-101 for a discussion of _De malo_, 1.4.

[28]_Summa theologiae_ III, 1.2 co/: "Et hoc quidem considerari potest quantum ad promotionem hominis in bono. Primo quidem, quantum ad fidem, quae magis certificatur ex hoc quod ipsi Deo loquenti credit. Unde Augustinus dicit, 'Ut homo fidentius ambularet ad veritatem, ipsa Veritas, Dei Filius, homine assumpto, constituit atque fundavit fidem.' Secundo, quantum ad

spem, quae per hoc maxime erigitur. Unde Augustinus dicit, 'Nihil tam necessarium fuit ad erigendam spem nostram quam ut demonstraretur nobis quantum diligeret nos Deus. Quid vero hujus rei isto indicio manifestius, quam ut Dei Filius naturae nostrae dignatus est inire consortium.' Tertio, quantum ad caritatem, quae maxime per hoc excitatur. Unde Augustinus dicit, 'Quae major causa est adventus Domini, nisi ut ostenderet Deus dilectionem suam in nobis?' Et postea subdit, 'Si amare pigebat, saltem reamare non pigeat.' Quarto, quantum ad rectam operationem, in qua nobis exemplum se praebuit. Unde Augustinus dicit, 'Homo sequendus non erat, qui videri poterat; Deus sequendus erat, qui videri non poterat. Ut ergo exhiberetur homini et qui ab homine videretur, et quem homo sequeretur, Deus factus est homo.' Quinto, quantum ad plenam participationem divinitatis, quae vere est hominis beatitudo, et finis humanae vitae. Et hoc collatum est nobis per Christi humanitatem; dicit enim Augustinus, 'Factus est Deus homo, ut homo fieret Deus.'"

^{29}Ibid., "Similiter etiam hoc utile fuit ad remotionem mali. Primo enim per hoc homo instruitur ne sibi diabolum praeferat et eum veneretur, qui est auctor peccati. Unde dicit Augustinus, 'Quando sic Deo conjungi potuit humana natura ut fieret una persona, superbi illi maligni ·spiritus non ideo se audeant homini praeponere quia non habent carnem.' Secundo, quia per hoc instruimur quanta sit dignitas humanae naturae, ne eam inquinemus peccando. Unde dicit Augustinus, 'Demonstravit nobis Deus quam excelsum locum inter creaturas habeat humana natura, in hoc quod hominibus in vero homine apparuit.' Et Leo Papa dicit, 'Agnosce, o Christiane, dignitatem tuam; et, divinae consors factus naturae, noli in veterem vilitatem degeneri conversatione redire.' Tertio, quia ad praesumptionem hominis tollendam, 'gratia Dei, nullis meritis praecedentibus, in homine Christo nobis commendatur,' ut dicitur in De Trinitate. Quarto, quia 'superbia hominis, quae maximum impedimentum est ne inhaereatur Deo, per tantam Dei humilitatem redargui potest atque sanari,' ut Augustinus dicit. Quinto, ad liberandum hominem a servitute. Quod quidem, ut Augustinus dicit, 'fieri debuit sic ut diabolus justitia hominis Jesu Christi superaretur.' Quod factum est Christo satisfaciente pro nobis. Homo autem purus satisfacere non poterat pro toto humano genere; Deus autem satisfacere non debebat. Unde oportebat Deum et hominem esse Jesum Christum. Unde et Leo Papa dicit, 'Suscipitur a virtute infirmitas, a majestate humilitas, ut, quod nostris remediis congruebat, unus atque idem Dei et hominum mediator et mori ex uno et resurgere posset ex altero. Nisi enim esset versus Deus, non afferret remedium; nisi esset homo verus, non praeberet exemplum.'"

[30]See Louis Richard, The Mystery of the Redemption, translated by J. Horn (Baltimore: Helicon, 1965), p. 178: Saint Anselm "is faithful to the theme of the victory of Christ who fought against sin, death and the devil in order to deliver us from their tyranny; and he deserves credit for having definitely brushed aside the theory (which was still presented in his day and which must have been deeply repugnant to him) of the 'abuse of power,' which attributed to the devil a right over sinful man." A detailed historical analysis of this problem can be found in Jean Rivière, Le dogme de la Rédemption au début du Moyen Age, (Paris, J. Vrin, 1934). See below Appendix, p. 262, n. 4.

[31]See Scriptum, Book Three, I.1.2, ag/4: see above, p. 72.

[32]Summa theologiae III, 1.2 ag/2: "Praeterea, ad reparationem humanae naturae, quae per peccatum collapsa erat, nihil aliud requiri videbatur quam quod homo satisfaceret pro peccato. Non enim Deus ab homine requirere plus debet quam possit; et, cum pronior sit ad miserendum quam ad puniendum, sicut homini imputat actum peccati, ita etiam videtur quod ei imputet ad deletionem peccati actum contrarium. Non ergo fuit necessarium ad reparationem humanae naturae Verbum Dei incarnari."

[33]Thomas (Cardinal Cajetan) deVio, Commentarium in Summa theologiae III (Rome: Leonine edition of the Summa theologiae, 1903), q.1, a.2 (#6): "Contra quartum dictum, scilicet quod 'omnis alia satisfactio efficax est ex satisfactione Christi,' occurrit ipsemet Auctor, in IV Sent., dist. xv, qu. 1, art. 2, ad 1, dicens: 'Alii dicunt quod etiam quantum ad aversionem pro peccato satisfieri potest virtute meriti Christi, quod quodammodo infinitum fuit. Et in hoc idem redit quod prius dictum est' (scilicet quod non potest satisfacere secundum aequalitatem, sed secundum acceptationem divinam): 'quia per fidem Mediatoris gratia data est credentibus. Si tamen alio modo gratiam daret, sufficeret satifactio per modum praedictum.' Ubi patet quod Auctor idem dat iudicium de satisfactione mea, sive habeam gratiam per fidem Iesu Christi, sive aliunde haberem gratiam. Ac per hoc, non fit ex

satisfactione Christi satisfaciens simpliciter, sed solum secundum acceptationem: cuius oppositum hic docere videntur. Et similiter non fit ex satisfactione Christi efficax: cuius oppositum expresse hic docet." See above pp. 62-63.

[34]Summa theologiae III, 1.2 ra/2: "Ad secundum dicendum quod aliqua satisfactio potest dici sufficiens dupliciter. Uno modo, perfecte, quia est condigna per quandam adaequationem ad recompensationem commissae culpae. Et sic hominis puri satisfactio sufficiens esse non potuit, quia tota natura humana erat per peccatum corrupta; nec bonum alicujus personae vel etiam plurium poterat per aequiparantiam totius naturae detrimentum recompensare. Tum etiam quia peccatum contra Deum commissum quandam infinitatem habet ex infinitate divinae majestatis; tanto enim offensa est gravior quanto major est ille in quem delinquitur. Unde opportuit, ad condignam satisfactionem, ut actio satisfacientis haberet efficaciam infinitam, utputa Dei et hominis existens. Alio modo potest dici satisfactio sufficiens imperfecte, scilicet secundum acceptationem ejus qui est ea contentus, quamvis non sit condigna. Et hoc modo satisfactio puri hominis est sufficiens. Et quia omne imperfectum praesupponit aliquid perfectum a quo sustentetur, inde est quod omnis puri hominis satisfactio efficaciam habet a satisfactione Christi."

[35]Anselm, Cur Deus homo? I, 21. See Appendix, pp. 261-266.

[36]Summa theologiae III, 1.2 ra/2: ". . . secundum acceptationem ejus qui est ea contentus. . ."

[37]Ibid., 1.3 co/: "Unde, cum in sacra Scriptura ubique incarnationis ratio ex peccato primi hominis assignetur. . . ."

[38]Ibid., I, 19.2 ra/2: "Unde, cum Deus alia a se non velit nisi propter finem qui est sua bonitas, . . . non sequitur quod aliquid aliud moveat voluntatem eius nisi bonitas sua."

[39]Colossians 1:20.

[40]This outline is found in O'Neill, Mediator, p. xxiv.

[41]For Saint Thomas's teaching on the Immaculate Conception see T.R. Heath, O.P., Our Lady, translation of Summa theologiae (3a. 27-30), Vol. 51 (New York: McGraw-Hill, 1969), appendix 3.

[42]See Etienne Gilson, L'esprit de la philosophie médiévale (Paris, J. Vrin, 1932), c. X, "Le personnalisme chrétien": "C'est dans le De duabus naturis de Boèce, c'est-à-dire dans un traité sur les deux natures du Christ, que se rencontre la définition de la personne dont tout le moyen âge s'inspira. . . ."

[43]Summa theologiae III, 1.2 co/: "Omne igitur quod inest alicui personae, sive pertineat ad naturam ejus sive non, unitur ei in persona. Si ergo humana natura Verbo Dei non unitur in persona, nullo modo ei unitur. Et sic totaliter tollitur incarnationis fides, quod est subruere totam fidem Christianam. Quia igitur Verbum habet naturam humanam sibi unitam, non autem ad suam naturam divinam pertinentem, consequens est quod unio sit facta in persona Verbi, non autem in natura."

[44]Ibid. I, 34.2 co/: "Dicendum quod Verbum proprie dictum in divinis personaliter accipitur et est proprium nomen personae Filii. Significat enim quamdam emanationem intellectus; persona autem quae procedit in divinis secundum emanationem intellectus dicitur Filius et hujusmodi processio dicitur generatio, ut supra ostensum est. Unde relinquitur quod solus Filius proprie dicatur Verbum in divinis.

[45]Ibid. III, 3.8 co/: "Secundo potest accipi ratio hujus congruentiae ex fine unionis, qui est impletio praedestinationis, eorum scilicet qui praeordinati sunt ad haereditatem caelestem, quae non debetur nisi filiis, secundum illud Rom., 'Filii et haeredes.' Et ideo congruum fuit ut per eum qui est Filius naturalis homines participarent similitudinem hujus filiationis secundum adoptionem, sicut Apostolus ibidem dicit, 'Quos praescivit et praedestinavit conformes fieri imagini Filii ejus.'"

[46]Ibid., "Tertio potest accipi ratio hujus congruentiae ex peccato primi parentis, cui per incarnationem remedium adhibetur. Peccavit enim primus homo appentendo scientiam, ut patet ex verbis serpentis promittentis homini 'scientiam boni et mali.' Unde conveniens fuit ut per Verbum verae sapientiae homo reduceretur in Deum, qui per inordinatum appetitum scientiae recesserat a Deo."

[47]Saint Thomas addresses himself to this theme of our sharing in the image of the Son in Summa theologiae III, 3.8 co/ where he describes why it was more fitting for the Son of God to become incarnate rather than the Father or the Holy Spirit: "Secundo potest accipi ratio huius congruentiae ex fine unionis, qui est impletio praedestinationis: eorum scilicet qui praeordinati sunt ad hereditatem caelestem, quae non debetur nisi filiis, secundum illus Rom. 8,17: 'Filli et heredes.'" It is also found in the biblical commentaries, for example, Super ad Ephesios, 1.2: "Nos autem sumus filii per adoptionem, inquantum scilicet sumus conformes Filio eius, et ideo quamdam participationem divini amoris habemus."

[48]Augustine, De trinitate, Book XIII, c. 18.

[49]Summa theologiae III, 4.6 co/: "Dicendum quod, sicut Augustinus dicit, 'poterat Deus hominem aliunde suscipere, non de genere illius Adae qui suo peccato obligavit genus humanum. Sed melius judicavit et de ipso quod victum fuerat genere assumere hominem Deus per quem generis humani vinceret inimicum.'"

[50]Augustine, De trinitate, Book XIII, c. 18, 23: "Victor primi Adam et tenens genus humanum, victus a secundo Adam et amittens genus humanum, liberatum ex humano genere ab humano crimine, per eum qui non erat in crimine quamvis esset ex genere. . . ."

[51]Summa theologiae III, 4.6 co/: "Et hoc propter tria. Primo quidem quia hoc videtur ad justitiam pertinere ut ille satisfaciat qui peccavit. Et ideo de natura per ipsum corrupta debuit assumi id per quod satisfactio erat implenda pro tota natura. Secundo, hoc etiam pertinet ad majorem hominis dignitatem, dum ex illo genere victor diabili nascitur quod per diabolum fuerat victum. Tertio, quia per hoc etiam Dei potentia magis ostenditur, dum de natura corrupta et infirma assumpsit id quod in tantam virtutem et dignitatem est promotum."

[52]Saint Thomas was aware of some of these heresies as he indicates in De articulis fidei et ecclesiae sacramentis, I (#606): "Secundus error est Manichaeorum dicentium, quod Christus non habuit verum corpus, sed phantasticum, contra quod est quod Dominus. Luc. ult., reprehendit errorem discipulorum suorum, qui conturbati et perterriti existimabant se spiritum videre; et Matth. XIV, 26: 'Videntes eum supra mare

ambulantem, turbati sunt dicentes, quia phantasma est, et prae timore clamaverunt:' quorum opinionem Dominus removit, dicens, vers. 27: 'Habete fiduciam, ego sum, nolite timere.' Tertius error est Valentini, qui dicit, Christum caeleste corpus attulisse, nihilique de Virgine assumpsisse, sed per ipsam tanquam per rivum aut fistulam sine ulla de illa assumpta carne transisse, contra quod dicitur Galat. IV, 4: 'Misit Deus Filium suum factum ex muliere.'"

[53]Summa theologiae III, 5.1 co/: "Secunda ratio sumi potest ex his quae in mysterio incarnationi sunt acta. Si enim non fuit verum corpus eius sed phantasticum, ergo nec veram mortem sustinuit; nec aliquid eorum quae de eo Evangelistae narrant, secundum veritatem gessit, sed solum secundum apparentiam quandam. Et sic etiam sequitur quod non fuit vera salutis hominis subsecuta: oportet enim effectum causae proportionari."

[54]Ibid., 14.1 co/: "Primo quidem, quia ad hoc Filius Dei, carne assumpta, venit in mundum, ut pro peccato humani generis satisfaceret. Unus autem pro peccato alterius satisfacit dum poenam peccato alterius debitam in seipsum suspicit. Hujusmodi autem defectus corporales, scilicet mors, fames et sitis, et hujus-modi, sunt poena peccati, quod est in mundum per Adam introductum, secundum illud Rom., 'Per unum hominem peccatum intravit in mundum, et per peccatum mors.' Unde conveniens fuit, quantum ad finem incarnationis, quod hujusmodi poenalitates in nostra carne susciperet, vice nostra, secundum illud Isaiae, 'Vere languores nostros ipse tulit.'"

[55]Ibid., ra/1: "Ad primum ergo dicendum quod satisfactio pro peccato alterius habet quidem quasi materiam poenas quas aliquis pro peccato alterius sustinet. Sed pro principio habet habitum animae ex quo inclinatur ad volendum satisfacere pro alio, et ex quo satisfactio efficaciam habet; non enim esset satisfactio efficax nisi ex caritate procederet. . . . Et ideo oportuit animam Christi perfectam esse quantum ad habitus scientiarum et virtutum, ut haberet facul-tatem satisfaciendi; et quod corpus ejus subjectum esset infirmitatibus, ut ei satisfactionis materia non deesset."

[56]Ibid., 14.4 co/: "Sunt autem tertii defectus qui in omnibus hominibus communiter inveniuntur ex peccato primi parentis, sicut mors, fames, sitis, et alia hujusmodi. Et hos defectus omnes Christus

suscepit. Quos Damascenus vocat 'naturales et in-
detractibiles passiones:' naturales quidem, quia
consequuntur communiter totam humanam naturam; inde-
tractibiles quidem quia defectum scientiae et gratiae
non important."

57Interestingly enough Saint Thomas excludes
Christ's having had the fomes peccati on the grounds
that they would not contribute to his having made
satisfaction, as he explains in III 15.2 co/: "Ad
rationem autem fomitis pertinet inclinatio sensualis
appetitus in id quod est contra rationem. Sic igitur
patet quod, quanto virtus fuerit magis in aliquo
perfecta, tanto magis debiliatur in eo vis fomitis.
Cum igitur in Christo fuerit virtus secundum perfectissimum gradum, consequens est quod in eo fomes peccati
non fuerit: cum iste defectus non sit ordinabilis ad
satisfaciendum, sed potius inclinat ad contrarium
satisfactioni."

58Summa theologiae III, 15.1 co/: "Dicendum quod,
sicut supra dictum est, Christus suscepit defectus
nostros ut pro nobis satisfaceret, et veritatem humanae
naturae comprobaret, et ut nobis exemplum virtutis
fieret. Secundum quae tria manifestum est quod defectum peccati assumere non debuit. Primo enim, peccatum
nihil operatur ad satisfactionem; quinimmo virtutem
satisfactionis impedit: quia, ut dicitur Eccl., 'dona
iniquorum non probat Altissimus.' Similiter etiam ex
peccato non demonstratur veritas humanae naturae:
quia peccatum non pertinet ad humanam naturam, cujus
Deus est causa, sed magis est contra naturam, 'per
seminationem diaboli' introductum ut Damascenus dicit.
Tertio, peccando exempla virtutum praebere non potuit,
cum peccatum contrarietur virtuti. Et ideo Christus
nullo modo assumpsit defectum peccati, nec originalis
nec actualis, secundum illud quod dicitur I Petr., 'Qui
peccatum non fecit, nec inventus est dolus in ore
ejus.'"

59Ibid., ag/4: "Praeterea, II Cor.5:21 dicitur
quod Deus 'eum qui non noverat peccatum,' scilicet
Christum, 'pro nobis fecit peccatum.' Sed illud vere
est quod a Deo factum est. Ergo in Christo vere fuit
peccatum."

60Ibid., ra/4: "Ad quartum dicendum quod Deus
'fecit Christum peccatum,' non quidem ut in se peccatum
haberet, sed quia fecit eum hostiam pro peccato. Sicut
Osee dicitur, 'Peccata populi mei comedent,' scilicet
sacerdotes, qui secundum legem comedebant hostias pro

peccato oblatas. Et secundum hunc modum dicitur Isaia quod 'Dominus posuit in eo iniquitates omnium nostrum:' quia scilicet eum tradidit ut esset hostia pro peccatis omnium hominum. Vel, 'fecit eum peccatum,' idest, 'habentem similitudinem carnis peccati,' ut dicitur Rom. Et hoc propter corpus passibile et mortale quod assumpsit."

[61]See above pp. 107-108.

[62]Summa theologiae III, 8.1 co/:   ". . . virtutem habuit influendi gratiam in omnia membra Ecclesiae. . ."

[63]Ibid., ra/1: "Ad primum ergo dicendum quod dare gratiam aut Spiritum Sanctum convenit Christo secundum quod Deus auctoritative; sed instrumentaliter ei convenit secundum quod est homo, inquantum scilicet ejus humanitas fuit 'instrumentum divinitatis ejus.' Et ita actiones ipsius ex virtute divinitatis fuerunt nobis salutiferae, utpote gratiam in nobis causantes et per meritum et per efficientiam quandam. Augustinus autem negat Christum, secundum quod est homo, dare Spiritum Sanctum per auctoritatem. Instrumentaliter autem, sive ministerialiter, etiam alii sancti dicuntur dare Spiritum Sanctum, secundum illus Gal., 'Qui tribuit vobis Spiritum Sanctum,' etc."

[64]See O'Neill, Mediator, p. 243.

[64a]Summa theologiae III, 7.9 co/:   "Sic enim recipiebat anima Christi gratiam ut ex quodammodo transfunderetur in alios. Et ideo oportuit quod haberet maximam gratiam: sicut ignis, qui est causa caloris in omnibus calidis, est maxime calidus.

[65]See Ibid., 48.5 co/: ". . . ad hoc quod aliquis redimat, duo requiritur: scilicet actus solutionis, et pretium solutum . . . utrumque istorum ad Christum pertinet immediate inquantum est homo: sed ad totam Trinitatem sicut ad causam primam et remotam. . . ."

[66]Ibid. 29.1 co/: "Et ideo solus Christus est perfectus Dei et hominum mediator, inquantum per suam mortem humanum genus Deo reconciliavit."

[67]Ibid. 29.2 co/: "Inquantum etiam est homo, competit ei conjungere homines Deo, praecepta et dona hominibus exhibendo, et pro hominibus ad Deum satisfaciendo et interpellando. Et ideo verissime dicitur mediator secundum quod homo."

[68]Some of the meanings listed by the Oxford Latin Dictionary (1971) for fundo, -ere are: (1) to pour (fluids from a vessel), pour out; (3) to drench (with); (5) to send forth in a stream; (6) to cause to rush forth; to expend or pour out lavishly; and for redundare: (1) to pour over, to stream forth, to overflow. Saint Thomas uses the traditional language of 'infusion,' which goes back to the Biblical language of 'pouring out,' in his discussion of the workings of grace, as in Summa theologiae I-II 113.2: "Utrum ad remissionem culpae, quae est justificatio impii, requiratur gratiae infusio."

[69]Summa theologiae III, 48.3 ra/1: ". . . licet veritas respondeat figurae quantum ad aliquid, non tamen quantum ad omnia: quia oportet quod veritas figuram excedat."

[70]Ibid., 48.2 ra/1: ". . . caput et membra sunt quasi una persona mystica."

[71]See Appendix, p. 266, n. 16.

[72]See above pp. 103-107.

[73]See above pp. 139-142.

[74]See O'Neill, Mediator, pp. xxv-xxvii.

[75]Ibid., p. xxv.

[76]Summa theologiae III, 22.1 co/: "Hoc autem maxime convenit Christo. Nam per ipsum divina bona hominibus sunt collata, secundum illud II Bet., 'Per quem,' scilicet Christum, 'maxima et retiosa nobis promissa donavit, ut per hoc efficiamini divinae consortes naturae.' Ipse etiam humanum genus Deo reconciliavit, secundum illud Col., 'In ipso,' scilicet Christo, 'complacuit omnem plenitudinem inhabitare, et per eum reconciliare omnia.' Unde Christo maxime convenit esse sacerdotem."

[77]Ibid., 22.2 co/: "Indiget igitur homo sacrificio propter tria. Uno quidem modo ad remissionem peccati per quod a Deo avertitur; et ideo Apostolus dicit, Heb., quod ad sacerdotem pertinet 'ut offerat dona et sacrificia pro peccatis.' Secundo, ut homo in statu gratiae conservetur, semper Deo inhaerens, in quo ejus pax et salus consistit; unde et in veteri lege immolabatur hostia pacifica pro offerentium salute,

ut habetur Levit. Tertio ad hoc quod spiritus hominis perfecte Deo uniatur, quod maxime erit in gloria; unde et in veteri lege offerebatur holocaustum, quasi totum incensum, ut dicitur Levit. Haec autem per humanitatem Christi nobis provenerunt. Nam primo quidem nostra peccata deleta sunt, secundum illud Rom., 'Traditus est propter delicta nostra.' Secundo gratiam nos salvantem per ipsum accepimus, secundum illud Heb., 'Factus est omnibus obtemperantibus sibi causa salutis aeternae.' Tertio per ipsum perfectionem gloriae adepti sumus, secundum illud Heb., 'Habemus fiduciam per sanguinem ejus in introitum sanctorum,' scilicet in gloriam caelestem. Et ideo ipse Christus, inquantum homo, non solum fuit sacerdos, sed etiam hostia perfecta, simul existens hostia pro peccato, et hostia pacifica, et holocaustum."

[78]Saint Thomas rarely speaks about the sinlessness of Christ without reference to what this subjective state of God-man enabled him to do pro nobis, as in Summa contra gentiles 4.55: "Manifestum est etiam ex praedictis quod oportuit Christum mortem pati, non solum ut exemplum praeberet mortem contemnendi propter veritatis amorem, sed ut etiam aliorum peccata purgaret. Quod quidem factum est dum ipse, qui absque peccato erat, mortem peccato debitam pati voluit, ut in se poenam aliis debitam, pro aliis satisfaciendo, susciperet. . . . Et quia alii homines pro seipsis hoc facere non poterant, Christus hoc pro omnibus fecit, mortem voluntariam ex caritate patiendo."

[79]Summa theologiae III, 22.3 ra/1: ". . . licet Christus non fuerit sacerdos secundum quod Deus, sed secundum quod homo, unus tamen et idem fuit sacerdos et Deus. . . . Et ideo, inquantum eius humanitas operabatur in virtute divinitatis, illud sacrificium erat efficacissimum ad delenda peccata."

[80]Ibid., co/: "Dicendum quod ad peccatorum perfectam emundationem duo requiruntur, secundum quod duo sunt in peccato, scilicet macula culpae et reatus poenae. Macula quidem culpae deletur per gratiam, qua cor peccatoris convertitur in Deum; reatus autem poenae totaliter tollitur per hoc quod homo Deo satisfacit. Utrumque autem horum efficit sacerdotium Christi. Nam virtute ipsius gratia nobis datur, qua corda nostra convertuntur ad Deum, secundum illud Rom., 'Justificati gratis per gratiam ipsius, per redemptionem quae est in Christo Jesu, quem proposuit Deus propitiatorem per fidem in sanguine ipsius.' Ipse etiam pro nobis plenarie satisfecit, inquantum 'ipse languores nostros

tulit, et dolores nostros ipse portavit.' Unde patet quod Christi sacerdotium habet plenam vim expiandi peccata."

[81]See above pp. 162-166.

[82]Summa theologiae III, 26.2 ra/3: "Ad tertium dicendum quod licet auctoritative peccatum auferre conveniat Christo secundum quod est Deus, tamen satisfacere pro peccato humani generis convenit ei secundum quod homo. Et secundum hoc dicitur Dei et hominum mediator."

[83]See ibid., 27. Introduction; also Heath, Our Lady, p. 3.

[84]Qq, 27-38 on the mystery of Christ's coming into the world as well as qq. 39-45 on the mission of Christ in his life and public ministry have been omitted from this schema.

[85]Adolph Harnack, History of Dogma, translated by W. M'Gilchrist, (London: Williams & Norgate, 1899), p. 196: "When we review the exposition given by Thomas, we cannot escape the impression created by confusion (multa, non multum)."

[86]These "méthodes 'd'investigation" are suggested by Lafont, Structures, pp. 406-412.

[87]Summa theologiae III, 46.1 ra/3: "Ad tertium dicendum quod hominem liberari per passionem Christi conveniens fuit et misericordiae et justitiae ejus. Justitiae quidem, quia per passionem suam Christus satisfecit pro peccato humani generis; et ita homo per justitiam Christi liberatus est. Misericordiae vero, quia cum homo per se satisfacere non posset pro peccato totius humanae naturae, ut supra dictum est, Deus ei satisfactorem dedit Filium suum, secundum illud, 'Justificati gratis per gratiam ipsius, per redemptionem quae est in Christo Jesu, quem proposuit Deus propitiatorem per fidem in sanguine ipsius:' et hoc fuit abundantioris misericordiae quam si peccata absque satisfactione dimisisset. Unde dicitur, 'Deus, qui dives est in misericordia, propter nimiam charitatem, qua dilexit nos, cum essemus mortui peccatis, convivificavit nos in Christo.'"

[88]Ibid., 46.2 ra/3: "Ad tertium dicendum quod haec etiam justitia dependet ex voluntate divina, ab humano genere satisfactionem exigente pro peccato.

Nam si voluisset absque omni satisfactione hominem a peccato liberare, contra justitiam non fecisset. Ille enim judex non potest salva justitia culpam sine poenam dimittere, qui habet punire culpam in alium commissam, puta vel in alium hominem vel in totam rempublican sive in superiorem principem. Sed Deus non habet aliquem superiorem, sed ipse est supremum et commune bonum totius universi. Et ideo si dimittat peccatum, quod habet rationem culpae, ex eo quod contra ipsum committitur, nulli facit injuriam: sicut quicumque homo remittit offensam in se commissam absque satisfactione, misericorditer et non injuste agit."

[89]Ibid., 46.3 co/: "Per hoc autem quod homo per Christi passionem est liberatus, multa occurrerunt ad salutem hominis pertinentia, praeter liberationem a peccato."

[90]Ibid., "Primo enim per hoc homo cognoscit quantum Deus hominem diligat, et per hoc provocatur ad eum diligendum, in quo perfectio humanae salutis consistit; unde Apostolus dicit Rom., 'Commendat suam charitatem Deus in nobis, quoniam cum inimici essemus Christus pro nobis mortuus est.' Secundo, quia per hoc dedit nobis exemplum obedientiae, humilitatis, constantiae, justitiae et caeterarum virtutum in passione Christi ostensarum, quae sunt necessariae ad humanam salutem: unde dicitur 1 Pet., 'Christus passus est pro nobis, vobis relinquens exemplum, ut sequamini vestigia ejus.' Tertio, quia Christus per passionem suam non solum hominem a peccato liberavit, sed etiam gratiam justificantem et gloriam beatitudinis ei promeruit. Quarto, quia per hoc est homini indicta major necessitas se immunem a peccato conservandi, secundum illud 1 Cor., 'Empti enim estis pretio magno; glorificate et portate Deum in corpore vestro.' Quinto, quia hoc ad majorem dignitatem hominis cessit, ut sicut homo victus fuerat et deceptus a diabolo, ita etiam homo esset qui diabolum vinceret; et sicut homo mortem meruit, ita homo moriendo mortem superaret. Unde dicitur 1 Cor., 'Deo gratias, qui dedit nobis victoriam per Dominum nostrum Jesum Christum.'"

The fifth reason is especially important for understanding Saint Thomas's rejection of the ransom from the devil theory (see above n. 30). In ag/3 attached to this article (46.3) it is argued that the devil would have been more fittingly dispossessed of his unjust servitude over man at a manifestation of Christ's power than by Christ's suffering. Note that in his response Saint Thomas contrasts the just punishment of man, to "be left by God in servitude to the devil," with the justice of the passion of Christ which liberated man from that servitude. Saint Thomas explains in 46.3 ra/3: "Ad tertium dicendum quod licet diabolus injuste invaserit hominem, tamen homo propter peccatum juste erat sub servitute diaboli derelictus a Deo. Et ideo conveniens fuit ut per justitiam homo a servitute diaboli liberaretur, Christo satisfaciente pro ipso per suam passionem. Fuit etiam hoc conveniens ad vincendam superbiam diaboli, qui est 'desertor justitiae et amator potentiae,' ut Christus 'diabolum vincere et hominem liberaret, non per solam potentiam Deitatis, sed etiam per justitiam et humilitatem passionis,' ut Augustinus dicit." There is no trace of the patristic tradition that it was to the devil that the ransom of Christ's blood was paid. A good example of this peculiar teaching is found in Gregory of Nyssa, The Great Catechism, translated by P. Schaff and H. Wace, (Grand Rapids: Eerdmans, 1976), c. 23: "The Enemy, therefore, beholding in Him such power, saw also in Him the opportunity for an advance, in exchange, upon the value of what he held. For this reason he chooses Him as a ransom for those who were shut up in the prison of death." Nor does Saint Thomas adopt Saint Augustine's modification of this doctrine, his abuse of the power of the devil theory (See De Trinitate XIII, 16-18), but chooses a text from the same author which simply compares the pride of the devil with the humility of Christ.

91Ibid., 46.4 co/: "Secundo, quia hoc genus mortis maxime conveniens erat satisfactioni pro peccato primi parentis, quod fuit ex eo quod contra mandatum Dei pomum ligni vetiti sumpsit. Et ideo conveniens fuit quod Christus ad satisfaciendum pro illo peccato seipsum pateretur ligno affigi, quasi restituens quod Adam sustulerat, secundum illud Ps., 'Quae non rapui, tunc exsolvebam.' Unde Augustinus dicit, 'Contempsit Adam praeceptum, accipiens ex arbore pomum; sed quidquid Adam perdidit Christus in cruce invenit.'"

92Ibid., 46.6 ra/2: "Et quia Stoici reputabant quod nulla tristitia esset ad aliquid utilis, ideo credebant quod totaliter a ratione discordaret, et per consequens quod totaliter esset sapienti vitanda. Sed secundum rei veritatem tristitia aliqua laudabilis est, . . . quando scilicet procedit ex sancto amore, utpote cum aliquis tristatur de peccatis propriis vel alienis. Assumitur etiam ut utilis ad finem satisfactionis pro peccato, secundum illud II Cor., 'Quae secundum Deum est tristitia, paenitentiam in salutem stabilem operatur.' Et ideo Christus, ut satisfaceret pro peccatis ommium hominum, assumpsit tristitiam, maximam quidem quantitate absoluta, non tamen excedentem regulam rationis."

[93]Ibid., 46.2 co/: "Sed ex aliqua suppositione facta, fuit impossible. Quia enim impossible est Dei praescientiam falli et eius voluntatem sive dispositionem cassari. . . ."

[94]Ibid., 47.3 co/: "Unde secundum tria Deus Pater tradidit Christum passioni. Uno quidem modo secundum quod sua aeterna voluntate praeordinavit passionem Christi ad humani generis liberationem, secundum illud quod dicitur Is., 'Dominus posuit in eo iniquitatem omnium nostrum;' et iterum, 'Dominus voluit conterere eum in infirmitate.' Secundo, inquantum inspiravit ei voluntatem patiendi pro nobis, infundendo ei charitatem: unde ibidem sequitur, 'Oblatus est, quia ipse voluit.' Tertio, non protegendo eum a passione, sed exponendo persequentibus: unde ut legitur Matt. quod pendens in cruce Christus dicebat, 'Deus meus, Deus meus, ut quid dereliquisti me?' quia scilicet potestati persequentium eum exposuit."

[95]Ibid., 47.2 ra/2: ". . . quod obedientia, etsi importet necessitatem respectu eius quod praecipitur, tamen importat voluntatem respectu impletionis praecepti. Et talis fuit obedientia Christi." ra/3: ". . . eadem ratione Christus passus est ex caritate, et obedientia: quia etiam praecepta caritatis nonnisi ex obedientia implevit; et obediens fuit ex dilectione ad Patrem praecipientem." Ibid., 47.1 ra/3: ". . . Christus simul violentiam passus est, ut moreretur, et tamen voluntarie mortuus fuit: quia violentia corpori eius illata est, quae tamen tantum corpori eius praevaluit quantum ipse voluit."

[96]See above pp. 143-151.

[97]How different is this perspective on satisfaction from the description which Aulén, Christus Victor, p. 150, offers of the Latin doctrine of redemption (for which Saint Thomas, in his view, is a chief exponent): "The actual atonement consists in the offering of satisfaction by Christ and God's acceptance of it; with this act men have nothing to do except insofar as Christ stands as their representative. Justification is a second act, in which God transfers or imputes to men the merits of Christ; here, again, there is no direct relation between Christ and men. Next, we have

Sanctification, a third act with no organic connection with the preceding two."

[98]See above pp. 114.

[99]See above pp. 26-28.

[100]J. Rivière, Le dogme de la Rédemption (Paris: Lecoffre, 1905), p. 8: "On reproche justement à nos prédicateurs d'être tombés dans ce défaut et, pour ne citer que les plus grands, il nous paraît difficile d'approuver, même dans Bossuet, des paroles comme celles-ci: 'Dieu montre à son Fils ce visage (de la justice); il lui montre cet oeil enflammé; il le regarde . . . de ce regard terrible qui porte le feu devant soi . . .; il le regarde enfin comme un pécheur et marche contre lui avec tout l'attirail de sa justice.'" See Bossuet, Oeuvres oratoires (Editions Lebarq) III, p. 382; 380; IV, pp. 286-287; V, p. 206 for similar examples of this kind of rhetorical excess. Another example is found in Bourdaloue, "Exhortation sur le crucifiement et la mort de Jésus-Christ" in Oeuvres complètes (Besançon, 1823) IX, p. 161: "Sous cette lèpre de péché, la justice de Dieu l'envisage comme un objet digne de toutes ses vengeances. Voilà pourquoi elle s'arme contre lui, pourquoi elle le poursuit le glaive à la main, pourquoi elle prononce l'arrêt de sa mort." · Also in "Mystères. Premier sermon sur la passion de Jésus-Christ," ibid. X, pp. 157,160.

[101]Summa theologiae III, 46.4 ra/1: "Loco autem materialis ignis, fuit in holocausto Christi ignis caritatis."

[102]Bernard Catão, Salut et Rédemption chez S. Thomas d'Aquin (Aubier, 1965), pp. 79-80: ". . . car pour lui (Saint Thomas) la satisfaction n'est pas la notion maîtresse, celle qui ferait comprendre en quoi consiste la valeur rédemptrice de la croix. Elle est simplement une bonne analogie, qui, entre autres, aide à comprendre pourquoi l'acte humain du Sauveur a été humiliation, souffrance et mort sur la croix."

[103]Summa theologiae III, 48.1 co/: "Dicendum quod, sicut supra dictum est, Christo data est gratia non solum sicut singulari personae, sed inquantum est caput Ecclesiae, ut scilicet ab ipso redundaret ad membra; et ideo opera Christi hoc modo se habent tam ad se quam ad sua membra, sicut se habent opera alterius hominis in gratia constituti ad ipsum."

[104]Ibid., 48.2 ra/1:   "Ad primum ergo dicendum quod caput et membra sunt quasi una persona mystica; et ideo satisfactio Christi ad omnes fideles pertinet sicut ad sua membra. In quantum etiam duo homines sunt unum in charitate, unus pro alio satisfacere potest."

[105]Ibid., co/: "Dicendum quod ille proprie satisfacit pro offensa qui exhibet offenso id quod aeque vel magis diligit quam oderit offensam. Christus autem ex charitate et obedientia patiendo majus aliquid Deo exhibuit quam exigeret recompensatio totius offensae humani generis: primo quidem propter dignitatem vitae suae, quam pro satisfactione ponebat; quae erat vita Dei et hominis; tertio, proper generalitatem passionis et magnitudinem doloris assumpti, . . . Et ideo passio Christi non solum sufficiens, sed etiam superabundans satisfactio fuit pro peccatis humani generis."

[106]Ibid., 48.3 co/: ". . . et hoc opus, quod voluntarie passionem sustinuit, fuit Deo maxime acceptum, utpote ex caritate proveniens. Unde manifestum est quod passio Christi fuit verum sacrificium."

[107]Ibid., ra/1: "(Caro Christi) quae est perfectissimum sacrificium . . . quia, ex hoc quod erat sine peccato, efficax erat ad emundanda peccata."

[108]Ibid., 48.4 co/: "Christus autem satisfecit, . . . dando id quod fuit maximum, seipsum scilicet pro nobis. Et ideo passio Christi dicitur esse nostra redemptio."

[109]Ibid., sc/: "Sed Contra est quod dicitur I Pet., 'Non corruptibilibus auro vel argento redempti estis de vana vestra conversatione paternae traditionis, sed pretioso sanguine quasi agni immaculati et incontaminati Christi;' . . ."

[110]Ibid., 48.2 sc/: "Sed contra est quod ex persona eius dicitur in Psalmo: 'Quae non rapui, tunc exsolvebam.' Non autem exsolvit qui perfecte non satisfecit. Ergo videtur quod Christus patiendo satisfecerit perfecte pro peccatis nostris."

[111]Ibid., 48.1 co/: "Manifestum est autem quod quicumque in gratia constitutus propter justitiam patitur, ex hoc ipso meretur sibi salutem, secundum illud Matt., 'Beati qui persecutionem patiuntur proper justitiam.'"

[112]Ibid., 48.6 ra/3: ". . . passio Christi, secundum quod comparatur ad divinitatem ejus, agit per modum efficientiae; in quantum vero comparatur ad voluntatem animae Christi, agit per modum meriti; secundum vero quod consideratur in ipsa carne Christi, agit per modum satisfactionis, in quantum per eam liberamur a reatu poenae; per modum vero redemptionis, in quantum per eam liberamur a servitute culpae; per modum autem sacrificii, in quantum per eam reconciliamur Deo."

[113]See above pp. 180-181.

[114]O'Neill, Mediator, pp. 243-244.

[115]See Summa theologiae III, 18.-19, especially 19.1 ra/3: ". . . operari est hypostasis subsistentis, sed secundum formam et naturam, a qua operatio speciem recipit. . . . Et similiter in Christo oportet quod sint duae operationes specie differentes, secundum eius duas naturas: quaelibet tamen operationum est una numero in Christo, semel facta, sicut una ambulatio et una sanatio."

[116]Lafont, Structures, pp. 421-432, especially p. 425: "Pour conclure ce thème du mérite capital, il faut souligner que c'est lui qui donne à l'activité concrète du Christ, à son 'acte extérieur' sa portée pour nous; . . . Mais si la rectitude intérieure de la volonté du Christ donne à son acte toute sa portée méritoire, elle ne le constitue pas totalement pour autant. Concrètement considéré, celui-ci est satisfaction, sacrifice, rédemption; . . . . Ces aspects complémentaires, dont la liste n'est pas exhaustive et qui d'ailleurs s'impliquent les uns les autres, sont successivement traités par Saint Thomas." The text cited by Lafont in support of this point is Summa theologiae III, 49.1 co/: "Secundo, passio Christi causat remissionem peccatorum per modum redemptionis. Quia enim ipse est caput nostrum, per passionem suam, quam ex charitate et obedientia sustinuit, liberavit nos tanquam membra sua a peccatis, quasi per pretium suae passionis; sicut si homo per aliquod opus meritorium quod manu exerceret redimeret se a peccato quod pedibus commisisset. Sicut enim naturale corpus est unum ex membrorum diversitate consistens, ita tota Ecclesia quae est mysticum corpus Christi computatur quasi una persona cum suo capite, quod est Christus."

[117]Summa theologiae III, 48.1 ra/2: "Christus a principio suae conceptionis meruit nobis salutem aeternam; sed ex parte nostra erant quaedam impedimenta, quibus impediebamur consequi effectum praecedentium meritorum: unde ad removendum illa impedimenta, oportuit Christum pati."

[118]J.-H. Nicolas, O.P. expresses a similar point of view in these words: "Si la passion a été méritoire, cela ne peut se comprendre qu'en la rattachant à la satisfaction. Car le principe du mérite est la charité, et n'importe quelle autre démarche du Christ, inspirée par la même charité, aurait été aussi méritoire. La notion de mérite à elle seule n'explique donc nullement pourquoi c'est précisément en souffrant et en mourant pour nous que le Christ nous a sauvés. Cela ne s'explique que par les exigences de l'amour pénitent, comme nous l'avons vu: donc par le sens satisfactoire de ces souffrances." Mimeographed notes from a course given at the University of Fribourg, summer 1977.

[119]Summa theologiae III, 49.1 sc/, co/: Merit: "Sicut si homo per aliquod opus meritorium. . ."; Satisfaction: ". . . quasi per pretium suae passionis."; Sacrifice: "'Dilexit nos, et lavit nos a peccatis nostris in sanguine suo.'"; Redemption: ". . . passio Christi causat remissionem peccatorum per modum redemptionis."; Efficient causality: ". . . caro, secundum quam Christus passionem sustinuit, est 'instrumentum divinitatis'."

[120]Ibid., 49.1 ra/3: "Sicut si medicus faciat medicinam ex qua possint etiam quicumque morbi sanari, etiam in futurum."

[121]See above p. 193, n. 90. Here Saint Thomas quotes Saint Augustine, De trinitate, Lib. XIII, c. 14: "Justitia Christi diabolus victus est: quia, cum in eo nihil morte dignum inveniret, occidit eum tamen; et utique iustum est ut debitores quos tenebat, liberi dimittantur, in eum credentes quem sine ullo debito occidit." One is reminded of Gregory of Nyssa's The Great Catechism, c. 24, where the devil is compared to a ravenous fish: "the hook of the Deity might be gulped down along with the bait of flesh, and thus, life being introduced into a house of death, and light shining in the darkness, that which is diametrically opposed to light and life might vanish. . . ."

[122]Summa theologiae III, 49.2 ra/3:   "Semper tamen per passionem Christi est paratum hominibus remedium . . . Sed si aliqui hoc remedio uti negligant, nil deperit efficaciae passionis Christi."

[123]Ibid., ra/1: ". . . non dicitur sic diabolus in homines potestatem habuisse quasi posset eis nocere Deo non permittente." Ibid., ra/2:   ". . . diabolus etiam nunc quidem potest, Deo permittente, homines tentare quantum ad animan. . . ." Ibid., ra/3: ". . . Deus permittit diabolo posse decipere homines. . . ."

[124]Ibid., 1.3 ra/3:   "Nihil autem prohibet ad aliquid maius humanum naturam productam esse post peccatum: Deus enim permittit mala fieri ut inde aliquid melius eliciat.   Unde decitur Rom. 5,20: 'Ubi abundavit iniquitas, superabundavit et gratia.' Unde et in benedictione Cerei Paschalis dicitur: 'O felix culpa, quae talem ac tantum meruit habere Redemptorem.'"

[125]Ibid., 49.3 co/:   "Dicendum quod per passionem Christi liberati sumus a reatu poenae dupliciter.   Uno modo directe, inquantum scilicet passio Christi fuit sufficiens et superabundans satisfactio pro peccatis totius humani generis: exhibita autem satisfactione sufficienti, tollitur reatus poenae.   Alio modo indirecte, inquantum scilicet passio Christi est causa remissionis peccati, in quo fundatur reatus poenae."

[126]Ibid., 4.1 ra/3:   ". . . deest congruitas ex parte necessitas: quia, etsi natura angelica in aliquibus peccato subiaceat, est tamen eius peccatum irremediable. . . ."

[127]Ibid., 49.3 ra/2:   "Ad secundum dicendum quod, sicut supra dictum est, ad hoc quod consequamur effectum passionis Christi, oportet nos ei configurari. Configuramur autem ei in baptismo sacramentaliter secundum illud Rom., 'Consepulti sumus ei per baptismum in mortem.' Unde bapitzatis nulla poena satisfactoria imponitur, quia sunt totaliter liberati per satisfactionem Christi.   Quia vero 'Christus semel tantum pro peccatis nostris mortuus est,' ut dicitur 1 Pet., ideo non potest homo secundario configurari morti Christi per sacramentum baptismi.   Unde oportet quod illi qui post baptismum peccant configurentur Christo patienti per aliquid poenalitatis vel passionis quam in seipsis sustineant; quae tamen multo minor sufficit quam esset condigna peccato, cooperante satisfactione Christi."

[128]Ibid., ra/3: "Ad tertium dicendum quod satis-factio Christi habet effectum in nobis, in quantum incorporamur ei, ut membra suo capiti, sicut supra dictum est. Membra autem oportet capiti conformari. Et ideo sicut Christus primo quidem habuit gratiam in anima cum passibilitate corporis, et per passionem ad gloriam immortalitatis pervenit, ita et nos, qui sumus membra ejus, per passionem ipsius liberamur quidem a reatu cujuslibet poenae, ita tamen quod primo recipiamus in anima spiritum adoptionis filiorum, quo ascribimur ad haereditatem gloriae immortalis, adhuc corpus passibile et mortale habentes; postmodum vero configurati passionbus, et morti Christi, in gloriam immortalem perducimur, secundum illud Apostoli Rom., 'Si filii, et haeredes, haeredes quidem Dei, cohaeredes autem Christi, si tamen compatimur, ut et conglorificemur.'"

[129]Ephesians 1: 9-10.

[130]Summa theologiae III, 49.4 co/: "Respondeo dicendum quod passio Christi est causa reconciliationis nostrae ad Deum dupliciter. Uno modo, inquantum removet peccatum, per quod homines constituuntur inimici Dei. . . ."

[131]Ibid., "Alio modo inquantum est sacrificium Deo acceptissimum. Est enim hoc proprie sacrificii effectus ut per ipsum placetur Deus; sicut etiam homo offensam in se commissam remittit proper aliquod obsequium acceptum, quod ei exhibetur. Unde dicitur I Reg., 'Si Dominus incitat te adversum me, odoretur sacrificium.' Et similiter tantum bonum fuit quod Christus voluntarie passus est, quod propter hoc bonum in natura humana inventum, Deus placatus est super omni offensa generis humani, quantum ad eos qui Christo passo conjunguntur secundum modum praemissum."

[132]Ibid., 49.4 ra/1: ". . . Deus diligit omnes homines quantum ad naturam, quam ipse fecit. Odit tamen eos quantum ad culpam, quam contra eum homines committunt . . ."

[133]Ibid., ra/2: "Ad secundum dicendum quod passio Christi non dicitur quantum ad hoc nos Deo reconcilias-se quod de novo nos amare inciperet cum scriptum sit Jer., 'In charitate perpetua dilexi te;' sed quia per passionem Christi sublata est odii causa, tum per ablationem peccati, tum per recompensationem acceptabilioris boni." A similar remark is found in

the commentary on Colossians 2:14, ". . . . having canceled the bond which stood against us with its legal demands; this he set aside, nailing it to the cross." In Super ad Colossenses 2.3: "Et ideo simul cum morte Christi, hoc chirographum est destructum, et ideo dicit 'tulit de medio,' id est sustulit de rerum natura, et hoc affigens 'illud cruce,' per quam satisfaciens Deo tulit peccatum nostrum."

134Summa theologiae III, 49.5 co/: "Dicendum quod clausio januae est obstaculum quoddam prohibens homines ab ingressu. Prohibentur autem homines ab ingressu regni coelestis propter peccatum, quia sicut dicitur Is., 'Via illa sancta vocabitur, et non transibit per eam pollutus.' Est autem duplex peccatum impediens ab ingressu regni coelestis. Unum quidem commune totius humanae naturae, quod est peccatum primi parentis: et per hoc peccatum praecludebatur homini aditus regni coelestis. Unde legitur Gen. quod post peccatum primi parentis 'collocavit Deus cherubim, et flammeum gladium atque versatilem, ad custodiendam viam ligni vitae.' Aliud autem est peccatum speciale uniuscujus- que personae, quod per proprium actum committitur uniuscujusque hominis. Per passionem autem Christi liberati sumus, non solum a peccato communi totius humanae naturae, et quantum ad culpam et quantum ad reatum poenae, ipso solvente pretium pro nobis, sed etiam a peccatis propriis singulorum, qui communicant ejus passioni per fidem, et charitatem, et fidei sacramenta. Et ideo per passionem Christi aperta est nobis janua regni coelestis. Et hoc est quod Apostolus dicit Heb., quod 'Christus assistens pontifex futurorum bonorum . . . per proprium sanguinem, introivit semel in sancta aeterna redemptione inventa.' Et hoc figura- tur Num. ubi dicitur, quod 'homicida manebit ibi,' scilicet in civitate refugii, 'donec sacerdos magnus, qui oleo sancto unctus est, moriatur;' quo mortuo poterit in domum suam redire."

135Ibid., ag/1: "Ergo videtur quod sancti Patres, qui operati sunt opera justitiae, fideliter consecuti essent introitum regni caelestis, etiam absque Christi passione."

136Ibid., ra/1: "Ad primum ergo dicendum quod sancti patres operando opera justitiae meruerunt introitum regni coelestis per fidem passionis Christi, secundum illud Heb., 'Sancti per fidem vicerunt regna, operati sunt justitiam:' per quam etiam unusquisque a peccato purgabatur, quantum pertinet ad emundationem propriae personae. Non tamen alicujus fides, vel justitia sufficiebat ad removendum impedimentum quod erat per reatum totius humanae creaturae; quod quidem remotum est pretio sanguinis Christi. Et ideo ante passionem Christi nullus intrare poterat regnum coeleste, adipiscendo scilicet beatitudinem aeternam, quae consistit in plena Dei fruitione."

[137]Ibid., 49.6 ra/1: "Et ideo perfectio animae Christi, quae fuit merendi principium, non debuit in eo acquiri per meritum. . . ."

[138]Ibid., 49.6 co/: "Ita enim, cum aliquis sibi ex justa voluntate subtrahit quod debebat habere, meretur ut sibi amplius aliquid superaddatur, quasi merces justae voluntatis."

[139]Ibid., 50.1 co/: "Est autem conveniens satisfaciendi pro alio modus cum aliquis se subiicit poenae quam alius meruit. Et ideo Christus mori voluit, ut, moriendo, pro nobis satisfaceret: secundum illud I Petr. 3, 'Christus semel pro peccatis nostris mortuus est.'"

[1]Lafont, Structures, pp. 421-425.

[2]The term "physical" is not frequently used in contemporary theological discussion to signify the universal dimension of Christ's saving mission. However, the notion that some kind of ontic communion exists between Christ and mankind can be traced back as far as Irenaeus of Lyon's recapitulation theory. The term should be understood in its etymological meaning, from physis, and therefore suggests a union on the level of common nature and not a mere mechanical incorporation of all (rational) creatures into Christ.

[3]Lafont, Structures, p. 424.

[4]Saint Thomas's explanation in De potentia 9.9 is an especially ample one: "Sic ergo oportet quod in divinis sit una tantum persona non procedens, et duae solae personae procedentes; quarum una persona procedit ut amor, et alia ut verbum; et sic est personarum ternarius numerus in divinis. Cuius quidem ternarii similitudoin creaturis apparet tripliciter: Primo quidem sicut effectus repraesentat causam; et hoc modo principium totius divinitatis, sclicet Pater, repraesentatur per id quod est primum in creatura, scilicet per hoc quod est in se una subsistens; verbum vero per formam cuiuslibet creaturae: nam in his quae ab intelligente aguntur, forma effectus a conceptione intelligentis derivatur; amor vero in ordine creaturae. Nam ex eo quod Deus amat seipsum, omnia ordine quodam in se convertit; et ideo haec similitudo dicitur vestigii, quod repraesentat pedem sicut effectus causam. Alio modo secundum eamdem rationem operationis; et sic repraesentatur in creatura rationali tantum, quae potest se intelligere et amare, sicut et Deus, et sic verbum et amorem sui producere, et haec dicitur similitudo naturalis imaginis; ea enim imaginem aliorum gerunt quae similem speciem praeferunt. Tertio modo per unitatem obiecti, in quantum creatura rationalis intelligit et amat Deum; et haec est quaedam unionis conformitas, quae in solis sanctis invenitur qui idem intelligunt et amant quod Deus."

[5]Summa theologiae III, 3.8 co/: "Dicendum quod convenientissimum fuit personam Filii incarnari. Primo quidem, ex parte unionis. Convenienter enim ea quae sunt similia uniuntur. Ipsius autem personae Filii, qui est Verbum Dei, attenditur uno quidem modo communis convenientia ad totam creaturam. Quia verbum artificis, idest conceptus ejus, est similitudo exemplaris eorum quae ab artifice fiunt. Unde Verbum Dei, quod est aeternus conceptus ejus, est similitudo exemplaris totius creaturae. Et ideo, sicut per participationem hujus similitudinis creaturae sunt in propriis speciebus institutae sed mobiliter, ita per unionem Verbi ad creaturam non participativam sed personalem conveniens fuit reparari creaturam in ordine ad aeternam et immobilem perfectionem. Nam et artifex per formam artis conceptam qua artificiatum condidit, ipsum, si collapsum fuerit, restaurat . . . . Secundo, potest accipi ratio hujus congruentiae ex fine unionis, qui est impletio praedestinationis, eorum scilicet qui praeordinati sunt ad haereditatem caelestem, quae non debetur nisi filiis, secundum illud Rom., 'Filii et haeredes.' Et ideo congruum fuit ut per eum qui est Filius naturalis homines participarent similitudinem hujus filiationis secundum adoptionem, sicut Apostolus ibidem dicit, 'Quos praescivit et praedestinavit conformes fieri imagini Filii ejus.'"

[6]Ibid., 61.1 ra/3: ". . . passio Christi est causa sufficiens humanae salutis. Nec propter hoc sequitur quod sacramenta non sint necessaria ad humanam salutem: quia operantur in virtute passionis Christi, et passio Christi quodammondo applicatur hominibus per sacramenta, secundum illud Apostoli, 'Quicumque baptizati sumus in Christo Jesu, in morte ipsius baptizati sumus.'"

[7]Ibid., 79.2 ra/1: "Ad primum ergo dicendum quod sicut passio Christi, ex cujus virtute hoc sacramentum operatur, est quidem causa sufficiens gloriae, non tamen ita quod statim per ipsam introducamur in gloriam, sed oportet ut prius simul compatiamur, ut postea simul glorificemur, sicut dicitur Rom., ita hoc sacramentum non statim nos in gloriam introducit, sed dat nobis virutem perveniendi ad gloriam, et ideo viaticum dicitur."

[8]Ibid., I, 95.4 ra/2: "Et tamen potest contingere quod aliquis ita prompta voluntate faciat opus aliquod facile, sicut alius difficile, quia paratus esset

facere etiam quod sibi esset difficile. Difficultas tamen actualis, inquantum est poenalis, habet etiam quod sit satisfactoria pro peccato."

[9]Ibid., I-II, 102.3 co/: "Et quia ex figurato sumitur ratio figurae, ideo rationes sacrificiorum figuralium veteris legis sunt sumendae ex vero sacrificio Christi."

[10]Ibid., ra/8: "Et quia hoc non esset satisfactio pro peccato: si enim cederet in usum eorum pro quorum peccatis offerebatur, idem esse videretur ac si non offerrent."

[11]Ibid., 114.2 co/: "Dicendum quod hominis sine gratia duplex status considerari potest, sicut supra dictum est. Unus quidem naturae integrae, qualis fuit in Adam ante peccatum; alius autem naturae corruptae, sicut est in nobis ante reparationem gratiae. Si ergo loquamur de homine quantum ad primum statum, sic una ratione non potest homo mereri absque gratia vitam aeternam per pura naturalia, quia scilicet meritum hominis dependet ex praeordinatione divina. Actus autem cujuscumque rei non ordinatur divinitus ad aliquid excedens proportionem virtutis quae est principium actus; hoc enim est ex institutione divinae providentiae, ut nihil agat ultra suam virtutem. Vita autem aeterna est quoddam bonum excedens proportionem naturae creatae; quia etiam excedit cognitionem et desiderium ejus, secundum illud I ad Cor., 'Nec oculus vidit, nec auris audivit, nec in cor hominis ascendit.' Et inde est quod nulla natura creata est sufficiens principium actus meritorii vitae aeternae, nisi superaddatur aliquod supernaturale donum, quod gratia dicitur. Si vero loquamur de homine sub peccato existente, additur cum hoc secunda ratio, propter impedimentum peccati. Cum enim peccatum sit quaedam Dei offensa excludens a vita aeterna . . ., nullus in statu peccati existens potest vitam aeternam mereri, nisi prius Deo reconcilietur dismisso peccato, quod fit per gratiam. Peccatori enim non debetur vita, sed mors, secundum illud Rom., 'Stipendia peccati mors.'"

[12]Ibid., II-II, 32.1 ra/2: ". . . nihil prohibet actum qui est proprie unius virtutis elicitive, attribui alteri virtuti sicut imperanti et ordinanti ad suum finem. Et hoc modo dare eleemosynam ponitur inter opera satisfactoria: inquantum miseratio in defectum patientis ordinatur ad satisfaciendum pro culpa. Secundum autem quod ordinatur ad placandum Deum, habet rationem sacrificii: et sic imperatur a latria."

[13]Ibid., I, 93.1 sc/: ". . . dicitur Gen. 1:26, 'Faciamus hominem ad imaginem et similitudinem nostram.'" Ibid., 93.6 co/: "Sic igitur in homine invenitur Dei similitudo per modum imaginis secundum mentis . . . ."

[14]Ibid., I-II, 107.1 ra/1: ". . . unitas fidei utriusque Testamenti attestatur unitati finis. Dictum est . . . quod objectum theologicarum virtutum, inter quas fides, est finis ultimus. Sed tamen fides habet alium statum in veteri et in nova lege; nam quod illi credebant futurum nos credimus factum."

[15]Ibid., ra/2: ". . . omnes differentiae quae assignantur inter novam legem et veterem accipiuntur secundum perfectum et imperfectum. Praecepta enim legis cujuslibet dantur de actibus virtutum. Ad facienda autem virtutum opera aliter inclinantur imperfecti qui nondum habent virtutis habitum, et aliter illi qui sunt per habitum virtutis perfecti. Illi enim qui nondum habent habitum virtutis inclinantur ad agendum virtutis opera ex aliqua causa extrinseca, puta ex comminatione poenarum, vel ex promissione aliquarum extrinsecarum remunerationum, puta honoris vel divitiarum vel alicujus hujusmodi; et ideo lex vetus, quae dabatur imperfectis, idest, nondum consecutis gratiam spiritualem, dicebatur 'lex timoris,' inquantum inducebat ad observationem praeceptorum per comminationem quarundam poenarum; et dicitur habere temporalia quaedam promissa. Illi autem qui habent virtutem inclinatur ad virtutis opera agenda propter amorem virtutis, non propter aliquam poenam aut remunerationem extrinsecam, et ideo lex nova, cujus principalitas consistit in ipsa spirituali gratia indita cordibus, dicitur 'lex amoris,' et dicitur habere promissa spiritualia et aeterna, quae sunt objecta virtutis, praecipue caritatis. Et ita per se in ea inclinantur non quasi in extranea, sed quasi in propria; et propter hoc etiam lex vetus dicitur 'cohibere manum, non animum,' quia qui timore poenae ab aliquo peccato abstinet non simpliciter ejus voluntas a peccato recedit, sicut recedit voluntas ejus qui amore justitiae, abstinet non simpliciter ejus voluntas a peccato recedit, sicut recedit voluntas ejus qui amore justitiae, abstinet a peccato; et propter hoc lex nova, quae est 'lex amoris,' dicitur 'animum cohibere.'"

[16]Ibid., 98.1 co/: ". . . absque omni dubio lex vetus bona fuit. Sicut enim doctrina ostenditur esse vera ex hoc quod consonat rationi rectae, ita etiam lex

aliqua ostenditur esse bona ex eo quod consonat rationi. Lex autem vetus rationi consonabat. . . . Finis
autem legis divinae est perducere hominem ad finem
felicitatis aeternae; qui quidem finis impeditur per
quodcumque peccatum, et non solum per actus exteriores,
sed etiam per interiores. Et ideo illud quod sufficit
ad perfectionem legis humanae, ut scilicet peccata
prohibeat et poenam apponat, non sufficit ad perfectionem legis divinae: sed oportet quod hominem totaliter
faciat idoneum ad participationem felicitatis aeternae.
Quod quidem fieri non potest nisi per gratiam Spiritus
Sancti, per quam 'diffunditur caritas in cordibus
nostris,' quae legem adimplet; 'gratia' enim 'Dei vita
aeterna, 'ut dicitur. Hanc autem gratiam lex vetus
conferre non potuit, reservabatur enim hoc Christo:
quia, ut dicitur, 'lex per Moysen data est; gratia
et veritas per Jesum Christum facta est.' Et inde
est quod lex vetus bona quidem est, sed imperfecta;
secundum illud, 'Nihil ad perfectum adduxit lex.'"

[17]Ibid., 106.1 co/: "Id autem quod est potissimum
in lege Novi Testamenti, et in quo tota virtus ejus
consistit, est gratia Spiritus sancti, quae datur per
fidem Christi. Et ideo principaliter lex nova est ipsa
gratia Spiritus sancti, quae datur Christi fidelibus."

[18]Ibid., 106.2 co/: ". . . ad legem Evangelii duo
pertinent. Unum quidem principaliter, scilicet ipsa
gratia Spiritus sancti interius data, et quantum ad hoc
nova lex justificat. Unde Augustinus dicit, 'Ibi,'
scilicet in Veteri Testamento, 'lex extrinsecus est
posita, qua injusti terrerentur; hic,' scilicet in
Novo Testamento, 'intrinsecus data est, qua jus-
tificarentur.' Aliud pertinet ad legem Evangelii
secundario, scilicet documenta fidei et praecepta
ordinantia affectum humanum et humanos actus; et
quantum ad hoc nova lex non justificat. Unde Apostolus
dicit II ad Cor., 'Littera occidit, spiritus autem
vivificat.'"

[19]Ibid., "Unde etiam littera Evangelii occideret,
nisi adesset interius gratia fidei sanans."

[20]Ibid., 114.8 co/: ". . . illud cadit sub
merito condigni ad quod motio gratiae se extendit.
Motio autem alicujus moventis non solum se extendit
ad ultimum terminum motus, sed etiam ad totum progres-
sum in motu. Terminus autem motus gratiae est vita
aeterna. Progressus autem in hoc motu est secundum
augmentum caritatis vel gratiae."

[21]Ibid., 114.7 ra/1: ". . . desiderium quo quis desiderat reparationem post lapsum justum dicitur, et similiter oratio, quia tendit ad justitiam; non tamen ita quod justitiae innitatur per modum meriti, sed solum misericordiae."

[22]Ibid., 114.1 ra/2: ". . . Deus ex bonis nostris non quaerit utilitatem, sed gloriam, idest manifestionem suae bonitatis; quod etiam ex suis operibus quaerit. Ex hoc autem quod eum colimus, nihil ei accrescit, sed nobis; et ideo meremur aliquid a Deo, non quasi ex nostris operibus aliquid ei accrescat, sed inquantum propter ejus gloriam operamur." It is important to read in connection with this text what Saint Thomas says about divine final causality, for example in Summa theologiae I, 44.4 co/: "Sed primo agenti, qui est agens tantum, non convenit agere propter acquisitionem alicuius finis; sed intendit solum communicare suam perfectionem, quae est eius bonitatis. Et unaquaeque creatura intendit consequi suam perfectionem, quae est similitudo perfectionis et bonitas divinae. Sic ergo divina bonitas est finis rerum omnium." See also ibid., 19.5.

[23]Ibid. III, 61.2 ra/1: ". . . homo in statu innocentiae gratia indigebat: non tamen ut consequeretur gratiam per aliqua sensibilia signa, sed spiritualiter et invisibiliter."

[24]Ibid., 61.3 ra/2: ". . . status humani generis post peccatum et ante Christum dupliciter potest considerari. Uno modo, secundum fidei rationem. Et sic semper unus et idem permansit: quia scilicet justificabantur homines per fidem futuri Christi adventus. Alio modo potest considerari secundum intensionem et remissionem peccati, et expressae cognitionis de Christo. Nam per incrementa temporum et peccatum coepit in homine magis dominari, intantum quod, ratione hominis per peccatum obtenebrata, non sufficerent homini ad recte vivendum praecepta legis naturae, sed necesse fuit determinari praecepta in lege scripta et cum his quaedam fidei sacramenta. Oportebat etiam ut per incrementa temporum magis explicaretur cognitio fidei: quia, ut Gregorius dicit, 'per incrementa temporum crevit divinae cognitionis augmentum.' Et ideo etiam necesse fuit quod in veteri lege etiam quaedam sacramenta fidei quam habebant de Christo venturo, determinarentur; quae quidem comparantur ad sacramenta quae fuerunt ante legem sicut determinatum ad indeterminatum, quia scilicet

ante legem non fuit determinate praefixum homini quibus sacramentis uteretur, sicut fuit per legem. Quod erat necessarium et propter obtenebrationem legis naturalis et ut esset determinatior fidei significatio."

25Ibid., 70.4 co/: "Et ideo dicendum quod in circumcisione conferebatur gratia quantum ad omnes gratiae effectus, aliter tamen quam in baptismo. Nam in baptismo confertur gratia ex virtute ipsius baptismi, quam habet inquantum est instrumentum passionis Christi jam perfectae. Circumcisio autem conferebat gratiam inquantum erat signum fidei passionis Christi futurae: ita scilicet quod homo qui accipiebat circumcisionem, profitebatur se suscipere talem fidem, vel adultus pro se vel alius pro parvulis. Unde et Apostolus dicit quod 'Abraham accepit signum circumcisionis, signaculum justitiae fidei;' qua scilicet justitia ex fide erat significata, non ex circumcisione significante. Et quia baptismus operatur instrumentaliter in virtute passionis Christi, non autem circumcisio, ideo baptismus imprimit characterem incorporantem hominem Christo, et copiosiorem gratiam confert quam circumcisio: major enim est effectus rei jam praesentis quam spei."

26Ibid., 62.6 co/: "Sic ergo patet quod sacramenta veteris legis non habebant in se aliquam virtutem qua operarentur ad conferendam gratiam justificantem."

27Ibid., "Et tamen per fidem passionis Christi justificabantur antiqui Padres, sicut et nos. Sacramenta autem veteris legis erant quaedam illius fidei protestationes, inquantum significabant passionem Christi et effectus ejus."

28Ibid., 61.4 co/: ". . . sicut antiqui Patres salvati sunt per fidem Christi venturi, ita et nos salvamur per fidem Christi jam nati et passi. Sunt autem sacramenta quaedam signa protestantia fidem qua homo justificatur. Oportet autem aliis signis significari futura, praeterita seu praesentia, ut enim Augustinus dicit, 'eadem res aliter annuntiatur facienda, aliter facta: sicut ipsa verba 'passurus' et 'passus' non similiter sonant.' Et ideo oportet quaedam alia sacramenta in nova lege esse, quibus significentur ea quae praecesserunt in Christo, praeter sacramenta veteris legis, quibus praenuntiabantur futura."

29Ibid., 62.1 co/: "Et hoc modo non potest causare gratiam nisi Deus: quia gratia nihil est aliud quam quaedam participata similitudo divinae naturae, secundum illud II Pet., 'Magna nobis et pretiosa promissa donavit, ut divinae simus consortes naturae.' Causa vero instrumentalis non agit per virtutem suae formae, sed solum per motum quo movetur a principali agente. Unde effectus non assimilatur instrumento, sed principali agenti: sicus lectus non assimilatur securi, sed arti quae est in mente artificis. Et hoc modo sacramenta novae legis gratiam causant: adhibentur enim ex divina ordinatione ad gratiam in eis causandam."

[30]Ibid., 62.5 co/: "Est autem duplex instrumentum: unum quidem separatum, ut baculus; aliud autem conjunctum, ut manus. Per instrumentum autem conjunctum movetur instrumentum separatum: sicut baculus per manum. Principalis autem causa efficiens gratiae est ipse Deus, ad quem comparatur humanitas Christi sicut instrumentum conjunctum, sacramentum autem sicut instrumentum separatum. Et ideo oportet quod virtus salutifera derivetur a divinitate Christi per ejus humanitatem in ipsa sacramenta."

[31]Ibid., "Gratia autem sacramentalis ad duo praecipue ordinari videtur: videlicet ad tollendos defectus praeteritorum peccatorum, inquantum transeunt actu et remanent reatu; et iterum ad perficiendam animam in his quae pertinent ad cultum Dei secundum religionem Chritianae vitae. Manifestum est autem ex his quae supra dicta sunt, quod Christus liberavit nos a peccatis nostris praecipue per suam passionem, non solum efficienter et meritorie, sed etiam satisfactorie. Similiter etiam per suam passionem initiavit ritum Christinae religionis, 'offerens seipsum oblationem et hostiam Deo,' ut dicit Ephes. Unde manifestum est quod sacramenta Ecclesiae specialiter habent virtutem ex passione Christi, cujus virtus quodammodo nobis copulatur per susceptionem sacramentorum. In cujus signum, de latere Christi pendentis in cruce fluxerunt aqua et sanguis, quorum unum pertinet ad baptismum, aliud ad Eucharistiam quae sunt potissima sacramenta."

[32]Ibid., "Et ideo oportet quod virtus salutifera derivetur a divinitate Christi per eius humanitatem in ipsa sacramenta."

[33]Ibid., 62.2 ra/2: "Ad secundum dicendum quod per virtutes et dona sufficienter excluduntur vitia et peccata quantum ad praesens et futurum, inquantum scilicet impeditur homo per virtutes et dona a

peccando. Sed quantum ad praeterita peccata, quae transeunt actu et permanent reatu, adhibetur homini remedium specialiter per sacramenta."

34See O'Neill, Mediator, p. 251: "Because it bestows a right to inheriting divine happiness adoptive sonship is essentially an eschatological reality. It is something which must be progressively realized in the members of Christ in virtue of his mediation. It does not, consequently, consist so much in a state of being as in a tendency towards the beatitude of heaven; for, while it is true that sanctifying grace gives a stable participation in the divine nature, it is no less true that grace is a divine source of activity, giving a dynamic impulsion towards God. Seen in this light, adoptive sonship falls into place in the scheme of the whole Summa Theologiae, deriving therefrom its theological intelligibility. Reciprocally, it throws the light of the Scriptures on the structure of the Summa. For fundamental to the concept of both adoptive sonship and the Summa is the notion of God as the Final Cause of all creation. The theological theme and the Christian reality are several times brought explicitly into harmony through the course of the Summa. Some of the principal places must be noticed before the central problem of adoptive sonship is approached."

35Summa theologiae·III, 69.1 co/: "Dicendum quod, sicut Apostolus dicit, 'quicumque baptizati sumus in Christo Jesu, in morte, ipsius baptizati sumus.' Et postea concludit, 'Ita et vos existimate mortuos quidem esse peccato, viventes autem Deo in Christo Jeso Domino nostro.' Ex quo patet quod per baptismum homo moritur vetustati peccati, et incipit vivere novitati gratiae. Omne autem peccatum pertinet ad pristinam vetustatem. Unde consequens est quod omne peccatum per baptismum tollatur."

36Ibid., 69.2 ag/2: ". . . sacramenta novae legis efficiunt quod figurant . . ." See ibid., 62.1 ra/1: "Ad primum ergo dicendum quod causa principalis non proprie potest dici signum effectus, licet occulti, etiam si ipsa sit sensibilis et manifesta. Sed causa instrumentalis, si sit manifesta, potest dici signum effectus occulti eo quod non solum est causa, sed quodammodo effectus, inquantum movetur a principali agente. Et secundum hoc, sacramenta novae legis simul sunt causae et signa. Et inde est quod, sicut communiter dicitur, 'efficiunt quod figurant.' Ex quo etiam patet quod habent perfecte rationem sacramenti: inquantum ordinatur ad aliquid sacrum non solum per modum signi, sed etiam per modum causae."

[37]Ibid. 69.2 ra/1: ". . . quia poena passionis Christi communicatur baptizato, inquantum fit membrum Christi, ac si ipse poenam illam sustinuisset, ejus peccata remanent ordinata per poenam passionis Christi."

[38]Ibid., 69.2 co/: ". . . per baptismum aliquis incorporatur passioni et morti Christi, secundum illud Rom., 'Si mortui sumus cum Christo, credimus quia etiam simul vivimus cum Christo.' Ex quo patet quod omni baptizato communicatur passio Christi ad remedium ac si ipse passus et mortuus esset. Passio autem Christi, sicut supra dictum est, est sufficiens satisfactio pro omnibus peccatis omnium hominum. Et ideo ille qui baptizatur liberatur a reatu omnis poenae sibi debitae pro peccatis, ac si ipse sufficienter satisfecisset pro omnibus peccatis suis."

[39]See above, pp. 239-240; also ibid., 69.2 ra/2: " . . . aqua non solum abluit, sed etiam refrigerat. Et ita suo refrigerio significat subtractionem reatus poenae, sicut sua ablutione significat emundationem a culpa."

[40]I Corinthians 15:54.

[41]See above p. 325, n. 22. What is suggested here is Saint Thomas's faithful interpretation of the Church's teaching on the working of divine grace and the absolute priority of God's initiative in bestowing it. See, for example, Summa theologiae I-II, 114.5 ra/1: "Sed si supponamus, sicut fidei veritas habet, quod initium fidei sit in nobis a Deo, jam etiam ipse actus fidei consequitur primam gratiam; et ita non potest esse meritorius primae gratiae. Per fidem igitur justificatur homo, non quasi homo credendo mereatur justificationem, sed quia dum justificatur credit, eo quod motus fidei requiritur ad justificationem impii . . . ."

[42]Summa theologiae III, 69.3 co/: "Et ideo conveiens est ut id agatur in membro incorporato quod est actum in capite. Christus autem a principio suae conceptionis fuit plenus gratia et veritate, habuit tamen corpus passible, quod per passionem et mortem est ad vitam gloriosam resuscitatum. Unde et Christianus in baptismo gratiam consequitur quantum ad animam,

352

habet tamen corpus passibile, in quo pro Christo possit pati; sed tandem resuscitabitur ad impassibilem vitam. Unde Apostolus dicit, 'Qui suscitavit Jesum Christum a mortuis, vivificabit et mortalia corpora nostra, propter inhabitantem Spiritum ejum in nobis.' Et infra eodem, 'Heredes quidem Dei, coheredes autem Christi: si tamen compatimur, ut et simul glorificemur.'"

[43]Ibid., 69.4 sc/:   "Sic ergo in baptismo datur gratia Spiritus Sancti et copia virtutum."

[44]Teresa of Avila, Castillo Interior 5.1.2 in Obras de Santa Teresa de Jesus, edited by P. Silverio de Santa Teresa, (Burgos: El Monte Carmelo, 1922), p. 587: "Por eso, hermanas mías, alto a pedir al Señor, que pues en alguna manera podemos gozar del cielo en la tierra . . . ."

[45]Romans 8: 19-24.

[46]Summa theologiae III, 69.5 co/:   ". . . per baptismum aliquis regeneratur in spiritualem vitam, quae est propria fidelium. Christi, sicut Apostolus dicit, 'Quod autem nunc vivo in carne, in fide vivo Filii Dei.' Vita autem non est nisi membrorum capiti unitorum, a quo sensum et motum suscipiunt. Et ideo necesse est quod per baptismum aliquis incorporetur Christo quasi membrum ipsius. Sicut autem a capite naturali derivتur ad membra sensus et motus, ita a capite spirituali, quod est Christus, derivatur ad membra ejus sensus spiritualis, qui consistit in cognitione veritatis, et motus spiritualis, qui est per gratiae instinctum. Unde Joan. dicitur, 'Vidimus eum plenum gratiae et veritatis: et de plenitudine ejus omnes accepimus.' Et ideo consequens est quod baptizati illuminentur a Christo circa cognitionem veritatis, et fecundentur ab eo fecunditate bonorum operum per gratiae infusionem."

[47]See above pp. 240-241.

[48]Summa theologiae III, 69.7 ra/1:   ". . . baptismus intantum aperit baptizato ianuam regni caelestis, inquantum incorporat eum passioni Christi virtutem eius homini applicando." Ibid., co/:   ". . . aperire ianuam regni caelestis est amovere impedimentum quo aliquis impeditur regnum caeleste intrare."

[49]See ibid., 49.5 ra/1 where Saint John explains that no one's faith or justice was sufficient to remove the impediment that kept men from entering into glory.

[50]See above pp. 240-241. See also ibid., 69.3
co/: ". . . baptismus habet virtutem auferendi poenalitates praesentis vitae: non tamen eas aufert in
presenti vita, sed eius virtute auferentur a justis in
resurrectione . . . . Et hoc rationabiliter . . . .
Secundo, hoc est conveniens propter spirituale exercitium: ut videlicet contra concupiscentiam et alias
passibilitates pugnans homo victoriae coronam acci-
peret."

[51]Ibid., 89.3 co/: ". . . homo per peccatum
duplicem dignitatem amittit . . . . Quantum autem ad
Deum, amittit duplicem dignitatem. Unam gratiam. Et
hanc dignitatem recuperat per poenitentiam. Quod
significatur Luc. 15, de filio prodigo, cui pater
poenitenti iussit restitui 'stolam primam et anulum et
calceamenta.'"

[52]Ibid., 84.10 ra/5: ". . . Baptismus habet
virtutem ex Passione Christi, sicut quaedam spiritualis
generatio cum spirituali morte praecedentis vitae.
'Statutum' autem 'est hominibus semel mori,' et semel
nasci; et ideo semel tantum debet homo baptizari. Sed
Poenitentia habet virtutem ex Passione Christi sicut
spiritualis medicina, quae frequenter iterari potest."

[53]O'Brien, Effects of Sin, appendix 2, provides
an excellent analysis of Saint Thomas's understanding
of mortal sin. See also Summa theologiae I-II, 87.3
co/ which expresses Saint Thomas's constant explanation
of mortal sin: sin that breaks the revealed, personal
union of man with God through charity.

[54]Summa theologiae III, 84.5 co/: ". . . aliquid
est necessarium ad salutem dupliciter; uno modo absolute, alio modo ex suppositione. Absolute quidem
necessarium est illud sine quo nullus salutem consequi
potest, sicut gratia Christi, et sacramentum Baptismi,
per quod aliquis in Christo renascitur. Ex suppositione autem est necessarium sacramentum Poenitentiae,
quod quidem est necessarium non omnibus, sed peccato
subjacentibus. 'Peccatum' autem, 'cum consummatum
fuerit, generat mortem,' ut dicitur Fac. I. Et ideo
necessarium est ad salutem peccatoris quod peccatum
removeatur ab eo; quod quidem non potest fieri sine
Poenitentiae sacramento, in quo operatur virtus Passionis Christi per absolutionem sacerdotis simul cum opere
poenitentis, qui cooperatur gratiae ad destructionem
peccati. Sicut enim dicit Augustinus super Jo., 'qui
creavit te sine te, non justificabit te sine te.' Unde

patet quod sacramentum Poenitentiae est necessarium ad salutem post peccatum, sicut medicatio corporalis postquam homo in morbum periculosum inciderit."

[55]Ibid., 84.7 co/: ". . . ex naturali enim ratione homo movetur ad poenitendum de malis quae fecit, sed quod hoc vel illo modo homo poenitentiam agat, est ex institutione divina. Unde et Dominus in principio praedicatonis suae indixit hominibus ut non solum poeniterent, sed etiam 'poenitentiam agerent,' significans determinatos modos actuum qui requiruntur ad hoc sacramentum. Sed id quod pertinet ad officum ministrorum, determinavit cum Matt. 16, dixit Petro, 'Tibi dabo claves regni coelorum,' etc. Efficaciam autem hujus sacramenti et originem virtutis ejus manifestavit post resurrectionem Luc. 24, ubi dixit quod 'oportet praedicari in nomine ejus poenitentiam et remissionem peccatorum in omnes gentes,' praemisso de Passione et Resurrectione, virtute enim nominis Jesu Christi patientis et resurgentis hoc sacramentum efficaciam habet in remissionem peccatorum. Et sic patet convenienter hoc sacramentum in Nova Lege institutum fuisse."

[56]Ibid., 86.4 ra/3: ". . . Passio Christi de se sufficiens est ad tollendum omnem reatum poenae non solum aeternae, sed etiam temporalis. Et secundum modum quo homo participat virtutem Passionis Christi, percipit etiam absolutionem a reatu poenae. In Baptismo autem homo participat totaliter virtutem Passionis Christi, utpote per aquam et Spiritum Christo commortuus peccato, et in eo regeneratus ad novam vitam; et ideo in Baptismo homo consequitur remissionem reatus totius poenae. In Poenitentia vero consequitur virtutem Passionis Christi secundum modum propiorum actuum, qui sunt materia Poenitentiae sicut aqua Baptismi . . . Et ideo non statim per primum actum poenitentiae quo remittitur culpa, solvitur reatus totius poenae, sed completis omnibus poenitentiae actibus."

[57]86.5 ra/1: ". . .Deus totum hominem perfecte curat; sed quandoque subito, sicut socrum Petri statim restituit perfectae sanitati, 'ita ut surgens ministraret illis,' ut legitur Luc. 4; quandoque autem successive, sicut dictum est de caeco illuminato, Mc. 8. Et ita etiam spiritualiter quandoque tanta commotione convertit cor hominis, ut subito perfecte consequatur sanitatem spiritualem, non solum remissa culpa, sed sublatis omnibus peccati reliquiis, ut patet

de Magdalena, Luc. 7. Quandoque autem prius remittit culpam per gratiam operantem, et postea per gratiam cooperantem successive tollit peccati reliquias.'"

[58]See *Summa theologiae*, I-II, 114.2-3. See Cornelius Ernst, O.P., *The Gospel of Grace*, translation of *Summa theologiae* (1a2ae. 106-114), Vol. 30 (New York: McGraw-Hill, 1972), appendix 4.

[59]*Summa theologiae* III, 86.4 ra/2: ". . . ad gratiam pertinet operari in homine justificando a peccato, et cooperari homini ad recte operandum. Remissio igitur culpae et reatus poenae aeternae pertinet ad gratiam operantem; sed remissio reatus poenae temporalis pertinet ad gratiam cooperantem, inquantum scilicet homo cum auxilio divinae gratiae patienter poenas tolerando, absolvitur etiam a reatu poenae temporalis. Sicut igitur prius est effectus gratiae operantis quam gratiae cooperantis, ita etiam prius est remissio culpae et poenae aeternae quam plena absolutio a poena temporali. Utrumque enim est a gratia, sed primum a gratia sola, secundum ex gratia et libero arbitrio."

[60]*Ibid.*, 90.2 co/: ". . . quia hic non quaeritur sola reintegratio aequalitatis iustitiae, sicut in iustitia vindicativa, sed magis reconciliatio amicitiae . . . ."

[61]*Ibid.*, 90.4 co/: "Est autem triplex immutatio a poenitente intenta. Prima quidem per regenerationem in novam vitam. Et haec pertinet ad poenitentiam quae est ante baptismu. Secunda autem immutatio est per reformationem vitae praeteritae iam corruptae. Et haec pertinet ad poenitentiam mortalium post baptismu. Tertia autem immutatio est in perfectiorem operationem vitae. Et haec pertinet ad poenitentiam venialium: quae remittuntur per aliquem ferventem actum caritatis . . . ."

[62]*Ibid.*, 85.3 co/: ". . . sed ex eo quod poenitens dolet de peccato commissio inquantum est offensa Dei, cum emendationis proposito."

[63]*Ibid.*, 85.3 ra/4: ". . . poenitentia, licet sit directe species justitiae, comprehendit tamen quodammodo ea quae pertinent ad omnes virtutes; inquantum enim est justitia quaedam hominis ad Deum, oportet quod participet ea quae sunt virtutum theologicarum, quae habent Deum pro objecto. Unde poenitentia est cum fide Passionis Christi, per quam justificamur a

peccatis, et cum spe veniae, et cum odio vitiorum, quod pertinet ad charitatem. Inquantum vero est virtus moralis, participat aliquid prudentiae, quae est directiva omnium moralium virtutum. Sed ex ipsa ratione justitiae non solum habet id quod justitiae est, sed etiam ea quae sunt temperantiae et fortitudinis, inquantum scilicet ea quae delectationem causant ad temperantiam pertinentem, vel terrorem incutiunt, quem fortitudo moderatur, in commutationem justitiae veniunt. Et secundum hoc ad justitiam pertinet et abstinere a delectabilibus, quod pertinet ad temperan tiam, et sustinere dura, quod pertinet ad fortitudinem."

[64]Ibid., 79.5 co/: "Inquantum vero est sacrificium, habet vim satisfactivam. Sed in satisfactione magis attenditur affectus offerentis quam quantitas oblationis. Unde et Dominus dicit Luc. de vidua quae obtulit duo aera quod 'plus omnibus misit.' Quamvis ergo haec oblatio ex sui quantitate sufficiat ad satisfaciendum pro omni poena, tamen fit satisfactoria illis pro quibus offertur, vel etiam offerentibus secundum quantitatem suae devotionis, et non pro tota poena."

[65]Ibid., 85.3 co/: "Et tale iustum consideratur in poenitentia. Unde poenitens recurrit ad Deum, cum emendationis proposito, . . . sicut filius ad patrem, secundum illud Luc. 15, 'Pater, peccavi in caelum et coram te.'"

[66]Romans 3: 23-26.

[1]F.-R. Hasse, De ontologico Anselmi pro existentia Dei argumento (Bonn: Leçon de maîtrise de la Fac. de Théologie Evangélique, 1849). For a more recent appreciation of Anselm's life and work see R.W. Southern, Saint Anselm and his Biographer. A Study of Monastic Life and Thought (Cambridge: University Press, 1966), especially pp. 77-121.

[2]René Roques, introduction to the French translation of Cur Deus homo?, Pourquoi Dieu s'est fait homme (Paris: Éditions du Cerf, 1963), p. 182.

[3]For a thorough treatment of the modern critics of Saint Anselm see J. McIntyre, St. Anselm and his Critics: a reinterpretation of the Cur Deus homo (Edinburgh, 1954). See also Spicilegium Beccense, I. Congrès international du IXe centenaire de l'arrivée d'Anselme au Bec (Paris: J. Vrin, 1959) for a collection of critical articles on various aspects of Anselm's thought.

[4]See above p. 162, n. 30. See also Jean Rivière, "Le droit du démon sur les pécheurs avant Saint Augustin," Recherches de théologie ancienne et médiévale (3) 1931, pp. 113-139; idem, "Réveil de la théorie du rachat au cours du moyen âge," Revue des sciences religieuses (13) 1933, pp. 353-392.

[5]Anselm, Proslogium c.1; see also Cur Deus homo? I,2.

[6]Etienne Gilson, History of Christian Philosophy in the Middle Ages (New York: Random House, 1955), p. 129.

[7]Cur Deus homo? II,5: "Dicamus tamen quia necesse est, ut bonitas Dei propter immutabilitatem suam perficiat de homine quod incipit, quamvis totum sit gratia bonum quod facit."

[8]Ibid., I, 13: "Necesse est ergo, ut aut ablatus honor solvatur aut poena sequatur."

[9]Ibid., I, 14:   "Deum impossibile est honorem suum perdere.   Aut enim peccator sponte solvit quod debet, aut Deus ab invito accipit."

[10]Ibid., I, 23:   ". . . quia peccator peccatorem justificare nequit."

[11]See ibid., I, 11:   "Hunc honorem debitum qui Deo non reddit, aufert Deo quod suum est, et Deum exhonorat; et hoc est peccare . . . .   Nec sufficit solummodo reddere quod ablatum est, sed pro contumelia illata plus debet redere quam abstulit."

[12]Ibid., II, 6:   ". . . maius quam omne quod praeter Deum est."

[13]Ibid., ". . . quam nec potest facere nisi Deus nec debet nisi homo: necesse est ut eam faciat Deus-homo."

[14]Ibid., I, 25:   "Quapropter si falsum est quia nullo aut alio aliquo modo potest hoc esse, necessere est fieri per Christum."

[15]Ibid., II, 18:   "Si propter justitiam se permisit occidi: nonne ad honorem Dei vitam suam dedit?"

[16]Ibid., II, 19:   "Si voluerit Filius quod sibi debetur alii dare: poteritne Pater jure illum prohibere, aut illi cui dabit negare?"

SELECTED BIBLIOGRAPHY

1. Primary Sources

Alexander of Hales. _Glossa in quatuor libros Sententiarum Petri Lombardi_. I. _Bibliotheca Franciscana Scholastica_, no. 12. Quaracchi: Ex typographia Collegii S. Bonaventurae, 1951.

_____. _Summa theologica_. Studio et cura PP. Collegii S. Bonaventurae. Quaracchi: Ex typographia Collegii S. Bonaventurae, 1930.

Anselm of Canterbury, Saint. _Pourquoi Dieu s'est fait homme_. Latin text, Introduction and notes by René Roques. _Sources chrétiennes_, no. 91. Paris: Les Editions du Cerf, 1963. (English translation: _Saint Anselm. Basic Writings_. Translated by S. N. Deane. LaSalle (IL): Open Court, 1962.)

Aquinas, Saint Thomas. _Scriptum super libros Sententiarum_. Four Books. First American edition, vols. VI, VII-1 and VII-2. New York: Musurgia, 1948-1950. A reprint of Parma _Opera Omnia_, vols. VI and VII. Parma: Fiaccadori, 1852-1873.

_____. _Summa contra gentiles_. Leonine version, vols. XIII (1918), XIV (1926) and XV (1930). Taken from the Casa Marietti edition, Torino-Rome: Marieti, 1961.

_____. _Summa theologiae_. Leonine version, vols. IV-XII (1888-1905). (English translation: Thomas Gilby, O.P., general editor, 60 vols. New York: McGraw-Hill, 1964-1975.)

_____. _De veritate_. Leonine version, vol. XXII-1,2,3 (1970-1972). (English translation: _On truth_, 3 vols. Translated by Mulligan-McGlynn-Schmidt. Chicago: Regnery, 1952-1954.

_____. _De malo_. Marietti, 1953.

_____. _De virtutibus in communi_. Marietti, 1953.

_____. _De caritate_. Marietti, 1953.

_____. _Quaestiones de quodlibet I-XII_. Marietti, 1956.

_____. _Contra errores Graecorum_. Leonine edition, vol. XL (1968).

_____. _De rationibus fidei contra Saracenos, Graecos et Armenos ad Cantorem Antiochiae_. Leonine edition, vol. XL (1968).

_____. _De perfectione spiritualis vitae_. Leonine edition, vol. XLI (1970).

_____. _De regno ad regem Cypri_. Marietti, 1954.

_____. _Compendium theologiae ad Reginaldum socium suum_. Marietti, 1954.

_____. _De articulis fidei et Ecclesiae sacramentis ad archepiscopum Panormitanum_. Marietti, 1954.

_____. _Expositio in Job "ad litteram."_ Leonine edition, vol. XXVI (1965).

_____. _Postilla super Isaiam_. Leonine edition, vol. XXVIII (1974).

_____. _Glossa continua super Evangelia_ (_Catena aurea_). Marietti, 1953.

_____. _Expositio et lectura super Epistolas Pauli Apostoli_, Marietti, 1953.

_____. _Postilla super Psalmos_. First American edition, vol. XIV. A reprint of the Parma edition, vol. XIV (1863).

_____. _Lectura super Matthaeum_. _Reportatio_. Marietti, 1951.

_____. _Lectura super Johannem_. _Reportatio_. Marietti, 1952.

St. Thomae Aquinatis Vitae Fontes Praecipuae, edited by A. Ferrua, O.P. Alba: Ed. Domenicane, 1968. Contains William of Tocco, _Hystoria beati Thomae_; Bernard Gui, _Legenda S. Thomae_; _Processus canonizationis Neapoli_ and selections from other of the _Fontes Vitae Sancti Thomae Aquinatis_, Toulouse: originally published as supplements to _Revue Thomiste_, 1911-1934.

Sancti Thomae Aquinatis Operum Omnium Indices et Concordantiae. Directed by Robert Busa, S.J. Stuttgart: Frommann-Holzboog, 1973-   .

Aristotle, Nicomachean Ethics. Translated by W.D. Ross. Basic Works of Aristotle. Edited by Richard McKeon. New York: Random House, 1941.

Bonaventure, Saint. Commentaria in quatuor libros Sententiarum III. Studio et cura PP. Collegii S. Bonaventurae. Quaracchi: Ex typographia Collegii S. Bonaventurae, 1887.

Petrus Lombardus. Sententiae in IV Libris Distinctae. Spicilegium Bonaventurianum, no. 4. Grottaferrata: Collegii S. Bonaventurae ad Claras Aquas, 1971.

Teresa of Avila, Saint. Obras de Santa Teresa de Jesus. Edited by Silverio de Santa Teresa, O.C.D. Burgos: Tipografía de "El Monte Carmelo," 1922.

        2. Secondary Sources (Books)

Aulén, Gustaf. Christus Victor. Translated by A.G. Hebert. New York: Macmillan Publishing Co., Inc., 1979.

Catão, Bernard. Salut et Rédemption chez S. Thomas d'Aquin. Théologie, no. 62. Lyon: Aubier, 1965.

Cerfaux, Lucien. Christ in the Theology of St. Paul. Translated by Geoffrey Webb and Adrian Walker. New York: Herder and Herder, 1966.

Chenu, M.-D. La théologie comme science au XIIIe siècle. Bibliothèque Thomiste, no. 33. Paris: Librairie J. Vrin, 1957.

_____. Toward Understanding Saint Thomas. Translated by A.-M. Landry and D. Hughes. Chicago: Henry Regnery Company, 1964.

Corbin, Michel. Le chemin de la théologie chez Thomas d'Aquin. Bibliothèque des Archives de Philosophie (nouvelle série), no. 16. Paris: Beauchesne, 1974.

Dodd, C.H. The Apostolic Preaching and its Development. New York: Harper & Row, 1964.

Duquoc, O.P., Christian. Christologie. Essai dogmatique: Le Messie. Paris: Les Editions du Cerf, 1972.

Ernst, Cornelius. The Gospel of Grace. Translation of Summa theologiae 1a2ae. 106-114. New York: McGraw-Hill Book Company, 1972.

Genovese, Paul. The Thomistic Concept of the Vicarious Mode of Satisfaction. Baltimore, 1950.

Gilby, Thomas. Christian Theology. Translation of Summa theologiae 1a.1. New York: McGraw-Hill Book Company, 1964.

_____. Purpose and Happiness. Translation of Summa theologiae 1a2ae. 1-5. New York: McGraw-Hill Book Company, 1969.

Gilson, Etienne. The Christian Philosophy of St. Thomas Aquinas. Translated by L.K. Shook. New York: Random House, 1956.

_____. History of Christian Philosophy in the Middle Ages. New York: Random House, 1955.

Gonzáles-Median, Salvador. La necesidad de la pasión: Un aspecto de la teología de la redención en S. Tomás. Freiburg, 1963.

Hardy, Louis. La doctrine de la Rédemption chez S. Thomas. Paris: Desclée, 1936.

Harnack, Adolph. History of Dogma. Translated by William M'Gilchrist. London: William & Norgate, 1899.

Haskins, Charles Homer. The Rise of Universities. Ithaca: Cornell University Press, 1957.

Hayen, André. Saint Thomas d'Aquin et la vie de l'église. Paris-Louvain: Publications Universitaires de Louvain, 1952.

Hill, Edmund. Man Made to God's Image. Translation of Summa theologiae 1a. 90-102. New York: McGraw-Hill Book Company, 1964.

Lafont, Ghislain. Structures et Méthode dans la Somme Théologique de Saint Thomas d'Aquin. Paris: Desclée de Brouwer, 1961.

Luyten, Norbert A., ed. L'anthropologie de Saint Thomas. Fribourg: Editions Universitaires, 1974.

O'Brien, T.C. Effects of Sin, Stain and Guilt. Translation of Summa theologiae 1a2ae. 86-89. New York: McGraw-Hill, 1974.

O'Collins, Gerald. The Calvary Christ. Philadelphia: The Westminster Press, 1971.

O'Neill, Colman E. The One Mediator. Translation of Summa theologiae 3a. 16-26. New York: McGraw-Hill, 1965.

Pannenberg, Wolfhart. Jesus--God and Man. Translated by Lewis L. Wilkins and Duane A. Priebe. Philadelphia: The Westminster Press, 1968.

Pelikan, Jaroslav. The Christian Tradition. A History of the Development of Doctrine. Vol. 1, The Emergence of the Catholic Tradition (100-600). Chicago: The University of Chicago Press, 1971.

Persson, Per Erik. Sacra Doctrina. Reason and Revelation in Aquinas. Translated by Ross MacKenzie. Philadelphia: Fortress Press, 1970.

Philippe, M.-D. Saint Thomas, Docteur, Témoin de Jésus. Fribourg-Paris: Saint Paul, 1956.

Philippe de la Trinité. La Rédemption par le sang. Paris: Fayard, 1959.

Richard, Louis. Le mystère de la Rédemption. Tournai: Desclée et Cie., 1959. (English translation: The Mystery of the Redemption. Baltimore-Dublin: Helicon Press, 1965).

Rivière, Jean. Le dogme de la Rédemption. Essai d'étude historique. Paris: Lecoffre, 1905. (English translation: The Doctrine of the Atonement. A Historical Essay. Translated by L. Cappadelta. 2 vols. St. Louis: B. Herder, 1909.)

_____. Le dogme de la Rédemption. Etude théologique. Paris: Gabalda, 1931.

_____. Le dogme de la Rédemption. Etudes critiques et documents. Louvain: Bibliothèque de la Revue d'Histoire Ecclésiastique, 1931.

_____. Le dogme de la Rédemption au début du moyen âge. Bibliothèque Thomiste, vol. 19. Paris: Librairie J. Vrin, 1934.

_____. Le dogme de la Rédemption dans la théologie contemporaine. Etude historique. Albi: Chez M. le Chanoine Lombard, 1948.

Robinson, John A.T. Wrestling with Romans. Philadelphia: The Westminster Press, 1979.

Smalley, Beryl. The Study of the Bible in the Middle Ages. Oxford: Clarendon Press, 1941.

Spicq, Ceslaus. Esquisse d'une histoire de l'Exégèse latine au moyen âge. Bibliothèque Thomiste, vol. 26. Paris: Librairie J. Vrin, 1944.

Southern, R.W. Saint Anselm and his Biographer. A Study of Monastic Life and Thought 1059-c.1130. Cambridge: University Press, 1966.

Turner, H.E.W. The Patristic Doctrine of Redemption. London: Mowbrays, 1952.

_____. Jesus the Christ. London: Mowbrays, 1976.

Weisheipl, James A. Friar Thomas D'Aquino. His Life, Thought, and Work. New York: Doubleday & Company, Inc., 1974.

3. Articles

Biffi, Inos. "Saggio bibliographico sui misteri della vita di Cristo in S. Tommaso d'Aquino." La Scuola Cattolica 99 (December 1971): 175-238.

Bourassa, François. "La satisfaction du Christ." Sciences Ecclésiastiques 15' (1963): 351-381.

Brajcić, Rudolf. "De loco, modis et comprobatione satisfactionis in opere Redemptionis." Divus Thomas (P) 67 (1964): 79-88.

Brugger, Walter. "Index Thomisticus." <u>Theologie und Philosophie</u> 52 (1977): 435-444.

DeLetter, P. "Theology of Satisfaction." <u>Thomist</u> 21 (1958): 1-28.

Deneffe, Auguste. "Das Wort Satisfactio." <u>Zeitschrift für Katholische Theologie</u> 43 (1919): 158-175.

Dondaine, Hyacinthe. "Le <u>Contra errores Groecorum</u> de S. Thomas et le IVe Livre du <u>Contra gentiles</u>." <u>Les Sciences Philosophiques et Théologiques</u> 30 (1941-1942): 156-162.

Galtier, P. "Satisfaction." <u>Dictionnaire de Théologie catholique</u>, Vol. 14: col. 1129-1210.

Gauthier, R.-A. "Les 'Articuli in quibus frater Thomas melius in Summa quam in Scriptis?'" <u>Recherches de Théologie ancienne et médiévale</u> 19 (1952): 271-326.

Geenem, Gottfried. "The Council of Chalcedon in the Theology of St. Thomas." <u>From an Abundant Spring</u>. New York: P.J. Kenedy & Sons, 1952.

Graystone, Geoffrey. "Modern Theories of the Atonement." <u>Irish Theological Quarterly</u> 20 (1953): 225-252.

Hacault, Antoine. "La satisfaction du Christ." <u>Studia Montis Regii</u> 3 (1960): 173-200; 4 (1961): 77-98; 133-184.

Journet, Charles. "La peine temporelle du péché." <u>Revue thomiste</u> (1927): "20-39; 89-103.

Laje, Enrique. "Satisfacción y Pena en el pensamiento de Santo Tomás." <u>Ciencia y Fe</u> 21 (1965): 267-289.

_____. "A propósito de una teologia de la redención en Santo Tomás de Aquino." <u>Stromata</u> 22 (1966): 79-81.

Lecuyer, Joseph. "Note sur une définition thomiste de la satisfaction." <u>Doctor Communis</u> 8 (1955): 21-31.

_____. "Prolégomènes thomistes à la théologie de la satisfaction." <u>Studi Tomistici</u> (Rome) 2 (1974): 82-103.

Mitros, Joseph. "Patristic Views of Christ's Salvific Work." Thought 42 (1967): 415-447.

// Moiser, Jeremy. "Why did the Son of God become Man?" The Thomist 37 (1973): 288-305.

Muscat, I. "De virtute satisfactoria." Divus Thomas (P) 40 (1937): 225-254; 329-349.

Nicolas, Jean-Hervé. "Réactualisation des mystères rédempteurs dans et par les sacrements." Revue Thomiste 58 (1958): 20-54.

_____. "Aimante et bienheureuse Trinité." Revue Thomiste 78 (1978): 271-292.

_____. "La seconde mort du pécheur et la fidélité de Dieu." Revue Thomiste 79 (1979) 25-49.

O'Neill, Albert. "De necessitate Incarnationis." Antonianum 7 (1932): 244-250.

Pelikan, Jaroslav. "'Imago Dei': An explication of Summa theologiae, Part 1, Question 93." Calgary Aquinas Studies. Toronto: Pontifical Institute of Medieval Studies, 1973: 26-48.

Plagnieux, Jean. "Le binôme justitia-potentia dans la sotériologie augustinienne et anselmienne." Spicilegium Beccense. Paris: Librairie J. Vrin, 1959: 141-154.

Richard, L. "Sens théologique du mot satisfaction." Revue des Sciences Religieuses 7 (1927): 87-93.

Rivière, Jean. "Sur les premières applications du terme 'satisfactio' à l'oeuvre du Christ." Bulletin de littérature ecclésiastique 25 (1924): 285-297; 353-369.

_____. "Sur l'origine des formules 'de condigno,' 'de congruo'." Bulletin de littérature ecclésiastique 28 (1927): 75-88.

Turner, C.H. "The Liber ecclesiasticorum dogmatum attributed to Gennadius." The Journal of Theological Studies 7 (1906): 78-99.